Operating Systems
A Systematic View

Fourth Edition

William S. Davis

Miami University
Oxford, Ohio

The Benjamin/Cummings Publishing Company, Inc.
Redwood City, California • Menlo Park, California
Reading, Massachusetts • New York • Don Mills, Ontario
Wokingham, U.K. • Amsterdam • Bonn • Sydney
Singapore • Tokyo • Madrid • San Juan

Library of Congress Cataloging-in-Publication Data

Davis, William S., 1943–
    Operating systems : a systematic view / William S. Davis.—4th
 ed.
    p.   cm.
    Includes index.
    ISBN 0–201–56701–6
    1. Operating systems (Computers)   I. Title.
 QA76.76.063D38 1992
 005.4′3—dc20   91–15887
                                            CIP

Sponsoring Editor: Peter Shepard
Production Supervisor: Helen Wythe
Text Design: To The Point and Patti Williams
Illustrations: ST Associates
Production Coordinator: Amy Willcutt
Cover Design: Peter Blaiwas

7 8 9 10 MA 99 98 97 96

P R E F A C E

The first edition of *Operating Systems: A Systematic View* was published in 1977. Six years later, a second edition updated the technology and added some new material. The third edition, a major revision, bore a 1987 copyright. Now, it's time for a fourth edition.

Although time-sharing and minicomputers did exist in the 1970s, batch processing was the accepted mode of computer access. The first edition reflected that standard, but today's users have come to expect interactive access. Thus, one change is the addition of screen editors and interactive job submission to the job control language chapters. The fourth edition also adds new chapters on IBM's AS/400 series and substantially updates the IBM VSE (formerly DOS/VSE) material. New versions of the instructor's manual and the student workbook are available to accompany this new edition.

In spite of these changes, *Operating Systems: A Systematic View* remains an *applied* introduction to operating systems. This is *not* a theoretical text. The intent of the previous editions was to show *why* operating systems are needed and *what*, at a functional level, they do. This new edition retains those objectives, along with the pace, level, and writing style of the first three editions. It also retains such pedagogical features as chapter overviews, summaries, key word lists, and exercises. As before, the numerous illustrations closely follow the narrative and visually reinforce the concepts.

The book looks at operating systems from an application programmer's point of view. It assumes little or no mathematics beyond high school algebra. The only prerequisites are a reasonable understanding of basic computer concepts and some programming experience. Part I, Chapters 2 through 4, reviews essential concepts; you should understand this material before moving on. Those students who need a brief review of number systems should read Appendix A.

Part II overviews key operating system concepts. Chapter 5 describes single user, microcomputer operating systems. Chapter 6 introduces multiple user systems, multiprogramming, and time-sharing. Later in the text, when you begin reading about the internals of several different operating systems, you'll encounter considerable detail, and it's easy to "miss the forest for the trees." The intent of this second part is to give you a "map" of an operating system's key functions.

Users and programmers communicate with an operating system through a job control or command language, the subject of Part III. Chapter 7 discusses the general functions of any command or job control language. MS-DOS (or PC-DOS) commands are introduced in Chapter 8. Chapter 9 discusses UNIX commands. Chapter 10 illustrates the job control language for IBM's AS/400 series computers. These first three command languages are presented in a tutorial format. IBM's VSE job control language is the subject of Chapter 11. Chapters 12 and 13 introduce IBM's MVS/JCL. Chapter 14 discusses libraries and the linkage editor and then illustrates key concepts with MVS/JCL examples. Each of these job control or command languages is summarized in an appendix.

Part IV moves inside the operating system. MS-DOS, the most popular microcomputer operating system, is covered in Chapter 15. Segmentation, paging, and virtual memory are essential concepts in many current operating systems, so they are introduced in Chapter 16. UNIX, the subject of Chapter 17, incorporates ideas that have influenced the design of many modern operating systems. Next (Chapter 18), IBM's OS/400 operating system is introduced. Chapter 19 discusses IBM System/370 principles of operation. Part IV ends with discussions of three operating systems designed to run in that environment: VSE (Chapter 20), MVS/VS1/VS2 (Chapter 21), and VM (Chapter 22).

User support software is the subject of Part V. The ongoing merger of computing and communication technologies is discussed in Chapter 23, with an emphasis on networks and network operating systems. The book ends with an overview of database management systems (Chapter 24). It is likely that the functions covered in this section will be incorporated in future operating systems.

Although the changes are substantial, the book is still aimed at those interested in using (rather than designing) computers.

Professional programmers, systems analysts, and technical managers should appreciate the applied orientation, too. I'm excited about this new edition, and I sincerely hope it meets your needs.

Acknowledgments

As the manuscript for the fourth edition of *Operating Systems: A Systematic View* was being written, Mr. Peter Shepard, the sponsoring editor, set in motion a substantial review process. I would like to thank the following reviewers for their contributions: Adrienne Haine-Schoenes, CDP, J Sargent Reynolds Community College; Shrohreh Hashemi, University of Houston; B.J. Honeycut, Clayton State College; Steve Kolars, San Antonio College; Rick Rhodes and Mike Snyder, IBM Corporation, Cincinnati; Alton Sanders and Doug Troy, Miami University, Oxford; I'd like to thank the following survey respondents as well: Claude "Mike" Fligg, Jr., University College, University of Denver; Dr. Helen C. Penny, Valdosta Technical Institute; John R. Shaw, Chemekta Community College; and E. James Williams, Jr., Florida Community College.

Most were positive. Some identified errors or oversights; to those reviewers I am particularly grateful. All were useful. Additionally, I would like to acknowledge the efforts of Helen Wythe (the production supervisor) and Addison-Wesley's production team who did their usual first class job.

WSD
Oxford, Ohio

C O N T E N T S

1

Introduction and Overview

This chapter introduces operating systems. Key topics include:

What is an operating system?

The programmer's environment

A look ahead

The final topic is a brief overview of the remainder of the book.

What Is an Operating System?

A computer fresh off the assembly line with no software in place can do absolutely nothing. It cannot accept characters from the keyboard, display data on a screen, execute, or even *load* an application program. Hardware presents a most unfriendly interface, and even experienced programmers find it difficult to communicate with the raw iron.

The **operating system** is a set of software routines that sits between the application program and hardware. All other software runs under the operating system's control, accessing the hardware *through* the operating system and following rules imposed by the operating system. Because the operating system serves as a hardware/software interface (Fig. 1.1), application programmers and users rarely communicate directly with the hardware.

At the hardware level, computers distributed by different manufacturers are often incompatible, using different rules for communicating with peripherals, reporting interrupts, and so on. Consequently, a program written for one computer will not work on another. However, if both machines support the same operating system, they can probably both run the same application software. Because their hardware/software interfaces are different, the operating system routines that communicate

Fig. 1.1   The operating system serves as an interface between the application program and the hardware.

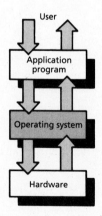

Fig. 1.2   The operating system can be viewed as a platform for writing application programs.

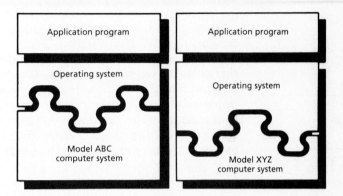

directly with the hardware might be quite different, but the routines that interface with the application program represent a consistent **platform** (Fig. 1.2). Because all communication with the hardware goes through the operating system, the application programmer can ignore the hardware differences.

The operating system's routines perform key support functions such as communicating with peripheral devices and accepting and carrying out user commands (load a program, copy a file, create a directory . . .). These seemingly simple tasks are, in reality, deceptively complex. They are also common to most applications, and it makes little sense to duplicate them in each and every application program.

Providing an easy-to-use hardware interface is the operating system's most obvious function, but that's not all it does. Although modern computers are quite powerful, the supply of such resources as processor time, memory space, disk space, and peripheral devices is still limited. The operating system manages these resources, ensuring that they are used efficiently and that conflicts over resource allocations do not degrade system performance.

The Programmer's Environment

Although the operating system represents the primary interface with the rest of the system, today's application programmers must communicate with other system software, too. Most organizations maintain a central database that is accessed through a **database management system.** Additionally, networks have become increasingly popular, and network access often involves **data communication software** or a **network operating system.**

Together, the operating system, the data communication software, and the database management system define the programmer's environment (Fig. 1.3). To access traditional files, printers, and most other peripheral devices, the programmer calls the operating system. Reading or writing the database means calling the database management system which, in turn, relies on the operating system to access the physical disk files that comprise the database. Network input/output (I/O) is performed by calling the data communication software; once again, physical I/O is controlled by the operating system.

Fig. 1.3   The modern programmer works within a very complex environment.

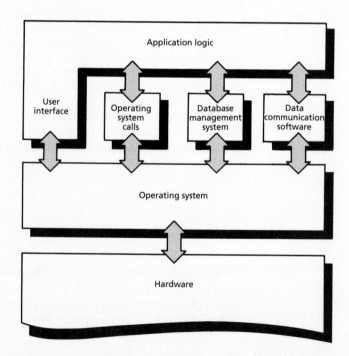

Note that the program's access to the outside world is defined, structured, and constrained by these three system modules. Consequently, a program written under such an environment actually deals with five different problems:

1. *the application logic;*
2. *the user interface* (screens, dialogues, and so on);
3. *the operating system interface* (read, write, and other I/O operations, plus control language commands);
4. *the database interface* (the logic to access the database management system);
5. *the network interface* (the logic to access the data communication software).

To the casual observer, the first component, the application logic, *is* the program, but professional programmers know better; indeed, the application logic is often the easy part. The user interface can be quite complex, and accessing the database, the data communication software, and the operating system requires three different sets of commands. Each module means a new interface, and each interface adds to the program's complexity.

Most programmers think of the system routines as black boxes. When programmers need support, they call the appropriate module, pass it some parameters, accept the results, and ignore precisely how the request is filled. That's fine to a point, but when given a few job control or database commands that work, too many programmers are content to simply use them without question. (And heaven help the programmer who changes anything.) The result can be inefficiency, low productivity, and maintenance nightmares.

The black box view of system software is fine; indeed, it is probably impossible for any one individual to be truly expert in operating systems, data communication, *and* database management. However, it is important that the application programmer have a sense of what happens inside each black box. The key word is *what.* It *is* possible for the average programmer to gain a *functional* understanding of operating systems, database management, and data communications.

Look carefully at Fig. 1.3 and note that *all* the software routines require the support of the operating system. The first step in really understanding how a program communicates with the system's other components is learning what the operating system does, because the database manager, the data communication software, user communications, and the application routine's I/O operations *all* go through the operating system.

Giving you a functional understanding of modern operating systems is the primary objective of this book.

A Look Ahead

This is *not* a theoretical text. Its focus is how system software impacts real-world tasks. More specifically, it assumes that you know how to program, and presents key concepts from an application programmer's perspective.

The book is divided into five parts. Part I, Chapters 2 through 4, covers a computer's basic hardware, software, and data resources; for many of you these three chapters will be review. Part II (Chapters 5 and 6) explains the essential functions performed by a modern operating system. Part III (Chapters 7 through 14) introduces the command and job control languages for several operating systems, including MS-DOS, UNIX, and IBM's OS/400, VSE, and MVS. Part IV (Chapters 15 through 22), explains how these operating systems work and introduces virtual memory and virtual machine concepts. Finally, Part V, Chapters 23 and 24, briefly introduces database management and data communication software.

Summary

An operating system serves as an interface between application programs and hardware and manages the system's resources. Because it represents the primary interface to the rest of the system, the operating system can be viewed as a platform on which applications are constructed.

The operating system, the database management system, and data communication software define the programmer's environment. It is important that a modern programmer gain at least a functional understanding of these system routines.

Key Words

database management
  system
data communication
  software

network operating
  system
operating system
platform

Exercises

1. Briefly, what is an operating system?

2. An operating system presents an application programmer with a relatively "friendly" hardware interface. What does this mean? Why is it important?

3. An operating system serves as a platform on which application programs are constructed. What does this mean and why is it important?

4. Briefly explain how an operating system, a database management system, and data communication software define the programmer's environment.

5. When a programmer writes a complex program, the application logic is often the easy part. Explain.

PART ONE

Basic System Resources

2

Hardware

This chapter briefly explains several key
hardware concepts, including:

Main memory
  Physical memory devices
  Addressing memory

The processor
  Machine cycles

  Microcode

Input and output devices

Secondary storage
  Diskette
  Hard disk
  Other secondary media
  Accessing secondary storage

Linking the components

For most readers, much of this material
will be review.

Main Memory

Physical Memory Devices

A computer's **main memory** holds binary digits, or **bits** (see Appendix A for a review of number system concepts). Almost any device that can assume either of two states can serve as storage, but most computers use integrated circuit chips (Fig. 2.1). A small computer might contain enough memory to store thousands of bits; a large machine might store millions. The difference is one of degree, not function.

Most main memory is random access memory (RAM). The programmer (through a program, of course) can read or write RAM; its contents are easy to change. Usually, this flexibility is an advantage. Sometimes, however, it makes sense to record key software or data in more permanent, read-only memory (ROM). A good example of a ROM-based program is the BASIC language interpreter found in many microcomputers. As the name implies, ROM can be read, but not written.

A single bit can hold either a 0 or a 1. Generally, however, the contents of memory are envisioned as groups of bits called bytes

Fig. 2.1   The main memory of most computers is composed of
                    integrated circuit chips.

and words. A **byte** contains enough bits (usually 8) to represent a single character. For example, the ASCII code for the letter A is 01000001. Within memory, an A is stored by recording that bit pattern in a single byte (8 bits).

Bytes are fine for storing characters but are too small to hold a meaningful number. Most computers are able to manipulate a group of bytes called a **word.** Some small computers have 8-bit words. Other, more powerful machines work with 16-bit (2-byte), 32-bit (4-byte), and even 64-bit words.

Memory is typically viewed as a hierarchy (Fig. 2.2). The basic unit of storage is the **bit.** Bits are grouped to form bytes, which in turn are grouped to form words. In one application, a given word might hold a binary number. In another, that word's bytes might hold individual characters, or a program instruction.

Throughout this book, the term "memory" will generally be used to mean "main memory."

Addressing Memory

A typical microcomputer contains 640K[1] or more bytes or words, while a large mainframe has millions. Each physical storage unit is assigned a unique **address.** On most computers, the

---

Fig. 2.2 In a computer's memory, bits are combined to form bytes, and bytes, in turn, are combined to form words.

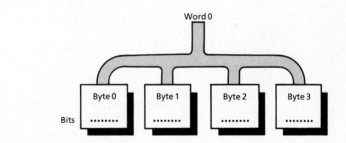

---

[1]The suffix K, which stands for kilo, means 1024, so a computer with 640K bytes of memory contains 655,360 actual memory locations.

bytes or words are numbered sequentially—0,1,2, and so on. The processor accesses a specific memory location by referencing its address. For example, if the processor needs the data stored in byte 1048, it asks memory for the contents of byte 1048. Since there is only one byte 1048, the processor gets the right data. Depending on the computer, bytes or words are the basic addressable units of memory. Data move between the processor and memory a byte or a word at a time.

The Processor

The **processor,** often called the central processing unit (CPU) or main processor, is the component that manipulates data. A processor can do nothing without a program to provide control; whatever intelligence a computer has is derived from software, not hardware. The processor manipulates data stored in memory under the control of a program stored in memory (Fig. 2.3).

A **program** is a series of **instructions,** each of which tells the computer to perform one of its basic functions: add, subtract, multiply, divide, compare, copy, start input, or start output. Each instruction has an operation code and one or more operands (Fig. 2.4). The operation code specifies the function to be performed, and the operands identify the memory locations that are to participate in the operation. For example, the instruction in Fig. 2.4 tells the computer to add the contents of memory locations 1000 and 1002.

Fig. 2.3   The processor manipulates data stored in memory under control of a program stored in memory.

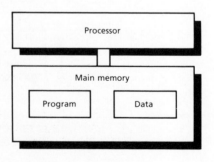

Fig. 2.4   An instruction is composed of an operation code and
                       one or more operands. The operation code tells the
                       computer what to do. The operand or operands identify
                       the addresses of the data elements to be manipulated.

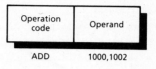

Operation code	Operand
ADD	1000,1002

The processor contains four key components (Fig 2.5). The
instruction control unit (ICU) fetches instructions from memory. The **arithmetic and logic unit** consists of the circuits that
add, subtract, multiply, and so on (the computer's instruction
set). It executes instructions. **Registers** are temporary storage
devices that hold control information, key data, and intermediate results. The **clock** generates precisely timed electronic
pulses that synchronize the other components.

Machine Cycles

Exactly how do a computer's internal components work together to execute instructions? Let's use a model of a simple

Fig. 2.5   A processor contains four key components.

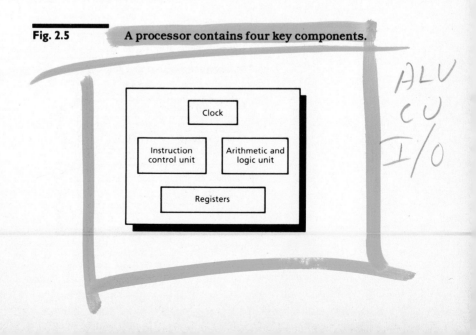

computer system (Fig. 2.6) to illustrate a few **machine cycles.**
Begin with the processor. In addition to the clock, it contains an
instruction control unit, an arithmetic and logic unit, and several registers, including an instruction counter, an instruction
register, and a work register called the accumulator. The
computer's other major component, memory, holds program instructions and data values. Note that each memory location is
assigned an address.

The process starts when the clock generates a pulse of current which activates the instruction control unit. The ICU's job
is to decide what the machine will do next. The computer is controlled by program instructions, and the instructions, remember, are stored in memory. The address of the next instruction to
be executed is found in the instruction counter (Fig. 2.6a). The

Fig. 2.6   A computer executes instructions by following a basic
machine cycle.

a. As the example begins, memory holds both program instructions
and data. The instruction register points to the first instruction to
be executed.

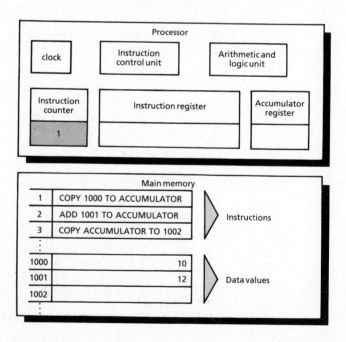

b. In response to a fetch command from the instruction control unit, the first instruction is copied from memory and stored in the instruction register. Note that the instruction counter points to the next instruction.

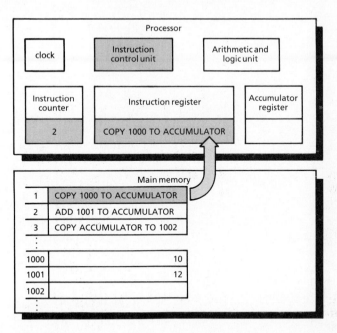

c. Next, the arithmetic and logic unit executes the instruction in the instruction register.

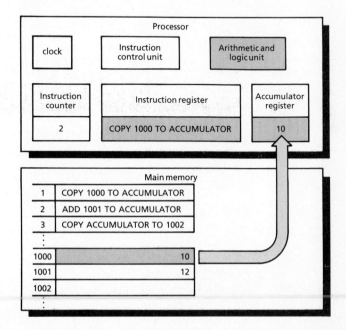

d. As the next cycle begins, the instruction control unit once again looks to the instruction register for the address of the next instruction.

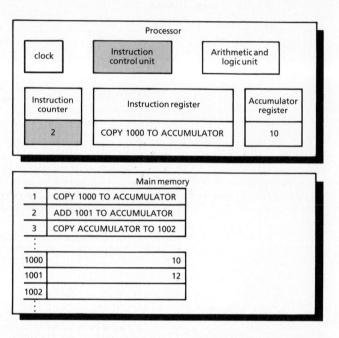

e. The next instruction is fetched into the instruction register. Note that the instruction counter points to the next instruction.

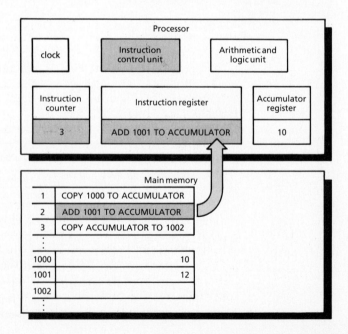

f. The arithmetic and logic unit executes the instruction in the instruction register.

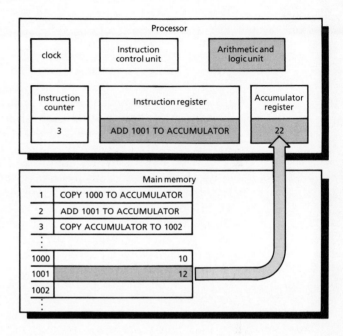

instruction control unit checks the instruction counter, finds the address, and fetches the instruction stored at that address, placing it in the instruction register (Fig. 2.6b). Fetching an instruction from memory takes time, giving the instruction control unit an opportunity to increment the instruction counter to point to the next instruction (Fig. 2.6b).

Next, the instruction control unit activates the arithmetic and logic unit, which executes the instruction stored in the instruction register (Fig. 2.6c). Note that, following execution of this instruction, a data value is copied from memory to the accumulator register.

Once again, the clock "ticks," activating the instruction control unit, and starting the next machine cycle (Fig. 2.6d). Referring to the instruction counter, the instruction control unit fetches the next instruction into the instruction register (Fig. 2.6e). Again, note that the instruction register now points to the next instruction. The arithmetic and logic unit then executes the instruction in the instruction register (Fig. 2.6f), adding a data value from memory to the accumulator.

Following the next clock pulse, the instruction control unit fetches the next instruction, which is subsequently executed by the arithmetic and logic unit. An instruction is fetched during **I-time**, or instruction time, and executed during **E-time**, or execution time (Fig. 2.7). This process is repeated again and again until the program is finished.

Note that the clock drives the process, generating pulses of current at precisely timed intervals. The rate at which the clock "ticks" determines the computer's operating speed. Clock speed is usually measured in megahertz (millions of cycles per second). Clearly, a computer with a 20 MHz clock is faster than a computer with a 10 MHz clock because it completes twice as many machine cycles per second.

Do be careful when comparing computers based on their clock speeds, however, because other factors influence computing speed, too. For example, some processors manipulate data in 16-bit increments, while others work with 32-bits at a time. All things being equal, a 32-bit word machine is faster than a 16-bit word machine because it can move twice as much data during each cycle. Also, not all instructions execute in the same amount of time. A simple instruction that adds the contents of two registers might be fetched and executed in a single machine cycle, but more complex instructions often need multiple cycles. Think of clock speed as *potential* operating speed.

Fig. 2.7   The basic machine cycle is repeated again and again, until all the instructions in the program have been executed.

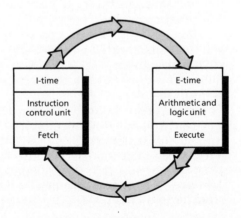

Figure 2.8   On many computers, a layer of **microcode** lies between
                    memory and the processor.

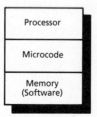

Microcode

On many computers, a layer of **microcode**, sometimes called
firmware, lies between memory and the processor (Fig. 2.8). On
a microcoded machine, object-level "machine-language" instructions are translated into lower-level microinstructions
before being executed by the processor. Because the microcode
insulates the software from the hardware, hardware changes
can be accommodated without affecting the operating system or
the application software. In some cases, key operating system
routines are actually implemented in microcode to improve efficiency. Additionally, microcoded systems are relatively difficult
to "clone," and that can give a company with a successful architecture a significant competitive advantage.

Input and Output Devices

Input and output devices provide a means for people to access a
computer. The basic **input** device on most small computer systems (Fig. 2.9) is a keyboard. As characters are typed, they are
stored in memory and then copied (or echoed) to the basic **output**
device, a display screen. In effect, the screen serves as a window
on memory, allowing the user to view its contents.

The image displayed on a screen is temporary; it fades as
soon as the power is cut. By routing the output to a printer, a
permanent copy (called a hard copy) is obtained. Character
printers print one character at a time, usually at rates varying
from 30 to perhaps 180 characters per second. The speed is fine

Fig. 2.9   A typical computer system. Input is provided by a
                       keyboard. Output goes to the screen or to the printer.

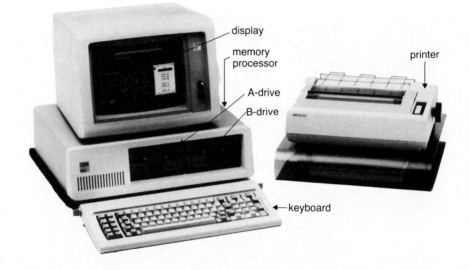

for a few pages of output, but it's much too slow for volume
printing. Laser printers are faster and generate high-quality
text and graphic output. Line printers print line by line instead
of character by character; rates of 1000 lines per minute (and
more) are common. Page printers, which churn out complete
pages at a time, are even faster. For more compact output or
long-term storage, there is computer output microfilm (COM).
Computers are not limited to displaying characters, of course;
graphic output is also possible. A plotter generates hard-copy
graphic output.

Several common input media rely on magnetic properties.
For example, the characters on the bottom of most checks are
printed with a special magnetic ink called MICR (magnetic ink
character recognition), and can be read electronically. Another
banking medium is the magnetic strip card. The strip of magnetic tape holds such data as a customer's account number and
credit limit, and is read much like sound recording tape.

Other media are read optically. For example, consider stan-
dardized test forms. Students use a black pencil to mark their
answers. The white paper reflects light; the black spots reflect

much less; variations in the intensity of the reflected light can be converted to an electronic pattern. OCR (optical character recognition) equipment uses the same principle to read typed or even handwritten material. Bar codes, such as the Universal Product Code (UPC) printed on most supermarket packages, can be read at a checkout station or by a hand-held scanner.

Often, terminals are linked to a central computer by cables or communication lines. A "dumb" terminal is simply a keyboard and a display screen. An intelligent terminal contains its own memory and processor and can perform many data processing functions independently. Other special-purpose terminals are designed for specific functions. Examples include automatic bank teller terminals and supermarket checkout stations.

Perhaps the most natural way of communicating with a computer is by voice. Voice response (output) is already used in such mundane applications as children's toys and video games. Due to the tremendous variety of human speech patterns, voice recognition (input) is much more difficult, but significant advances have been made.

Secondary Storage

There are numerous problems with main memory. For one thing, it's expensive, and the supply on most machines is limited. More significant is its volatility; RAM loses its contents when the power is cut. **Secondary storage** is a fast, accurate, inexpensive, high-capacity, nonvolatile extension of main memory.

Diskette

The most common microcomputer secondary storage medium is **diskette** (Fig. 2.10), a thin circular piece of flexible polyester coated with a magnetic material. Data are recorded on one or both flat surfaces. A diskette drive works much like a record turntable. The round hole in the center of the disk allows the drive mechanism to engage and spin it; an access mechanism, analogous to the tone arm, reads and writes the surface.

The data are recorded on a series of concentric circles called tracks (Fig. 2.11). The access mechanism steps from track to track, reading or writing one at a time. The tracks are subdivided into sectors; it is the contents of a sector that move between the diskette and main memory. To distinguish the

Fig. 2.10   The most popular microcomputer secondary storage
                     medium is diskette.

sectors, they are addressed by numbering them sequentially—1,
2, 3, and so on. (Sector 0 exists, but it is used by the system.)

When a program instruction requesting diskette input is executed, the processor sends a control signal to the drive. In response, the drive spindle is engaged, and the disk begins to spin,
quickly reaching a constant rotational speed (Fig. 2.12a). Next,
the access mechanism is moved to the track containing the desired data (Fig. 2.12b). The time required to bring the drive up to
speed and position the access mechanism is called seek time. Remember that data are transferred between the diskette and
memory one sector at a time. The desired sector may be anywhere on the track. The time required for the sector to rotate to
the access mechanism (Fig. 2.12c) is called rotational delay.

Hard Disk

Although diskette is quite fast, data access still means a delay of
at least a fraction of a second. Many common personal computer
applications involve only limited disk access, so the delay is
hardly noticeable. On other applications, however, waiting can
be intolerable. The solution is often a **hard disk.**

A diskette drive spins only when data are being read or written. The drive must be brought up to operating speed before the
read/write heads can be moved and the data accessed, and that

Fig. 2.11   Data are recorded on a series of concentric circles
called tracks. The tracks, in turn, are subdivided into
sectors. Data move between the disk surface and
main memory a sector at a time.

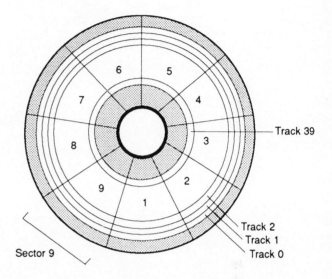

takes time. A hard disk, in contrast, spins constantly. Since it is
not necessary to wait for the drive to reach operating speed before moving the access mechanism, seek time is significantly
reduced, often to a few thousandths of a second. Further improvements are gained by spinning the disk more rapidly (1000
revolutions per minute or more), which reduces rotational delay.
Data stored on hard disk can be accessed far more rapidly than
data stored on diskette. Another advantage of hard disk is its
storage capacity. A typical double-sided diskette might hold
360,000 to 1.44 million characters. A hard disk for a microcomputer system might store 20 to 80 million characters.

Although single-surface **disks** do exist, most large computers use disk packs consisting of several recording surfaces
stacked on a common drive shaft (Fig. 2.13). Typically, each surface has its own read/write head. The heads are arrayed on a single, comblike access mechanism, so they all move together.
Imagine, for example, that the access mechanism is positioned

Fig. 2.12   Reading a sector from disk.

a. First, the disk drive is brought up to operating speed.

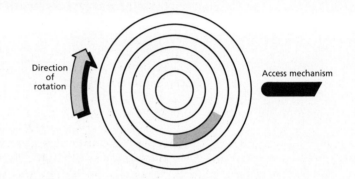

b. Next, the access mechanism is positioned over the track that holds
    the desired data. The time required to perform steps a and b is
    called seek time.

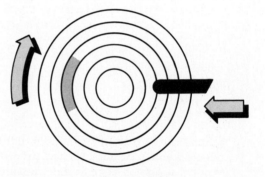

c   Finally, the system waits until the desired sector rotates to the
    read/write head (rotational delay) and the data are transferred into
    memory.

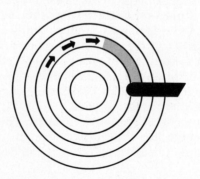

over track 30. The top read/write head will access track 30 on surface 0. Moving down, surface by surface, the second head will be over track 30 on surface 1, the third over track 30 on surface 2, and so on. One position of the access mechanism corresponds to one track on each surface. This set of tracks is called a cylinder.

Accessing disk begins with seek time. The access mechanism is moved to a selected cylinder, and a selected head is activated. The system is now looking at a single track. Next, the desired data rotate to the read/write head—rotational delay. Finally, the data are read and transferred into the computer.

On some hard disks, tracks are divided into fixed-length sectors, and data move between the disk's surface and memory a sector at a time. Other hard disks, particularly on large mainframes, are track addressed, with tracks subdivided into physical records or blocks. A physical record can be any length, from a single byte to a full track; the physical record length (or block size) is chosen to fit the application. Data are transferred between secondary and main storage a block at a time.

Given the tremendous capacity of a disk pack, losing one, through human error, fire, flood, or similar disaster, can destroy

Fig. 2.13   On a disk pack, each surface has its own read/write head. The heads are arrayed on a single, comblike access mechanism, so they all move together.

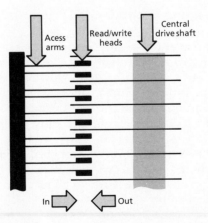

a great deal of important data. In most large computer centers, the data are regularly backed up by copying them. Should a disk pack be lost, the **backup** copy is used to restore its contents.

Other Secondary Media

The least expensive secondary storage medium is magnetic cassette, the same cassette tape used to record music. Data are output to a tape recorder. By playing the recording back, the material is restored to memory. Cassettes are inexpensive and compact, but they are also relatively slow and error prone. They are used on some small home computer systems or for archival storage.

Magnetic tape (similar to reel-to-reel recording tape) is a common backup medium. Accessed through high-speed drives, tape is fast, with data transfer rates comparable to disk. Its storage capacity is high, and a reel of tape is inexpensive. Unfortunately, data can be read or written only in a fixed sequence, which limits tape to a few applications.

Today, dictionaries, encyclopedias, clip-art libraries, and similar reference materials can be purchased on CD-ROM (compact disk, read-only memory); and WORM (write-once, read many) technology allows a user to create personalized reference files. Because data on these media are read and written by laser beam, there is no physical contact between the recording surface and the access mechanism, and that tends to minimize wear and tear. Look for high capacity CD-based read/write secondary storage in the near future (perhaps by the time you read this).

Accessing Secondary Storage

Because of its storage capacity, a single disk can hold hundreds of programs or the data for dozens of different applications. If you are a computer user, however, you want a particular program, and you want to access a particular set of data. How does the computer find the right program or the right data?

Start by reviewing how data are stored on disk. The surface is divided into tracks, which, in turn, are divided into sectors or blocks. The tracks are numbered sequentially. The outer track is 0. Moving toward the disk's center, the next track is 1, then 2, and so on. The sectors (or blocks) on a track are also numbered sequentially, starting with 1. Track 5, sector 8 is a particular sector; track 5, sector 9 is a different sector; and track 6, sector

8 is yet another one. Each sector has a unique track/sector address; each physical record has a unique track/block address.

Depending on the operating system, when a program is stored on disk it is either recorded in consecutive sectors (or blocks) or its sectors are in some way linked sequentially. Consequently, if the computer can find the program's first sector, it can find the entire program. To record the starting address of each of its programs, a portion of the disk's first track is set aside to hold a **directory** (Fig. 2.14). When the program is first written to disk, it is assigned a name. The program's name is then recorded in the directory, along with the track and sector (or track and block) address where it begins. Later, to retrieve

Fig. 2.14 The programs and files stored on a disk are listed in the disk's directory.

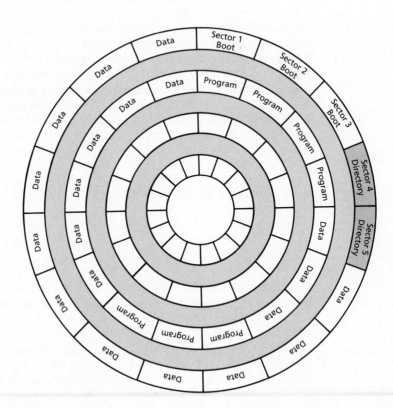

the program, a user enters the program's name. Given a name, the computer reads the directory, searches for the name, finds the address where the program begins, and reads the program.

Data are accessed in much the same way. The data for a given application are grouped to form a file. Each file is assigned a name. The file name and the address of its first sector or block are recorded in the disk's directory. Knowing the file's start address allows the system to find its other blocks or sectors.

Some hard-disk systems support an optional search-by-key feature. In addition to the normal block number, a logical key (for example, a social security number) is recorded with each physical record. During seek time, the access mechanism is positioned over the selected cylinder, and a selected read/write head is activated. Normally, the track is then searched by count for a particular sector or block. When the search-by-key feature is utilized, the track is searched for a logical key.

Secondary storage is an extension of main memory, not a replacement for it. A computer cannot execute a program on disk unless it is first copied into memory, not can it manipulate data on a secondary medium until they have been copied into memory. Main memory holds the current program and the current data; secondary storage is long-term storage.

The input and output devices described earlier provide human access to the computer system; taken together, they are sometimes called the computer's front end. Secondary storage is a machine readable medium. Data are stored in a form convenient to the computer and can be read and written only by the machine; taken together, a computer's secondary storage devices form its back end. The only way people can access the data stored on a disk is by instructing the computer to read them into memory and then write them to the screen or to a printer.

Linking the Components

Data are stored in a computer as patterns of bits. Within a given machine, the patterns are consistent; for example, if the code for the letter A is 01000001, this pattern, and *only* this pattern, will be used to represent an A.

The rule does not apply to input, output, or secondary storage devices, however. On a keyboard, each key generates one character. A printer represents characters as patterns of dots or positions on a print wheel. An optical device reads light intensity, while a disk drive records and reads magnetized spots. Each peripheral device represents or interprets data in its own unique way, and the signals used by a device may or may not match the signals stored inside the computer. If these dissimilar devices are to communicate, translation is necessary. This is the function of the **interface** board.

Consider, for example, a keyboard. When a key is pressed, an electronic signal is sent to the keyboard's interface. In response, the interface generates the code that represents the character inside the computer, and transfers the coded data into memory (2.15a). Change the device to a printer (Fig. 2.15b). As output begins, the data are stored in memory as binary-coded characters. Assume that the printer requires a dot pattern. Clearly translation is necessary. The coded characters are sent to the printer's interface, which translates the computer's binary codes to printer form.

The printer and the keyboard are different; the signals that physically control them and the electronic patterns they use to represent data are device dependent. However, because the device-dependent tasks are assigned to interface boards, both can be attached to the same computer. On input, an interface translates external signals into a form acceptable to the computer. Output signals are electronically converted from the computer's internal code to a form acceptable to the peripheral device. Because they are electronically different, a printer and a keyboard require different interface boards.

Secondary storage devices are linked to the system through interfaces, too. The interface physically controls the disk drive, accepting seek, read, and write commands from the processor, positioning the access mechanism, and managing the flow of data between the disk surface and memory. Because the disk drives attached to a given computer are virtually identical, a single interface often controls two or more peripherals. Consequently, only one drive can be active at a time.

Many interfaces contain buffers. A **buffer** is temporary memory or storage used to adjust for the speed differential between adjacent devices. For example, if you've ever waited for a lengthy paper to print, you know that a printer is much slower than a computer. If waiting for the printer is a problem, add a buffer to the printer interface. Then, instead of the computer sending the contents of memory directly to the printer, it can send the information to the buffer at computer speed. Subsequently, as the characters are dumped from the buffer to the

Fig. 2.15   The functions of an interface board.

a. Input from the keyboard enters the interface and is converted to the computer's internal form.

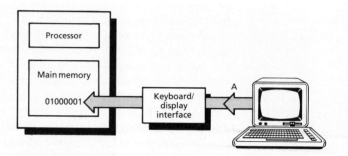

b. Data stored in memory are sent to the printer interface, converted to printer form, and output.

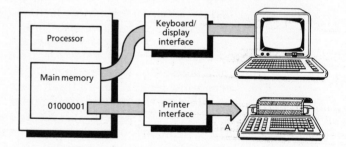

printer at printer speed, the computer can be used for some other task.

Assigning one interface to each device is reasonable on a microcomputer system. However, on a large system with hundreds of peripherals, this approach is simply unworkable. Instead, input and output devices are linked to a large computer system through channels and control units.

Certain functions (for example, deciding where the next byte can be found or stored in memory and counting the characters transferred to or from an external device) are common to almost all types of input and output. On a microcomputer, they are performed by each interface or by the main processor. On larger machines, these common functions are assigned to data **channels** (Fig. 2.16).

Note that a channel performs device-independent functions. Such device-dependent functions as interpreting magnetic patterns or moving a disk's access mechanism are implemented through **I/O control units** or interface units. Each physical device has its own control unit. The channel communicates with the computer in the computer's language; the control unit communicates with the external device on the device's terms; the channel and the control unit, working together, translate.

A typical large computer system may have three or four channels, with numerous control units attached to each one. Some channels overlap or multiplex the operation of several slow input and output devices. Other selector channels link dozens of secondary storage devices to the system, often "selecting" one high-speed device at a time and serving as a data path between it and the computer. When a given data transfer is complete, the channel is then free to select another secondary storage device. With channels and control units, hundreds of input

Fig. 2.16   On a large computer system, peripheral devices are
                       linked to the system through a channel and an I/O
                       control unit.

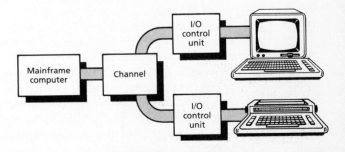

and output devices can access the computer through only a few easy-to-control data paths.

Summary

A computer is a binary machine. Its memory stores bits. Generally, memory is grouped into bytes, or words, or both (depending on the system), and each basic storage unit is assigned an address. Using this address, the processor can read or write selected bytes or words.

The processor consists of a clock, an instruction control unit, an arithmetic and logic unit, and registers. Once a program is stored in memory, the processor can execute it. During I-time, the instruction control unit fetches an instruction from memory; during E-time, the arithmetic and logic unit executes that instruction. Precisely timed electronic pulses generated by the clock drive this basic machine cycle. On many computers, a layer of microcode lies between the processor and memory. People access a computer through its input and output devices.

Because of its cost, limited capacity, and volatility, main memory cannot be used for long-term or for volume storage. Secondary storage is a solution. The most popular microcomputer medium is diskette. Data are stored on the disk's surface on a series of concentric circles called tracks. The tracks are subdivided into sectors. On input, the contents of one sector are copied from disk to memory; on output, one sector moves from memory to the disk's surface. To access disk, it is first necessary to bring the drive up to operating speed and then move the access mechanism over the track containing the desired data (seek time). Additional time is lost waiting for the desired sector to rotate to the read/write head (rotational delay).

Unlike diskette, a hard disk spins constantly, so a major component of seek time is eliminated. Because hard disk rotates faster than diskette, it has less rotational delay. Hard disk has more storage capacity, too. Often, several surfaces are stacked on a single drive shaft to form a disk pack. A disk pack normally has one read/write head per surface, with the heads grouped on a single access mechanism. One position of the access mechanism defines a cylinder consisting of one track on each surface. On many hard disks, tracks are divided into sectors. On others, tracks are divided into physical records or blocks, with the block size chosen to fit the application. Because data are so valuable, disk packs are normally backed up. Magnetic tape is a common backup medium.

A single disk can contain numerous programs and data files. To distinguish them, a directory is maintained. The directory identifies the programs and data files and indicates the track and sector (or track and block) address where each one begins. Given the address of the first sector, the other sectors can be located.

Secondary storage is an extension of main memory. The computer cannot execute a program until it has been loaded into memory, nor can it process data until they have been copied into memory.

Each peripheral device is electronically different, but the computer always deals with a common code. An interface serves to bridge this gap. A buffer can help to adjust for the speed differential between adjacent devices. On larger computers, each peripheral device is linked to a control unit, the control units are plugged into channels, and the channels are connected to the computer. The channel performs device-independent tasks; those function unique to a given peripheral device are assigned to the control unit.

Key Words

address	directory	I-time
arithmetic and	disk	machine cycle
logic unit	diskette	main memory
backup	E-time	microcode
bit	hard disk	output
buffer	input	processor
byte	instruction	program
channel	instruction	register
clock	control unit	secondary storage
control unit (I/O)		word

Exercises

1. Computers manipulate *binary* data and execute *binary* instructions. Why binary?

2. Distinguish between reading and writing memory. Distinguish between ROM and RAM.

3. Distinguish between physical memory and its contents.

4. Define the terms bit, byte, and word, and describe how they relate to each other.

5. How is a computer's main memory addressed? Why is addressing memory important?

6. Draw a sketch showing the key components of a processor. Add blocks representing memory, a program, and data.

7. Explain step-by-step, what happens during a single machine cycle.

8. What are registers? Where are they located? Why are they needed?

9. How are input/output and secondary storage devices similar? How are they different?

10. Why is secondary storage necessary?

11. Distinguish between cylinders, tracks, and sectors. Distinguish between sectors and blocks.

12. Briefly explain the process of reading data from or writing data to disk.

13. Distinguish between diskette and hard disk. What advantages are associated with using hard disk?

14. What is the purpose of a disk's directory? Why is it needed?

15. What is the purpose of an interface? Why are interfaces needed?

16. Distinguish between a microcomputer interface and the channel/control unit used on mainframes. How are they similar? How are they different?

17. Why do computer manufacturers use channels and control units instead of simple interface boards on large computer systems?

18. What is a buffer? Why are buffers used?

19. Briefly distinguish between a selector channel and a multiplexer channel.

20. Exercise 6 asked you to sketch a computer's internal components. Add channels, control units, I/O devices, and secondary storage devices to your sketch.

3

Software and Data

This chapter briefly explains several key software and data concepts, including:

Hardware and software

Software
  Instructions
  Programming languages
  Libraries
  Reentrant code

Data
  Data management
  Data elements
  Data structures
  Access techniques
  Database management

For many readers, this material will be review.

Hardware and Software

A computer is a machine (hardware) that processes data under control of a stored program. All three elements—the hardware, the data, and the software—must be present or the system cannot function. Software and data are stored on the hardware; they exist as nothing more substantial than patterns of bits, electronic impulses, that can be destroyed or changed in far less than the blink of an eye. One pattern of bits might represent a machine-level instruction. Another might hold EBCDIC or ASCII coded data. Yet another might hold a pure binary integer, or a floating-point number. Hardware is physical; software and data are logical.

Software

Instructions

A **program** is a series of instructions that guides a computer through a process. Each **instruction** tells the machine to perform one of its basic functions: add, subtract, multiply, divide, compare, copy, request input, or request output. The processor fetches and executes a single instruction during each machine cycle. A typical instruction (Fig. 3.1) contains an **operation code** that specifies the function to be performed and a series of **operands** that specify the memory locations or registers holding the data to be manipulated. For example, the instruction

ADD 3,4

Fig. 3.1   An instruction is composed of an operation code and one or more operands. The operation code tells the computer what to do. The operand or operands specify the addresses of the data elements to be manipulated.

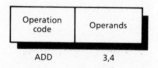

Operation code	Operands
ADD	3,4

tells a hypothetical computer to add the contents of registers 3 and 4.

Because a computer's instruction set is so limited, even simple logical operations call for several instructions. For example, imagine two data values stored in main memory. To add them on many computers, both values are first loaded (or copied) into registers, the registers are added, and then the answer is stored (or copied) back into memory. That's four instructions: LOAD, LOAD, ADD, and STORE. If four instructions are needed to add two numbers, imagine the number of instructions in a complete program.

A computer is controlled by a program stored in its own memory. Because memory stores bits, the program must exist in binary form. Figure 3.2 shows the binary, machine-level instructions needed to load two numbers into registers, add them, and store the answer in memory. If programmers had to write in **machine language** there would be very few programmers.

Programming Languages

One option is to write instructions in an **assembler language**; for example, Fig. 3.3 shows how two numbers might be added in IBM mainframe assembler. The programmer writes one mnemonic (memory-aiding) instruction for each machine-level instruction. AR (for add registers) is much easier to remember than the equivalent binary operation code: 00011010. L (for load) is much easier to remember than 01011000. The operands use labels, such as A, B, and C, instead of numbers to represent memory addresses, and that simplifies the code, too.

Fig. 3.2   Because a computer's main memory stores bits, the
                      program must exist in binary form. These four
                      instructions add two numbers on an IBM mainframe
                      computer.

```
01011000001100001100000000000000
01011000010000001100000000000100
0001101000110100
01010000001100001100000000001000
```

Fig. 3.3   An assembler program reads a programmer's
                    mnemonic source statements, translates each one to a
                    single machine-level instruction, and then combines
                    them to form an object module.

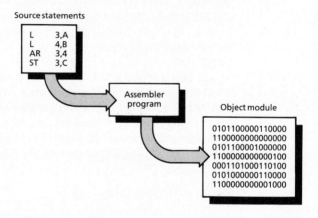

Source statements

L	3,A
L	4,B
AR	3,4
ST	3,C

Assembler program

Object module

```
0101100000110000
1100000000000000
0101100001000000
1100000000000100
0001101000110100
0101000001110000
1100000000001000
```

There are no computers that can directly execute assembler language instructions. Writing mnemonic codes may simplify the programmer's job, but computers are still binary machines that require binary instructions, so translation is necessary. An assembler program (Fig. 3.3) reads a programmer's **source code,** translates the source statements to binary, and produces an **object module.** Because the object module is a machine-level version of the programmer's code, it can be loaded into memory and executed.

An assembler language programmer writes one mnemonic instruction for each machine-level instruction. Because of the one-to-one relationship between the language and the machine, assemblers are machine dependent, and a program written for one type of computer won't run on another. On a given machine, assembler language generates the most efficient programs possible, so assembler is often used to write operating systems and other system software. However, when it comes to application programs, machine dependency is a high price to pay for efficiency, so application programs are rarely written in assembler.

A computer needs four machine-level instructions to add two numbers, because that's the way a computer works. Human beings shouldn't have to think like computers. Why not simply

allow the programmer to indicate addition and assume the other
instructions? For example, one way to view addition is as an algebraic expression:

C = A + B

Why not allow a programmer to write statements in a form similar to algebraic expressions, read those source statements into
a program, and let the program generate the necessary machine-
level code (Fig. 3.4)? That's exactly what happens with a **compiler.** Compare the binary instructions in Figs. 3.3 and 3.4;
they're identical.

Many compiler languages, including FORTRAN, BASIC, Pascal, PL/1, and ALGOL, are algebraically based. The most popular
business-oriented language, COBOL, calls for statements that
resemble brief English-language sentences (Fig. 3.5). Note, however, that no matter what language is used, the objective is the
same. The programmer writes source code. An assembler program accepts mnemonic source code and generates a machine-
level object module. A FORTRAN compiler accepts FORTRAN
source code and generates a machine-level object module. A
COBOL compiler accepts COBOL source code and generates a
machine-level object module.

With an assembler, each source statement is converted to a
single machine-level instruction. With a compiler, a given source

Fig. 3.4   A compiler reads a programmer's source statements,
translates each one to one or more machine-level
instructions, and then combines them to form an
object module.

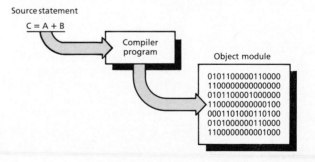

Fig. 3.5   COBOL source statements resemble brief
                          English-language sentences.

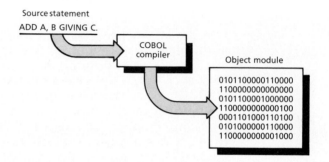

statement may be converted to any number of machine-level instructions. An option is to use an **interpreter.** An assembler or a
compiler reads a complete source program and generates a complete object module. An interpreter, on the other hand, works
with one source statement at a time, reading it, translating it to
machine level, executing the resulting binary instructions, and
then moving on to the next source statement. Both compilers
and interpreters generate machine-level instructions, but the
process is different.

Each language has its own syntax, punctuation, and spelling
rules, so a Pascal source program is meaningless to a COBOL
compiler or a BASIC interpreter. However, no matter what language is used, the objective is the same: defining a series of steps
to guide the computer through a process.

Libraries

Picture a programmer writing a large routine. As source statements are typed, they are manipulated by an editor program and
stored on disk in a source statement **library** (Fig. 3.6).

Eventually, the source program is completed and compiled.
The resulting object module might be loaded directly into memory, but more often, it is stored on an object module library (Fig.
3.7). Because object modules are binary, machine-level routines,
there is no inherent difference between one produced by an as-

Fig. 3.6   Source statements are typically typed, manipulated by an editor, and stored on a source statement library. Eventually, the source statements are compiled and an object module is created.

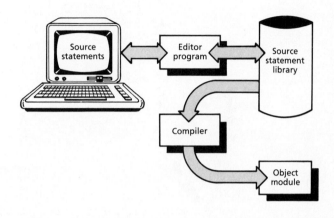

sembler and one produced by a FORTRAN compiler (or any other compiler for that matter). Therefore, object modules generated by different source languages can be stored on the same library.

Some object modules can be loaded into memory and executed. Others, however, include references to subroutines that are not part of the object module. For example, imagine a program that simulates a game of cards. If, some time ago, another programmer wrote an excellent subroutine to deal cards, it would make sense to reuse that logic.

Picture the new program after it has been written, compiled, and stored on the object module library (Fig. 3.8). The subroutine that deals cards is stored on the same library. Before the program is loaded, the two routines must be combined to form a **load module** (Fig. 3.9). An object module is a machine-language translation of a source module, and may include references to other subroutines. A load module is a complete, ready-to-execute program with all subroutines in place. Combining object modules to form a load module is the job of the **linkage editor** or **loader** (Fig. 3.10). A linkage editor prepares a complete load module and copies it to a library for immediate or eventual loading. A loader, on the other hand, simple creates a load module in memory and starts its execution.

Fig. 3.7

Object modules can be stored on a library, too. Because an object module is a binary, machine-level routine, there is no inherent difference between one produced by an assembler and one produced by a FORTRAN compiler, so both can be stored on the same library.

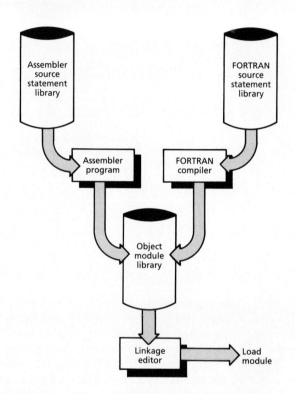

Fig. 3.8

In this example, the just created object module is incomplete because it includes a reference to an independent subroutine.

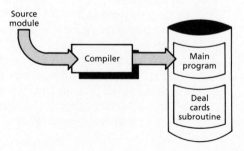

Fig. 3.9   Before the program can be loaded and executed, the object modules for the main program and the subroutine must be combined to form a load module.

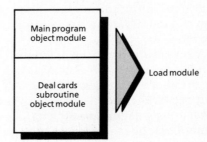

Fig. 3.10   The linkage editor combines object modules to form a complete, ready-to-execute load module.

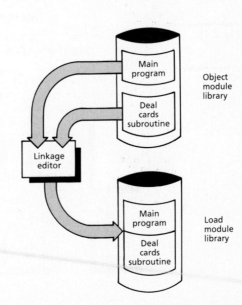

Reentrant Code

Many programs modify themselves as they run, changing key data values and even executable instructions. Imagine two users concurrently accessing the same program. Any attempt to share the code would be doomed because changes made by one user could have unforeseen consequences for the other. If the program can modify itself, there must be two copies in memory, one for each user.

A **reentrant** program or program module does *not* modify itself. Consequently, since the code does not change, two or more programmers can share the same logic. Often, the secret to creating reentrant code is breaking the program into two components: a logic segment and a data segment (Fig. 3.11). The data segment belongs to an individual user and can be modified as the program runs. The logic segment, on the other hand, consists of program instructions that cannot be changed. Given such segmentation, it is possible to assign each of several users their own data segments and allow them to share a single logic segment (Fig. 3.11). Avoiding duplication of program logic can save a great deal of memory space.

An operating system is composed of system software modules that support application programs. On a large system, several applications may execute concurrently. It makes little sense to include multiple copies of the same support logic, so almost

Fig. 3.11   Given reentrant code, it is possible for several users to share the same logic segment. This saves memory space.

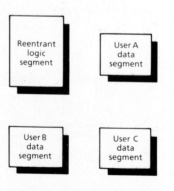

by definition, an operating system contains shared, reentrant code.

Data

Data Management

Like software, data are stored on hardware as patterns of bits. Simply storing the data is not enough, however, A typical computer system, even a small one, can have dozens of disks and tapes, each holding data for dozens of different applications, and for any given application, one and only one set of data will do. A computer system must be able to store, locate, and retrieve the specific data needed by a given program. That is the concern of **data management.**

A single diskette can hold numerous programs, or data for several different applications, or both. For a given application, one and only one set of data will do, and finding the right data is much like finding the right program. There are differences between accessing programs and accessing data, however. When a program is needed, all its instructions must be loaded into memory. Data, on the other hand, are processed selectively, a few elements at a time. Thus, it is not enough merely to locate the data; you must be able to distinguish the individual data elements, too.

Data Elements

A **data element** is a single, meaningful unit of data, such as a name, a social security number, or a temperature reading. Most computers can store and manipulate pure binary integers, floating-point numbers, decimal numbers, and character or string data. (See Appendix A for a review of these data types.)

Data Structures

The key to retrieving data is remembering where they are stored. If the data elements are stored according to a consistent and well-understood structure, it is possible to retrieve them by remembering that structure.

The simplest **data structure** is a list. For example, data for a program that computes an average might be stored as a series of numbers separated by commas. The commas distinguish the individual data elements.

Most programming languages support a more complex data structure called an array (Fig. 3.12). Each array element holds one data value. Each element is assigned a unique identifying number or numbers, and individual data elements can be inserted, extracted, or manipulated by referencing those numbers. For example, in the array pictured in Fig. 3.12, elements are identified by a row number and a column number, and row 1, column 3 (element 1,3) contains the value 29. Once an array has been filled, it can be written to disk, tape, or any other secondary medium and later read back into memory for processing.

Consider a program that generates name and address labels. For each label, you need a name, a street address, a city, a state, and a zip code. If you needed only a few labels, you might store the data in a list, but separating the elements would soon become tedious. An option is to set up an array of names and addresses, with each row holding the data for a single label. The only problem is that the entire array must be in memory before the individual elements can be accessed, and memory space is limited. Thus, even with an array, you could generate relatively few labels.

Fig. 3.12   Most programming languages support a data
                     structure called an array.

1,1	1,2	1,3	1,4	1,5
71	38	29	90	70
2,1	2,2	2,3	2,4	2,5
91	13	56	77	20
3,1	3,2	3,3	3,4	3,5
68	18	54	63	56
4,1	4,2	4,3	4,4	4,5
12	38	68	39	74
5,1	5,2	5,3	5,4	5,5
82	80	35	98	61

A better solution is to organize the data as a **file** (Fig. 3.13). All computer data begin as patterns of bits. On a file, the bits are grouped to form characters. Groups of characters, in turn, form meaningful data elements called fields. A group of related fields is a record; the file is a set of related records. For example, in a name and address file, an individual's name is a field. Each record holds a complete set of data for a single individual (a name, a street address, and so on). The file consists of all the records.

The data in a file are processed record by record. Normally, the file is stored on a secondary medium such as a disk. Programs are written to read a record, process its fields, generate the appropriate output, and then read and process another record. Because only one record is in main memory at a time, very little memory is needed. Because many records can be stored on a single disk, a great deal of data can be processed in this limited space.

Fig. 3.13 Characters are grouped to form fields. Fields are grouped to form records. A file is a group of related records.

File

Name	Street address	City	State	Zip code
Melinda Atkins	142 Maple St.	Oxford	Ohio	450781718
Charles Baker	713 Main Street	Cincinnati	Ohio	457033304
Thomas Bates	42 South Blvd.	Atlanta	Georgia	352170315
Lisa Campanella	8 Tower Square	San Jose	California	953214450
Shen Chan	State Route 77	Binghamton	New York	127561495
Tomas Garcia	473 Dixie Highway	Lexington	Kentucky	434101236
⋮	⋮	⋮	⋮	⋮
Arthur White	Northside Mall	Orlando	Florida	214504372
Character				
Field	Field	Field	Field	Field
Record				

Access Techniques

How can a computer locate specific records in a file? The key to many storage and retrieval techniques is the **relative record number.** Imagine a string of 100 records. Number the first one 0, the second 1, the third 2, and so on. The numbers indicate a given record's position relative to the first record in the file. The file's first record (relative record 0) is at "start of file plus 0"; its second record is at "start of file plus 1," and so on.

Now, store the records on disk (Fig. 3.14); to keep the initial example simple, store one per sector. Number the sectors relative to the start of the file—0, 1, 2, and so on. Note that the relative record number, a logical concept, and the relative sector number, a physical location, are identical. Given a relative record number, it is possible to compute a relative sector number. Given a relative sector number, it is possible to compute a physical disk address.

Assume a file begins at track 30, sector 1, and that one logical record is stored in each sector. As Fig. 3.15 shows, relative record 0 is stored at track 30, sector 1, relative record 1 is at track 30, sector 2, and so on. Where is relative record 10? Track 30, sector 11. In this example, the relative record number indicates how many sectors away from the beginning of the file the record is stored. The file starts at track 30, sector 1. Relative record 10 is stored 10 sectors away, at track 30, sector 11.

Fig. 3.14   A relative record number indicates a record's position relative to the first record in a file. Given a relative record number, it is possible to compute a physical disk address.

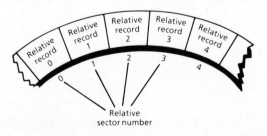

Fig. 3.15   Given the start of a file address (from open) and a
                       relative record number, a physical disk address can be
                       computed.

Relative record number	Actual location on disk	
	Track	Sector
0	30	1
1	30	2
2	30	3
3	30	4
4	30	5
5	30	6
6	30	7
7	30	8
8	30	9
9	30	10
10	30	11
.	.	.
.	.	.
.	.	.

You might complicate matters by storing two or more logical
records in each sector, or by creating a file extending over two or
more tracks, but in either case it is still possible to develop a simple algorithm to compute a record's physical location, given its
relative record number. Many different algorithms are used.
Some allow records to be stored or retrieved sequentially.
Others allow individual records to be accessed in random order.
Let's examine a few common **data access** techniques.

Imagine preparing meeting announcements for a club. You
need a set of mailing labels, and each member's name and address is recorded on an index card. Probably the easiest way to
generate the labels is to copy the data from the first card, turn to
the second card and copy it, and so on, processing the records
sequentially, from the beginning of the file to the end.

Magazine publishers face the same problem with each new
issue, but need mailing labels for tens of thousands of subscrib-
ers. Rather than using index cards, they store customer data on
disk or magnetic tape, one record per subscriber. The easiest
way to ensure that all labels are generated is to process the records in the order in which they are stored, proceeding sequen-

tially from the first record in the file to the last. To simplify handling, the records might be presorted by zip code or a mailing zone, but the basic idea of processing the data in physical order still holds.

How does this relate to the relative record number concept? A relative record number indicates a record's position on the file. With sequential access, processing begins with relative record 0, then moves to relative record 1, 2, and so on. Accessing data sequentially involves little more than counting. For example, imagine a program has just finished processing relative record 14. What is the next record? Obviously, relative record 15. Simply by counting records, it is possible to read them, or write them, in physical order.

Processing records in sequence is not always acceptable. For example, when a subscriber moves, his or her address must be changed in the file. Searching for that subscriber's record sequentially is like looking for a telephone number by starting with the first page of the telephone book and reading line by line. That's not how you use a telephone book. Instead, knowing the records are stored in alphabetical order, you quickly narrow your search to a portion of a single page, and then begin reading the entries, ignoring the bulk of the data. The way you use a telephone book is a good example of direct, or random, access.

A disk drive reads or writes one sector at a time. To randomly access a specific record, all the programmer must do is remember the address of the sector that holds the record and ask for it. The problem is remembering all those disk addresses. One solution is to maintain an index of the records. Use the names and address file as an example. As the file is created, records are written, one at a time, in relative record number order. Additionally, as each record is written, the customer name and the associated relative record number are recorded in an array or index (Fig. 3.16). After the last record has been written to disk and its position recorded on the index, the index is itself stored.

Once the index has been created, it can be used to find individual records. Assume, for example, that Susan Smith has changed her address. To record her new address on the file, a program could:

1. read the file index,
2. search the index for her name,
3. find her relative record number,
4. compute the disk address, and read her record,
5. change her address, and
6. rewrite the record to the same place on disk.

Fig. 3.16   A file index can help when records must be accessed
directly.

Key	Relative record
Atkins, Melinda	0
Baker, Charles	1
Bates, Thomas	2
Campanella, Lisa	3
Chan, Shen	4
Garcia, Tomas	5
.	.
.	.

Note that this specific record is accessed directly, and that no
other records in the file are involved.

The basic idea of direct access is assigning each record an
easy-to-remember, logical key, and then converting that key to a
relative record number. Given this relative location, a physical
address can be computed, and the record accessed. Using an
index is one technique for converting keys to physical addresses. Another is to pass a numeric key to an algorithm and
compute a relative record number.

Not all data access techniques rely on relative *record* numbers; in fact, some computer experts consider the very concept
of a record an unnecessary anachronism left over from the days
of punched cards. On many modern operating systems there are
no records. Instead, data stored on disk are treated as simple
strings of characters or bytes, and no other structure is imposed. On such systems, programmers address data by relative
byte number (the same way they address main memory).

Database Management

There are problems with traditional data management. Many of
these result from viewing applications independently. For example, consider payroll. Most organizations prepare their payrolls
by computer because using a machine instead of a small army of

clerks saves money. Thus, the firm develops a payroll program to process a payroll file. Inventory, accounts receivable, accounts payable, and general ledger are similar applications, so the firm develops an inventory program, an inventory file, an accounts receivable program, an accounts receivable file, and so on. Each program is independent, and each processes its own independent data file.

Why is this a problem? For one thing, different applications often need the same data elements. For example, schools generate both bills and student grade reports. View the applications independently. The billing program reads a file of billing data, and the grade report program reads an independent file of grade data. The outputs of both programs are mailed to the students' homes, so student names and addresses must be redundantly recorded on both files. What happens when a student moves? Unless both files are updated, one will be wrong. Redundant data are difficult to maintain.

Data dependency is a more subtle problem. There are many different file organizations, each has its own rules for storing and retrieving data, and certain tricks of the trade can significantly improve the efficiency of a given program. If the programmer takes advantage of these efficiencies, the program's logic becomes dependent upon the physical structure of the data. When a program's logic is tied to its physical data structure, changing that structure will almost certainly require changing the program. As a result, programs using traditional access methods can be difficult to maintain.

The solution to both problems is organizing the data as a single, integrated **database.** The task of controlling access to all the data can then be concentrated in a centralized database management system (Fig. 3.17).

How does a centralized database solve the data redundancy problem? All data are collected and stored in a single place; consequently, there is one and only one copy of any given data element. When the value of an element (an address, for example) changes, the single database copy is corrected. Any program requiring access to this data element gets the same value, because there is only one value.

How does a database help to solve the data dependency problem? Since the responsibility for accessing the physical data rests with the database management system, the programmer can ignore the physical data structure. As a result, programs tend to be must less dependent upon their data and are generally much easier to maintain.

Fig. 3.17   Many of the problems associated with traditional data
                       access techniques can be solved by using a database.

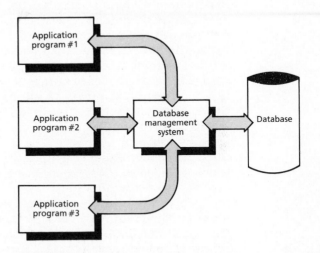

Summary

A program is a series of instructions that guides a computer
through a process. Each instruction tells the machine to perform one of its basic functions. Because computers are binary
machines, the program stored in a computer's main memory
must be in binary form.

An assembler programmer writes one mnemonic instruction
for each machine-level instruction. A compiler reads source
statements, translates each one into one or more machine-level
instructions, and combines them to form an object module. An
interpreter works with one source statement at a time, translating it and executing the resulting machine-level code before
moving on to the next instruction.

Source code is stored on a source statement library. An assembler or compiler reads the source code and stores the resulting object module on an object module library. A linkage editor
or loader combines object modules to form a load module. An object module is a machine-level translation of a programmer's
source code that may include references to other subroutines. A
load module is a complete, ready-to-execute program.

The key to retrieving data is remembering where they are stored. Often, the secret is storing them in a well-defined structure. The simplest data structure is a list. Most programming languages support arrays; individual data elements are identified by numbering the array's cells.

In a file, individual characters are grouped to form fields, fields are grouped to form records, and a set of related records forms the file. Accessing the data on a file involves reading and writing individual records. Often, the key to finding a specific record is its relative record number. The records in a file are numbered sequentially, with each relative record number indicating the record's position relative to the first one in the file. Given its relative record number, it is possible to compute a record's physical location.

With sequential access, data are stored and retrieved in a fixed order, essentially by counting records. With direct or random access, individual records can be retrieved without regard for their positions on the physical file. Not all data access techniques rely on relative record numbers, however. Some treat the data stored on disk as simple character or byte strings and use relative byte values to address them.

With traditional data management, because different applications often require the same data, certain data elements may be stored redundantly. Also, a program's logic can be too closely linked to the physical structure of its data. The solution is to collect all the organization's data in a centralized database. With a database, there is only one copy of each data element, so the data redundancy problem is eliminated. Because every program must access data through a database management system, programs are insulated from the physical data structure,so data dependency is reduced.

Key Words

assembler language	instruction	object module
compiler	interpreter	operand
data access	library	operation code
data element	linkage editor	program
data management	load module	reentrant
data structure	loader	relative record
database	machine language	number
file		source code

Exercises

1. Without a program to provide control, a computer is little more than an expensive calculator. Do you agree? Why, or why not?

2. Relate the idea of an instruction to a computer's basic machine cycle.

3. Why are programming languages necessary?

4. Distinguish between an assembler and a compiler.

5. Distinguish between a compiler and an interpreter.

6. What is a library? Why are libraries useful?

7. Distinguish between a source module, an object module, and a load module.

8. When a program is accessed, all its instructions are accessed. Data, on the other hand, are accessed selectively. Explain.

9. What is a data element? Describe several different types of data elements.

10. What is a data structure? Why are data structures important?

11. Briefly relate the terms character, field, record, and file.

12. Briefly explain the relative record concept.

13. Distinguish between sequential and direct access. Relate both techniques to the relative record concept.

14. Some modern operating systems don't even recognize records, treating data stored on disk as simple strings of bytes. What advantages might you expect from such an approach? What disadvantages?

15. What is a database? Why are databases useful?

4

Linking the Components

This chapter explains how a computer's
components are physically linked. Key
topics include:

Linking internal components
  Bus lines
  Word size

Machine cycles

Architectures
  Single-bus architecture
  Interfaces
  Channels and control units
  Multiple-bus architecture

Logical and physical I/O
  Primitives
  Open
  Accessing data

These concepts are crucial to
understanding how an operating system
works.

Linking Internal Components

Bus Lines

A computer is a system, with data and instructions flowing between its components in response to processor commands. Clearly, those components must be physically linked. Inside a computer, speed is essential, so internal components are normally linked by **bus** lines. A bus is a ribbonlike set of parallel wires that can carry several bits at a time.

Some bus lines transmit power. Others carry instructions, data, addresses, or commands. On some computers, a single bus might serve two or more purposes; on others, the data, address, and command buses are separate. Basically, however, a computer's internal components are linked by bus lines.

Word Size

Communication between components is greatly simplified if they are electronically similar. Thus, on most systems, the internal components are designed around a common **word** size. For example, on a 32-bit computer, the processor manipulates 32-bit numbers, memory and the registers store 32-bit words, and data and instructions move between the components over 32-bit bus lines.

A computer's word size affects its processing speed, memory capacity, precision, and instruction set size. Consider speed first. A 32-bit bus contains 32 wires, and thus can carry 32 bits at a time. A 16-bit bus has only 16 parallel wires, and thus can carry only 16. Because the wider bus moves twice as much data in the same amount of time, the 32-bit machine is clearly faster. Generally, the bigger the word size, the faster the computer.

Memory capacity is also a function of word size. To access memory, the processor must transmit over a bus the address of a desired instruction or data element. On a 32-bit machine, a 32-bit address can be transmitted. The biggest 32-bit number is roughly 4 billion in decimal terms, so the process can access as many as 4 billion different memory locations. On the other hand, a 16-bit computer transmits a 16-bit address, limiting it to roughly 64,000 memory locations. Generally, the bigger its word size, the more memory a computer can access.

There are 16-bit microcomputers that access considerably more than 64k bytes of memory. How is that possible? A 16-bit machine can access more than 64K if addresses are broken into two or more parts and transmitted during successive machine cycles. Each cycle takes time, however, so memory capacity is gained at the expense of processing speed.

Next, consider the size of the numbers each machine can manipulate. Registers generally hold one word. The processor's internal circuitry is usually most efficient when manipulating numbers one word in length. A 32-bit mainframe adds 32-bit numbers; a 16-bit machine adds 16-bit numbers. Clearly, the machine with the bigger word size is more precise. While the 16-bit machine may be able to add two 32-bit numbers, it will need several machine cycles to do so, once again sacrificing speed.

What about instructions? They, too, must move from memory to the processor over a bus. A 32-bit bus can carry a bigger instruction than a 16-bit bus. The bigger instruction size means more bits are available for the operation code. A machine with a 6-bit op code can have only 64 different instructions, while a machine with an 8-bit op code can have as many as 256 different instructions.

Machine Cycles

Perhaps the easiest way to envision how the various components of a computer are linked is to follow, in detail, a typical **machine cycle.** Consider the computer pictured in Fig. 4.1a. Note that a single bus line links the processor, the registers, and memory. The system registers hold key control information and are not, normally, available to the application programmer. The work registers can be used by the programmer for computations or addressing.

During instruction time, or I-time, the instruction control unit fetches the next instruction from memory. The address of the next instruction is found in the instruction counter. The instruction control unit extracts this address and sends it as part of a fetch **command** over the bus to the memory controller (Fig. 4.1a). The memory controller accepts the command, reads the requested memory location, and copies its contents onto the bus (Fig. 4.1b). This takes time, giving the instruction control unit an opportunity to increment the instruction counter to point to the *next* instruction. Meanwhile, the current instruction moves over the bus and into the instruction register (Fig. 4.1c).

During E-time, the arithmetic and logic unit executes the instruction in the instruction register (Fig. 4.1d). Assume it calls for loading a main memory word into a work register. Responding to the instruction, the arithmetic and logic unit issues, again

Fig. 4.1   A machine cycle.

a. Obtaining the address of the next instruction from the instruction counter, the instruction control unit sends a fetch command to memory.

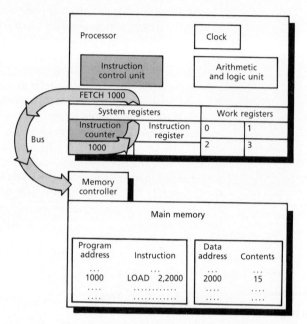

b. The memory controller responds to the fetch command by copying the contents of the requested memory location onto the bus.

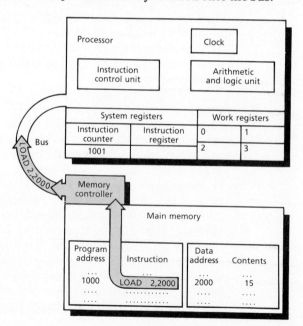

c. The instruction moves over the bus and into the instruction register.

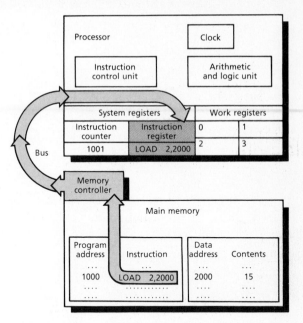

d. During E-time, the arithmetic and logic unit executes the instruction in the instruction register.

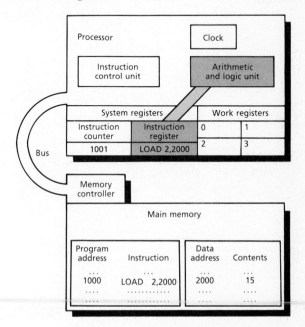

e. The instruction calls for copying data from memory into a register, so the arithmetic and logic unit sends a fetch command to memory.

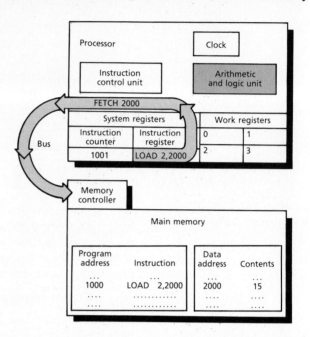

f. The memory controller responds by copying the contents of the requested memory location onto the bus. The data value then flows over the bus and into a work register.

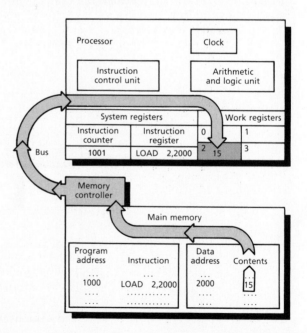

over the bus, a command to fetch the contents of a specified memory location (Fig. 4.1e). As before, the memory controller reads the requested word, copies the contents onto the bus, and the data flow into a work register (Fig. 4.1f).

Note carefully how the components are coordinated. Instructions, addresses, and data flow over the bus in response to commands issued by the processor. Controlling everything, of course, are the clock's precisely timed pulses.

Not all instructions can be executed in a single machine cycle. For example, contrast an instruction that adds the contents of two registers with one that adds two values stored in main memory. In the first case, the data are already in the processor. In the second case, the arithmetic and logic unit will have to fetch both values before adding them, and that takes time. Adding two registers might call for a single machine cycle. Adding memory contents to a register might take two machine cycles, while adding two memory locations might require four. More complex instructions (such as multiplying two decimal numbers) might consume a dozen or more.

Recently, several firms have announced reduced instruction set computers (RISC technology). The idea is simple. Instead of offering a complete instruction set (for example, one including binary, decimal, floating-point, and string operations) the number of available instructions is reduced and the hardware is optimized to execute each of them in one or two machine cycles. While not ideal for every application, reduced instruction set computers offer significant advantages for such compute-bound tasks as engineering graphics, simulation, and network management.

Architectures

Not all computers are designed in exactly the same way. Computer scientists use the term **architecture** to describe the relationships between a computer's components.

Single-Bus Architecture

Most microcomputers are constructed around a motherboard (Fig. 4.2), a metal framework containing a series of slots linked, through a bus, to a processor (Fig. 4.3). Memory is added by plugging a memory board into one of the open slots (Fig. 4.4). Additional boards tie input, output, and secondary storage devices to the system. The components pictured in Fig. 4.4 are linked by a

Fig. 4.2   A microcomputer is constructed around a metal
                     framework called a motherboard.

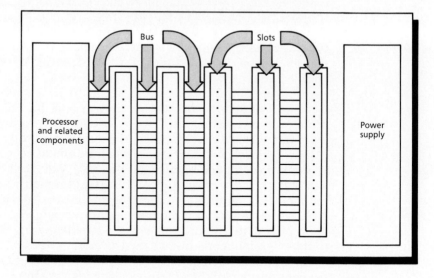

Fig. 4.3   A schematic drawing showing a processor and a
                     motherboard. A bus links the processor with a
                     number of slots into which components can be
                     plugged.

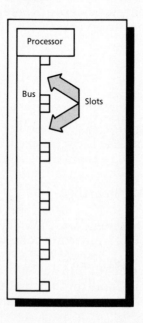

Fig. 4.4   Input devices, output devices, and secondary storage
devices are added to the system by plugging the
appropriate interface into an open slot and then
running a cable from the external device to the
interface.

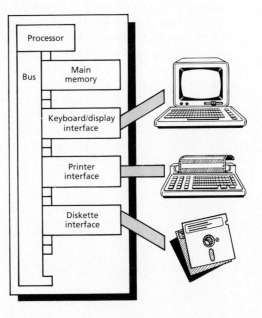

Fig. 4.5   A typical microcomputer uses a single-bus
architecture, with all internal components linked by a
single bus line.

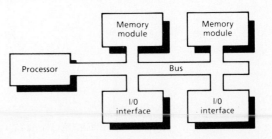

common bus; this arrangement is called **single-bus architecture** (Fig. 4.5). All communications between the components flow over this single bus.

Interfaces

Because the electronic signals controlling a keyboard/display unit, a printer, and a diskette drive are different, each peripheral device has its own **interface.** One side of the interface communicates with the computer, using internal codes (Fig. 4.6). The other side is device dependent, communicating with the external device in its own terms. The basic function of the interface is translation.

For example, the letter A is represented physically both as a key on a keyboard and as a dot pattern on a printer. When a user types *A,* an electronic pulse enters the keyboard/display interface where it is translated to the binary code that represents an *A* inside the computer. Later, on output, this same code is sent to a printer interface, where it is translated to the electronic signals needed to form the proper dot pattern. Note that the computer always uses the same binary code, no matter what peripheral device is involved. To the processor all peripherals look alike.

Channels and Control Unit

Microcomputers are designed for single users, so single-bus architecture is reasonable. A mainframe with a 32-bit processor, a million or more bytes of memory, scores of secondary storage devices, and numerous input and output devices is much too powerful and expensive to dedicate to a single user, however. Consequently, mainframes often execute several programs con-

---

Fig. 4.6   The basic function of an interface is to translate between internal and external data forms.

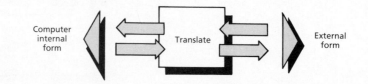

currently. A mainframe's basic machine cycle is identical to a microcomputer's—its processor still fetches and executes one instruction at a time. How can such a machine execute two or more programs concurrently? The key is freeing the main processor from responsibility for controlling I/O.

Controlling input and output involves such logical functions as selecting the path over which the data are to flow, counting characters, and computing memory addresses. Because the main processor is the only source of logic on a microcomputer system, the processor must directly control each input and output operation. While it is controlling I/O, the processor is not available to execute application program instructions, but given the nature of a microcomputer system, this is a minor problem.

Most mainframes assign the task of controlling I/O to **channels** (Fig. 4.7). A channel is a micro- or minicomputer with its own processor. Thus it can perform logical functions in parallel with the computer's main processor, freeing the main processor to do other things.

Some I/O functions are device dependent; for example, controlling the movement of an access arm is a disk problem, while converting characters to a dot pattern is unique to a dot matrix printer. Other tasks, such as selecting a data path, counting characters, and computing memory addresses, are common to all input and output operations, no matter what peripheral

Fig. 4.7   On a mainframe, device-independent functions are assigned to a channel, and device-dependent functions are assigned to an I/O control unit.

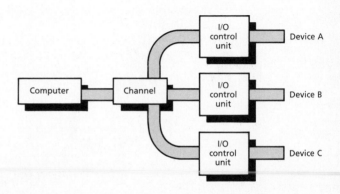

Fig. 4.8   Most mainframes use multiple-bus architecture.

a. The main processor starts an I/O operation by sending a signal to
   the channel.

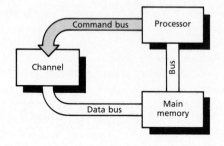

b. The channel assumes responsibility for the I/O operation, and the
   processor turns its attention to another program.

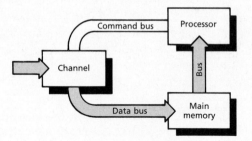

c. The channel sends an interrupt to the processor to signal the end of
   the I/O operation.

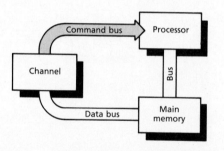

device is involved. The channel performs these device-*independent* functions, while the device-*dependent* functions are assigned to an I/O **control unit.** Each physical device has its own control unit.

Multiple-Bus Architecture

Single-bus architecture creates a number of problems on a multiple-user system. Channel communication is one of the easiest to visualize. A channel moves data between memory and a peripheral device. The computer's processor manipulates data in memory. Allowing a channel and a processor to simultaneously access memory won't work on a microcomputer system, because the single-bus architecture provides only one physical data path. Simultaneous access requires independent data paths, so most mainframes use **multiple-bus architecture** (Fig. 4.8).

Start with a channel. Typically, two bus lines link it with the computer (Fig. 4.8a). As an input or output operation begins, the main processor sends a "start I/O" command over the command bus to the channel's processor. In response, the channel assumes responsibility for the input or output operation, establishing a link with the external device and controlling the transfer of data into main memory over the data bus (Fig. 4.8b). (Note that the *channel's* memory serves as a buffer between the peripheral device and *main* memory. Meanwhile, the main processor can turn its attention to another program. Note that both the main processor and the channel's processor can directly access memory.

The channel is an independent, asynchronous device with its own processor. It controls the I/O operation. Because the channel and the computer are independent, the main processor has no way of knowing when the I/O operation is complete unless the channel's processor tells it, so as the last character of data flows across the channel, the channel processor sends the main processor an electronic signal called an **interrupt** (Fig. 4.8c). When it receives the interrupt, the main processor knows the requested I/O operation has been completed, and can take appropriate action. The interrupt process will be discussed in detail in Chapters 5 and 6.

Logical and Physical I/O

Picture a sequential file on disk. Imagine a program designed to process the file's records. Whenever a READ statement is executed, the programmer expects the next record to be copied from disk into main memory. What exactly is meant by the "next" record? It's a logical concept. In effect, the programmer is saying, "Get me the next record, and I don't care what physical steps are involved." It's not that easy. The data must be copied from one device to another, and that involves considerable logic.

Primitives

Peripheral devices are controlled by interfaces or control units that are limited to a few **primitive** operations. For example, a disk interface or control unit can:

1. move the access mechanism to a specific track (seek),
2. read a specific sector, or
3. write a specific sector.

Because printers, tape drives, and terminals are so different, they are controlled by different sets of primitive operations, and thus by different interfaces. Interfaces and control units execute special programs, called I/O or **channel programs,** that consist of primitive commands.

Open

Because computers and their peripherals are physically independent, their electronic signals must be carefully synchronized before they can begin communicating. Often, an initial electronic link is established by exchanging a set of prearranged protocol signals at **open** time. After a device is officially opened, the computer knows it exists and knows how to communicate with it.

Often, open involves more than simply establishing communication with a peripheral device. For example, a single disk can hold hundreds of programs and data files. For a given application, only one program and only one set of data will do. How does the system select the right program or the right data file?

The files stored on a disk are identified by name in the disk's directory (see Chapter 2). On a given system, the directory is always stored in the same place (for example, track 0, sector 2). Once initial contact with the disk drive has been established, the open logic can issue the primitive commands to read the directory (seek track 0, read sector 2). Once the directory is in memory, the open logic can search it for the file's name. Recorded along with the file name is the disk address where the file begins. Given the address of a file's first sector, the location of its other sectors can be computed.

Accessing Data

A disk controller is limited to a few primitive functions, including:

1. seek to a track,
2. read a sector,
3. write a sector.

The concept of the "next" record is meaningless at this level. To find data physically on disk, you must specify a track and issue a seek command, and then specify a sector and issue a read command. The programmer is concerned with **logical** I/O. The device is limited to **physical** I/O.

The task of bridging this gap starts when the application program issues a logical I/O request. The problem is converting this logical request into a series of primitive physical I/O operations. Often, the key is the relative record number.

A relative record number indicates a record's position relative to the beginning of a file. One function of the open logic was reading the disk's directory, searching it for the file's name, and extracting the file's start address. In general, once a file has been opened, its start address is known, so the location of any record on that file can be computed by using the appropriate relative record number.

Once again, imagine a program reading data sequentially. As the program begins, the file is opened. The disk address of its first record is now known. The file's first record is relative record 0; its second record is relative record 1, and so on. Accessing individual records involves little more than counting them. For example, imagine that relative record 5 has just been read. Clearly, the "next" record is relative record 6. Where is it physically located? Given the start of file address (from open), and knowing that the desired record is at "start of file plus 6," its disk address can be computed and the necessary primitive commands issued.

Now, picture a direct access application. A program needs data for student number 123456. In some way, that student number must be converted to a relative record number. One option is to use a randomizing algorithm. Another is to store a

Fig. 4.9   Often, responsibility for converting a programmer's
logical I/O requests into primitive physical commands
is assigned to the operating system.

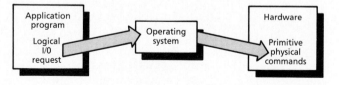

table of student numbers and their associated relative record
numbers and do a table look-up. Once the student number has
been converted to a relative record number, the process of computing a disk address, given the start of file address, is easy.
Given the disk address, the necessary primitive commands can
be issued.

Of course, few programmers communicate directly with peripheral devices at a primitive level. Generally, the responsibility for translating a programmer's logical I/O requests to
physical commands is assigned to the operating system (Fig.
4.9). Because there are so many data access techniques available, some mainframe computers assign application-dependent
portions of this translation process to special subroutines called
access methods (Fig. 4.10), keeping only application-*independent* logic in the operating system. An access method is added to
a program load module by the linkage editor (Fig. 4.11), so

Fig. 4.10   On many mainframe computers,
application-dependent portions of the
logical-to-physical I/O conversion are performed by
an access method.

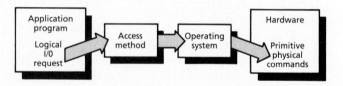

application-dependent I/O logic occupies memory only when the application program occupies memory. Another option is to assign responsibility for all database access to a database management system.

Once a record's physical location has been determined, the process of communicating with the peripheral device can begin. Typically, the access method identifies the necessary primitive commands, sets up a channel program, and calls the operating system. The operating system then sends a "start I/O" signal to the channel, which accesses memory, finds the channel program, and transfers it to the I/O control unit. Once the data have been transferred, the channel notifies the operating system through an interrupt, and the program can resume processing. The elements involved in this operation are summarized in Fig. 4.12.

Many students are surprised to learn that a task as apparently simple as reading data from disk can be so complex. In fact, the complexity associated with physical I/O is one of the major reasons why operating systems and systems software came into being. Remember the basic function of an operating

Fig. 4.11   Access methods are added to a program load module by the linkage editor.

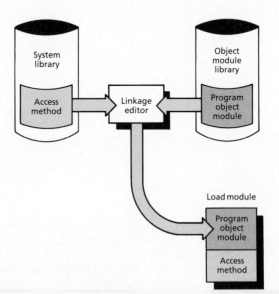

Fig. 4.12   This figure summarizes the process of converting a
                     logical I/O request to primitive physical commands.

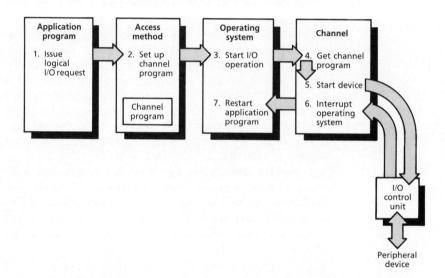

system: to present the programmer with a relatively friendly interface. Physical I/O is one of those rough spots in the hardware.

Access methods were among the first system programs, and
input/output control forms the core of most modern operating
systems. We are, however, getting ahead of ourselves. In the
chapters that follow, you will study key operating system concepts in some detail. An operating system is a resource manager—its job is to manage the hardware, software, and data
resources of a computer system. The intent of Chapter 2, 3, and
4 was to provide you with a summary of these resources and a
feel for how they fit together.

Summary

A computer's internal components are linked by bus lines. On
most computers, the internal components are designed around a
common word size. The choice of a word size affects a
computer's speed, memory capacity, precision, instruction set
size, and cost. Sometime, memory capacity and precision can be
increased by sacrificing processing speed.

A microcomputer is constructed around a metal framework called a motherboard. Features are added by plugging memory boards and various interface boards into available slots; the number of slots limits the number of peripherals that can be added. Typically, each peripheral device requires its own interface board.

Mainframes often support multiple concurrent users. Rather than wasting the main processor's time controlling input and output, the responsibility for I/O is transferred to a channel, which communicates with the external device, performing a number of device-independent functions. Those tasks that depend on the external device are assigned to control units. Because a channel contains its own processor, it can work simultaneously with the main processor. When a channel completes an I/O operation, it notifies the main processor by sending it an electronic signal called an interrupt. For a channel and a main processor to simultaneously access the same main memory, independent data paths are needed, so most mainframes use multiple-bus architecture.

An I/O control unit executes primitive commands to physically control a peripheral device. These primitive commands are given to the control unit in the form of an I/O or channel program.

The first step in accessing a peripheral device is opening it. When a shared device such as disk is opened, the open logic establishes a data path, reads the disk's directory, searches for the file name, and extracts the file's disk address. Given the address of the file's first sector, the location of any data in the file can be computed from a relative record number. Few programmers actually deals with primitive I/O operations. Instead, they assign responsibility for translating logical I/O requests to physical form to the operation system, an access method, or a database management system.

Key Words

access method	control unit	open
architecture	interface	physical I/O
bus	interrupt	primitive
channel	logical I/O	single-bus
channel program	machine cycle	architecture
command	multiple-bus	word
	architecture	

Exercises

1. How are a computer's internal components physically linked?

2. On most computers, all internal components are designed around a common word size. Why?

3. Explain how a computer's word size affects its processing speed, main memory capacity, precision, and instruction set size.

4. What is meant by a computer's architecture?

5. In describing a microcomputer's architecture, the text used the terms motherboard, slot, and bus. Define these terms and discuss how they are related to each other.

6. On a typical microcomputer system, each input, output, and secondary storage device has its own interface. Why?

7. Distinguish between single-bus architecture and multiple-bus architecture.

8. On a mainframe computer, channels and control units are used instead of simple interfaces. Why?

9. What is a primitive operation?

10. Briefly explain what happens when a file is opened.

11. Distinguish between logical and physical I/O.

12. On small computers, responsibility for converting logical I/O requests to physical commands is assigned to the operating system, while on large mainframes, access methods are often used. Why?

PART TWO

Basic Operating System Concepts

5

Microcomputer Operating Systems: The Hardware/Software Interface

This chapter discusses the functions performed by a typical single-user microcomputer operating system. Key topics include:

An operating system's basic functions

Communicating with the user
 The command processor
 The command language
 Batch commands
 Shells

Communicating with the hardware
 The input/output control system
 The file system

Memory management

Interrupts

The boot

Utilities

These functions are common to virtually all operating systems.

An Operating System's Basic Functions

The operating system serves as an interface, insulating both the user and the application software from the hardware. Its most basic functions are communicating with the user and communicating with the hardware. Many single-user, microcomputer operating systems perform these basic functions and little more, while multiple-user operating systems build on them.

Communicating with the User

The Command Processor

Computers are not intelligent. Before the operating system can perform one of its functions, the person using the computer must tell it what to do. The user, much like a military officer, issues orders. The operating system responds like a sergeant, gathering the necessary resources and carrying out each command. The operating system module that accepts, interprets, and carries out commands is called the **command processor** (Fig. 5.1).

Fig. 5.1   The operating system module that accepts, interprets, and carries out commands is called the command processor.

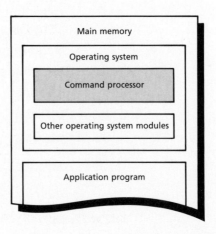

The Command Language

The command processor is composed of a number of routines, each of which performs a single task (Fig. 5.2). For example, one module contains the instructions that guide the computer through the process of loading a program from disk into memory, while another contains the instructions that transfer control of the computer to that program. The programmer or user tells the command processor which functional routine to execute by typing **commands** such as LOAD, RUN, FORMAT, COPY, and so on. The command processor interprets each command and gives control to the appropriate functional module. The set of available commands and their syntax rules form a **command language.**

For example, consider the task of loading and executing a program. As the process begins, a **prompt** is displayed on the screen; it indicates that the operating system is waiting for a command. In response, the user types

Fig. 5.2   The command processor is composed of a number of routines, each of which performs a single, logical function.

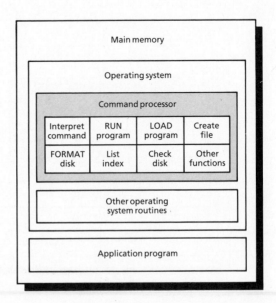

LOAD MYPGM

presses the enter key, and the command flows into memory (Fig. 5.3a). The command processor then evaluates it, recognizes a LOAD command, and transfers control to the program-loading module (Fig. 5.3b), which reads the requested program from disk. Once the program is loaded, the command processor gets control again, displays another prompt, and waits for the next command (Fig. 5.3c).

Assume the next command is

RUN

It tells the operating system to execute the application program stored in memory, so the command processor calls the module that starts the application program (Fig. 5.3d). When the appli-

Fig. 5.3   The operating system is responsible for loading an application program and starting it.

a. Responding to the operating system's prompt, a user types a load command. The command processor then interprets the command.

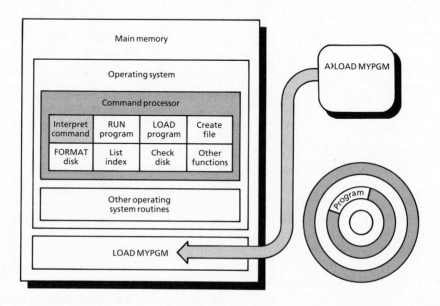

b. The command says to load a program, so the command processor's
    program loading module is called.

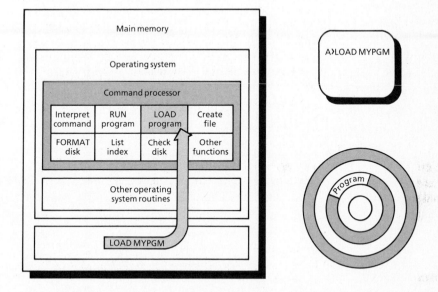

c. After the program is loaded, the command processor gets control,
    displays its prompt, and waits for the next command.

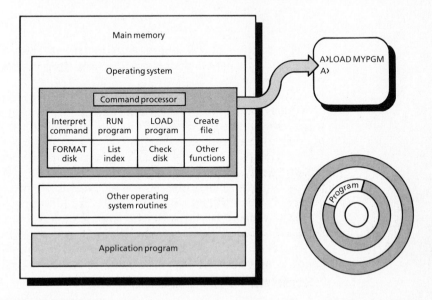

d. The next command tells the operating system to run the program in memory, so the command processor calls the module that starts the application program.

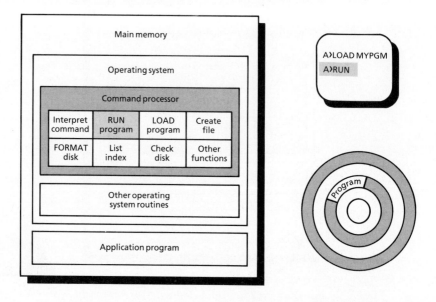

cation program is finished executing, it returns control to the command processor, which displays a prompt and waits for the next command.

On most microcomputers, the command processor is the operating system's main control module, accepting commands, interpreting them, and determining which lower-level routines are needed to carry them out. Some of those lower-level routines communicate directly with the hardware; others perform application tasks. (In fact, the application program itself runs under the command processor.) When a lower-level routine finishes processing, it returns control to the command processor, which displays a prompt and waits for the next command. Such systems are said to be **command driven.**

Incidentally, the task of loading and then executing a program is so common that, in many command languages, both steps are implied when you type the program's name.

Batch Commands

Imagine a payroll application in which input data are verified, sorted, and processed before the checks are printed. Three programs plus a sort operation are required. The commands to perform these functions might include:

LOAD VERIFY

RUN VERIFY

SORT TIMEDATA

LOAD PAYROLL

RUN PAYROLL

LOAD PAYPRINT

RUN PAYPRINT

Payroll is run weekly, so the same seven commands must be typed once a week.

Computers are much better than people at repetitive tasks. That is why most operating systems support **batch files.** To create a batch file, the programmer types a set of commands and saves them in a file. Given the batch file, the application can subsequently be run by typing the file name; for example,

payroll

The command processor responds by searching the system disk for a batch file named *payroll*, reading the file, and then carrying out the specified commands.

Shells

It is useful to visualize the command processor as a **shell** surrounding the operating system (Fig. 5.4). Programmers and users communicate with the shell through commands. The shell, in turn, interprets the commands and uses various operating system functions to access the hardware.

Most microcomputer operating systems include a standard shell that interprets standard commands, but it is possible to

Fig. 5.4   The command processor is sometimes called a shell.

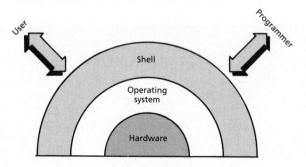

replace or augment the standard shell with a custom shell. For example, while experienced programmers might be comfortable with cryptic DOS or UNIX commands, a nontechnical user might find them intimidating. A custom shell designed for nontechnical users might display available commands as visual images or icons (for example, an open file drawer for SAVE, or a wastebasket for DELETE), and allow the user to select a command by pointing to its image. Another common approach is listing commands in a menu. An operating environment such as Microsoft *Windows* is a good example.

While custom shells can make a computer easier to use, they occupy more memory and consume more processor time than a standard shell. For many users, however, the advantages are worth the cost.

Communicating with the Hardware

The Input/Output Control System

There is a great deal of logic involved in communicating with hardware. For example, consider the problem of accessing data on disk. A disk drive is limited to a few primitive operations, including:

1. seek to a track,
2. read a sector from that track,
3. write a sector to that track.

The only way to read a program or a set of data from disk into memory is to send the drive a series of primitive commands asking it to seek and read the contents of one or more sectors. Note that the disk drive must be told exactly where to position the access mechanism, and exactly which sectors to read.

Imagine if you had to communicate at a primitive level. If your program needed the data stored on track 20, sectors 8 and 9, you would have to tell the system to:

SEEK 20

READ 8

SEEK 20

READ 9

All you want, however, are the data; the primitive hardware details associated with accessing them are (or should be) the computer's concern. That is where the **input/output control system,** or IOCS (Fig. 5.5), comes into play.

The input/output control system communicates directly with the computer's peripheral devices. Each device is controlled by its own unique set of primitive commands. Application programs issue *logical* requests to start input or to start output. The input/output control system accepts these logical I/O requests and generates the primitive commands needed to *physically* control the peripheral device (Fig. 5.6).

Establishing communication with an external device in-

Fig. 5.5   Most operating systems also contain an input/output control system. The IOCS is the module that communicates directly with the peripheral equipment.

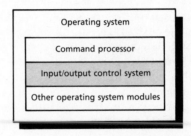

Fig. 5.6   The application program passes logical I/O requests
                    to the input/output control system, which interprets
                    each request and generates the primitive commands
                    needed to control the physical I/O operation.

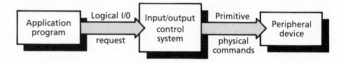

volves more than just generating primitive commands, however.
For example, if two independent hardware components (such as
a computer and a disk drive) are to communicate with each
other, their electronic signals must be carefully synchronized.
Synchronization involves exchanging a predetermined set of
signals called a **protocol.** Starting or checking these protocols is
a tedious process usually assigned to the IOCS.

Other problems arise from the difference between logical
and physical data structures. For example, imagine a program
written to process a series of 56-byte logical records stored on
disk. A disk is physically accessed one sector at a time. Assume
that each sector holds 512 bytes. Storing one 56-byte logical record in each 512-byte physical sector means wasting 456 bytes
per sector. Clearly, wasting that must space is unacceptable.

The solution is to **block** the data, storing several logical records in each sector (Fig. 5.7). A *physical* record is the unit of
data (in this case, a sector) that is transferred between an external device and memory by a single physical I/O operation. A *logical* record is the unit of data requested by a single logical read or
write instruction in an application program. On output, the
input/output control system collects logical records, builds a
block or sector in memory, and starts a physical output operation when the block is filled. On input, the IOCS reads a physical
block or sector, extracts the requested logical record, and makes
it available to the application program.

Some applications involve lengthy records. For example, the
academic history of a college senior might not fit in a single 512-
byte sector (Fig. 5.8). In this case the logical record (a single
student's grade history), is bigger than the physical record (a
single sector). Thus, a single logical read calls for two or more
physical input operations, while a single logical write means two
or more physical writes.

Fig. 5.7   Better utilization of disk space can be achieved by
                      blocking data, storing several logical records in a
                      single sector (physical record).

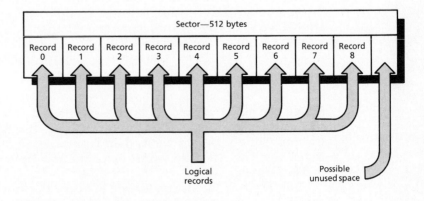

On input, the input/output control system accepts **logical I/O**
requests from an application program, performs whatever **physical I/O** operations are necessary to obtain the requested data,
either selects or combines the physical data to form a logical record, and returns the logical record to the application program.
On output, the IOCS either assembles several small logical records or disassembles a lengthy one before starting physical

Fig. 5.8   Sometimes, a logical record can be bigger than a
                      single physical record.

output. As a result, the application programmer can ignore physical I/O and concentrate on logical I/O.

Incidentally, not all operating systems work with records. Some treat the data stored on disk or moving between memory and a peripheral device as simple strings of bytes. However, the principle is the same. On input, the IOCS accepts a complete block or sector and extracts selected groups of bytes. On output, the IOCS collects bytes until it has enough to fill a block and then starts the physical output operation.

The File System

A disk can hold hundreds of different files and programs, but if you want to load a particular program, only that program will do, and if the program needs data from a particular file, only that file will do. The **file system** helps the user keep track of data and programs.

The location (or start address) of every file stored on a disk can be found by searching the disk's directory (Fig. 5.9). (*Note:* A program is a special type of file.) For a given operating system the directory is always stored at the same location on every disk, so the file system can always find it. Accessing, searching, and maintaining the directory are three of the primary tasks performed by the file system.

For example, the process of loading a program begins with a command, such as

LOAD SPACEWAR

The command processor interprets the command and calls the program-loading module. That module, in turn, calls the file system, which reads the directory. Once the directory is in memory, the file system searches it. Each program is identified by name as shown in Fig. 5.9; note that *SPACEWAR* is the third entry. Following the program's name is its physical location (in other words, the track and sector holding its first instructions). Using this information, the input/output control system can generate the seek and read commands needed to copy the program into memory.

When a program is first written to disk, its name and physical location are recorded in the directory. To retrieve the program, the directory is read and searched for the name, the program's physical location is extracted, and the necessary primitive commands are issued. When a program is deleted, its

Fig. 5.9 The directory found on each disk is the key to accessing programs and files by name.

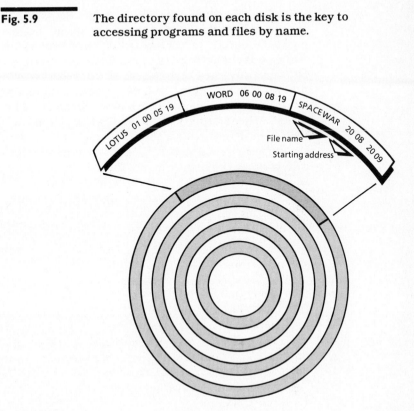

entry is removed from the directory. The file system manages the directory.

Programs are normally saved and loaded in response to operating system commands. Data files, on the other hand, are created and accessed by programs. To create a new file or find an existing file, the programmer codes an **open** instruction. When a file is opened, the file system gets control, reads the directory, finds the directory entry for an old file or creates a directory entry for a new file, and notes the file's start address for subsequent use. Generally, when a program is finished with a file, the file is closed. In response to a **close** instruction, the file system updates the directory to indicate such information as the file's length and ending address. Programs are saved and loaded; files are opened and closed; records are read and written.

The file system is also responsible for allocating space on disk. Ideally, when a file is created, its data are stored in a series of consecutive sectors, but, because many different files share the same disk, that is not always possible. For example, imagine a file created on Wednesday and updated on Thursday. Wednesday's data might occupy consecutive sectors, but data belonging to some other file might lie between Wednesday's data and Thursday's data. The file system bridges this gap.

Often, a table of sectors is maintained on disk (Fig. 5.10). When a file is created, the file system records the number of its first sector in the directory. When that first sector is filled, the disk allocation table is searched, and the next available sector is allocated to the program. (In this example, available sectors are identified by a 0 table value.) Note that the next available sector might not be physically adjacent to the first one.

To link the sectors, the second sector's number is recorded in the first sector's table entry. Follow the chain of pointers in Fig. 5.10. The directory tells you that file A starts in sector 6.

Fig. 5.10   Many operating systems use a table of sectors to allocate disk space. Sectors belonging to a particular file are linked by pointers. A zero table entry might indicate an unallocated sector. The table is itself stored on disk.

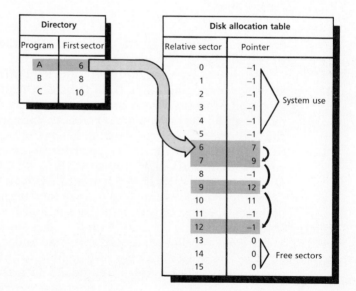

The table entry for sector 6 points to sector 7; sector 7's entry points to sector 9; and sector 9's table entry points to sector 12. Because sector 12's table entry holds a sentinel value, it marks the end of the file. Of course, not all file systems use 0 to mark free sectors and -1 as a sentinel value, but this example gives you a sense of how disk allocation techniques work.

One potentially confusing point is the difference between the file system and the input/output control system. Generally, the IOCS is the module that communicates *directly* with peripheral devices at a primitive level. The file system, on the other hand, performs such logical functions as managing the directory and allocating disk space. The file system uses the IOCS to read and write the directory, the disk allocation table, and data sectors.

Memory Management

The operating system is a collection of software modules that, among other things, loads application programs and supports them as they run. Clearly, the operating system must itself occupy memory. Generally, the first few hundred bytes of low memory are set aside to hold key operating system control information (Fig. 5.11). Next come the input/output control system

Fig. 5.11   Generally, control information is stored in low memory, while transient logic occupies high memory.

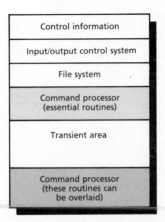

and the file system, followed by the command processor. The remaining memory (sometimes called high memory) is the **transient area;** this is where application programs and less essential operating system routines are loaded.

Some operating system modules, such as the ones that control physical I/O, directly support application programs as they run, so they must be **resident.** Others, such as the routine that formats disks, are used only occasionally. These modules can be stored on disk and read into memory only when needed; they are called **transients.** Given that memory space is limited, keeping only essential logic resident is a good idea.

Loading application programs is not always as simple as it seems. The amount of space needed by a program can change as it runs, so some programs make use of **overlay** structures. The idea of overlays was developed during the second generation when the amount of available memory was quite limited. The problem, in a nutshell, was how to fit a 32K program into a 16K machine. The solution was breaking the program into modules.

For example, imagine a program with four 8K modules (Fig. 5.12a). Module 1 holds the main control logic and key data common to the entire program. Module 2 processes valid input data. Occasionally, errors or unusual data values call for the logic in module 3. Module 4 generates end-of-program statistics, so it is needed only when the program terminates.

Clearly, module 1 must remain in memory at all times. If no errors are encountered, there is no need for module 3. If an error occurs, module 3's logic must be executed, but modules 2 and 4 are superfluous. Thus, as the program begins, modules 1 and 2

Fig. 5.12   With overlay structures, only the necessary portions of a program are kept in memory.

a. The complete program consists of four modules.

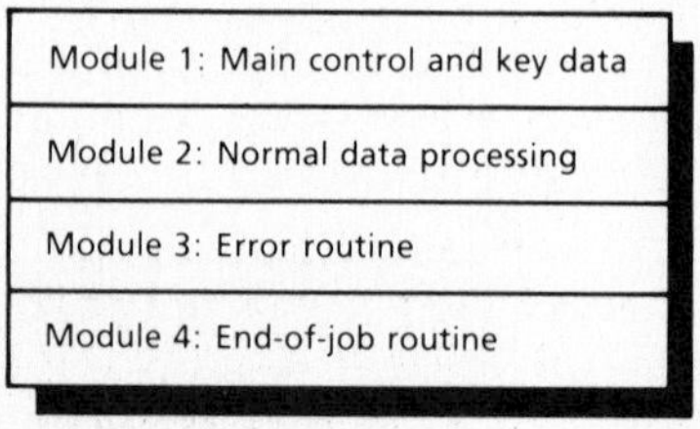

| Module 1: Main control and key data |
| Module 2: Normal data processing |
| Module 3: Error routine |
| Module 4: End-of-job routine |

b. Under normal conditions, only modules 1 and 2 are in memory.

c. When errors are encountered, module 3 overlays module 2.

d. At end-of-job, only modules 1 and 4 are needed.

are in memory (Fig. 5.12b). When an error is encountered, module 3 overlays module 2 (Fig. 5.12c). It stays in memory until the next valid set of data is read; at that time module 2 replaces it. Finally, just before the program ends, module 4 overlays 2 or 3 (Fig. 5.12d) and generates its statistics.

Memory is not nearly so limited on modern microcomputers, but overlays are still used. Some programming languages support a chain function that allows new programs or subroutines to be loaded in response to program-generated requests, and many commercial programs use overlays for special features.

Because the amount of memory required by a program can change as it runs, the operating system maintains a table of unused space. When a program issues a chain or overlay request, it transfers control to the operating system, which scans its free memory list, determines if there is adequate space to hold the new module, allocates the space, and reads the module into memory. (The process is just like loading a program.) Finally, the operating system returns control to the application program.

Sometimes, the resident operating system is itself partially overlaid. When an application program is running, it needs the support of the input/output control system, the file system, and some of the command processor's functions, but has little or no use for other command processor features. Consequently, part of the command processor occupies high memory (Fig. 5.11) and, if extra space is needed, those functions can be overlaid. (Of course, when the program finishes executing, the complete command processor must be restored to memory.) If you have ever noticed a slight delay or sensed unexpected disk drive activity as you used an application program, you might have encountered an overlay.

Interrupts

Because their operation is synchronized by the clock, communication between the processor and memory is simple. A computer and its peripheral devices, on the other hand, are asynchronous. They function independently, and that creates communication problems.

The processor, of course, is in charge, and can always initiate communication with a peripheral device. Before an external device can talk to the processor, however, it must get the processor's attention. On most computers, a peripheral establishes communication with the processor by sending an electronic signal called an **interrupt.** When hardware senses an interrupt, it saves the control information needed to resume processing the current program and transfers control to an operating system routine.

For example, pressing a key on most microcomputer keyboards generates an interrupt. The computer responds by stopping the currently executing program, saving necessary control information in a series of registers or on a memory stack, and branching to the operating system's interrupt handling routine. The operating system then checks the incoming character. In most cases, the character is stored in memory and echoed to the screen, control information is reset, and the application program resumes processing. Occasionally, a special character such as *Control-break, Print screen,* or the "hot" key that activates a personal notepad or a screen capture routine is pressed, and the operating system responds by taking the appropriate action before returning control to the application program.

Interrupts can also be generated by software. The operating system contains support routines that are utilized by application programs. For a programmer to call a particular routine, he or she would have to know a great deal about the operating system's structure. Fortunately, most systems allow the programmer to store key control information in a register and issue an interrupt. Following the interrupt, the operating system gets control, reads the register's contents, and activates the routine responsible for the requested service. Once the operating system is finished, control returns to the application program.

On many computers, interrupts also allow the machine to sense, and thus react to, errors. When a hardware component fails, an interrupt transfers control to the operating system, which attempts to recover. If a program tries an illegal operation, such as a zero divide, the operating system might display an error message or generate a dump before terminating the program.

An interrupt is an electronic signal. It is sensed by hardware; the hardware responds by (1) saving the information needed to resume the current program and (2) transferring control to an operating system routine. At this point, the interrupt itself ends. The operating system then responds to (or handles) the interrupt. Eventually, assuming no unrecoverable errors, control returns to the program that was executing at the time the interrupt occurred.

The Boot

Loading and executing a program starts with a command that is read and interpreted by the operating system. Clearly, the operating system must be in memory before the command is issued. On some systems, the operating system resides in read-only memory. ROM is permanent; it keeps its contents even when power is lost. A ROM-based operating system is always there.

However, the main memory of most computers is composed of RAM, or random access memory. RAM is volatile; it loses its contents when power is cut. Consequently, the operating system must be loaded each time the computer is turned on

Unfortunately, you can't simply type a command, such as LOAD OS, and let the operating system take care of loading itself because, when the computer is first turned on, the operating system is not yet in memory and thus cannot possible read, interpret, and carry out commands.

Typically, the operating system is stored on disk. The idea is to copy it into memory. This objective is achieved by a special program called a **boot** (Fig. 5.13). Generally, the boot is stored on the first sector (or two) of a disk. Hardware is designed to read this sector automatically whenever the power is turned on (Fig. 5.13a). The boot consists of only a few instructions, but they are sufficient to read the rest of the operating system into memory (Fig. 5.13b); note how it is seemingly "pulled in by its own bootstraps." Now a user can type the commands to load and execute an application program.

Loading the operating system from scratch is called a *cold boot* or cold start. If the computer is already running, it is often possible to *warm boot* or warm start the operating system by pressing a specific key combination. (For example, press *Ctrl/Alt/Del* on an IBM PC.) Because key control information is already in place, a warm boot can bypass certain preliminary tasks, and that saves time.

Fig. 5.13　　　　Booting the operating system.

a. When the computer is first turned on, hardware automatically reads the boot program from the first few sectors of a disk.

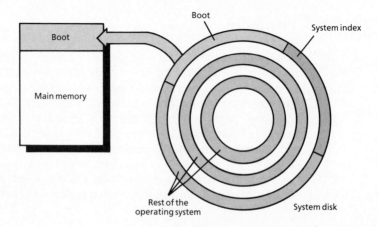

b. The boot routine contains the instructions that read the rest of the operating system from disk into memory.

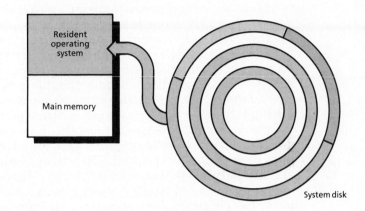

Utilities

Most operating systems incorporate a set of transient **utility** routines such as linkage editors, loaders, line editors, disk formatting modules, sort routines, debugging features, library management routines, and many others. Additional utility routines designed to recover lost data, convert data from one format to another, optimize the way data are stored on a disk, make backup copies of files or disks, and perform similar support functions can be purchased. Such utilities are invaluable.

Summary

Users communicate with an operating system through a command language. The command processor accepts, interprets, and carries out the commands. Often, a batch feature supports repetitive commands. One way to view the command processor is as a shell. Sometimes, custom shells are substituted for the standard shell. Most microcomputer operating systems are command driven.

Each input and output device is controlled by its own primitive commands. The input/output control system accepts logical I/O requests and generates the necessary physical I/O operations. Sometimes, this involves blocking and deblocking. The IOCS assembles and/or disassembles physical records as necessary, allowing the application routines to focus on logical I/O.

Files and programs are accessed by name through the file system. Each file name is recorded in a disk directory. The file system reads the directory, searches it by file name, and extracts the file's start address. Programs are loaded or saved in response to commands. Data files are opened and closed in response to program instructions. The input/output control system communicates with the physical devices; the file system manages the directory and allocates disk space.

The resident portion of the operating system normally occupies low memory. Following the resident operating system, in high memory, is a transient area where application programs and operating system transients are loaded. Because the amount of memory used by a program can vary as the program runs, the operating system must keep track of available memory. Overlay structures were covered briefly. Portions of the operating system can be overlayed.

An interrupt is an electronic signal that causes the computer to stop the current program, save its control information, and transfer control to the operating system. After the interrupt is handled, the program that was executing when the interrupt occurred typically resumes processing.

Because a computer's memory is volatile, the operating system must be loaded each time the computer is activated. The routine that loads the operating system is called a boot.

Most operating systems include several transient utility routines.

Key Words

batch file	file system	prompt
block	input/output	protocol
boot	control system	resident
close	interrupt	shell
command	logical I/O	transient
command driven	open	transient area
command language	overlay	utility
command processor	physical I/O	

Exercises

1. What is a command language? What is a batch command file?

2. Many microcomputer operating systems are command driven. What does this mean?

3. A command processor is sometimes called a shell. Why? Distinguish between the standard shell and a custom shell.

4. What functions are performed by the input/output control system?

5. Distinguish between logical I/O and physical I/O. Distinguish between a physical record and a logical record.

6. What functions are performed by the file system?

7. Briefly distinguish between the input/output control system and the file system.

8. What happens when a file is opened? What happens when a file is closed?

9. Sketch the main memory layout of a typical microcomputer operating system.

10. Distinguish between resident and transient modules.

11. Briefly explain overlay structures.

12. What is an interrupt? Why are interrupts important?

13. What is a boot? Why is a boot needed?

14. What is a utility?

6

Resource Management

This chapter discusses the resource
management tasks performed by a
multiple-user operating system.
Key topics include:

The multiple-user environment

Multiprogramming
  Memory management
  Memory protection
  Managing the processor's time
  Interrupts
  Peripheral device allocation
  Deadlock
  Scheduling and queuing
  Jobs and tasks
  Spooling
  A multiprogramming operating system

Time-sharing
  Roll-in/roll-out
  Time-slicing
  Polling
  Other factors

The Multiple-User *Programs* Environment

Microcomputers are inexpensive, so no one is concerned if they sit idle much of the time. Mainframes, on the other hand, are quite expensive. They represent potential computing power that simply should not be wasted, so efficient resource utilization is crucial on a mainframe.

Given the speed disparity between a computer and its peripherals, input and output operations significantly impact on efficiency. For example, picture a computer with a single program in memory. The program cannot process data it does not yet have, and success cannot be assumed until an output operation is finished, so the program waits for input or output. Since the program controls the computer, the computer waits, too. Typically, computers spend far more time waiting for I/O than processing data.

Why not put two programs in memory? Then, when program A is waiting for data, the processor can turn its attention to program B. And why stop at two programs? With three, even more otherwise wasted time is utilized (Fig. 6.1). Generally, the more

Fig. 6.1   With more than one program in memory, much of the
                        computer's wait time can be utilized.

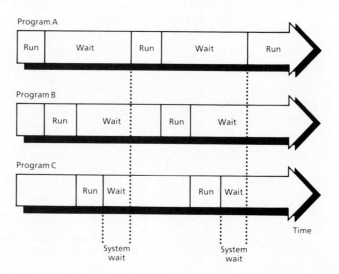

programs in memory, the greater the utilization of the processor.

The processor fetches and executes a single instruction during each machine cycle. If the processor can execute only one *instruction* at a time, it cannot possibly execute two or more programs at a time; although multiple programs can share memory, only one can be active. Simultaneous means "at the same instant." No processor can execute two or more programs simultaneously. Concurrent means "over the same time period." A processor can certainly execute two or more programs concurrently.

The advantage of concurrently executing multiple programs is obvious: the processor can do more work in the same amount of elapsed time. However, while a mainframe's resources are substantial, they are limited and, with two or more concurrent users, conflicts over processor time, memory space, and peripheral device allocation are inevitable. When these conflicts occur, they must be resolved. Since human operators cannot function at computer speeds, key decisions must be made by the computer itself. Because the operating system acts as the hardware/software interface, it is the ideal place to implement resource management.

Multiprogramming

Multiprogramming is a common approach to resource management. Originally developed to support batch processing applications, multiprogramming operating systems take advantage of the extreme speed disparity between a computer and its peripheral devices. Traditionally, the key measures of effectiveness are throughput (run time divided by elapsed time) and turnaround (the time between job submission and job completion).

The essential components of a single-user operating system include a command processor, an input/output control system, a file system, and a transient area. A multiprogramming operating system builds on this base, subdividing the transient area to hold several independent programs and adding resource management routines to the operating system's basic functions.

Memory Management

If memory is to hold multiple programs, memory space must be managed. The simplest approach, **fixed-partition memory management** (Fig. 6.2), divides the available space into fixed-length

Fig. 6.2   Under fixed-partition memory management, the
available memory space is divided into a series of
fixed-length partitions.

Operating system
Partition A
Partition B
Partition C
Partition D

partitions each of which can hold one program. Partition sizes
are generally set when the system is booted, so the memory allocation decision is made before the actual amount of space
needed by a given program is known. Imagine a 32K program. If
the partition size is 256K, fully 224K will be wasted when that
program runs. Fixed-partition memory management wastes
space. Its major advantage is simplicity.

Under **dynamic memory management**, the transient area is
treated as a pool of unstructured free space. When the system
decides to load a particular program, a **region** of memory just
sufficient to hold it is allocated from the pool. Because a program gets only the space it needs, relatively little space is
wasted. Consequently, more programs can occupy the same
amount of memory space, and that means more efficient utilization.

Dynamic memory management does not completely solve
the wasted space problem, however. Assume, for example, that a
120K program has just finished executing (Fig. 6.3). If there are
no 120K programs available, the system might load a 60K program and a 50K program. Note that 10K remains unallocated. If
there are no 10K or smaller programs available, the space will
simply not be used. Over time, little chunks of unused space will
be spread throughout memory, creating a **fragmentation** problem.

Most load modules are addressed relative to their first byte.

Fig. 6.3   Over time, dynamic memory management leaves
                      small fragments of unused space spread throughout
                      memory.

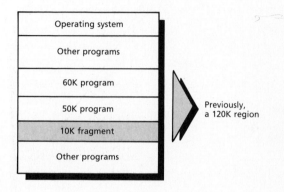

Consequently, although the load module can be placed anywhere
in memory, it must occupy *contiguous* space. Taken together,
the unused fragments of memory might represent enough space
to hold a complete program, but, because they are not contiguous, they cannot be used.

There is no law that requires load modules to be contiguous.
An alternative is breaking a program into logical **segments,** assigning addresses relative to segment entry points, and loading
the segments into *noncontiguous* memory (Fig. 6.4). Most programmers are trained to write independent, single-function
modules linked by a control structure. Those modules represent
possible break points, so segmentation makes logical sense. Because a program's segments can be spread throughout memory,
occupying whatever small fragments of memory that might be
available, still more programs can fit in the same amount of
memory. Once again, more programs means more efficient processor utilization.

Another approach is dividing programs into fixed-length
pages, addressing memory relative to the start of a page, and
loading pages into noncontiguous memory. The basic difference
between segmentation and paging is that segment size can vary
to match the logic of the program, while the page size is fixed.
The disadvantage of paging is that break points are arbitrary

Fig. 6.4   Under segmentation, a program is broken into
                      segments. Because the instructions and data within a
                      segment are addressed relative to the *segment's*
                      beginning address, a program's segments can be
                      loaded into noncontiguous memory.

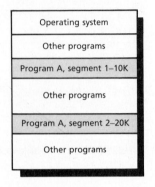

relative to the program logic. The advantage is that all pages are
the same size, and that simplifies memory management.

If a processor can execute only one instruction at a time, why
must the entire program be in memory before processing can
begin? Under a **virtual memory** system, programs are divided
into pages or segments and stored on disk. Subsequently, only
active modules are read into memory.

Consider, for example, the computer system sketched in Fig.
6.5a. Imagine that main memory (called *real* memory) is large
enough to hold four pages. Three programs are stored on virtual
memory (disk). The first page in program A (page A-0) is copied
into real memory and starts to execute. Soon it requests an I/O
operation and drops into a wait state, so the first page in program B (page B-0) is loaded.

Eventually memory comes to resemble Fig. 6.5b, with all
real pages filled. Assume program A has just requested input.
Program B is next in line, but its next instructions are on page
B-1, which is not yet in real memory. The processor cannot execute instructions residing on disk, so page B-1 must be loaded.
Program A has moved on to its second page and no longer needs
page A-0, so the operating system sends page A-0 back to virtual

Fig. 6.5   Under virtual memory, only necessary portions of a program are stored in real memory.

a. The first page, A-0, is read from virtual into real memory.

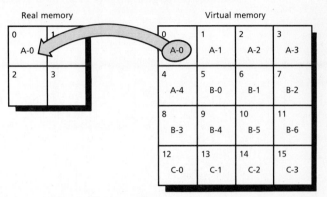

b. Eventually, as additional pages are read, real memory is filled.

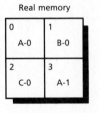

c. To make room in real memory, an inactive page is copied back to virtual.

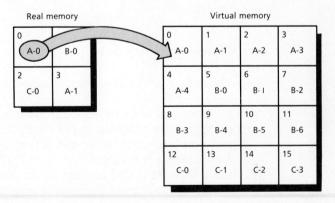

d. A new page is then read into real memory.

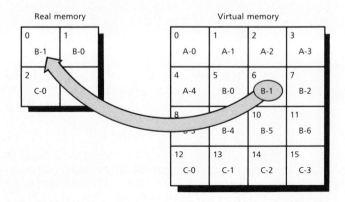

memory (Fig. 6.5c) and copies page B-1 into the vacated real
page (Fig. 6.5d). Now the instructions on page B-1 can be executed.

By swapping pages between secondary storage and real
memory, virtual memory management allows a computer to
concurrently execute many more programs than could possibly
be supported by the available real memory, and that means more
efficient processor utilization. Historically, the amount of available memory limited program size and forced the programmer to
pay close attention to memory management. An additional ben-
efit of virtual memory is that it gives the programmer the illu-
sion of almost unlimited memory. Many experts view the
relaxation of space constraints as the primary advantage of virtual memory.

Memory Protection

There is more to **memory management** than simply allocating
space, however. The contents of random access memory are easily changed. With multiple programs sharing memory, it is possible for one program to destroy the contents of memory space
belonging to another, so the active programs must be protected
from each other. Generally, the operating system keeps track of
the space assigned to each program. If a program attempts to
modify (or, sometimes, even to read) the contents of memory locations that do not belong to it, the operating system's **memory**

protection logic intervenes and (usually) terminates the program.

Managing the Processor's Time

Imagine several programs occupying memory. Some time ago, program A requested data from disk (Fig. 6.6). Because it was unable to continue until the input operation was completed, it dropped into a **wait state** and the processor turned to program B. Assume the input operation has just been completed. Both programs are now in a **ready state**; in other words, both are ready to resume processing. Which one gets the processor? Computers are so fast that a human operator cannot effectively make such real-time choices. Instead, the processor's time is managed by an operating system routine called the **dispatcher**.

Consider a system with two partitions: foreground and background (Fig. 6.7). The dispatcher checks the program in the foreground partition first; if the program is ready, it gets control. Only if the foreground program is still in a wait state does the dispatcher check the background partition. The foreground has high priority; the background has low priority.

This idea can be extended to larger systems, with the dispatcher checking partitions in a fixed order until a ready-state program is found. The first partition checked has highest priority; the last has lowest priority. The only way the low-priority

Fig. 6.6   With multiple concurrent users, it is possible that two or more programs will be ready to execute at the same time. When this happens, an operating system module must resolve the conflict, deciding which program goes first.

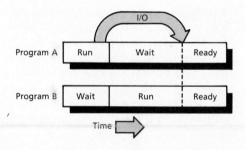

Fig. 6.7   Often, the dispatcher looks for a ready program by
                      checking partitions in priority order.

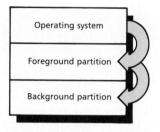

program can get control is if all the higher-priority partitions are
in a wait state.

There are a number of control fields that must be maintained
in support of each active program. Often, a **control block** is created to hold a partition's key control flags, constants, and variables (Fig. 6.8). These control blocks (one per partition) might be
linked by pointers or stored in a table. The dispatcher typically
determines which program is to be given control by following a
chain of pointers from control block to control block, or by moving through the table from top to bottom.

It is also possible to implement more complex priority
schemes. For example, a program's priority can be set by a job
control or command language statement, or computed dynamically, perhaps taking into account such factors as program size,
time in memory, peripheral device requirements, and other measures of the program's impact on system resources. The dispatcher can then search control blocks in priority order.

Interrupts

A program normally surrenders control of the processor when it
requests an I/O operation and is eligible to continue when that
operation is completed. Consequently, the key to multiprogramming is recognizing when input or output operations begin or
end. The operating system knows when these events occur because they are marked by interrupts.

An **interrupt** is an electronic signal. Hardware senses the
signal, saves key control information for the currently execut-

Fig. 6.8   A control block holds key control information for each partition. Often these control blocks are stored in a table or linked by pointers. The dispatcher looks for a ready program by following the pointers from control block to control block.

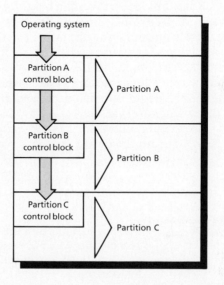

ing program, and transfers control to the operating system's **interrupt handler** routine. At that instant, the interrupt ends. The operating system then handles the interrupt, and the dispatcher, subsequently, starts an application program. Eventually, the program that was executing at the time of the interrupt resumes processing. Note that the interrupt is merely a signal. Distinguish between the interrupt itself and the logic that handles it.

For example, follow the steps in Fig. 6.9. When an application program needs data, it issues an interrupt (Fig. 6.9a). In response, hardware transfers control to the interrupt handler routine. Once it gets control, the interrupt handler drops the application program into a wait state (Fig. 6.9b) and calls the input/output control system to start the I/O operation. Finally, control flows to the dispatcher, which starts another application program (Fig. 6.9c).

Later, when the I/O operation is finished, the channel issues an interrupt (Fig. 6.9d). Once again the interrupt handler gets control (Fig. 6.9e). After verifying that the operation was successfully completed, it resets the program that initially requested the data (program A) to a ready state. Then it transfers control to the dispatcher, which starts an application program (Fig. 6.9f). Because A is the highest priority ready-state program, it goes next, even though program B was running at the time the interrupt occurred.

Note that interrupts can originate in either hardware or software. A program issues an interrupt to request the operating system's support (for example, to start an I/O operation). Hardware issues interrupts to notify the processor that an asynchronous event (such as the completion of an I/O operation or a hardware failure) has occurred. Other types of interrupts might signal an illegal operation (a zero divide) or the expiration of a preset time interval.

Interrupts mark events. In response, hardware transfers control to the interrupt handler routine, which performs the

Fig. 6.9   The key to managing the processor's time is recognizing when input and output operations begin and end. Generally, these crucial events are signaled by interrupts.

a. The program requests the operating system's support by issuing an interrupt.

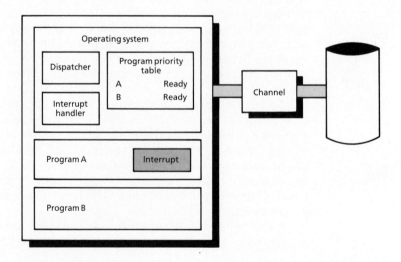

b. Following the interrupt, the interrupt handler routine sets the program to a wait state.

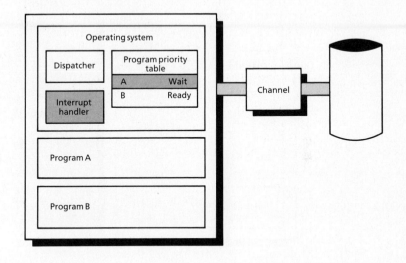

c. After the interrupt handler starts the requested input or output operation, the dispatcher starts another application program.

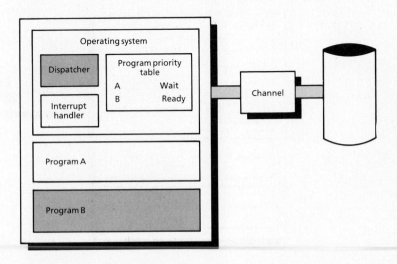

d. Eventually, the channel signals the end of the I/O operation by sending the computer an interrupt.

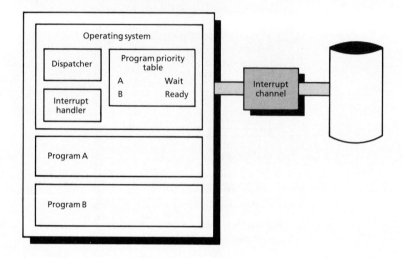

e. Following the interrupt, the interrupt handler resets program A to
a ready state.

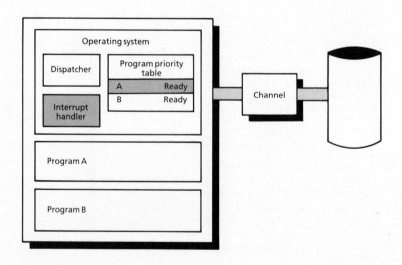

f. Finally, the dispatcher selects an application program and starts it.

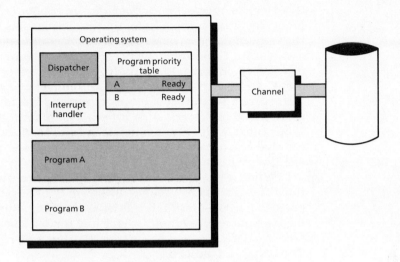

appropriate logical functions and, if necessary, resets the affected program's state. Following each interrupt, the dispatcher starts the highest priority ready program. That, in a nutshell, is the essence of multiprogramming.

Peripheral Device Allocation

If two programs take turns writing to the same printer, the output is useless. If two programs send primitive commands to the same tape drive, neither one gets the right data. Clearly, with multiple programs sharing the computer's resources, access to peripheral devices must be carefully managed.

Generally, the operating system maintains a list of available devices. Some (such as printers and tape drives) cannot be shared; for example, if a printer is allocated to an existing program, a new program requesting the same printer might not be loaded until the device is freed. Other peripherals (such as disk) *can* be shared, but interference between the various programs' read and write commands must be avoided. Many operating systems maintain a queue of pending disk operations and issue them in priority or time sequence.

Deadlock

Deadlock is one possible consequence of poor resource management. Imagine, for example, that two programs need data from the same disk. Program A issues a seek command and drops into a wait state. Subsequently, program B gets control and issues its own seek command. Eventually, the first seek operation is completed and control returns to A, which issues a read command. Unfortunately, the second seek command has moved the access mechanism, so A reissues its seek command and once again drops into a wait state. Soon B issues its read command, discovers that the access mechanism is in the wrong place, and reissues its seek command.

Consider the outcome of this nightmare. Program A positions the access mechanism. Program B moves it. Program A repositions it; program B does the same thing. Picture the access mechanism moving rapidly back and forth across the disk's surface. No data are read or written. Neither program can proceed. The result is deadlock.

Deadlock is not limited to peripheral devices; it happens when two (or more) programs each control *any* resource needed by the other. Neither program can continue until the other "gives in," and if neither is willing to give in, the system, almost literally, "spins its wheels." At best, that leads to inefficiency. At worst, it can bring the entire system to a halt.

One solution is prevention; some operating systems will not load a program unless all its resource needs (including peripheral devices and memory space) can be guaranteed. Other operating systems allow some deadlocks to occur, sense them, and take corrective action.

Scheduling and Queuing

Processor management is concerned with the *internal* priorities of programs already in memory. A program's *external* priority is a different issue. As one program finishes processing and space becomes available, which program is loaded into memory next? This decision typically involves two separate modules, a **queuing** routine and a **scheduler**. As programs enter the system, they are placed on a queue by the queuing routine (Fig. 6.10). When space becomes available, the scheduler selects a program from the queue and loads it into memory (Fig. 6.11).

Generally, the first program on the queue is loaded first, but more sophisticated priority rules can be used. Sometimes, more

Fig. 6.10   When a program first enters a multiprogramming
                       system, a queuing routine copies it to a queue.

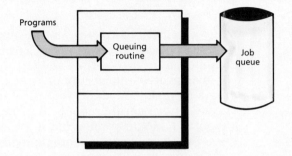

than one queue is maintained. Often, a program is placed on a
particular queue based on its resource needs; for example, programs requiring magnetic tape or special printer forms can be
separated from those calling for more normal setup. Grouping
programs with similar resource needs simplifies scheduling.

Clearly distinguish between a program's internal and external priorities. Once a program is in memory, the dispatcher uses
its internal priority to determine its right to access the processor. In contrast, the program's external priority has to do with

Fig. 6.11   Later, when space becomes available, the scheduling
                       routine loads a program from the queue into memory.

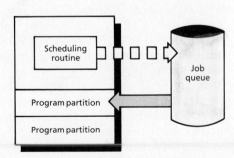

loading it into memory in the first place. Until the program is in memory, it has no internal priority. Once in memory, its external priority is no longer relevant.

Jobs and Tasks

Many applications require the execution of several related programs. For example, testing a program often means executing a compiler, a linkage editor, and then the program load module; whereas processing weekly payroll might call for separate programs to verify the data, sort the data, compute payroll, print checks, and generate reports. A group of related programs that supports a single application is called a **job,** and a single program (more accurately, a single load module) on the computer and ready to execute is called a **task.** (*Note: Job* and *task* are IBM terms; some other manufacturers use different words to describe these two basic units of work.)

A programmer communicates with a multiprogramming system's command processor through commands or job control language statements. Generally, one statement identifies the job, while other statements (one per program) identify the tasks that comprise that job. The programmer submits a job. The operating system's queuing routine places that job on a queue. The scheduler subsequently loads and the processor executes one task at a time. The active task shares the computer's resources with other tasks from other jobs.

Spooling

Compared to a single-user system, a multiprogramming operating system allows a computer to execute more programs in the same amount of time. If the turnover rate of those programs can be increased, even greater efficiencies can be realized. For example, imagine a system with five concurrent programs. Assume that each one occupies memory for ten seconds. As soon as a program finishes executing, another one replaces it, so the computer can run thirty programs a minute. If each program's run time could be reduced to five seconds, sixty programs could run in that same minute.

Imagine a program that generates payroll for 1000 employees. Reading 1000 time cards takes at least two minutes. Printing 1000 checks takes a few minutes more, so the program will need at least four or five minutes to run. But if the slow card reader and printer were replaced by a disk, the program would run in much less time. Consequently, memory would be freed for another program much more quickly.

That is the essential idea behind **spooling.** Even with multiprogramming, it is common for all application programs to be waiting for I/O. When this happens, the processor has nothing to do. During these idle periods, the operating system's spooling module reads data from such slow devices as card readers or terminal keyboards and stores them on a high-speed medium such as disk, even before the program needing those data has been loaded into memory. Later, when the program is loaded, its input data can be read from disk. On output, data are spooled to disk and later dumped to the printer. Because the application program deals only with high-speed I/O, it finishes processing and thus frees space for another program much more quickly.

A Multiprogramming Operating System

A multiprogramming operating system begins with the same basic functions as a single-user operating system (Fig. 6.12). Generally, key tables and control blocks occupy low memory. They are followed by an input/output control system, a file system, and a command processor. Next comes logic to manage the system's resources, including memory management and memory protection routines, a dispatcher, one or more interrupt handler routines, device allocation modules, logic to deal with or prevent deadlocks, a queuing routine, a scheduler, and a spooler.

A multiprogramming system is designed to take advantage of otherwise wasted input and output time, so application programs are generally assigned internal priorities based on their I/O needs. For example, interactive programs are highly I/O-bound, with widely spaced transactions calling for only limited processing. Because such programs voluntarily surrender control of the processor quickly, it makes sense to assign them high priority. Traditional batch processing applications also involve a great deal of I/O, but typically call for more memory space and more processing time; they are good candidates for second priority. Compute-bound applications (such as statistical analysis) involve a great deal of processing and relatively little I/O. They have low priority.

Because of their relative priorities, a batch task is processed only when there are no ready interactive tasks, and a compute-bound task in executed only when there are no ready batch tasks. Fortunately, the interactive and batch routines spend most of their time waiting for I/O, so there is plenty of time left

Fig. 6.12   The components of a typical
                     multiprogramming operating system.

Tables and control blocks		
Input/output control system	File system	Command processor
Memory management	Memory protection	Dispatcher
Interrupt handler	Peripheral device allocation	Deadlock routine
Queuing routine	Scheduler	Spooler
Other resident operating system routines		
High-priority interactive programs		
Intermediate-priority batch programs		
Low-priority compute-bound programs		
Operating system transient routines		

over for the compute-bound task. What prevents the statistical
routine from hogging the processor once it gets control? Interrupts. A task waiting for input represents a *pending* interrupt.
When that interrupt happens, the dispatcher eventually gets
control and starts the highest priority ready task. Consequently, if *any* interactive or batch task is ready, it gets the processor before the compute-bound task does.

Time-Sharing

Time-sharing systems are different. They are designed with interactive processing in mind. Users enter brief transactions

through relatively slow keyboard terminals. Programs are usually small and process relatively little data. Perhaps the most important measure of effectiveness is response time, the elapsed time between entering a transaction and seeing the first character of the system's response appear on the screen.

Before you begin this section, note that time-sharing and multiprogramming are not mutually exclusive. In fact, it is common for an interactive, time-sharing system to run in the high priority partition of a large, multiprogrammed mainframe.

Roll-in/Roll-out

Picture a typical time-sharing application. Transactions (a single program statement, a line of input data, or a command) are typed through a keyboard. In most cases, very little actual processing is required. Typing is slow; two transactions per minute is the best most people can do. To the computer, each user represents a string of brief, widely spaced processing demands.

As a transaction is processed, the system knows that considerable time will pass before that user's next transaction arrives, so the work space can be rolled out to secondary storage, making room for another application in memory. Later, when the first user's next transaction arrives, his or her work space is rolled back in. Most time-sharing systems use such **roll-in/roll-out** (or swap-in/swap-out) techniques to manage memory space.

Time-Slicing

Imagine that you have just spent twenty minutes typing the data for a statistical analysis program. Each line of data was one brief transaction; your work to this point is a typical time-sharing application. Your last transaction is different, however. It is a command that tells the system to process the data, and that command causes the computer to begin a computational routine that can easily run for a few minutes. While your transaction is being processed, the other users on the system will have to wait, and, given the objective of maintaining good response time, that is intolerable.

The solution is **time-slicing**. Each program is restricted to a maximum "slice" of time, perhaps 0.01 second. Once a program gets control, it runs until one of two things happens. If the program requires input or output before exhausting its time slice, it calls the operating system and "voluntarily" drops into a wait state, just like a multiprogramming application. If, however, the program uses up its entire time slice, a timer interrupt transfers control to the operating system, which selects the next program.

Polling

Often, a **polling** algorithm is used to determine which program is activated next. Imagine a table of program control blocks (Fig. 6.13). Starting at the top, the operating system's dispatcher checks program 1's status. If it's ready, it gets control. If not, the dispatcher moves on to the second control block.

Assume that program 2 is ready. It begins executing and then, one time slice later, surrenders control again, so the dispatcher must select another program. Because the last program to have control was number 2, polling begins with the third table entry; note that program 2 is now at the end of the line. Eventually, the dispatcher works its way through the entire table. At this point, it returns to the top and repeats the process. Program 2 will get another shot only after every other program has a chance.

There are alternatives to simple round-robin polling. Two (or even more) tables can be maintained, with high-priority pro-

---

Fig. 6.13   A time-sharing dispatcher selects the next program by polling.

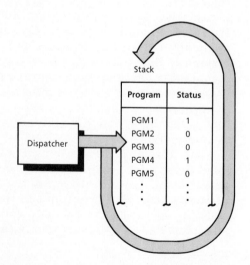

grams on the first one and background or low-priority routines on the second. Another option is to place multiple references to a crucial program on the table, thus giving it several shots at the processor on each polling cycle. Some systems use a priority scheme and recompute priorities every second or two. A common priority algorithm is dividing actual run time by elapsed residency time. The limit of this computation is 1, and that is considered low priority. The more processor time a program uses, the worse its priority becomes, so compute-bound tasks tend to drop to the end of the line.

Other Factors

Time-sharing systems still process interrupts. External devices still communicate with the processor, programs still need the operating system's support, and program and hardware failures still occur. An interrupt represents a transition point—an opportunity to transfer control to another program. On a multiprogramming system, the dispatcher follows a priority algorithm after any interrupt, no matter what program had control when the interrupt occurred. On a time-sharing system, the program that was processing at the time of the interrupt normally resumes processing until it either issues its own interrupt or exceeds its time limit.

External device allocation can be quite dynamic on a multiprogramming system, with a given program asking for almost any imaginable combination of peripherals. Consequently, a multiprogramming operating system must contain considerable logic to prevent or deal with device allocation conflicts.

Most time-sharing systems rely on defaults to minimize this exposure. Each user has a keyboard and a screen that serve as standard input and output devices, a work space that is rolled-in and rolled-out between disk and memory, and a certain amount of disk space to hold programs and files. Spooling is often used for printed output. Generally, peripheral device requests beyond these defaults must be approved by the system manager before they are needed. Defaults simplify both application programming and the operating system's device allocation and deadlock routines, but they also limit the programmer's flexibility.

A programmer who decides to work on a time-sharing system either walks to the computer center or accesses the system via a communication line. If no terminal is available or the system is too busy to accept additional users, programming is postponed. On a time-sharing system, equipment availability determines external priority.

A well-designed time-sharing system is configured for peak-load conditions. A high-priority user can be assigned a personal terminal linked to the system by a dedicated line, and to ensure quick response, this terminal can be polled several times in each polling cycle or assigned an interrupt code that overrides the normal dispatching algorithm. Otherwise, scheduling and external priorities are not factors on time-sharing systems. Scheduling is a batch concept.

Incidentally, the concept of a job is not as applicable to interactive systems as it is to batch systems. Instead, the user's basic unit of work consists of all activities performed between log-on and log-off. Some manufacturers call this unit of work a **session**.

Summary

A mainframe computer is much faster than its peripheral devices, and generally spends more time waiting for I/O than processing data. On a multiprogramming system, two or more programs are loaded into memory and executed concurrently. With multiple programs competing for the computer's resources, conflicts are inevitable. Most are resolved by the operating system.

The simplest form of memory management divides memory into fixed-length partitions and loads one program in each one. Greater efficiency can be achieved by using dynamic memory management, segmentation, or paging. With virtual memory management, programs are stored on disk, and only active portions are loaded into memory. A memory protection routine prevents one program from destroying the contents of another's memory space.

When two or more programs are ready to use the processor, a dispatcher selects the next program by following a priority algorithm. Interrupts mark the beginning and end of input and output operations, alerting the system that the affected program's state should be reset. Following each interrupt, the dispatcher starts the highest priority ready-state program.

Peripheral devices must be carefully managed. Deadlock occurs when two programs each control a resource needed by the other but neither is willing to give up its resource. Some operating systems are designed to prevent deadlock; others sense deadlock and take corrective action.

When programs enter a multiprogramming system, they are stored on a queue. Later, when memory space becomes available, a scheduler selects the next program from the queue and loads it into memory. A load module in memory and ready to execute is called a task. A job is a group of related tasks. To improve the turnover rate of tasks, data are often spooled.

Time-sharing is used for interactive applications. Because the time between successive transactions is relatively lengthy, memory space can be managed by roll-in and roll-out techniques. To eliminate the risk of one program tying up the system and forcing all other users to wait, time-slicing is used to manage the processor's time. Often, the dispatcher follows a polling algorithm to determine which program gets the processor next. External device allocation and external priority are not as significant on a time-sharing system as they are on a multiprogramming system. The standard unit of work on a time-sharing system, a session, consists of all activities performed between log-on and log-off.

Key Words

control block	job	region
deadlock	memory	roll-in/roll-out
dispatcher	management	scheduler
dynamic memory	memory	segment
management	protection	session
fixed-partition	multiprogramming	spooling
memory	page	task
management	partition	time-sharing
fragmentation	polling	time-slicing
interrupt	queuing	virtual memory
interrupt handler	ready state	wait state

Exercises

1. Generally, the more programs in memory, the greater the utilization of the processor. Explain why this is so.

2. Why assign resource management to a multiprogramming operating system? Why can't the human operator do that?

3. Distinguish fixed-partition memory management, dynamic memory management, segmentation, and paging.

4. What is virtual memory? How can virtual memory help improve throughput?

5. Why is memory protection necessary?

6. What does the dispatcher do? What are control blocks, and why are they necessary? Relate these two ideas.

7. What is an interrupt? Explain the relationship between interrupts and the dispatcher.

8. Distinguish between an interrupt and the logic that handles the interrupt.

9. What is deadlock?

10. Explain how the queuing routine and the scheduler work together to load application programs.

11. Distinguish between a job and a task.

12. Distinguish between a program's internal priority and its external priority.

13. What is spooling? How does spooling help throughput and turnaround?

14. Compare roll-in/roll-out to multiprogramming memory management. In particular, compare roll-in/roll-out and virtual memory. How are they similar? How are they different?

15. What is time-slicing? Why is it necessary on a time-sharing system?

PART THREE

Command and Job Control Languages

7

Command Languages

This chapter introduces several concepts
that are common to most command and job
control languages. Key topics include:

Command language functions
 Identifying users
 Identifying programs
 Specifying device requirements
 Run-time intervention

Sources of commands

Learning a command language

Command Language Functions

An operating system is an interface between a computer's programs or users and its hardware (Fig. 7.1). Programs request operating system support by issuing interrupts. People communicate directly with the operating system by typing **commands** or **job control language** statements. The operating system coordinates and manages resources; the command language provides guidance and direction.

Identifying Users

One key operating system function is identifying users. On time-sharing or interactive systems, a person normally begins a session by typing a user number and a password. Most batch jobs start with a job control language statement that identifies the application and the responsible programmer or user.

User identification is an essential security feature. Computer resources are expensive, and the data and software stored on a computer can be crucial to an organization, so unauthorized access must be denied. Additionally, user identification can serve as a basis for setting priorities or for limiting access. For example, in an academic system, a faculty ID might give a professor high priority and the right to access any student's work space, while a student ID restricts the user to standard priority and his or her own work space.

Fig. 7.1   Users communicate with an operating system through commands or job control language statements.

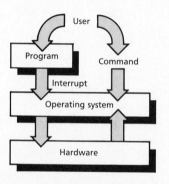

Identifying Programs

A second major function is identifying programs. Normally, operating system routines and utilities, application programs, compilers, editors, and other support routines are assigned names. It's the user's responsibility to specify, through the command language, the name of the program or routine to be executed. On interactive systems, the command often consists of little more than the program name, followed, perhaps, by some run-time options. On a batch system, several different programs might be identified on a series of job control statements, with the order of the statements indicating the order in which the programs are to be run.

Specifying Device Requirements

The user also specifies peripheral device requirements through the command language. This is often a minor concern on interactive systems, which tend to rely on default device assignments, but it can be significant on a batch system. Generally, a batch user is expected to define each program's peripheral device needs through job control language statements. Given a list of device needs, the operating system can determine if the necessary resources are available before loading a program.

Most batch and interactive systems allow users to name and set access limits on files. Some operating systems allocate disk space dynamically, as programs request it. Others expect job control statements to specify the required number of cylinders, tracks, sectors, or blocks, or even absolute disk addresses.

Run-time Intervention

Finally, most command languages support run-time intervention. The simplest example is a control break on a single-user system; if a program gets into an endless loop or begins generating clearly invalid results, the programmer can usually stop it by simultaneously pressing control and break (or some other combination of keys). The result is an interrupt that terminates the program and transfers control to the operating system.

Run-time intervention can be considerably more complex on a multiple-user system. Many support an automatic time-out feature that terminates long-running programs; often a command language parameter sets expected run time. Occasionally, an unexpected "hot" job enters the system and demands immediate attention. When this happens, the operator must be able to override normal priorities. Occasionally, jobs or sessions must be canceled; once again the command language provides a means.

Sources of Commands

Users and programmers are the most common sources of operating system commands. Casual users might issue commands through a shell by selecting them from a menu or by pointing and clicking on icons. On interactive systems, single-line commands are typed as work progresses. On batch systems, a series of commands, called a **job stream,** is prepared and submitted before the first program is loaded (Fig. 7.2). Job stream commands identify the user, define (in order) the programs to be run, and request peripheral device support for each program.

The operator's console is a second source of commands (Fig. 7.3). At the start of the day, the operator boots the system by following initial program load (IPL) procedures to set such key variables as default main memory space allocations, internal priority rules, system device assignments, the system date and time, and others. As the system runs, other commands are used to halt, terminate, or load a program, check the status of the system, identify a user, and, in general, control the flow of work. At the end of the day, other commands allow the operator to shut down the system.

Fig. 7.2   On batch processing systems, a series of commands often enters through the job stream.

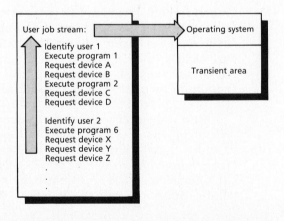

Fig. 7.3 The system operator enters real-time commands through the system console.

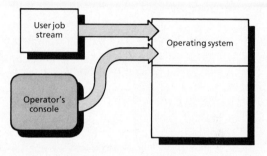

Generally, software belongs to the programmer, while the operator controls the hardware. Where do the data fit? Many large organizations assign responsibility for secondary storage space, data maintenance, backup, security, and accessibility to a database administrator. Other systems identify a super user who has overall responsibility for managing the entire system. The database administrator's or super user's console represents a third source of commands (Fig. 7.4).

Imagine if every user were given access to a complete set of system commands. Be honest: wouldn't you be tempted to cancel a friend's program as a joke if you had the opportunity? The set of commands available to a user is often quite limited. The operator, on the other hand, can issue all user commands plus several others, such as cancel a program, change a user's priority, postpone a batch job, and so on. The system administrator represents yet a higher level of control. Often this individual is empowered to issue any user command, any operator command, and several others as well. Thus, the complete command language is available only to the system administrator, the operator is limited to a subset, and users to a still smaller subset.

Learning a Command Language

The best way to learn a command language is to issue some commands. The next seven chapters are designed to help you do exactly that. Chapter 8 introduces the command language for a popular microcomputer operating system, MS-DOS (or PC-DOS). Chapter 9 investigates UNIX and its command language. Most

Fig. 7.4   On many systems, the database administrator's or
                      super user's console is yet another source of
                      commands.

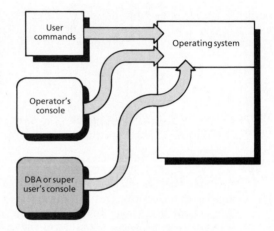

MS-DOS and UNIX commands are interactive, so Chapters 8 and
9 are written as tutorials. Chapter 10 introduces IBM's OS/400
command language, while Chapter 11 presents a batch job control language for IBM's VSE operating system. Perhaps the best
known batch job control language, IBM's MVS/JCL, is covered in
Chapters 12 and 13. Part III ends (Chapter 14) with a discussion
of libraries and the linkage editor, using MVS/JCL examples.

   Most job control and command languages are quite "rich,"
with features that allow a skilled expert to do just about anything. However, the average programmer needs only a small subset of a command language. The intent of these chapters is to
focus on that small subset. Ideally, you should be able to read a
chapter, gain an appreciation for a command language, complete some exercises, and learn enough to begin using a system.
As your skill increases, you will find it necessary to consult a reference manual to learn more advanced features.

   It is unlikely that anyone but a future system programmer
will use, on a regular basis, all five command languages, so a
good approach is to select one or two for in-depth study. Carefully read about the command languages you (or your instructor) have selected, and work through the tutorial or complete the
end-of-chapter programming exercises. Read the other chapters.

Note how the other command languages are similar to, and yet different from, the ones you are studying.

The material in this brief chapter is general and relates to all command languages. Much of Chapter 14 is also general and should be read carefully; specific examples are clearly identified and can be skipped by those who choose not to study MVS/JCL. Near the end of the book, you'll find a series of appendices summarizing these command and job control languages; you should find them useful references.

Summary

People communicate with an operating system through a command or job control language. Command language statements identify users, identify programs to be executed, request peripheral device support, name files, set access limits on files, and request secondary storage space. Other commands allow operators, programmers, and users to intervene as a program runs.

The most common sources of commands are users and programmers. Time-sharing commands are entered interactively, as work progresses. Batch commands are prepared before any programs are loaded and submitted to the operating system through the job stream. Operator commands enter the system through the operator's console. A third source is the database administrator's or super user's console. Often, only the super user has access to a complete set of commands, with the operator limited to a subset and users to a still smaller subset.

Key Words

command	job control language	job stream

Exercises

1. Identifying users is not a major problem on single-user systems. Why not?

2. Why must multiprogramming and time-sharing users be identified?

3. Generally, users or the operator must issue commands identifying the program or programs to be executed by a computer. Why?

4. Distinguish between interactive commands and batch commands. Hint: the key is timing.

5. Deadlocks were introduced in Chapter 6. Relate a user's requests for peripheral device support to the deadlock concept.

6. Why is the ability to intervene as a program runs an important command language feature?

7. Many systems limit users to a subset of the command language. Why?

8

MS-DOS Commands

MS/DOS (or PC/DOS) is a popular
microcomputer operating system. This
chapter introduces DOS commands.
Key topics include:

MS-DOS

Getting started
  Formatting a disk

The file system
  File names
  Directories
  Path names
  Viewing a directory
  Creating directories
  Creating files
  Changing directories
  Manipulating files

Pipes, filters, and redirection

Batch files

Other useful commands

MS-DOS

Since its release in the fall of 1981, the IBM personal computer, better known as the PC, has become an industry standard. Its operating system, PC-DOS, was developed for IBM by Microsoft Corporation. It, too, has become a standard and is available in a generic version called MS-DOS. IBM PCs run PC-DOS; compatible microcomputers from other suppliers run MS-DOS; the two operating systems are functionally identical.

The general form of a **command** is shown in Fig. 8.1. The **default drive** and the system **prompt** are displayed by the operating system. The user responds by typing a command name followed by necessary **parameters.** A **delimiter,** usually a space, separates the command from the parameters, and, if there are several, the parameters from each other.

Some DOS commands are **resident;** in other words, they reside in memory whenever the operating system is loaded. Others are **transient;** they remain on disk and are read into memory only when needed. Resident commands can be issued even if the system disk is not in a drive; transient commands cannot.

This introduction to DOS commands is presented as a tutorial. Don't just read it. Instead, find an IBM PC or compatible computer, and, as you read about a command, enter it and see

Fig. 8.1   All DOS commands follow this general format.

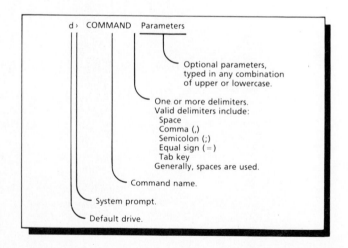

for yourself how the computer responds. You'll need a copy of MS-DOS or PC-DOS (version 2.0 or higher) and a blank diskette. Later, you'll find Appendix B a useful reference.

The tutorial assumes that your system has two diskette drives, that drive A is the boot drive, and that you have a working copy of either MS-DOS or PC-DOS on diskette. If your system boots from the hard drive (usually C), ignore instructions to insert your DOS disk, and as you read, mentally substitute drive C for drive A. If your system accesses DOS over a network, ask your instructor for the default drive identifier. In any case, format a work diskette and use it to hold any directories and files you create. That way, if you make a mistake, it won't impact anyone else.

The examples in this chapter were tested on a Zenith Data Systems Z-286-LP personal computer with MS-DOS 3.3 Plus and on an IBM PS/2 Model 55SX with PC-DOS version 4.00. The sample screens were generated from PC-DOS version 4.00. If you use a different version of DOS, the messages on your screen might be slightly different, but the format should be similar.

Getting Started

Main memory is volatile, so when a computer is first turned on, the operating system is not in memory. Instead, it resides on disk, and must be loaded before any commands can be issued. Start with the DOS disk in drive A (the leftmost or top drive). When you switch on the computer, hardware automatically reads, from disk, a routine called the **boot,** which, in turn, loads the rest of the operating system. (If the computer is already running, simultaneously pressing Ctrl, Alt, and Del has the same effect.) Try it.

Once the operating system is loaded, it issues two commands: *DATE* and *TIME* (Fig. 8.2). When asked to "Enter new date:", you have two choices. One is simply to press enter and accept the default date. The second is to type the current date and *then* press enter. When asked to "Enter new time:", you have the same choices. For now, press enter in response to both commands.

DOS stamps every file it creates or modifies with the date and time. Many programming languages include features that get the date and time from the operating system. If you don't set them correctly, they won't be reported correctly. Many computers contain a battery that supplies sufficient power to maintain the date, the time, and other key parameters even when the

Fig. 8.2   Once it's loaded, DOS issues two commands: *DATE*
and *TIME*. The last line on this screen shows the
standard system prompt.

```
Current date is Thu 03-28-1991
Enter new date (mm-dd-yy):
Current time is 15:45:42.20
Enter new time:


IBM DOS Version 4.00
            (C) Copyright International Business Machines
                   Corp 1981, 1988
            (C) Copyright Microsoft Corp 1981–1986


A>
```

computer's primary power is cut. If your computer has such a
battery, the date and the time displayed by DOS when you start
the system will probably be correct.

The last line in Fig. 8.2 reads

A>

That's the standard system prompt. The default drive is A; unless it is told otherwise, the operating system will expect to find
programs, routines, and data files on the disk in drive A. The
greater-than symbol (>) is the prompt; it means DOS is waiting
for you to enter the next command. Change the default drive by
typing *B:* (Fig. 8.3). Use either upper or lowercase; DOS converts
everything to uppercase. Press enter. Note that the next prompt
reads

B>

The default drive is now B. Type *A:*, and press enter. The default
drive should be A again.

When you first booted the system, you accepted the default
date and time. To correct the date, issue a *DATE* command (Fig.
8.4). Following the command, *DATE*, are the parameters month,
day, and year, separated by dashes or hyphens. The month must

Fig. 8.3   To change the default drive, type a drive letter
                    followed by a colon.

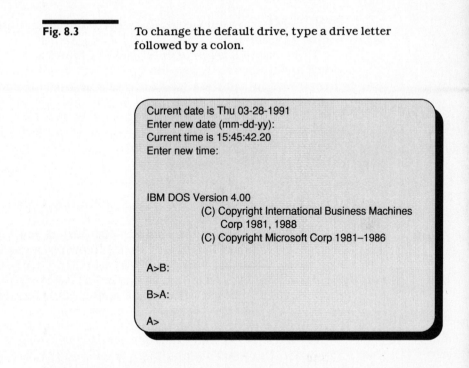

Current date is Thu 03-28-1991
Enter new date (mm-dd-yy):
Current time is 15:45:42.20
Enter new time:

IBM DOS Version 4.00
            (C) Copyright International Business Machines
                Corp 1981, 1988
            (C) Copyright Microsoft Corp 1981–1986

A>B:

B>A:

A>

lie between 1 (or 01) and 12; the day must lie between 1 and 31.
Years between 1900 and 1999 can be typed as two-digit (91) or
four-digit (1991) numbers; years after 2000 (or before 1900)
must be typed as four-digit numbers (2037). If you type a bad

Fig. 8.4   The *DATE* command allows a user to check and/or set
                    the system date.

DATE

or

DATE   mm-dd-yy

                                    Year. Enter 00 through 99 for years
                                    between 1900 and 1999. After 1999,
                                    enter four digits; for example, 2037.

                                Day of the month (1–31).

                            Month (1–12).

date, the system responds with an error message. Simply reenter the date correctly.

There are two ways to enter a *DATE* command. If you type *DATE* and then press enter, the system will display its version of the current date and ask you to enter a new one. If you respond by pressing enter again, the system will continue to use its current date. To change the date, type a new one. An option is to enter *DATE*, a space, and then type the new date before pressing return; for example,

DATE 07-04-91

If it's given a date, the operating system won't prompt you to enter a new one.

The *TIME* command is similar (Fig. 8.5). If you type *TIME*, the system displays its current time and prompts you to enter a new value. Hours are based on 24-hour military time; for example, 10 a.m. is 10, and 3 p.m. is 15. Generally, you should enter the time to the nearest minute; few applications require greater accuracy. If you type hours and minutes (separated by a colon), the values of seconds and hundredths of a second are set to zero.

Try a few *DATE* and *TIME* commands. They can be typed in any order. Use any combination of upper and lowercase letters

Fig. 8.5   The *TIME* command allows a user to check and/or set
                        the system time.

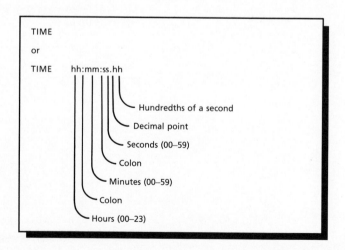

(remember, DOS converts everything to uppercase). Lie to the computer; it doesn't care. Of course, you should set the date and time correctly before actively using the system, but the computer will accept whatever you tell it as long as the format is correct.

Some applications require a particular version of DOS. The version number was displayed when the system was booted, but that first line may have scrolled off the screen by now. To view the version number, type

VER

and press enter. (By now you should know that you must press enter to issue the command after you type it.) There are no parameters. In response, the system displays its version number.

Formatting a Disk

Later in the chapter you'll need a work disk. Before a disk can be used, it must be formatted. The formatting process writes a pattern of sectors on the disk surface, records a copy of the boot routine on the first sector, and initializes control information. The *FORMAT* command (Fig. 8.6) is used to format a disk.

The simplest form of the command consists of a single word: *FORMAT*. If you issue such a command, DOS will format a disk

---

Fig. 8.6   The *FORMAT* command allows a user to format a disk.

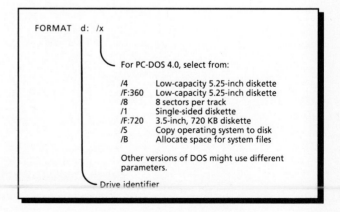

in the default drive at that drive's default density. Do be careful, however, because *FORMAT* is a destructive command. When you format a disk, you erase whatever data might be stored on it, and recovering those data is virtually impossible. *Caution:* if your default drive is a hard disk (usually, drive C), *do not,* under any circumstances, format that disk. You could destroy your system.

The safest way to format a disk is to specify the target drive. For example, type the command

FORMAT B:

The *FORMAT* command is transient, so you will notice a slight delay as DOS reads it into memory. The B: parameter identifies drive B as the target drive. A message will tell you to insert the disk to be formatted into drive B and press enter (or return). (*Note:* if your boot drive is C and you have only one diskette

---

Fig. 8.7   The *FORMAT* command generates its own prompts to guide a user through the process of formatting a disk.

```
A>FORMAT B:
Insert new diskette for drive B:
and press ENTER when ready . . .

Format complete

Volume label (11 characters, ENTER for none)? DOSDEMO

         1457664 bytes total disk space
         1457664 bytes available on disk

       512 bytes in each allocation unit
      2847 allocation units available on disk

Volume Serial Number is 367A-0AC9

Format another (Y/N)?N
A>
```

drive, most systems allow you to reference it as drive A *or* B, so the B: parameter will still work.) After you press enter, the target disk will be formatted. If your version of DOS asks you to enter a volume label, type *DOSDEMO* and press enter. Figure 8.7 summarizes the system messages; different versions of DOS might generate slightly different messages.

Several optional parameters are summarized in Fig. 8.6. Unless it is told otherwise, *FORMAT* assumes the target drive's maximum density. Some of the options change this default. Coding /S records a copy of the operating system on the new disk.

The File System

File Names

The DOS **file system** allows a user to identify, save, and retrieve files by name. (A program is a type of file.) A **file name** (Fig. 8.8) is composed of the name itself and an optional extension. The name consists of from 1 to 8 characters. A few file names are reserved by the system, and delimiters may not be used; otherwise, just about any combination of characters you can type is legal. The file name is separated from its 1- to 3-character extension by a period. Some extensions have special meaning to the operating system; they are summarized in Fig. 8.8. The extension is sometimes used to identify a version of a program or data file; for example, *VITA.1*, *VITA. 2*, and so on.

Directories

Directory management is a key function of the DOS file system. The first time a file is written to disk, its name, disk address, creation date, and other information are recorded in the **directory** (Fig. 8.9). Later, when the file is retrieved, the operating system reads the directory and searches it by name. When the file is modified, the file system updates the directory entry. When the file is deleted, its directory entry is deleted, too.

When a disk is first formatted, a single **root directory** is created. Using a single directory is fine for a few files, but as the number of files increases, distinguishing them becomes increasingly difficult. For example, imagine a work disk that holds several different types of files. Letters and correspondence are generated by a word processor. Chapters for a book are output by the same word processor, but they clearly represent a

Fig. 8.8   This figure summarizes the rules for defining a file name.

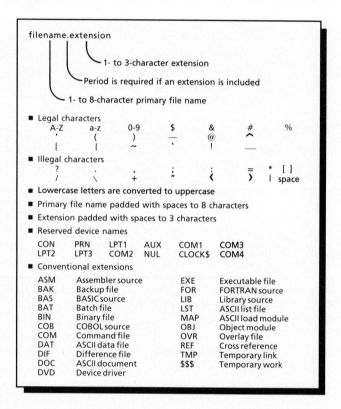

separate group of files. Finally, BASIC programs form another group of files.

To simplify keeping track of such files, DOS allows the user to create special files called **subdirectories.** For example, Fig. 8.10 shows three subdirectories. *LETTERS* holds letters and correspondence. A book's chapters are stored under subdirectory *BOOK.* Finally, BASIC programs are grouped under *PRO-GRAMS.* Think of a subdirectory as a file folder that allows you to group related files and thus organize a disk. Given the number of files that can be stored on its surface, subdirectories are almost essential on a hard disk.

Fig. 8.9   A file's name and starting address are recorded in the
disk directory.

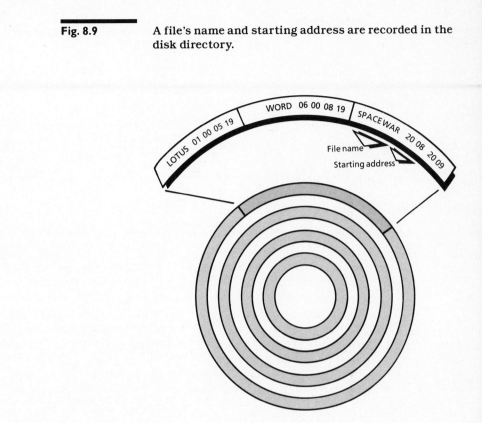

Path Names

When subdirectories are used, you need more than a simple file
name to find a file. For example, it is possible to have files named
PAY recorded under two different directories. A reference to *PAY*
would thus be ambiguous—which *PAY* do you mean? To identify
a file, you need a complete **path name** (Fig. 8.11); for example,

\LETTERS \PAY

The first back slash (on an IBM PC keyboard, the back slash key
is just above and to the left of the space bar) references the root
directory. The second back slash separates the directory name
from the file name. The path name just above tells DOS to start

Fig. 8.10   Subdirectories help to organize the data stored on a
                     disk.

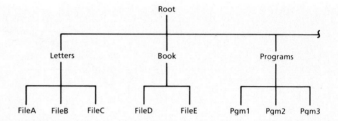

with the root directory, find a subdirectory named *LETTERS*,
and search the subdirectory for the file name *PAY.*

It is possible to divide a subdirectory into lower level directories. For example, Fig. 8.12 shows *LETTERS* broken into three
subdirectories. One, *CLUB*, is further subdivided into *ROTARY*
and *JCC*. To retrieve a letter named *MEMBER.3* from the *RO-
TARY* subdirectory, code

\LETTERS \CLUB\ROTARY \MEMBER.3

Fig. 8.11   This figure summarizes the rules for defining path
                     names.

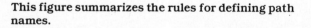

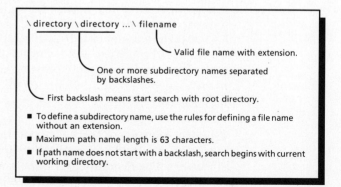

\ directory \ directory ... \ filename

Valid file name with extension.

One or more subdirectory names separated
by backslashes.

First backslash means start search with root directory.

- To define a subdirectory name, use the rules for defining a file name
  without an extension.
- Maximum path name length is 63 characters.
- If path name does not start with a backslash, search begins with current
  working directory.

Fig. 8.12   Directories can be subdivided into lower-level subdirectories.

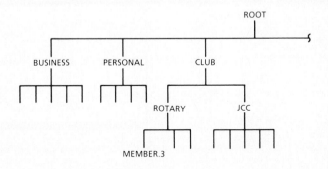

Note how the path name leads from directory to directory until, finally, you reach the desired file.

At first glance, subdirectories seem to complicate rather than simplify accessing files. In practice, people rarely use such lengthy path names. Instead, they select a working directory and allow the operating system to add the directory names needed to complete a path name. Later in the chapter, you'll learn how to select a working directory.

Viewing a Directory

Before you begin creating and manipulating directories, it might be wise to look through an existing one. There are numerous programs and files on the DOS disk, so insert it into drive A. Then type a check disk *(CHKDSK)* command (Fig. 8.13)

CHKDSK

This command is transient, so you'll notice a slight delay as the routine is read from disk. Because there are no parameters, DOS will check the disk in the default drive. The output is shown in Fig. 8.14; your screen might show different numbers, and not all versions of DOS display volume information, but the format should be similar. You now know how many files are stored on the DOS disk and how much free space remains.

Fig. 8.13   The check disk *(CHKDSK)* command checks a disk's
directory and reports on its contents.

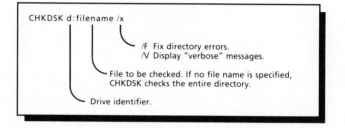

```
CHKDSK d:filename /x

                        /F  Fix directory errors.
                        /V  Display "verbose" messages.

                      File to be checked. If no file name is specified,
                      CHKDSK checks the entire directory.

                Drive identifier.
```

Fig. 8.14   The check disk command reports on the contents of
the designated disk.

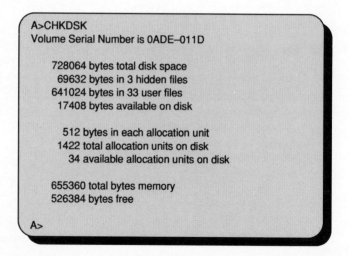

```
A>CHKDSK
Volume Serial Number is 0ADE–011D

     728064 bytes total disk space
      69632 bytes in 3 hidden files
     641024 bytes in 33 user files
      17408 bytes available on disk

        512 bytes in each allocation unit
       1422 total allocation units on disk
         34 available allocation units on disk

     655360 total bytes memory
     526384 bytes free

A>
```

Next, look at the names of the programs stored on that disk. Type a directory *(DIR)* command (Fig. 8.15)

DIR

Unlike *CHKDSK*, *DIR* is resident, so the operating system will respond much more quickly. Because there are no parameters, DOS will look to the disk in drive A. Part of the output is shown in Fig. 8.16; the complete DOS directory is too big to fit on a single screen. For each file, you can see a file name and extension, the file size, and the date and time the file was created.

A variation of the *DIR* command is particularly useful for displaying the contents of a lengthy directory. Type the command

DIR/W

and press enter. The /W parameter indicates wide mode. After the command is executed, you'll see a list of file names arrayed across the screen (Fig. 8.17). Note that such details as the file's size and creation date do not appear.

Are any of these files subdirectories? To find out, type a *TREE* command (Fig. 8.18)

TREE

In response, DOS reads the directory and displays only directory paths. As Fig. 8.17 shows, the DOS disk contains only a root directory.

Fig. 8.15   The directory *(DIR)* command displays a directory's contents.

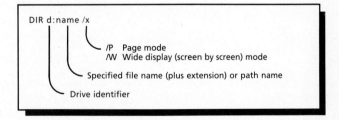

Fig. 8.16   The DOS directory is too big to fit on a single screen.

```
KEYB        COM    14759    06-17-88    12:00p
KEYBOARD    SYS    23360    08-03-88    12:00p
MODE        COM    23056    08-03-88    12:00p
PRINTER     SYS    18946    06-17-88    12:00p
REPLACE     EXE    17199    06-17-88    12:00p
SELECT      DAT    22453    08-03-88    12:00p
SELECT      EXE    99545    08-03-88    12:00p
SELECT      HLP    27562    08-03-88    12:00p
SELECT      PRT     1594    08-03-88    12:00p
SHARE       EXE    10301    08-03-88    12:00p
SYS         COM    11472    06-17-88    12:00p
VDISK       SYS     6376    06-17-88    12:00p
XCOPY       EXE    17087    06-17-88    12:00p
XMAZEMS     SYS    29249    08-03-88    12:00p
XMAEM       SYS    19312    06-17-88    12:00p
EGA         CPI    49052    06-17-88    12:00p
LCD         CPI    10592    06-17-88    12:00p
4201        CPI     6404    06-17-88    12:00p
4208        CPI      641    06-17-88    12:00p
5202        CPI      402    06-17-88    12:00p
012345      678      109    06-17-88    12:00p
AUTOEXEC    BAK       39    06-17-88    12:00p
           33 File(s)              17408 bytes free

A>
```

Creating Directories

Next, use a make directory *(MKDIR)* command (Fig. 8.19) to create a few subdirectories on the work disk you just formatted. Start with *LETTERS*. Insert the blank work disk in drive B. The default drive is A, so you'll have to identify the output drive. To create a directory named *LETTERS* on drive B, code

MKDIR B:\LETTERS

(Fig. 8.20). The back slash (\) indicates that *LETTERS* is a subdirectory of the root directory. Use similar commands to create two more directories: *BOOK* and *PROGRAMS*. When you're finished, type a directory command

Fig. 8.17   Note, near the bottom of this screen, that DOS has no
                  subdirectories.

```
A>DIR /W

   Volume in drive A has no label
   Volume Serial Number is 0ADE–011D
   Directory of A:\

ANSI     SYS  COMMAND COM  CONFIG    SYS  COUNTRY SYS  DISKCOPY COM
DISPLAY  SYS  DRIVER  SYS  FASTOPEN  EXE  FDISK   COM  FORMAT   COM
IFSFUNC  EXE  KEYB    COM  KEYBOARD  SYS  MODE    COM  PRINTER  SYS
REPLACE  EXE  SELECT  DAT  SELECT    EXE  SELECT  HLP  SELECT   PRT
SHARE    EXE  SYS     COM  VDISK     SYS  XCOPY   EXE  XMAZEMS  SYS
XMAEM    SYS  EGA     CPI  LCD       CPI  4201    CPI  4208     CPI
5202     CPI  012345       678       AUTOEXEC BAK
         33 File(s)       17408 bytes free

A>TREE
Directory PATH listing
Volume Serial Number is 0ADE–011D
A:.
No sub-directories exist


A>
```

Fig. 8.18   The *TREE* command displays the directory paths on
                  the specified disk.

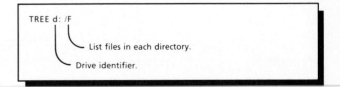

Fig. 8.19   The make directory *(MKDIR)* command creates a new
                  directory.

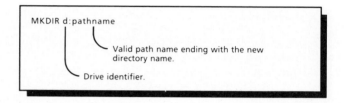

```
MKDIR d:pathname

                    Valid path name ending with the new
                    directory name.

              Drive identifier.
```

DIR B:

As Fig. 8.20 shows, three subdirectories have been added to the
work disk's root directory.

   MKDIR creates a directory; MD is an acceptable abbrevia-
tion. To remove a directory, code a remove directory (*RMDIR*, or
RD) command.

Fig. 8.20   This screen shows the commands to create three
                  subdirectories. The *DIR* command near the bottom of
                  the screen lists the subdirectories.

```
A>MKDIR B:\LETTERS

A>MKDIR B:\BOOK

A>MKDIR B:\PROGRAMS

A>DIR B:

   Volume in drive B is DOSDEMO
   Volume Serial Number is 367A–0AC9
   Directory of B:\

LETTERS        <DIR>        03–28–91      3:12a
BOOK           <DIR>        03–28–91      3:13a
PROGRAMS       <DIR>        03–28–91      3:13a
          3 File(s)              1456128 bytes free

A>
```

Creating Files

Most files are created by programs, such as the DOS line editor, compilers and interpreters, word processors, spreadsheet programs, and database managers. Another option is to copy an existing file. When DOS carries out a *COPY* command (Fig. 8.21), it reads the file specified in the first parameter (the source file), and copies it to the file described in the second parameter (the destination file).

One of the simplest ways to create a file is to copy the data from the console. For example, type

COPY CON B:\LETTERS \JIM

The first file name, *CON*, stands for the console. To DOS, it means input data will be typed through the keyboard. After you enter the command, the cursor will appear directly under the command line (you'll see no prompt). At this point, you can type whatever you want. When you reach the end of a line, press return. When you've typed all your lines, press function key F6 (the *COPY* command's sentinel value) and then press enter.

Copy the three files you see in Fig. 8.22 to directory *LETTERS*. Then copy a portion of a BASIC program to *PROGRAMS* and the first line of chapter 1 to *BOOK* (Fig. 8.23). If you prefer, use the BASIC interpreter to create a few BASIC programs and

---

Fig. 8.21 The *COPY* command copies one or more files from a source to a destination.

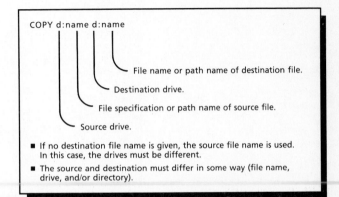

Fig. 8.22   Copy these three files to directory *LETTERS*.

```
A>COPY CON B:\LETTERS\JIM
Looking forward to spring break!
See you in Florida.
^Z
        1 File(s) copied

A>COPY CON B:\LETTERS\SALLY
Sorry, Jim.
I'm going skiing!
^Z
        1 File(s) copied

A>COPY CON B:\LETTERS\TOM
Math assignment.
Chapter 8, problems 10–14.
^Z
        1 File(s) copied

A>
```

Fig. 8.23   Copy this partial BASIC program to *PROGRAMS* and
this opening sentence to *BOOK*.

```
A>COPY CON B:\PROGRAMS\ASGN1.BAS
REM   THIS IS A BASIC COMMENT.
REM   THIS IS ANOTHER ONE.
^Z
          1 File(s) copied

A>COPY CON B:\BOOK\CHAPT1
It was a dark and stormy night.
^Z
          1 File(s) copied

A>
```

store them under directory *PROGRAMS*, use your favorite word processor to create a few text files and store them under directory *BOOK*, and copy a few *LETTERS* files from the console.

Some operating systems require a programmer or user to specify a file's size when creating it. That's not necessary under DOS. You will learn how DOS dynamically allocates disk space in Chapter 15.

Changing Directories

Now that the work disk holds some directories and files, investigate it. Start with a check disk command

CHKDSK B:

Clearly, the work disk contains three directories and several files (Fig. 8.24). Next, type

---

Fig. 8.24 The check disk command's output shows that five user files have been added to the work disk.

```
A>CHKDSK B:

Volume DOSDEMO        created 03–28–1991 3:03a
Volume Serial Number is 367A–0AC9

    1457664 bytes total disk space
       1536 bytes in 3 directories
       2560 bytes in 5 user files
    1453568 bytes available on disk

        512 bytes in each allocation unit
       2847 total allocation units on disk
       2839 available allocation units on disk

     655360 total bytes memory
     526384 bytes free

A>
```

DIR B:

Only the three directories (the contents of the root directory) are listed (Fig. 8.25). To view the contents of the *LETTERS* directory, type

DIR B:\LETTERS

Your screen should look something like the bottom half of Fig. 8.25 (your file names may be different of course).

Look carefully at Fig. 8.25. Directory *LETTERS* contains two unusual files: (.) and (..). The single dot refers to the direc-

---

Fig. 8.25   The first directory command lists the contents of the root directory. The second command lists the contents of subdirectory *LETTERS.*

```
A>DIR B:

    Volume in drive B is DOSDEMO
    Volume Serial Number is 367A–0AC9
    Directory of B:\

    LETTERS          <DIR>        03–28–91       3:12a
    BOOK             <DIR>        03–28–91       3:13a
    PROGRAMS         <DIR>        03–28–91       3:13a
             3 File(s)           1453568 bytes free

A>DIR B:\LETTERS

    Volume in drive B is DOSDEMO
    Volume Serial Number is 367A–0AC9
    Directory of B:\LETTERS

    .                <DIR>        03–28–91       3:12a
    ..               <DIR>        03–28–91       3:12a
    JIM                    55 03–28–91           3:14a
    SALLY                  32 03–28–91           3:17a
    TOM                    46 03–28–91           3:18a
             5 File(s)           1453568 bytes free

A>
```

tory itself; the double dot is a reference to its parent (in this case, the root directory).

Finally, type a *TREE* command

TREE B:

As Fig. 8.26 shows, the root directory contains three sub-directories, none of which holds lower level directories. (Note: other versions of DOS simply list subdirectories and do not draw lines to link them.)

The root directory is the current **working directory**. To shift to a different working directory, type a change directory (*CHDIR,* or *CD*) command (Fig. 8.27); for example, enter the command

CHDIR B:\LETTERS

Now type

DIR B:

The output should resemble the bottom half of Fig. 8.25. If you don't specify a directory, DOS starts with your current working directory. The change directory command allows you to specify a working directory.

Fig. 8.26   The root directory contains three subdirectories, none of which holds lower-level directories.

```
A>TREE B:
Directory PATH listing for Volume DOSDEMO
Volume Serial Number is 367A–0AC9
B:.
    ├────LETTERS
    ├────BOOK
    └────PROGRAMS

A>
```

Fig. 8.27   The change directory *(CHDIR)* command changes the
                         current working directory.

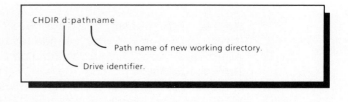

Manipulating Files

Earlier, you copied text from the console to a disk file. More generally, existing files are copied. The *COPY* command's first parameter specifies a source file; the second parameter identifies the destination. If drive designators are prefixed to a parameter, a file on one disk can be copied to another. If a file name is specified for the destination file, the new file name is used; if not, the source file name is assigned to the destination file. For example,

COPY A:\LETTERS \ TOM B:

copies a file named *TOM* from drive A to drive B and assigns it path name *\LETTERS\TOM.* (Don't issue this copy command.) The command

COPY B:\LETTERS \ TOM B:\LETTERS \ TAMMY

reads file *TOM*, makes another copy on drive B, and assigns it path name *\LETTERS\TAMMY.* Make sure your work disk is in drive B, and try this one.

    Special **wild card** characters allow a user to generalize the parameters. A question mark (?) represents any single character; for example, the file name

TERM.?

identifies *TERM.1*, *TERM.2*, *TERM.C*, and any other file named
TERM with a 1-character extension. An asterisk (*) represents
multiple characters; for example,

TERM. *

stands for every file named *TERM* with a 1-, 2-, or 3-character
extension, including *TERM.1*, *TERM.V6*, and *TERM.ABC*.

Imagine you've been working on a BASIC program. Your
source module is called *MYPGM.BAS*; the object module is
MYPGM.OBJ. You want to copy both. You have two options. One
is to issue two *COPY* commands. The other is to reference
MYPGM. * or *MYPGM.???*. Seeing the wild card characters, DOS
will look for all files that fit, so a single command will copy both.

Wild card characters are particularly useful for making
backup copies of selected files or an entire disk. For example,

*COPY *.* B:*

copies every file on the disk in drive A to the disk in drive B,
while

*COPY *.BAS B:*

copies every file with extension *BAS* (generally, BASIC programs) from drive A to drive B.

Occasionally, you'll want to rename a file or assign it to another directory without actually copying it. Use a *RENAME* command. To remove a file, use an *ERASE* command.

To display a file's contents on the screen, you could code a
COPY command with *CON* as its second parameter; for example,

COPY B:\LETTERS\JIM CON

Try it. The contents of the file will appear on the screen. An option is to code a *TYPE* command, such as

TYPE B:\LETTERS\JIM

TYPE reads the specified file and displays it on the screen. You
should see the same output.

A program is a special kind of file. Executable programs are
assigned extensions *COM* or *EXE*. To load and execute a program, simply type its file name (with or without its extension) as

though it were a command. If no extension is given, DOS will look for a resident command with the specified name. If it finds none, it will search for the file name with a *.COM* extension, then for a *.EXE* file, and finally for a *.BAT* file. (Batch files will be explained shortly.)

Pipes, Filters, and Redirection

Many DOS commands assume a standard input or output device; for example, the directory command sends its output to the screen. By using **redirection** parameters (Fig. 8.28), a user can change those defaults.

Consider a few examples. Insert the DOS disk in drive A. To print the DOS directory, code

DIR > PRN

To copy drive A's directory to a file on drive B, code

DIR > B:DFILE

If a program you have written expects its input from the standard input device (the keyboard), and for testing purposes, you

Fig. 8.28   Many DOS commands and filters deal with standard input and output devices. Redirection parameters allow a user to change to a specified file or device.

Parameter	Meaning	Example
⟨	Change source to a specified file or device	⟨MYFILE.DAT
⟩	Change destination to a specified file or device	⟩PRN
⟩⟩	Change destination, usually to an existing file, and append new output to it	⟩⟩HOLD.DAT
I	Pipe standard output to another command or to a filter	DIR I MORE

want to get input data from a text file, you can code something like

MYPGM < B:TESTDATA. I

It's much easier than modifying the program and recompiling it.

A **filter** is a special type of command. It accepts input from the standard input device, modifies (or filters) the data in some way, and sends the results to the standard output device. For example, *SORT* (Fig. 8.29) accepts data from the keyboard, sorts the data values into alphabetical or numerical sequence, and outputs the sorted data to the screen. With redirection, you can override or change the standard input device, output device, or both. For example, to sort the contents of a file and display the result on the screen, insert your work disk in drive B and enter the command

SORT < B:\LETTERS\JIM

(Note: if an error message indicates "Bad command," replace the DOS disk in drive A with DOS disk #2 and issue the command again.) To sort a file and store the output in a different file, code something like

SORT < MYFILE > RESULT

The *MORE* command (Fig. 8.30) is another useful filter. It sends output to the terminal one screen at a time. *MORE* is generally used with pipes.

A **pipe** causes one command's standard output to be used as the standard input to another command. Pipes are designated by a vertical line (|); on an IBM PC, press shift and the back slash key. For example, try displaying the DOS directory. Type

Fig. 8.29   The function of the *SORT* filter should be obvious.

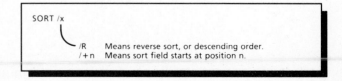

```
SORT /x

    /R    Means reverse sort, or descending order.
    /+n   Means sort field starts at position n.
```

Fig. 8.30   The filter *MORE* reads text from the standard input
                  device and displays it one screen at a time.

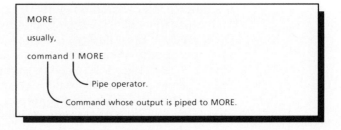

Fig. 8.31   *MORE* displays data one screen at a time.

```
Volume in drive A has no label
Volume Serial Number is 0ADE–011D
Directory of A:\

ANSI      SYS      9148   06–17–88        12:00p
COMMAND   COM     37637   06–17–88        12:00p
CONFIG    SYS        96   06–17–88        12:00p
COUNTRY   SYS     12838   06–17–88        12:00p
DISKCOPY  COM     10428   06–17–88        12:00p
DISPLAY   SYS     15741   06–17–88        12:00p
DRIVER    SYS      5274   06–17–88        12:00p
FASTOPEN  EXE     16302   06–17–88        12:00p
FDISK     COM     70151   06–17–88        12:00p
FORMAT    COM     22923   06–17–88        12:00p
IFSFUNC   EXE     21653   08–03–88        12:00p
KEYB      COM     14759   06–17–88        12:00p
KEYBOARD  SYS     23360   08–03–88        12:00p
MODE      COM     23056   08–03–88        12:00p
PRINTER   SYS     18946   06–17–88        12:00p
REPLACE   EXE     17199   06–17–88        12:00p
SELECT    DAT     22453   08–03–88        12:00p
SELECT    EXE     99545   08–03–88        12:00p
SELECT    HLP     27562   08–03–88        12:00p
— More —
```

Fig. 8.32 If the DOS directory is piped through *SORT* and then through *MORE,* the output is displayed one screen at a time in alphabetical order.

```
       33 File(s)            17408 bytes free
  Directory of A:\
  Volume in drive A has no label
  Volume Serial Number is 0ADE-011D
  012345      678        109    06-17-88    12:00p
  4201        CPI       6404    06-17-88    12:00p
  4208        CPI        641    06-17-88    12:00p
  5202        CPI        402    06-17-88    12:00p
  ANSI        SYS       9148    06-17-88    12:00p
  AUTOEXEC    BAK         39    06-17-88    12:00p
  COMMAND     COM      37637    06-17-88    12:00p
  CONFIG      SYS         96    06-17-88    12:00p
  COUNTRY     SYS      12838    06-17-88    12:00p
  DISKCOPY    COM      10428    06-17-88    12:00p
  DISPLAY     SYS      15741    06-17-88    12:00p
  DRIVER      SYS       5274    06-17-88    12:00p
  EGA         CPI      49052    06-17-88    12:00p
  FASTOPEN    EXE      16302    06-17-88    12:00p
  FDISK       COM      70151    06-17-88    12:00p
  FORMAT      COM      22923    06-17-88    12:00p
  IFSFUNC     EXE      21653    08-03-88    12:00p
  KEYB        COM      14759    06-17-88    12:00p
  -More-
```

DIR

The first several file names will scroll off the screen before you have time to read them. Now type

DIR | MORE

The directory command's standard output will be routed to the *MORE* filter rather than directly to the screen. *MORE* will display one screen and then wait until you press enter before displaying the next one (Fig. 8.31).

Try another experiment. Sort the DOS directory, and then display it one screen at a time. It's easy. Just code

DIR | SORT | MORE

Note that the data are displayed one screen at a time in alphabetical order (Fig. 8.32).

Pipes, filters, and redirection are powerful tools. As you become more experienced with DOS, you'll find many uses for them.

Batch Files

While most DOS applications are interactive, you will occasionally encounter a need to issue the same set of commands over and over again. For example, the manuscript for this book was written on a word processor called WordPerfect. Loading Word-Perfect requires four commands: *DATE, TIME, B:* (the data disk's default drive), and *A:WP* (where *WP* is the program name). Typing those same commands every day is annoying. An option is to create a **batch file.**

The normal boot procedure includes *DATE* and *TIME*, but nothing else. You can replace the normal procedure with your own boot sequence that includes all four commands by creating an *AUTOEXEC.BAT* file. (The extension *BAT* means batch.) When the computer is booted, the operating system searches the default drive's directory for a file named *AUTOEXEC.BAT*. If such a file exists, DOS reads it and issues its commands in order. If not, the standard boot sequence is followed.

To create an *AUTOEXEC.BAT* file, use the text editor or simply copy the commands from the console; for example,

COPY CON B:AUTOEXEC.BAT

(The sentinel value, remember, is function key F6.) The commands you type will be stored on a batch file on drive B. Subsequently, when the system is booted with that disk in the default drive, the commands in *AUTOEXEC.BAT* will replace the standard boot sequence. You may not have WordPerfect, but consider creating an *AUTOEXEC.BAT* file for your favorite software package.

An expansion board with a battery-operated clock is a popular option on many personal computer systems. If your system is equipped with a clock, you can obtain the current date and time from it rather than from the keyboard by creating an *AU-*

TOEXEC.BAT file. Check your expansion board user's guide for details.

Other types of batch files can be created, too. For example, imagine a payroll application that calls for entering data to a verification program, sorting those data, processing the data through a payroll program, and, finally, printing the checks. Four programs must run to complete this application. Week after week, the same four programs must be run in the same order. Instead of expecting an operator to enter the necessary commands, a better approach is to create a batch file; for example,

```
ECHO Insert payroll data disk in drive B.
VERIFY
SORT < B:TIMEDATA > B:TIMESORT
PAYROLL
CHECKS
```

This file of commands might be called *PAY.BAT*. To run the complete payroll application, the operator enters a single line

```
PAY.BAT
```

DOS responds by reading the batch file and carrying out the commands in order.

The *ECHO* command is new. It displays comments or messages on the screen. Another use for *ECHO* is turning on or off the printing of other commands. Normally, when a command is issued it is displayed on the screen. Adding *ECHO OFF* suppresses this display; adding *ECHO ON* reactivates it. The default is *ON*.

Other Useful Commands

DOS is a powerful operating system, and you have barely scratched the surface of its command language. However, assuming you have actually tried the commands described in this chapter, you should be able to read the reference manual and determine how to use additional commands on your own. For example, *COMP* compares two files and is used to verify a copy operation; *DISKCOPY* copies an entire disk, track by track; *DISCOMP* compares the contents of two disks. Another useful command, *RECOVER*, allows you to salvage at least portions of a file from a disk that contains bad sectors. Find an MS-DOS or PC-DOS reference manual and read about the *RECOVER* command.

You have already considered two filters: *MORE* and *SORT*. Another filter, *FIND*, searches the standard input stream or, using redirection, a file, for a specified series of characters. Although it isn't a filter, the clear screen (*CLS*) command is useful. If you can't guess what it does, try it.

Many applications generate graphic output. If you'd like to print a copy of what appears on the screen, use the *GRAPHICS* command. Simply type *GRAPHICS*, press return, and then load your application program. The graphics command loads a copy of a graphics routine immediately after the operating system. With this routine in place, pressing Shift-PrtSc sends the contents of the screen to the printer in graphics mode rather than character mode. You must have a graphics printer, and it might run slowly, but you'll get a very nice graphic image.

Finally, consider the *PRINT* command. It places one or more text files in a print queue. The contents of the queue are then printed in the background, in parallel with other DOS commands; in other words, as the printer prints, you can type other commands and work on other applications concurrently. Once you learn how to use the *PRINT* command, you will never again be willing to wait for the printer.

Summary

This chapter introduced the DOS command language. The basic structure of a command was illustrated and the difference between resident and transient commands explained. Normal boot procedures, *DATE* and *TIME*, the default drive, the standard system prompt, the *VER* command, and the Format command were all explained.

The file system is a key element of DOS. The rules for defining file names, hierarchical directory structures, the root directory, subdirectories, and path names were introduced. Using the DOS disk as an example, the *CHKDSK*, *DIR* and *TREE* commands were illustrated.

The next step was creating several directories and files on the work disk formatted earlier. Using *MKDIR*, three directories were created. Next, several files were added to the work disk and *DIR* and *TREE* commands were used to verify their presence. *CHDIR* changes the working directory. Wild card characters can be used to copy multiple files. The *TYPE* command displays a file's contents on the screen.

Many commands and utilities expect input from the standard system input device and send output to the standard system output device. Redirection allows a user to substitute files or other devices for these standard devices. Filters are routines that accept data from a standard input device, modify them, and send the results to a standard output device. Filters are often used with pipes. *MORE* and *SORT* were introduced and then combined to generate some interesting output.

When faced with a need to issue the same set of commands again and again, a user can create a batch file. *AUTOEXEC.BAT* files replace the system's normal boot procedure. Other batch files can be used for repetitive applications. To invoke the commands in a batch file, simply code the file's name as though it were a command.

The chapter ended with a brief overview of several other DOS commands. For a more detailed summary of command formats, see Appendix B.

Key Words

batch file	file name	resident
boot	file system	root directory
CHDIR	filter	*SORT*
CHKDSK	*FORMAT*	subdirectory
command	*MKDIR*	*TIME*
COPY	*MORE*	transient
DATE	parameter	*TREE*
default drive	path name	*TYPE*
delimiter	pipe	*VER*
DIR	prompt	wild card
directory	redirection	working directory

References

1. IBM (1988). *Using Disk Operating System Version 4.00.* Armonk, New York: International Business Machines Corporation.

2. Norton, Peter (1989). *Peter Norton's DOS Guide,* third edition. New York: Brady/Simon & Schuster.
3. Wood, Craig A. (1990). *PC-DOS & MS-DOS.* Reading, Massachusetts: Addison-Wesley Publishing Company.
4. Zenith Data Systems (1988). *MS-DOS Version 3.3 Plus.* St Joseph, Michigan: Zenith Data Systems Corporation.

Exercises

1. If you haven't already done so, work through the chapter tutorial.

2. Describe the general form of a DOS command. What are parameters? What are delimiters?

3. Distinguish between resident and transient commands.

4. Why is it important to set the date and time before using a system?

5. What is the significance of the default drive?

6. Why must a diskette be formatted before use?

7. What is the significance of a file name extension?

8. Briefly describe a hierarchical directory structure. What advantages does it offer over a simple linear structure?

9. Distinguish between a path name and a file name.

10. Distinguish between creating a directory and creating a file.

11. Distinguish between the root directory and a working directory.

12. What are wild card characters? Why are they useful? Why can't they be part of a file's legal name?

13. Briefly explain redirection.

14. What are filters? What are pipes? Briefly explain how they work together.

15. What is a batch file? Why are batch files useful?

16. If you normally use a particular application program such as a word processor or a spreadsheet, create an *AUTOEXEC.BAT* file of the commands needed to boot it.

17. Create a set of directories to help keep track of your DOS text files or programs. Add your existing files to the directory (rename them).

9

UNIX Commands and Utilities

This chapter introduces the command language for UNIX, a popular interactive, multiple-user operating system. Key topics include:

UNIX

Logging on

The file system
  File names
  Directories
  Pathnames
  Viewing a directory
  Creating directories
  Changing working directories
  Creating files
  Manipulating files

Pipes, filters, and redirection

Shell scripts

Other useful commands

UNIX

UNIX was developed at Bell Laboratories, a division of AT&T, in the 1970s. Largely the work of two individuals, Ken Thompson and Dennis Ritchie, the system's main thrust was providing a convenient working environment for programming. In addition to gaining wide acceptance, particularly in the academic world, UNIX has influenced the design of many modern operating systems. For example, current releases of DOS incorporate numerous UNIX features. Experienced programmers consider UNIX simple, elegant, and easy to learn. Beginners, on the other hand, sometimes find it terse, and not very friendly.

UNIX commands are processed by a **shell** that lies between the user and the resident operating system (Fig. 9.1). The shell is not really part of the operating system, so it can be changed. Professional programmers might choose a technical shell. Beginners might prefer a graphical user interface (GUI) with its menus and icons. The idea of a command processor that is independent from the operating system was an important UNIX innovation.

Two command-line shells are in common use. The **Bourne shell** was developed at Bell Laboratories. A second, the **C shell**, is taken from Berkeley UNIX. They are similar; in fact, you can follow the chapter tutorial and complete the end-of-chapter exercises using either one. As you become more experienced, you will want to write shell programs; at that point, the differences become significant.

Figure 9.2 shows the general form of a UNIX command. The system **prompt** (often, a dollar sign for the Bourne shell or a percent sign for the C shell) is displayed by UNIX. Command names

Fig. 9.1   UNIX commands are processed by a shell that lies between the user and the resident operating system.

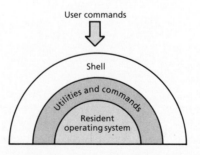

Fig. 9.2   The general form of a UNIX command.

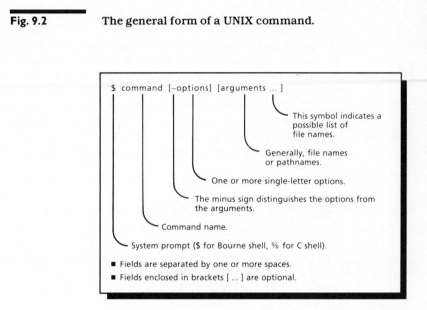

are generally terse (*ed* for editor, *cp* for copy a file), but meaning-ful. One or more spaces separate the command name from the options. If they are included, the options are usually preceded by a minus sign to distinguish them from the arguments. Most options are designated by a single lowercase letter, and more than one can be coded. One or more spaces separate the options from the arguments (generally consisting of one or more file names).

This introduction to UNIX commands and utilities is pre-sented as a tutorial. The examples were run on a Digital Equip-ment Corporation MicroVax computer under the Bourne shell. Don't just read it. Instead, find a UNIX system, and as you read about a command enter it and see for yourself how the computer responds. You'll need a user name and a password; see your in-structor or your system's super user. Later, you'll find Appen-dix C a useful reference.

Logging On

Usually, a system administrator or super user is responsible for such startup procedures as booting the system and setting the date and time, so the UNIX user can ignore these tasks. When you sit down at a terminal, the system should be up and running.

Every UNIX session begins with a request for a **login id** and a **password** (Fig. 9.3). In response to the first prompt, type your login name and press enter. Next, you'll be asked for your password. Type it and press enter; for security reasons, passwords are never displayed. Note that you always press enter to issue a command after typing it.

On some systems, you'll be expected to select your own password the first time you log on. Use any combination of up to eight keyboard characters. UNIX prefers relatively lengthy passwords and may ask you to try again if you suggest fewer than six characters.

Figure 9.3 shows a normal logon sequence, and then illustrates several commands. Use the *passwd* utility (Fig. 9.4) to change your password. The *date* utility (Fig. 9.5) displays the system date and time. To identify users currently logged on your system, type *who* (Fig. 9.6). A user working on more than one project may have two or more login names, and that can be confusing. The command

---

Fig. 9.3   Your system's super user or your instructor will
                    assign you a login name and a password. This screen
                    shows a normal log on sequence and illustrates
                    several commands.

```
login: bill
password:

Welcome to UNIX!

$passwd
Changing password for bill
Old password:
Type new password:
Retype password:
$date
Tues Mar 26 10:32:15 EST 1991
$who am i
bill        tty1 Mar 26 10:21
$
```

Fig. 9.4   Use the *passwd* utility to change your password

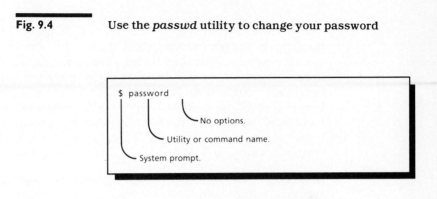

Fig. 9.5   The *date* utility displays the system date and time.

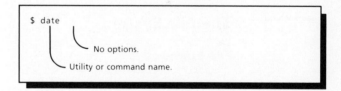

Fig. 9.6   The *who* utility displays the names of users currently
                                logged on the system.

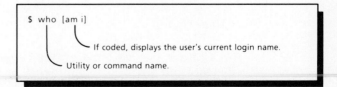

who am i

displays his or her current login id.

The *write* utility (on some systems, it's *talk*) allows two users to exchange real-time messages, while *mail* sends and receives electronic mail. Many larger UNIX systems feature an on-line reference manual. To obtain a description of any utility, code *man* followed by the utility name. For example,

man who

displays a description of the *who* utility. Because of space limitations, microcomputer versions of UNIX might not support *man.*

Two shells, the Bourne shell and the C shell, are considered UNIX standards; on most systems, one of them is started after logon. While the examples in this text will work under either shell, you can select one. To activate the Bourne shell, type *sh;* to switch to the C shell, type *csh.* To terminate a shell and return to your original login shell (or to log off once you get there), press control-D (the Ctrl key and either an uppercase or lowercase D).

The File System

File Names

The UNIX **file system** allows a user to identify, save, and retrieve files by name. (A program is a type of file.) A **file name** (Fig. 9.7) consists of from 1 to 256 characters. Don't use slashes (/), and avoid starting a file name with a minus sign or hyphen; otherwise, virtually any combination of characters is legal. Note that UNIX distinguishes between uppercase and lowercase; *A* and *a* are different. If you include a period, the characters following it are considered the file name **extension.** The extension is significant to some compilers and to the linkage editor; otherwise, it's simply part of the file name. An **invisible file**'s name starts with a period; invisible file names are not normally displayed when a directory is listed.

Directories

Imagine a user who maintains several different types of files. Letters and other correspondence are generated by a text editor, chapters for a book are output by a word processor, and C pro-

Fig. 9.7   The rules for defining UNIX file names.

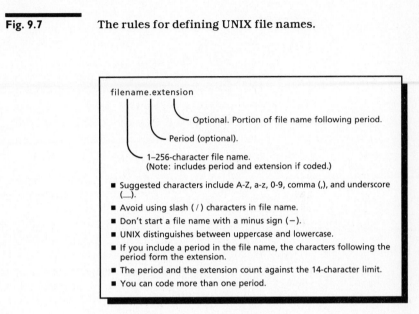

- Suggested characters include A-Z, a-z, 0-9, comma (,), and underscore (_).
- Avoid using slash (/) characters in file name.
- Don't start a file name with a minus sign (−).
- UNIX distinguishes between uppercase and lowercase.
- If you include a period in the file name, the characters following the period form the extension.
- The period and the extension count against the 14-character limit.
- You can code more than one period.

grams form another group. Dozens, perhaps even hundreds of different users will have similar needs. Keeping track of all those files in a single **directory** is almost impossible. Instead, UNIX uses a flexible hierarchical directory structure (Fig. 9.8).

The structure begins with a **root directory**. Growing from the root are several "children." Some hold references to utilities and other system routines. One, *usr,* contains several children of its own, one of which, *users,* holds all the user directory names. Note that *bill* is *users* child, a grandchild of *usr,* and a great grandchild of the root directory. Under *bill* come subdirectories to hold letters, book chapters, and programs. Incidentally, a directory is a special type of file, so the rules for naming directories and files are the same.

Pathnames

With all these directories, you need more than a simple name to uniquely identify a file. For example, it is possible to have files named *pay* recorded under two different directories. A reference to *pay* would thus be ambiguous—which *pay* do you mean? To identify a file, you need a complete **pathname** (Fig. 9.9); for example,

Fig. 9.8   UNIX uses a hierarchical directory structure.

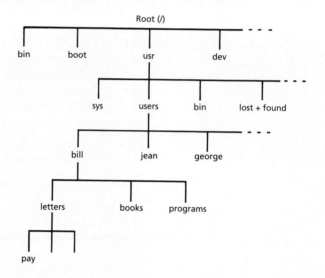

Fig. 9.9   Because UNIX uses a hierarchical directory structure,
                     you must specify a complete pathname to identify
                     uniquely a file.

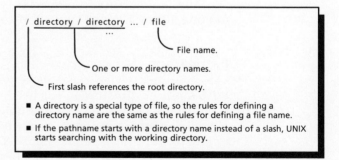

/usr/users/bill/letters/pay

Look at Fig. 9.8, and follow the pathname. The first slash (/) indicates the root directory. Move down to *usr*, then *users*, then *bill*,
then *letters*, and finally to the file.

At first glance, subdirectories seem to complicate rather
than simplify accessing files. In practice, however, people rarely
use such lengthy pathnames. Instead, when you log on, UNIX selects your **home directory** (its name usually matches your login
id) as your initial **working directory**. Unless it is told otherwise,
the operating system searches for files starting with your working directory, so

letters/pay

is typically all you need to find file *pay*. Later in the chapter,
you'll see how to change working directories.

Viewing a Directory

Before you begin creating and manipulating directories, look
through some existing ones. Start by printing or displaying your
working directory. Just type

pwd

and then press enter; the results are shown in Fig. 9.10 (your
working directory name will be different).

Even if this the first time you've logged on, your home directory should contain a few files. To view their names, type an *ls*
(list directory) command (Fig. 9.11)

ls -a

The output is shown in Fig. 9.12 (your output may differ). The
file names that begin with a period are usually invisible; had the
-*a* option not been coded, they would not have been listed.

Two files, (.) and (..) are particularly interesting. The single
period stands for the working directory; the double period is a
synonym for its parent. They are useful shorthands for writing
pathnames.

Try a few variations; some sample results are shown in Fig.
9.13. For example, code

ls

Fig. 9.10   The *pwd* (print working directory) command displays
the pathname of your current working directory.

```
$pwd
/usr/users/bill
$
```

Fig. 9.11   The list directory (*ls*) command displays, normally in
alphabetical order, the names of the files in the
specified directories. If no directories are coded, the
contents of the current working directory are listed.

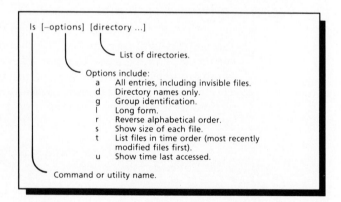

```
ls  [-options]  [directory ...]

                              List of directories.

                 Options include:
                    a     All entries, including invisible files.
                    d     Directory names only.
                    g     Group identification.
                    l     Long form.
                    r     Reverse alphabetical order.
                    s     Show size of each file.
                    t     List files in time order (most recently
                          modified files first).
                    u     Show time last accessed.
                 Command or utility name.
```

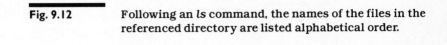

Fig. 9.12   Following an *ls* command, the names of the files in the referenced directory are listed alphabetical order.

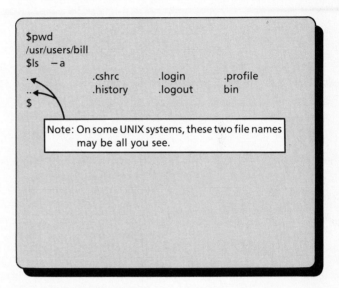

with no options. File names beginning with a period should no longer appear. In fact, on many systems, absolutely nothing is displayed because initially there are no regular files. If you ask for a list of files, and there are none, UNIX displays nothing, not even a "directory empty" message. To experienced programmers, that makes sense. A beginner might find such terseness a bit intimidating, however.

To list only directories, code a *d* option

ls -d

Next, take a look at the long form

ls - l

Finally, list everything, including invisible files, in long form

ls -la

Fig. 9.13   Experiment with the *ls* command by coding several
options.

```
$pwd
/usr/users/bill
$ls    − a
.                 .cshrc          .login          .profile
..                .history        .logout         bin
$ls
bin
$ls    − d
.                     ..

$ls    − l
total  1
d rw x r− x r − x   2 bill      24 Mar 25 05:05 bin
$ls    − 1a
total  9
d rw x r− x r − x   3 bill     512 Apr 14 10:02 .
d rw x r− x r − x  68 root    1536 Mar 26 16:32 ..
− rw x r− x r − x   1 bill     414 Mar 25 05:05 .cshrc
− rw x r− x − − −   1 bill     588 Mar 25 10:07 .history
− rw x r− x r − x   1 bill     245 Mar 25 05:05 .login
− rw−r− − − − −     1 root      44 Mar 26 16:33 .logout
− r x wr− x r − x   1 bill     103 Mar 25 05:05 .profile
d rw x r− x r − x   2 bill      24 Mar 25 05:05 bin
$
```

To indicate more than one option, simple code all the option letters one after another.

A long-form line shows a file's owner, size, and the date and
time it was most recently modified. The first 10 characters indicate the file type and its access permissions (Fig. 9.14). The file
can be an ordinary file (data or a program), a directory, or a special file that corresponds to an input or output device. Three sets
of permissions are included—one for the file's owner, a second
for users in the owner's group, and a third for all other users.
Based on the recorded values, a given user or group can be
granted read (r), write (w), or execute (x) permission, or any combination. A minus sign indicates no permission. To change access permissions, use the *chmod* utility.

Fig. 9.14   The first 10 characters in a long-form directory line indicate the file's type and access permissions. Use *chmod* to change them.

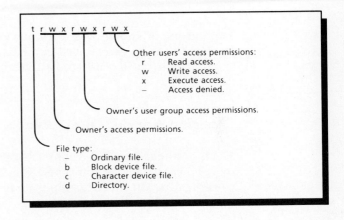

Creating Directories

The make directory command (Fig. 9.15) creates a subdirectory. For example, the command

mkdir letters book programs

creates three subdirectories under the home directory. Note that the command is followed by a list of directory names separated

Fig. 9.15   Directories are created by the make directory (*mkdir*) utility.

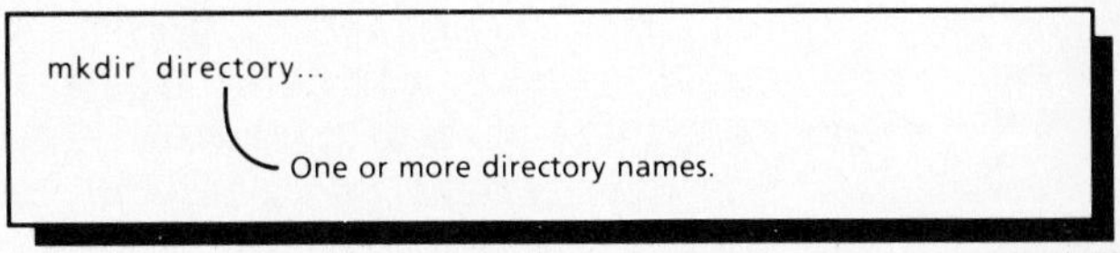

```
mkdir  directory...
              └── One or more directory names.
```

by spaces. UNIX will respond by creating the requested directories, but will not display a confirmation message (after all, you didn't tell it to).

To find out if the directories actually were created, type

ls -d

The output is shown in Fig. 9.16. Compare it with Fig. 9.13; clearly, the three directories now exist.

The *mkdir* utility creates a directory. Use *rmdir* to remove or delete one.

Changing Working Directories

The *ls* command lists the contents of the current working directory. You can use a *cd* command (Fig. 9.17) to change the current working directory. For example, code

cd /

Fig. 9.16   After a make directory command is executed, a directory list should reveal the new directories' names.

```
$mkdir  letters  book  programs

$ls   − d

.           ..          book          letters          programs

$
```

Fig. 9.17   Use a *cd* (change directory) command to switch to a
                 new working directory.

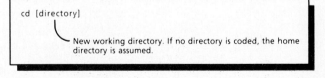

The slash identifies the root directory. UNIX will display no confirmation message, but the root directory will be your new working directory. Now code

ls -a

The output (on the author's system) is shown in the top half of
Fig. 9.18.
        Next, switch to a lower level, or child, directory. Type

cd /usr/users

On many UNIX systems, *users* contains each user's home directory. Once again, list your working directory's contents; the output (on the author's system) is shown in the bottom half of Fig.
9.18.
        Finally, move back to your home directory. Type

cd

with no options or arguments. To verify that you've returned to
your home directory, type a *pwd* (print working directory) command. Once again, list the directory's contents.

Creating Files

Most files are created by programs, such as editors, compilers,
interpreters, word processors, spreadsheets, and data base man-
gers. Most UNIX systems incorporate both a line editor (*ed*) and
a full-screen "visual" editor (*vi*). While an in-depth discussion of

Fig. 9.18

This screens shows the contents of the root directory and of directory *users* on the author's UNIX system. You may see a different list of files on your system.

```
$cd  /
$ls  −a
.            .profile     etc          save         verify.log
..           TEST         flp          sys          vmunix
.cshrc       bin          fverify      test
.hostabbr    boot         lib          tmp
.login       core         lost+fnd     tp
.logout      dev          mnt          usr

$cd  /usr/users
$ls  −a
.            datacom3     jj2eossa     mb52ossb     rw42ossa
..           datacom4     jk3rossb     md4gossa     sk4ossa
ab2bossb     db5nossb     jm1xossb     m19nossa     sn0bossb
ab7cossa     dc1zossb     jm6bossb     mt7nossb     sr6dossa
ac7sossa     dg44ossb     jm8vossb     mv3oossb     sr71ossb
bac          d12nossb     jm0sossb     nr5hossa     st7vossa
bc9gossb     dw00ossa     jw6wossa     pa31ossa     sw3kossb
bd41ossb     dw1gossa     kc1uossb     pb1possb     tb8hossa
bh5tossa     er8oossa     kc4iossb     pg4nossb     tg3uossb
bill         es19ossb     kg0xossa     ph7oossb     tw6sossa
c136ossa     guest        kr6fossb     rb2aossb     tr41ossa
dat          hp1qossa     ks9kossb     rh22ossa     wsd
datacom1 jd8vossb         lt9fossa     rs6iossa

$
```

its features is beyond the scope of this book, you can use *vi* to create a few simple files. First, however, change the current working directory to *letters*. It's a subdirectory of your home directory, which, if you've been following the tutorial, is your current working directory. Unless you specify otherwise, UNIX always assumes that a file reference starts with the current working directory, so

cd letters

changes the working directory to *letters*.

Fig. 9.19   The visual editor (*vi*) can be used to create text files and source modules.

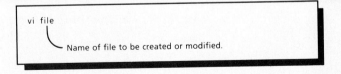

Start by requesting the visual editor (Fig. 9.19). For example, to create (in the working directory) a file named *jim*, code

vi jim

Except for a message at the bottom, the screen should go blank or display tildes. The visual editor has two operating modes: command and insert. As you begin, you're in command mode. To enter insert mode, press the *i* key. You'll get no confirmation, but you should be able to begin entering text. (Note: you may have to tell *vi* your terminal type—check with your instructor or your system administrator.)

Type anything you want. (Refer back to Fig. 8.22 for some suggested file contents.) When you're done, exit insert mode by pressing the escape key (or on some systems, a function key), and then type :*wq* (for write quit). Some systems accept a pair of capital Zs as a command to exit *vi*. You should see a system prompt indicating that you're back in the shell. Type an *ls* command to verify that the file is on disk. Repeat this procedure to create two more files named *sally* and *tom* (Fig. 9.20).

Some operating systems require a programmer or user to specify a file's size when creating it. That's not necessary under UNIX. You will learn how UNIX dynamically allocates disk space in Chapter 17.

Manipulating Files

Now that you've created some files, you can manipulate them. For example, the concatenate (*cat*) utility (Fig. 9.21) displays the contents of selected files. To display *tom*, code

cat tom

Fig. 9.20   This screen shows the message displayed by the
                     visual editor after it has created a file.

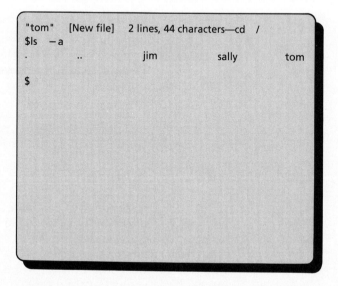

```
"tom"    [New file]    2 lines, 44 characters—cd    /
$ls   — a
.                .              jim           sally          tom

$
```

Fig. 9.21   Use the concatenate (*cat*) utility to display the
                     contents of one or more files.

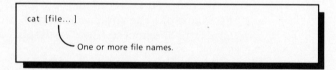

```
cat  [file... ]

          └── One or more file names.
```

The file should appear on your screen. To list the contents of more than one file, code a series of file names; for example,

cat jim sally tom

produces something like the output shown in Fig. 9.22. (You should see whatever you typed through *vi*.)

Imagine that a file named *resume* contains enough data to fill several screens. If you code

cat resume

much of the data will scroll off the screen before you can read it. To display the file's contents one screen at a time, code

more resume

Fig. 9.22   The word concatenate means "to join together." Thus, if several file names follow a *cat* command, the contents of all the files are displayed one after another.

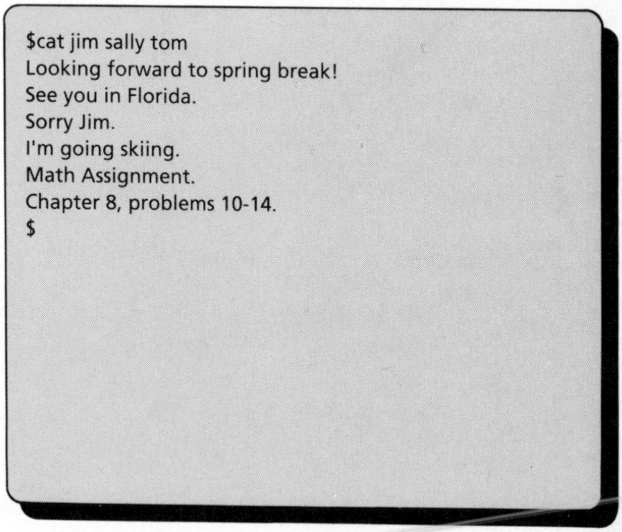

```
$cat jim sally tom
Looking forward to spring break!
See you in Florida.
Sorry Jim.
I'm going skiing.
Math Assignment.
Chapter 8, problems 10-14.
$
```

Press the space bar to view another screen, or the delete key to end the program. The *more* utility is not available on all versions of UNIX. If your system doesn't have *more*, you might be able to suspend a display by pressing control-s, and resume the display by pressing control-q.

Your current working directory is *letters*. Switch back to your home directory by coding

cd

Now try

cat sally

You should get an error message. Try

cat letters/sally

You should get valid output. Why? List your working directory

ls -a

Do you see a file named *sally*? No. However, the directory *letters* does appear. If you follow a path from your current directory, through *letters*, you'll find *sally*.

To copy a file, use the copy (*cp*) utility (Fig. 9.23). For example, code

---

Fig. 9.23   To copy a file, use the copy (*cp*) utility.

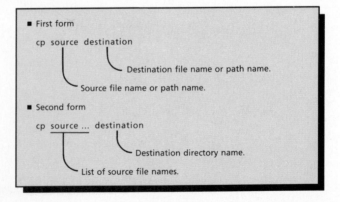

cp letters/jim book/chapt.2

Now,

cat book/chapt.2

should display the contents of the newly created file (Fig. 9.24). List the directory

ls -a book

File *chapt.*2 should appear in the list.
    The same file can be referenced in more than one directory by creating a link (Fig. 9.25). For example, code

ln letters/sally book

followed by

Fig. 9.24   When a file is copied, its name appears in the new directory.

```
$cd
$cp    letters/jim   book/chapt.2
$cat   book/chapt.2
Looking forward to spring break!
See you in Florida.
$ls    −a     book
.              ..                    chapt.2
$
```

Fig. 9.25   The same file can be referenced in more than one
                       directory by creating a link.

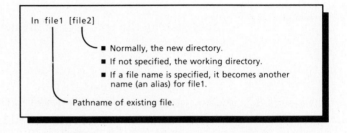

ls -a book

and compare the output to Fig. 9.24. You should see a new entry
in the list. Copy duplicates a file. Link does not; it merely assigns
another name to the same file by creating a new directory entry.

  To rename a file, code an *mv* (move) command. To delete a
file, code an *rm* (for remove link) command. If a file has multiple
links, *rm* will not delete it; you'll still be able to access it through
other links. When you remove the last link to a file, however, it's
gone.

  Wild card characters make it easy to reference a number of
related file names. A question mark (?) represents any single
character; for example, the file name

term?

expands to *term1, term2, termc,* and any other file named *term*
followed by any single character. An asterisk (*) represents multiple characters; for example,

term

stands for *term1, term.v6, term.abcdefgh,* and any other file
named *term* followed by any combination of characters (the
limit, remember, is 256).

  Imagine you've been working on a C program. Your source
module is called *mypgm.c;* the object module is *mypgm.o.* You

want to copy both. You have two options. One is to issue two *cp* commands. The other is to reference *mypgm.*[*] or *mypgm.?.* Seeing the wild card characters, the shell will look for all files that fit, so a single wild card name references both.

Pipes, Filters, and Redirection

Many UNIX utilities and commands assume a standard input or output device; for example, *cat* sends its output to the screen, while *vi* gets its input from the keyboard. By using **redirection** operators (Fig. 9.26), a user can tell the shell to change those defaults.

You already know that a *cat* command followed by a file name displays the contents of the file. Try coding *cat* with no options

cat

Since no inputs or outputs are specified, the shell assumes the standard input and output devices (the keyboard and the screen), so whatever you type is echoed back to the screen. Try typing a few lines (Fig. 9.27). Press return at the end of each line; when you're finished, press control-D (the end-of-file sentinel

Fig. 9.26   Many UNIX commands and filters deal with the standard input and output devices. Redirection operators and pipes allow a user to change to a specified file or device.

Parameter	Meaning	Example
<	Change source to a specified file or device	<myfile
>	Change destination to a specified file or device	>tempfile
>>	Change destination, usually to an existing file, and append new output to it	>>master.pay
|	Pipe standard output to another command or to a filter	cat file1|sort

Fig. 9.27   This series of *cat* commands illustrates redirection.

```
$cat
The quick brown fox
jumped over the lazy dog.
The quick brown fox
jumped over the lazy dog.
^D
$cat >book/intro
There was a young man from Nantucket
who ...
^D
$ls   —a   book
.            ..              chapt.2        intro
$
```

value). Some UNIX systems echo line by line; others display all the output only after you press control-D; in either case, data are copied from the standard input to the standard output device.

Redirect that output. Type

cat > book/intro

followed by several lines of text (Fig. 9.27). Press control-D when you're finished. Now, list your directory

ls *-a book*

You should see the new entry.

A **filter** accepts input from the standard input device, modifies (or filters) the data in some way, and sends the results to the standard output device. For example, consider *sort* (Fig. 9.28). It's a utility that reads input from the specified file or files (or the standard input device), sorts them into alphabetical or nu-

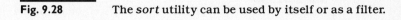

Fig. 9.28   The *sort* utility can be used by itself or as a filter.

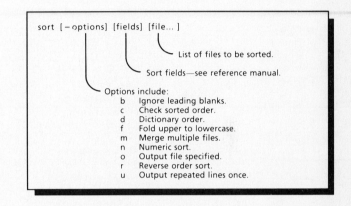

merical sequence, and outputs the sorted data to the screen. It can also be used as a filter.

A **pipe** causes one utility's standard output to be used as another utility's standard input. Pipes are designated by a vertical line (|). For example, earlier in the chapter, you coded

cat jim sally tom

Repeat that command. Now, try

cat jim sally tom | sort

As the bottom half of Fig. 9.29 shows, the standard output has been routed through *sort,* and the file contents are displayed, line by line, in alphabetical order.

UNIX utilities can be viewed as tools. Each one performs a single function. Instead of writing a massive program to perform a series of functions, it makes sense to use the existing tools. Pipes, filters, and redirection make it easy to link programs and utilities. As you become more experienced with UNIX, you'll find many uses for them.

Incidentally, most utilities send error messages to the standard error device—usually, the screen. The shell does not redirect error messages, so they won't be lost in an output file or down a pipe.

Fig. 9.29   With pipes, one utility's standard output becomes
                              another utility's standard input.

```
$cat jim sally tom
Looking forward to spring break!
See you in Florida.
Sorry Jim.
I'm going skiing.
Math Assignment.
Chapter 8, problems 10-14.

$cat jim sally tom  |  sort
Chapter 8, problems 10-14.
I'm going skiing.
Looking forward to spring break!
Math Assignment.
See you in Florida.
Sorry Jim.
$
```

This marks the end of the chapter tutorial. When you're
ready, log off the system by pressing control-D. An option (on
some systems) is to type a *logout* or *logoff* command.

Shell Scripts

Many data processing applications are run daily, weekly, or at
other regular intervals. Others, for example, a program test, are
repeated many times. When such applications are run, a set of
commands must be issued. Repeating the application means repeating the commands. Retyping the same commands over and
over again is annoying and error prone. An option is to write a
shell script.

A shell script is a file that consists of a series of commands.
(It's much like a DOS BAT file.) The shell is actually a highly sophisticated, interpretive programming language, with its own
variables, expressions, sequence, decision, and repetitive structures. Writing shell scripts is beyond the scope of this book, but
it is a powerful UNIX feature that you will eventually want to
learn more about.

Other Useful Commands

You have barely scratched the surface of the UNIX command language. However, assuming that you have actually tried the commands described in this chapter, you should be able to read a reference manual or a UNIX textbook and determine how to use additional commands on your own. For example, check *lpr*. It sends the contents of a file to the line printer. Then check *pr*. This filter prepares output for the line printer, adding page headers, page numbers, and so on. Try using pipes to direct the output from *cat*, through *pr*, and then to *lpr*.

You used the visual editor, *vi*, to create some files. Several other utilities transform text prepared under *vi* into printable form. For example, *nroff* formats text, *troff* prepares output for a phototypesetter, *eqn* sets up equations, *tbl* formats tables, and *spell* checks for spelling errors. Learn to use them; they are powerful tools.

Some tasks, for example, printing the contents of a file or performing a lengthy compile, can be time-consuming. Instead of idly waiting for such a process to finish executing, you can take advantage of UNIX's multiprogramming capability and run it in the **background.** While it runs, the terminal is free to support another program.

To run a program in the background, type an ampersand (&) at the end of the command line; for example,

lpr names &

Usually, the shell starts a command as soon as you enter it, and then waits for it to terminate before displaying the next prompt. The ampersand tells the shell to start the process, immediately display a process identification number, and give you another prompt (see Chapter 17 for additional details). Respond by typing your next command. To check the status of your background command, type a process status (*ps*) command.

Two other utilities support communications between systems. Call UNIX (*cu*) is a terminal emulator that allows a user to dial a remote computer and access it. UNIX-to-UNIX copy (*uucp*) transfers files between UNIX systems.

Summary

UNIX commands are processed by a shell. The basic structure of a command was illustrated, and normal logon procedures introduced. The *passwd* utility can be used to change a password; the *date* utility displays the system date and time, and *who* displays a list of users logged on the system.

The UNIX file system allows a user to store, retrieve, and manipulate files by name. The rules for defining file names were explained. Because UNIX uses a hierarchical directory structure, a pathname must be specified to completely identify a file. The *pwd* command displays the current working directory's pathname. You used *ls* to list a directory's contents, trying several different options. Next, you used *mkdir* to create three directories and experimented with the change directory (*cd*) command. Finally, you used the visual editor (*vi*) to create some files, and manipulated those files with, *cat, cp,* and *ln* commands.

Many UNIX utilities and commands assume the standard input or output device. Redirection tells the shell to change these defaults. A filter accepts data from the standard input device, modifies them in some way, and sends the results to the standard output device. Pipes allow a user to link utilities and other programs, treating the standard output generated by one as the standard input for another. The *sort* utility was used to illustrate pipes and filters.

Many data processing jobs are run frequently, so the same set of commands must be entered again and again. An option is to write a shell script. The chapter ended with a brief overview of several other UNIX commands and a discussion of background processing.

Key Words

background	filter	prompt
Bourne shell	home directory	redirection
C shell	invisible file	root directory
cat	login id	shell
cd	*ls*	shell script
cp	*mkdir*	*sort*
date	password	*vi*
directory	*passwd*	*who*
extension	pathname	wild card
file name	pipe	working directory
file system		

References

1. Bourne, S.R. (1983). *The UNIX System.* Reading, MA: Addison-Wesley Publishing Company.
2. Parker, Tim (1990). *UNIX Survival Guide.* Reading, MA: Addison-Wesley Publishing Company.
3. Sobell, Mark G. (1989). *A Practical Guide to the UNIX System,* second edition. Menlo Park, California: The Benjamin Cummings Publishing Company, Inc.
4. Troy, Douglas (1990). *UNIX Systems.* Reading, Massachusetts: Addison-Wesley Publishing Company.

Exercises

1. If you haven't already done so, work through the chapter tutorial.

2. What is a shell? Relate the UNIX shell to the command processor introduced in Chapter 5.

3. Describe the general form of a UNIX command.

4. Chapter 8 discussed DOS. Typically, start-up procedures included booting the operating system and setting the date and time. A UNIX user can ignore these tasks, but must provide a login name and a password. Why are these two operating systems so different?

5. Briefly describe a hierarchical directory structure. What advantages does if offer over a simple linear structure?

6. Distinguish between a pathname and a file name.

7. Distinguish between the root directory, your home directory, and your working directory.

8. Explain the significance of the (.) and (..) file names. What do they mean? Why are they useful?

9. Distinguish between creating a directory and creating a file.

10. When you log on, your home directory is your working directory. Why would you want to change that?

11. What are wild card characters? Why are they useful? Why can't they be part of a file's legal name?

12. Briefly explain redirection.

13. What are filters? What are pipes? Briefly explain how they work together.

14. What is a shell script? Compare a shell script to a DOS batch file.

15. What is the advantage of running selected programs in the background?

10

OS/400 Control
Language

This chapter introduces the control language
used on IBM's AS/400 computer systems.
Key ideas include:

The IBM AS/400

OS/400 control language

Sign-on procedures
  The sign-on screen
  The MAIN menu
  Signing off

OS/400 menus

On-line education

On-line help

OS/400 Commands
  Changing your password
  The command log
  The prompt feature
  Listing libraries and objects
  Creating a library
  Creating an object
  The SIGNOFF command

AS/400 program development

The IBM AS/400

The **AS/400,** IBM's successor to the System/36 and System/38, is a popular midrange multiple-user computer system designed to be accessed interactively through workstations. The **control language** is conversational, so this chapter is presented as a tutorial, but students who do not have access to an AS/400 system can still gain a sense of the control language by reading it.

Function keys F1 through F24 are arrayed across the top of a standard AS/400 keyboard. The enter (or return) key is in the bottom row just to the right of the space bar. Two keys above it (where the enter key is found on many keyboards) is the field exit key; press it when you finish typing a field to delete any characters that remain. The reset key is in the bottom row to the left of the space bar. The help key is located near the middle of a supplemental keypad at the keyboard's left. Locate the delete, backspace, cursor control, and other common keys, too.

An AS/400 system can be accessed via many different keyboards, so yours might be different. If it is, find the equivalent keys.

OS/400 Control Language

The format of an **OS/400** control language **command** is summarized in Fig. 10.1; an example can be seen near the bottom of the figure. The **command name** is formed by concatenating a series of abbreviations, one for each word in the descriptive command name. For example, *SNDMSG* means send (*SND*) message (*MSG*), while *DSPUSRPRF* is display (*DSP*) user (*USR*) profile (*PRF*). Most of these abbreviations are three characters long, but there are exceptions. For example, *CPYF* is the copy (*CPY*) file (*F*) command and the call command is *CALL*. There are roughly 700 different OS/400 commands, but the use of mnemonics makes them relatively easy to remember (or to guess).

The command name consists of a verb or action followed by a noun or phrase that identifies the receiver of the action. Under OS/400, documents, files, folders, libraries, programs, and other entities that can be stored and/or retrieved are represented as **objects.** (The significance of this object orientation will be explored in Chapter 18.) The command's action is applied to one or more objects, and the affected objects are specified by name in the **parameters.** Most parameters are key word in nature, but some can be specified positionally. If multiple parameters are coded, they are separated by blanks.

Fig. 10.1   The format of an OS/400 command.

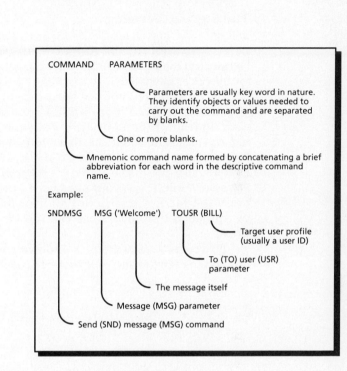

Commands are generally entered interactively from a workstation. Rather than memorizing a string of parameters, most users take advantage of the **prompt** feature by typing the command name and then pressing function key F4. The system responds by listing the necessary parameters and prompting the user for values.

You can also generate commands by selecting choices from a series of **menus.** (In fact, the menus make it possible to effectively utilize an AS/400 system without ever learning the control language.) However, working through menus can be tedious. Typing commands is sometimes called the fast path.

OS/400 commands can also be entered as part of the batch job stream or as instructions in a **control language program.** Control language programs are compiled and accessed much like application programs or DOS batch commands. They can also be called from an application program.

Sign-on Procedures

The Sign-on Screen

Before you sign onto an AS/400 system, you need a **user ID** and
(generally) a **password.** They are assigned by the system officer
(or by your instructor).

    The first screen you see should be the AS/400 **sign-on** screen
(Fig. 10.2). (If your workstation shows a different screen, ask
your instructor for help before you proceed.) The cursor (a blink-
ing box) should mark the line identified as *User;* if it doesn't,
press the tab key one or more times until it does. Then type your
user ID and press the tab key. The cursor will advance to the
Password line. Type your password (it will *not* be displayed) and
press the tab key again. Not all installations use passwords. If
yours doesn't simply press the tab key to skip over the password.

    The cursor should mark *Program/procedure.* This line can
be used to identify the program or procedure to be executed once

Fig. 10.2   The AS/400 sign-on screen.

```
                        Sign On
                            System  . . . . .  : SYS00001
                            Subsystem   . . .  : QBASE
                            Display   . . . . .  : DSP03



    User. . . . . . . . . . .    ▌_____
    Password. . . . . . . .
    Program/procedure. . . . .      _____
    Menu. . . . . . . . . . .       _____
    Current library. . . . . . .    _____



                (C) COPYRIGHT IBM CORP. 1980, 1988

    _____

    1                                            6/53
```

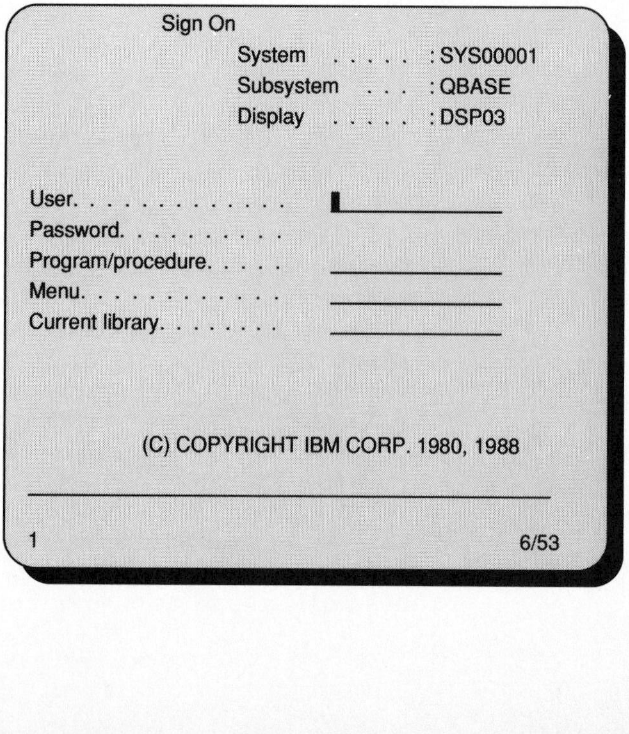

start-up is completed. Press the tab key to skip to the next line, *Menu*, which specifies the menu to be displayed following start-up. Type MAIN. The MAIN menu is the normal default, so there was probably no need to type it, but some systems are different. The fifth line, *Current library*, can be used to identify the name of the user's initial current library, but the system default (whatever it might be) is fine for this tutorial.

Press enter to complete the sign-on procedure. You might see a message displayed on your screen. If you do, press the enter key to clear it.

The MAIN Menu

Following successful start-up, the AS/400 **MAIN menu** (Fig. 10.3) will appear on your screen. It lists 11 possible choices

---

Fig. 10.3   The OS/400 MAIN menu.

```
MAIN                    Main Menu
                                              System SYS00001

Select one of the following:

       1. User tasks
       2. Office tasks
       3. General system tasks
       4. Files, libraries, and folders
       5. Programming
       6. Communications
       7. Define or change the system
       8. Problem handling
       9. Display a menu
      10. User support and education
      11. PC support tasks

      90. Sign off

Selection or Command
=== > |

F3=Exit     F4=Prompt    F9=Retrieve     F12=Cancel
F13=User support      F23=Set initial menu
```

(your screen might not show them all) plus option 90, *Sign off*. The cursor should be three or four lines up from the bottom just to the left of the arrow under *Selection or Command*. Menu choices and commands are entered on this line. The last two lines identify the function keys that are valid when this screen is displayed.

Signing Off

As an exercise, type 90 (for menu option 90) and then press enter to exit or sign off the system. After a brief delay, the sign-on screen will reappear. Should you find it necessary to quit before you complete the tutorial, remember how to exit the system.

OS/400 Menus

Repeat the sign-on procedure by retyping your user ID and password, typing *MAIN* after *MENU*, and pressing enter. The MAIN menu lists 11 (or fewer) choices. Type 1, press enter, and the USER menu (Fig. 10.4) will appear. Type 60 and press enter again to see the USER2 menu. Select the first option from the USER2 menu by typing 1 and pressing enter. The REMOTE menu will appear. Press F12 to cancel the last operation and the USER2 menu will reappear. Then press F3 to return to the MAIN menu. F12 backs you up one screen; F3 (usually) sends you back to the MAIN menu.

   Some operations call for negotiating a series of menus, and that can become tedious. An alternative is to go directly to the desired menu by issuing a *go to menu (GO)* command (Fig. 10.5). Each menu has a name; look back at Figs. 10.3 and 10.4 and note the name in the menu's top left corner. The *GO* command consists of the command verb, one or more blanks, and the target menu name. For example, on the MAIN menu's command line, type

GO SUPPORT

and press enter. The SUPPORT menu will appear. On the SUPPORT menu's command line, type

GO MAIN

Fig. 10.4   The USER menu.

```
 USER          User Tasks
                                        System SYS00001

 Select one of the following:

      1. Display or change your job
      2. Display messages
      3. Send message
      4. Submit a job
      5. Work with your spooled output files
      6. Work with your batch jobs
      7. Display or change your library list
      8. Change your password
      9. Change your user profile

     60. More user task options

     90. Sign off

 Selection or Command
 === > █_____

 ──────────────────────────────────────────────
 F3=Exit     F4=Prompt    F9=Retrieve    F12=Cancel
 F13=User support    F16=System main menu
 ──────────────────────────────────────────────
 (C) COPYRIGHT IBM CORP. 1980, 1990
```

Fig. 10.5   The *go menu* command takes the user directly to the specified menu.

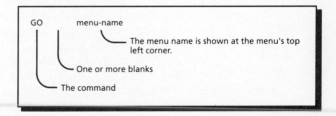

and press enter to return to the MAIN menu. (Pressing function key F3 is another way to return to the MAIN menu.)

As you begin to use an AS/400 system, you will quickly identify frequently used menus, and issuing *GO* commands to by-pass intermediate menus can save a great deal of time. For a complete list of menu names, see the AS/400 *Display Station User's Guide.*

On-line Education

Now that you know how to sign-on the system and navigate the menus, you can access the AS/400 **on-line education** feature. (*Note:* This portion of the tutorial is optional.) On the main menu, select option 10, *User support and education,* or issue a *GO SUPPORT* command. Then select option 9, *Online education,* from the SUPPORT menu. You might see a screen entitled *Start Education Administration;* if you do, select option 3, *Work as student.* Next, you might be asked to specify your name. If so, type your first name, press the tab key, type your last name, and press enter.

A list of available courses will be displayed on the *Select Course* screen. Press tab key several times until the cursor marks the *Tutorial System Support* course. Then type 1 and press enter. After a brief delay, the course will begin; just follow the instructions that appear on the screen. When you finish the tutorial, press F3 to exit on-line education. Then press F3 again to return to the MAIN menu.

On-line Help

On-line **help** is another valuable AS/400 feature. Start with the MAIN menu. Find the help key, press it, and the *MAIN Menu Help* screen will appear (Fig. 10.6). Note the word *More* near the lower right. It indicates that there is too much information to fit on a single screen. To see the next screen, press the roll forward (roll up) or page down (PgDn) key. An option is to press function key F14 to send the information to the printer. Press F3 to exit help and return to the MAIN menu.

The AS/400 supports **contextual help**; in other words, the help message you see is a function of the screen you were on when you requested help. For example, on the MAIN menu, type 1 and press enter to get to the USER menu. Then press the help

Fig. 10.6   The *Main Menu Help* screen.

```
MAIN                    AS/400  Main Menu
                  Main (MAIN) Menu - Help

     The AS/400 Main (MAIN) menu allows you to select the
     general task you want to do.

  How to use a menu

     To select a menu option, type the option number and
     press Enter. To run a command, type the command and
     press the Enter key. For assistance in selecting a com-
     mand, press F4 (Prompt) without typing anything. For
     assistance in entering a command,  type the command
     and press F4 (Prompt). To see the last command you
     entered, press F9 (Retrieve).

     To go to another menu, use the Go to menu (GO) com-
     mand. Type GO followed by the menu ID, then press
     the Enter key. For example, to go to the User Task
     (USER) menu, type GO USER and press the Enter
                                            More. . .
     F3=Exit help        F10=Move to top   F11=Search index
     F13=User support    F12=Cancel    F14=Print help
  [ ]                                               3/4
```

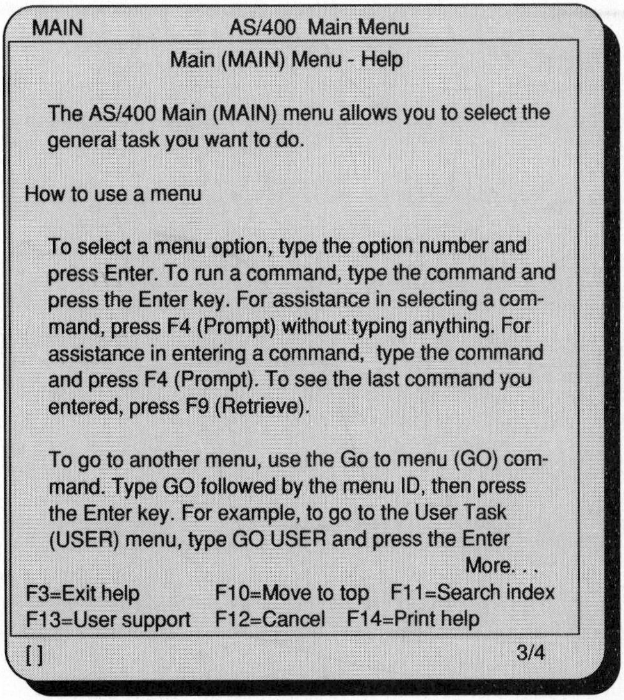

key and the *User Tasks Help* screen will appear. Press F3 to return to the USER menu. Then press F3 again to return to the
MAIN menu.

   The **search index** option allows you to find specific help information by typing a few key words. Start with the MAIN menu
and press the help key. When the *Main Menu Help* screen appears, press F11. A message at the bottom of the next screen will
ask you to enter a search string (Fig. 10.7). As an example, type
Folder and press enter. In response, the system will display a list
of references that include the search string (Fig. 10.8).

   Note that options 5 (*display*) and 6 (*print*) are listed near the
top of the *Main Help Index* screen. Press the tab key to select a
specific reference; for example, press tab twice to advance to the
third topic, *Add library list entry (ADDLIBLE) command.* Then
type 5 to request more detail on that topic. You can use the tab

Fig. I0.7

After you press function key F11 on the *Main Menu Help* screen, the system asks you to enter a search string.

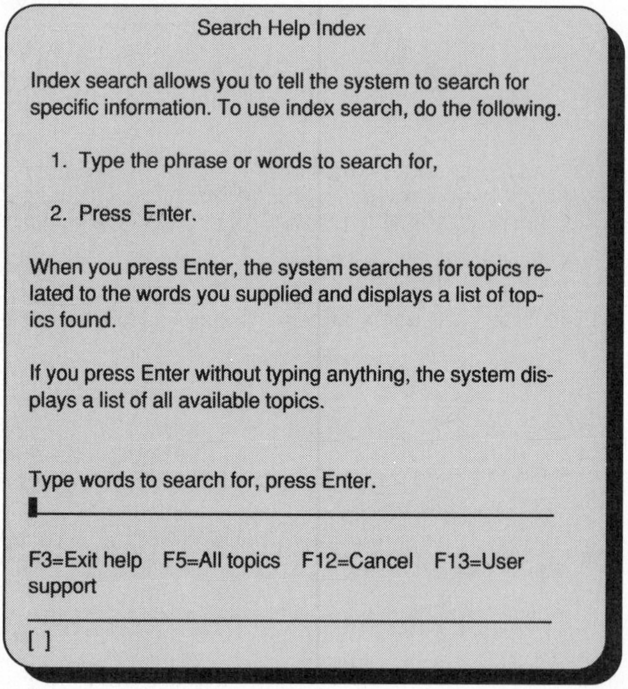

```
                     Search Help Index

Index search allows you to tell the system to search for
specific information. To use index search, do the following.

   1. Type the phrase or words to search for,

   2. Press Enter.

When you press Enter, the system searches for topics re-
lated to the words you supplied and displays a list of top-
ics found.

If you press Enter without typing anything, the system dis-
plays a list of all available topics.


Type words to search for, press Enter.
_____

F3=Exit help   F5=All topics   F12=Cancel   F13=User
support
_____
[ ]
```

key to select additional topics and type 5 or 6 in front of as many as you wish, but one is enough to illustrate the concept. Press enter to issue the request, and the next screen will display more detail on the selected topic. Press F3 to exit help.

OS/400 Commands

Changing Your Password

Because stolen passwords are a common security problem, it's a good idea to change your password frequently. Additionally, some systems expect new users to select a password the first

Fig. 10.8   The *Main Help Index* lists general topics that match the search string. You can display or print additional details for selected topics.

```
                     Main Help Index for AS/400

Type options, press Enter.
    5=Display topic      6=Print topic


Option  Topic
   –      Access code
   –      Add document library object authority (ADDDLOAUT) command
   –      Add library list entry (ADDLIBLE) command
   –      Change current library (CHGCURLIB) command
   –      Change document library object authority (CHGDLOAUT) command
   –      Change document library object owner (CHGLOOWN) command
   –      Change library (CHGLIB) command
   –      Change library list (CHGLIBL) command
   –      Change system library list (CHGSYSLIBL) command
   –      Chack document library object (CHKDLO) command
   –      Clear library (CLRLIB) command
   –      Convert to folder (CUTTOFLR) command
                                                           More. . .
or to search again, type new words and press Enter.
    Folder


F3=Exit help     F5=All topics     F12=Cancel     F13=User support
```

time they use the system, so you should know how to issue a *change password* command.

An AS/400 password can be virtually any combination of from one to ten characters. An installation can specify a minimum or maximum length, and it is also possible to have the system reject passwords for repeating digits or characters. Avoid using your name, your social security number, your telephone number, or other obvious patterns; they are easy to remember, but they are equally easy to guess. As a general rule, select a character string that you can remember but that cannot be lifted directly from your wallet, a telephone book, your resume, or any other source that might fall into a potential intruder's hands. Some installations assign each user a random character string.

Start with the MAIN menu. Type 1 (*User tasks*) and press enter to get the USER menu (Fig. 10.4). Then type 8 (*Change your password*), press enter, and the *Change Password* screen (Fig. 10.9) will appear. Changing your password is a three-step process. Start by typing your current password and pressing the tab key. Next type your new password and press the tab key again. (Follow your installation's guidelines or use your initials and today's date.) Finally, retype the new password and press enter. After your password is changed, the USER menu will reappear. Press F3 to return to the MAIN menu.

Instead of working through the menus, you can issue a *CHGPWD* command (Fig. 10.10). Note the mnemonic command name; *CHG* means change and *PWD* means password. On the MAIN menu's command line, type *CHGPWD* and then press enter. (There are no parameters, and you can type in either upper or lower case.) The *Change Password* screen will appear. Because you just changed your password, press F3 to return to the MAIN menu.

Fig. 10.9   The *Change Password* screen.

```
                    Change Password

Password last changed  . . . . . . . . . . . . : 03/15/91

Type choices, press Enter.

   Current password . . . . . . . . . . . . . . :

   New password . . . . . . . . . . . . . . . . :

   New password (to verify) . . . . . . . . . . :




F3=Exit                        F2=Cancel
[ ]
```

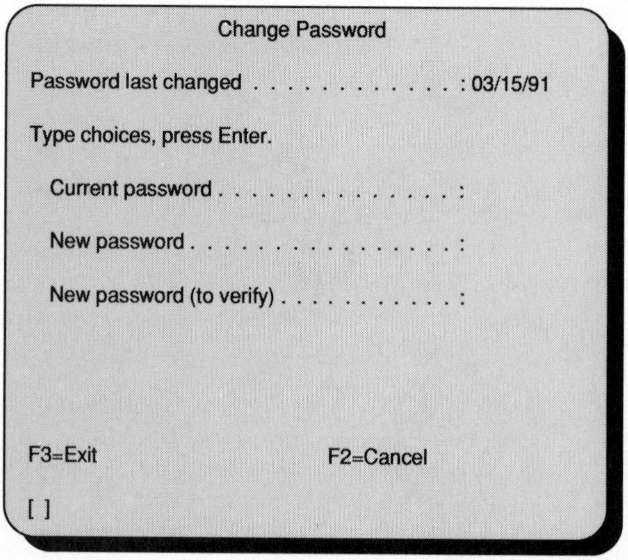

Fig. 10.10   The change password command.

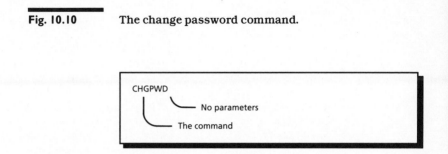

The Command Log

OS/400 maintains a log of all the commands you issue between sign-on and sign-off. To view your most recent command (*CHGPWD*), press function key F9 (*Retrieve*). Then press F9 again to view the previous command. Pressing F9 repeatedly allows you to step back, one by one, through all your commands. If you press the enter key while a command is displayed, that command is reissued. Take advantage of this feature if you find yourself issuing a series of similar commands.

The Prompt Feature

The *CHGPWD* command is easy to code because it has no parameters. However, many commands have numerous parameters. Rather than trusting their memories or searching through a reference manual, most experienced OS/400 users allow the system to identify the necessary parameters by taking advantage of the prompt feature.

For example, linked to each user ID is a **user profile** that defines an operating environment. Display your user profile. Start at the MAIN menu and try to guess the name of a *display a user profile* command. *DSP* suggests display. *USR* is short for user. *PRF* makes sense for profile. Put them together and you get *DSPUSRPRF*, which just happens to be the command name. Type

DSPUSRPRF

directly over the command that appears on the screen; note that the new characters replace the old ones as you type. If any characters from the old command remain, press the field exit key. Then press F4 (*prompt*), and a *Display User Profile* prompt screen will appear (Fig. 10.11).

Fig. 10.11   The *Display User Profile* prompt screen.

```
               Display User Profile (DSPUSRPRF)

Type choices, press Enter.

User profile . . . . . . . . . . .   _____Name, generic*, *ALL
Type of information . . . . . . .    *BASIC_____ *BASIC, *ALL, *CMDAUT. . .
Output  . . . . . . . . . . . .      *_____ *, *PRINT, *OUTFILE








                                                                  Bottom
F3=Exit  F4=Prompt  F5=Refresh  F12=Cancel  F13=How to use this display
F24=More keys
```

The prompt screen lists all the parameters the command
needs. First comes the user profile name—type your user ID.
User profile information can be displayed at several levels of detail. The basic level will do for this illustration, so accept the default, *BASIC, for the second parameter. (The asterisk identifies
*BASIC as a system value.) Finally, you can direct the output to
the display screen (*), the printer (*PRINT), or to a file; once
again accept the default (the display screen). All three parameters are defined, so press enter to issue the command.

The resulting display should resemble Fig. 10.12. Note that
your user profile specifies such attributes as your user class, au-
thorities, current library, initial menu, and initial program.
When you finish reviewing your user profile, press F3 to return
to the MAIN menu. Then press F9 (*Retrieve*) to see the command
you just issued. It should read

DSPUSRPRF USRPRF(username)

Fig. 10.12   A typical user profile display.

```
         Display User Profile – Basic

 User Profile . . . . . . . . . . . . . . . . :   BILL

 Previous sign-on . . . . . . . . . . . . . :   03/12/91 10:04:53
 Sign-on attempts not valid  . . . . . . :   0
 Date password last changed  . . . . :   03/12/91
 Password expiration interval . . . . . :   *SYSVAL
 Set password to expired . . . . . . . . :   *NO
 User class . . . . . . . . . . . . . . . . . :   *USER
 Special authority . . . . . . . . . . . . :   *NONE
 Group profile . . . . . . . . . . . . . . . :   *NONE
 Owner . . . . . . . . . . . . . . . . . . . . :   *USRPRF
 Group authority . . . . . . . . . . . . . :   *NONE
 Current library . . . . . . . . . . . . . . :   *CRTDTF
 Initial menu . . . . . . . . . . . . . . . . :   MAIN
      Library . . . . . . . . . . . . . . . . . :     *LIBL
 Initial program . . . . . . . . . . . . . . :   *NONE
      Library . . . . . . . . . . . . . . . . . :
                                             More . . .
 Press Enter to continue

 F3=Exit     F12=Cancel
 (C) COPYRIGHT IBM CORP. 1980, 1990.
```

where (*username*) is your user ID. You could have typed the entire command and then pressed enter, but it's much easier to use the prompt feature.

Listing Libraries and Objects

Under OS/400, files, programs, and other entities are stored as objects. Objects hold information; for example, a file holds data, while a program holds instructions. Objects are stored in **libraries.** Every user has access to several system libraries, a default **current library** (*CURLIB*), and, perhaps, additional user libraries.

To obtain a list of available libraries, issue a *display library list* command. Once again try to guess the command name—*DSP*, plus *LIB*, plus *L* seems to make sense. This time type the complete command

DSPLIBL OUTPUT(*)

Delete any leftover characters from the previous command or
press the field exit key. Then press enter. Your screen should resemble Fig. 10.13; note that it lists several libraries by name and
by type. Press F3 to return to the MAIN menu.

To display the contents of a selected library, issue a *display
library* command. Type the command name

DSPLIB

and press F4. You must specify the library name on the prompt
screen; unless it is already listed as the default, type *CURLIB.
The other defaults are fine, so press enter to get a list of the
names and types of the objects stored on your current library.
Your screen should resemble Fig. 10.14; don't worry if your list
of objects is different. Once again, press F3 to return to the MAIN
menu.

Fig. 10.13   A typical library list.

```
                         Display Library List
                                        System: SYS00001

Type options, press Enter.
    5=Display  objects in library

Opt    Library        Type     Text
 –     QSYS           SYS      System library
 –     QHLPSYS        SYS
 –     QUSRSYS        SYS      * In use
 –     QTEMP          USR
 –     QGDDM          USR
 –     QGPL           USR      General purpose library




                                                   Bottom
F3=Exit   F12=Cancel   F17=Top   F18=Bottom
(C) COPYRIGHT IBM CORP. 1980, 1990.
```

Fig. 10.14   The contents of a typical library.

```
                            Display Library
Library . . . . . . . :  QGPL     Number of objects . . :  443
Type . . . . . . . . :  PROD     ASP of library . . . . :  1

Type options, press Enter.
  5=Display full attributes        8=Display service attributes

Opt   Object     Type    Attribute   Freed   Size    Text
 –    @MAIL02    *PGM    CLP         NO      19968   Member added by COP
 –    ACZAA      *PGM                        0       *Not authorized
 –    ACZPAA     *PGM                        0       *Not authorized
 –    ACZPAX     *PGM                        0       *Not authorized
 –    AIR702     *PGM    RPG         NO      50688   Office integration
 –    AMZAA      *PGM                        0       *Not authorized
 –    AMZPAA     *PGM    CLP         NO      9216    M7X 09199
 –    AMZPAX     *PGM    CLP         NO      3072    M7X 09199 CL driver
 –    AMZPUP     *PGM                        0       *Not authorized
 –    BATRUN     *PGM    CLP         NO      9216
 –    BREAK      *PGM    CLP         NO      7680    Put QSYSOPR in BREA
 –    CALWDW     *PGM    RPG         NO      32768   Calendar window
                                                                   More . . .
F3=Exit  F12=Cancel  F17=Top  F18=Bottom
(C) COPYRIGHT IBM CORP. 1980, 1990.
```

To obtain a list of objects of a particular type, display them by type, for example, *DSPDOC* (documents), *DSPFLR* (folders), *DSPMSG* (messages), and *DSPPGM* (programs). Use a *CHGCURLIB* command to change your current library. (Can you guess the full descriptive command name associated with *CHGCURLIB*?)

Creating a Library

As you begin using an AS/400 system, you will probably want to create your own libraries to hold your work. To create a library, type

CRTLIB

on the command line and press F4. When the prompt screen appears, give the library a name. If your installation has standard library naming conventions, follow them; otherwise, use your initials. After you type the library name, press enter to accept the remaining defaults, and the library will be created; note the "library created" message near the bottom of the screen.

Creating an Object

To create an object, you can issue a create command such as *CRTDOC* (document), *CRTFLR* (folder), *CRTLIB* (Library), or *CRTPF* (physical file). Filling the object is a bit more difficult, however. Source information (data, code) typically enters the system through an application program, an editor, or a system utility. Rather than spending time introducing a particular data entry routine (which your system might not support), it makes more sense to copy an object that already exists. All AS/400 systems contain a set of RPG source code called QRPGSRC stored on a system library called QGPL. Copy that source code to the library you just created.

The desired operation is *create duplicate object.* Type the command

CRTDUPOBJ

and press F4. A prompt screen will appear; Fig. 10.15 shows the completed screen. Start by defining the source. After *From object* type the file name, *QRPGSRC*; after *From library* type *QGPL*; after *Object type,* type*FILE. (*Remember:* Press the tab key to advance to the next parameter and, if necessary, press field exit to delete stray characters at the end of a line.)

Now define the target object. The *To library* is the one you created earlier, so type its name. (*BILL* is the file name the author used). If necessary, press field exit to delete stray default characters. Make sure the *New object* is *OBJ, and press enter. A new line, *Duplicate data,* will appear; type *YES, press enter again, and the new object will be created.

Now that you have an object on your library, display the library's contents by coding

DSPLIB

and pressing F4. On the prompt screen, type the name of your library, press field exit, and then press enter. You should be able to identify the new library member (Fig. 10.16). Press F3 to exit the library display.

Fig. 10.15   The prompt screen for a *create duplicate object*
                     command.

```
                     Create Duplicate Object (CRTDUPOBJ)

Type choices, press Enter.

From object . . . . . .    QRPGSRC_____      Name, generic*, *ALL
From library . . . . . .   QGPL_____      Name, *CURLIB
Object type . . . . . .    *FILE_____     *ALL, *ALRTBL, *AUTL. . .
      + for more values
To library . . . . . . .   BILL_____      Name, *SAME, *FROMLIB. . .
New Object . . . . . .     *OBJ_____      Name, *SAME, *OBJ
Duplicate data . . . . .   *YES_____      *NO, *YES




                                                                    Bottom
F3=Exit  F4=Prompt  F5=Refresh  F12=Cancel  F13=How to use this display
F24=More keys

[ ]                                                                  5137
```

To display the contents of a physical file member, issue the
command

DSPPFM

and press F4. The *File* is *QRPGSRC* and the *Library* is the one
you just created; press field exit to delete left-over default characters. Following the prompt for *Member,* type *PROOF* and then
press enter. The display should resemble Fig. 10.17. (Your
screen might show compressed characters.) If you know RPG,
the code should make sense. If you don't, this program, when
compiled, prints a verification message that shows RPG was correctly installed.

OS/400 objects are assigned a one- to ten-character name.
Some special symbols are legal but, rather than memorizing the

Fig. 10.16   The library you just created contains a single member.

```
                          Display Library

Library . . . . . . . :  BILL      Number of objects . . :  1
Type . . . . . . . . :  PROD      ASP of library . . . . :  1

Type options, press Enter.
   5=Display full attributes      8=Display service attributes

Opt   Object        Type      Attribute   Freed   Size    Text
 –    QRPGSRC       *FILE     PF          NO      24064   File for RPG source



                                                              Bottom
F3=Exit   F12=Cancel   F17=Top   F18=Bottom
(C) COPYRIGHT IBM CORP. 1980, 1990.
```

rules, use letters and digits. Avoid starting object names with
the letter Q. Otherwise, just about any unique combination of
characters can be used, although a good name should suggest
the object's use or contents. An object name can be qualified; for
example,

PAYLIB/PAYPGM

might represent a payroll program on the payroll library. Two or
more objects can have the same name as long as they are different types or are stored on different libraries.

The *SIGNOFF* Command

This completes the tutorial. To sign off the system, type the command

Fig. 10.17   A typical physical file member display.

```
                    Display Physical File Member
File . . . . . . : QRPGSRC  Library . . . . . : BILL
Member . . . . : PROOF      Record . . . . . : 1
Control . . . .             Column . . . . . : 1
Find . . . . . .
*. . .+. . .1. . . .+. . .2. . . .+. . .3. . . .+. . .4. . . .+. . .5. . . .+. . .6. . . .+. . .7. . . .+. . .8
000100000000   H
000200000000   FQSYSPRT 0  F       132                 PRINTER
000300000000   E                   ARRY        1   3   8
000400000000   C                   MOVE ARRY,2          ARRY,3
000500000000   C                   SETON                             LR
000600000000   OQSYSPRT T 1 1  LR
000700000000   O                                        21 'INSTALLATION'
000800000000   O                                        24 'OF'
000900000000   O                                        28 'THE'
001000000000   O                                        35 'AS/400'
001100000000   O                                        43 'RPG/400'
001200000000   O                                        52 'COMPILER'
001300000000   O                                        55 'IS'
001400000000   O                                        64 'VERIFIED'
001500000000**
001600000000COMPILE
001700000000TIME
001800000000ARRAY
F3=EXIT  F12=Cancel  F19=Left  F20=Right  F24=More keys
```

SIGNOFF

and press enter. (There are no parameters.) An option is to type 90 on the MAIN menu and press enter. The sign-on screen will reappear.

AS/400 Program Development

The standard program development environment for the AS/400 is defined by IBM-licensed package called **programming development manager** (PDM). It is an object manager for programmers that incorporates several useful, integrated tools.

Fig. 10.18   To execute an application program, call it.

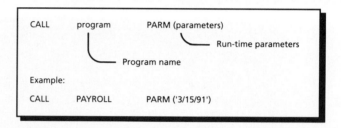

File descriptions are created using the data file utility (DFU) and stored as objects. Screens are created using the screen design aid (SDA), and the screen descriptions are also stored as objects. An editor allows the programmer to enter source code, merge the independently created file and screen descriptions into the program, and compile the source code. The editor can also be used to prepare batch jobs and control language programs.

To run an application program under OS/400, you call it by issuing a *CALL* command (Fig. 10.18). In response, the system finds the program and starts it. *CALL* commands can be issued interactively, as part of a batch job, or as part of a control language program.

See Appendix D for a summary of OS/400 control language commands.

Summary

The IBM AS/400 is a midrange, multiple-user computer system. An OS/400 control language command consists of a mnemonic command name followed by parameters that describe the objects affected by the command. Commands can be entered interactively, as part of a batch job, or as part of a control language program.

In addition to the user ID and password, the sign-on screen allows a user to specify an initial program, menu, and/or current library. The normal default is the system MAIN menu. To move to a new menu, you can type a menu choice and press enter or issue a *go menu (GO)* command. To sign off the system, code a

SIGNOFF command or select option 90 from the MAIN menu. The AS/400 supports on-line education and on-line contextual help. The help feature's search index option allows a user to search for information by key words.

The *change password (CHGPWD)* command was introduced, issued through the menus, and then reissued by typing it. Next, a *display user profile (DSPUSRPRF)* command was issued using the prompt feature. A library list was generated, and the contents of the user's current library (*CURLIB*) were then displayed. A new library was created. Then, a duplicate object, a set of RPG source code from QGPL, was created on the new library and subsequently displayed.

The standard program development environment for the AS/400 is defined by an IBM-licensed package called programming development manager (PDM). It is an object manager that helps the programmer create file descriptions, screen descriptions, source programs, batch jobs, and control language programs. To execute an AS/400 application program, you call it.

Key Words

AS/400	library	programming
command	MAIN menu	development
command name	menu	manager
contextual help	object	prompt
control language	on-line education	search index
control language	OS/400	sign-on
program	parameter	user ID
current library	password	user profile
help		

References

1. Hoskins, Jim (1990). *IBM AS/400, a Business Perspective,* second edition. New York: John Wiley & Sons, Inc.
2. IBM Corporation (1989). *Application System/400. Programming: Control Language Programmer's Guide,* second edition. Rochester, Minnesota: International Business Machines Corporation. Publication Number SC21-8011.

3. IBM Corporation (1988). *Application System/400. Programming: Control Language Reference,* second edition. Rochester, Minnesota: International Business Machines Corporation. Publication Number SBOF-0481 (six volumes).
4. IBM Corporation (1989). *Application System/400. System Concepts.* Rochester, Minnesota: International Business Machines Corporation. Publication Number GC21-9802.
5. IBM Corporation (1988). *Application System/400. Technology: Advantage AS/400.* Rochester, Minnesota: International Business Machines Corporation. Publication Number SA21-9540.

Exercises

1. If you haven't already done so, work through the chapter tutorial.

2. If you haven't already done so, complete the on-line education tutorial entitled *Tutorial System Support.*

3. Briefly outline the general format of an OS/400 control language command.

4. Explain how to sign on to an AS/400 system. How do you sign off the system?

5. Briefly explain how OS/400 commands are generated by selecting choices from menus. Why is the *go menu (GO)* command so useful?

6. What is meant by contextual help? Explain how you might use the search index feature to find HELP information about system libraries.

7. Why should a user change his or her password regularly?

8. Briefly explain how OS/400 command names are formed. Give several examples.

9. Explain how the prompt feature helps the user generate commands. Why is the prompt feature so valuable?

10. Distinguish between displaying a library list and displaying a library's contents.

11. Briefly explain how to create a library. Briefly explain how to create an object.

12. With your instructor's permission, use OS/400 control language commands to perform the following functions:
    a. Create a library using your user ID as the library name.
    b. Create a duplicate object in that library by copying the file QRPGSCR from library QGPL.
    c. Make another copy of QRPGSCR on your library, changing the file name to *MYFILE*.
    d. Display the contents of *MYFILE* member PROOF on the default printer.

11

VSE Job Control Language

This chapter introduces a subset of IBM's VSE job control language. Key topics include:

VSE

Job control language

The Editor

The JOB statement

The EXEC statement
  Compiling and link editing
  Cataloging programs

I/O control
  The ASSGN statement

VSE
  Power and the job stream

Cataloged procedures

Other job control functions

The chapter focuses on those job control language statements that a typical application programmer might expect to use.

VSE

During the computer's second generation, such accounting applications as payroll, accounts receivable, accounts payable, and general ledger were dominant. These applications run on a scheduled basis, so most second-generation systems were batch oriented. Punched cards were the standard input medium. Programmers prepared decks of cards containing program statements and data, and submitted them to a computer operator along with detailed instructions for running them. The operator scheduled the work and returned the results later.

IBM's 1964 announcement of the System/360 computer series heralded the arrival of the third generation. The application base remained relatively constant, but multiprogramming significantly changed the operator's job. Using written instructions to control several applications concurrently is almost impossible, so it became necessary to insert control statements into the job stream.

IBM's disk operating system (DOS) was written to support small- and medium-size computer systems. Initial versions were limited to two concurrent programs. As virtual memory gained acceptance, DOS evolved into DOS/VSE (for Virtual Storage Extended). Today's version, known simply as VSE, can concurrently execute up to 12 application programs plus the resident operating system.

Job Control Language

VSE was originally developed as a batch processing operating system. On an interactive system, commands are issued as the work progresses. On a batch system, all commands must be prepared before the first one is submitted.

Under VSE, programmers or users prepare complete jobs consisting of instructions, data, and JCL statements. A job might contain almost any number of related programs; for example, a data verification program, a sort program, a payroll program, and a check writing program might form a payroll job. To a programmer or a user, a complete job is a single unit of work. Once prepared, jobs are submitted to a computer operator or a job scheduler and combined with other jobs to form a job stream (Fig. 11.1).

Fig. 11.1   On batch processing systems, program instructions,
                      data, and control statements enter through the job
                      stream.

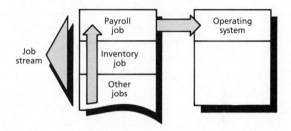

Look carefully at the job stream pictured in Fig. 11.1.
Clearly, the payroll job and the inventory job are different, and,
even though they might be submitted together, they must be
kept separate. Job separation and identification are essential
job control language functions. Within a job, programs must be
identified, so program identification is a second job control language function. As a program runs, certain default peripheral
device assignments can be assumed, but any deviations from
these defaults must be clearly communicated to the operating
system; this is a third job control language function. Finally, a
number of options are communicated through command statements.

Figure 11.2 shows the general form of a VSE job control language statement. The two slashes (//) in positions 1 and 2 must
be coded. Position 3 must be blank. Following one or more
blanks is an operation such as JOB (job identification), EXEC
(program identification), ASSGN (device assignment), or OP-
TION. One or more blanks separate the operation from the operands. Optional comments are separated from the operands by
one or more blanks; note that blanks serve as field separators.
Should it be necessary to continue a JCL statement on a second
line, code a continuation character (usually, the letter C) in position 72.

Because VSE JCL is a batch command language, a tutorial
approach is inappropriate. Instead, the various commands will
be introduced one by one, with several complete examples illus-

Fig. 11.2   The general form of a VSE job control language
                        statement.

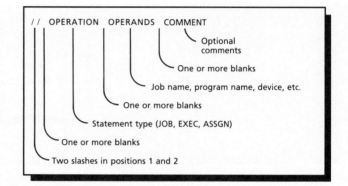

trating typical jobs. The nature of batch JCL makes it particularly important that you complete the end-of-chapter exercises.

Incidentally, the job control language described in this chapter is a subset of the VSE system command language. Any job
control statement can be entered through the operator's console. Additionally, the operator has a set of system initialization
and job control commands that cannot be submitted through the
job stream.

The Editor

Back in the 1960s when DOS was first developed, punched cards
were the standard system input medium. Today, punched cards
have been largely replaced by screens, keyboards, and diskettes,
but the 80-character "card image" is still the standard for VSE
job control language.

VSE job control statements are typically entered through a
workstation under control of a line or screen **editor** (Fig. 11.3).
The electronic card images are then stored on a library and subsequently submitted to the job stream. Many different editors
can be used. For example, VSE systems running under IBM's VM
(Virtual Machine) facility might use CMS (Conversational Monitor System). Perhaps the most common editor is **VSE/ICCF** (In-

Fig. 11.3   VSE job control statements are typically entered
                       through a workstation under control of a line or
                       screen editor.

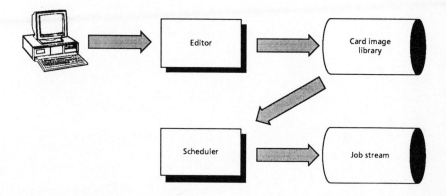

teractive Computing and Control Facility). The balance of this
section will use a few basic ICCF commands to illustrate editors;
if your installation has a different editor, you might want to skip
ahead.

To begin an ICCF session, type a *LOGON* command such as

/LOGON userid

where *userid* is the user identification code assigned by the system administrator (or by your instructor). ICCF will respond by
prompting you for your password. Once your identification code
and password are approved, the ICCF work screen appears (Fig.
11.4).

Note that *LOGON* is an *editor* command. Editor commands
consist of a single slash, an operation code (for example, *LIB* to
list a library directory, *LIST* to list a file's contents, *SAVE* to
copy a file to disk, or *LOGOFF* to exit ICCF), and possibly one or
more operands. Editor commands are different from job control
language commands. They manipulate text. (Think of ICCF as a
word processor). Job control language commands, on the other
hand, function at a higher level, defining or specifying programs, peripheral devices, files, and other system resources.

To access the full-screen editor, type

ED filename

Fig. 11.4   The VSE/ICCF work screen.

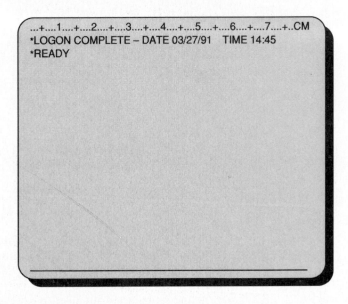

```
...+....1....+....2....+....3....+....4....+....5....+....6....+....7....+..CM
*LOGON COMPLETE – DATE 03/27/91    TIME 14:45
*READY
```

and press enter. Note that there is no slash. ED is not a command; it's a macro that defines a series of previously coded ICCF
commands. The (optional) *filename* references a library member. If a file name is coded, the requested file is retrieved and you
can edit its contents. If no file name is coded, a temporary file is
created in the ICCF input area, and you can save it under a file
name later.

Figure 11.5 shows an ICCF editor screen. Editor commands
are entered from the top line. Line commands are entered at the
right of the screen; they allow you to insert, copy, delete, move,
and duplicate text. (See Appendix E for a summary of ICCF editor and line commands.) Job control language statements (and
job stream data) are entered, one statement per line, on the editor screen.

When you finish typing a job, issue a *SAVE* or *FILE* command
to copy the statements to disk. Later, when you are ready to submit the job to VSE, code the ICCF macro

SUBMIT filename operands

Fig. II.5   The ICCF editor screen.

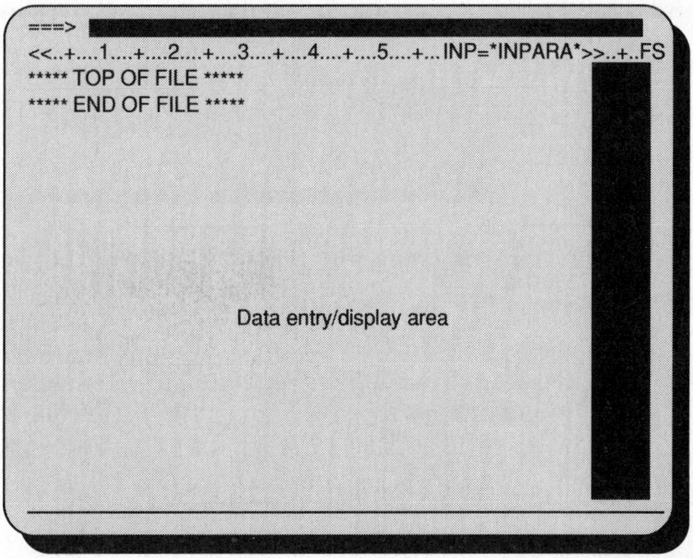

```
===>
<<..+....1....+....2....+....3....+....4....+....5....+... INP=*INPARA*>>..+...FS
***** TOP OF FILE *****
***** END OF FILE *****




                              Data entry/display area
```

The operands allow you to route the output (see Appendix E). After the job is submitted, other ICCF commands allow you to monitor the job's status and retrieve the output.

This brief introduction barely scratches the surface of ICCF. The intent here is to convey a sense of how an editor works. Your installation might use a different editor; there are many choices, and attempting to cover all of them would destroy the continuity of this chapter. By far the best way to learn an editor is to use it.

The JOB Statement

Jobs are separated and identified by **JOB statements** (Fig. 11.6). The two slashes (//) must appear in positions 1 and 2. One or more blanks separate the slashes from the keyword JOB. The **job name** is chosen by the programmer to identify the job. Accounting information is optional, although some installations require it.

Fig. 11.6   The general form of a VSE JOB statement.

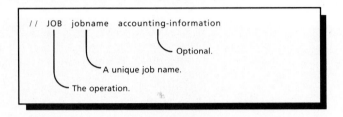

A job name consists from 1 to 8 characters. The first one must be a letter; otherwise, any combination of letters and digits is valid. It makes sense, however, to use meaningful job names. For example, a programmer named Sue might code

// JOB SUE

To distinguish jobs, she might choose

// JOB SUE1
.
.
.
// JOB SUE2

and so on. Often, jobs are assigned a prefix followed by a sequence number; for example,

// JOB PC0015

might identify the production control department's fifteenth job. An option is to choose a functional job name, such as

// JOB PAYROLL

Every job submitted to a VSE system must begin with a JOB statement.

The EXEC Statement

Programs are identified by **EXEC** (execute) **statements** (Fig. 11.7). Once again, the statement begins with slashes in positions 1 and 2. One or more blanks separate the slashes from the key word EXEC. Additional blanks separate the command from the **program name**, which identifies a load module stored in a library.

It should be noted that the program name bears absolutely no relationship to the job name. Like the job name, it consists of from 1 to 8 alphanumeric characters, but there the similarity ends. A job name serves to identify a job being run on the computer right now; when the job ends, the job name ceases to exist. A program name, on the other hand, serves to identify a program on a system library. When the current job terminates, the program still exists, ready, perhaps, to be included in another job.

A job is composed of one or more **job steps**. For example, consider the job illustrated in Fig. 11.8. In the first step, labor data are read into an edit program that eliminates certain data entry errors. The good data are sorted, and the sorted data are then read, along with a master year-to-date-earnings file, into a payroll program. The final job step is an audit program that prepares reports for the accounting department. The job ends with a /& (slash-ampersand) statement. Each job step is one program. Each program requires its own EXEC statement. When VSE reads

```
// EXEC PAYEDIT
```

it loads a copy of program PAYEDIT into memory.

Note that the job and the third program are both named PAYROLL (Fig. 11.8). That's perfectly legal, but it's pure coincidence. The operating system doesn't care; you could have coded

Fig. 11.7   The general form of a VSE EXEC statement.

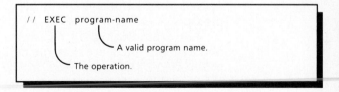

Fig. 11.8   Jobs start with a JOB statement. Programs are
                       identified by EXEC statements. A single job might
                       include several programs.

```
// JOB      PAYROLL
// EXEC     PAYEDIT
// EXEC     SORT
// EXEC     PAYROLL
// EXEC     PAYAUDIT
/&
```

// JOB MELVIN

and still referenced the same programs.

Compiling and Link Editing

VSE assumes that the program referenced in an EXEC statement
is stored on a library in load module form. The first step in creating a load module is compilation. A compiler is a program that
converts source statements into an object module. Like any program, the compiler is loaded by the operating system when an
EXEC statement references it; for example, the commands to
compile a COBOL program are shown in Fig. 11.9. The /* **statement** marks the end of the source module. The /& **statement**
marks the end of the job. The output will include a listing, compiler error messages, and an object module.

Once a clean assembly or compilation is obtained, the programmer will almost certainly want to test the program. This requires a new job control statement, the **OPTION statement** (Fig.
11.10). It allows the programmer to override a default system
option. One option, **LINK**, is particularly important. It tells the
compiler to write the object module to a file where it can be accessed by the linkage editor program and converted to a load
module.

For example, Fig. 11.11 shows a COBOL compile, link edit,
and execute job. Note that the OPTION statement precedes the
associated EXEC statement. In this example, the OPTION statement provides information for the COBOL compiler. Note also

Fig. 11.9   Compiling a COBOL source program calls for these
                       VSE JCL statements.

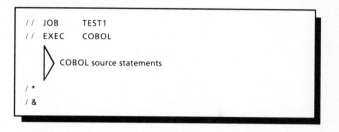

```
//   JOB     TEST1
//   EXEC    COBOL

            ▷  COBOL source statements

/ *
/ &
```

the last EXEC statement. No program name is specified. When
the program name field is blank, VSE selects the load module
most recently created by the linkage editor.

   The /* statements mark the end of the source module and the
end of the job stream data. By convention, programs treat /*
statements as sentinel values. To VSE, they are null commands;
the operating system basically ignores them. Some programmers use them to separate job steps.

   Because the compile, link edit, execute sequence is so common, VSE supports a **GO option** on the EXEC statement (Fig.
11.12). It implies an automatic link edit and execute after the
program has been compiled. Serious compiler or linkage editor
errors will terminate the job, of course.

Fig. 11.10   The OPTION statement allows a programmer to
                       specify run-time options.

```
//  OPTION    option1,option2,option3...

                        └─────┐  └─ List of options, such as NODECK and LINK.
                              └─ The operation.
```

Fig. 11.11   Testing a program calls for three job steps—compile,
                      link edit, and execute. The OPTION statement tells the
                      compiler to write the object module to a system file
                      where the linkage editor can find it.

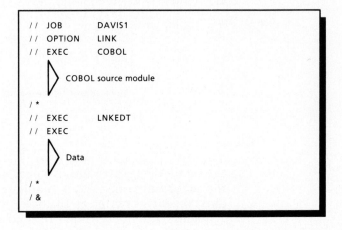

```
/ /  JOB        DAVIS1
/ /  OPTION     LINK
/ /  EXEC       COBOL

        ▷  COBOL source module

/ *
/ /  EXEC       LNKEDT
/ /  EXEC

        ▷  Data

/ *
/ &
```

Fig. 11.12   A VSE programmer can invoke the compile, link edit,
                      and execute sequence by adding a GO parameter to
                      the EXEC statement.

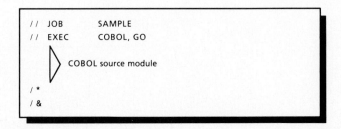

```
/ /  JOB        SAMPLE
/ /  EXEC       COBOL, GO

        ▷  COBOL source module

/ *
/ &
```

Cataloging Programs

An EXEC statement must reference a load module (called a **phase** under VSE). To add a program to the library, the programmer must provide a phase name by coding a **PHASE statement.** Figure 11.13 illustrates the commands needed to assemble a program, link it, and catalog the resulting load module. Once a load module is cataloged, executing it requires only the following control statements:

```
// JOB WHATEVER
// EXEC MYPGM
    } data
/*
/&
```

The PHASE statement's second operand (Fig. 11.13) is an asterisk (*). It indicates that the phase is to be created with a relative load address so it can be executed in any available partition. (The load point address can be specified in several different ways, but that's a detail we won't explore.) Note that position 1

Fig. 11.13   An OPTION CATAL statement tells the linkage editor to catalog the load module (or phase) under the specified PHASE name.

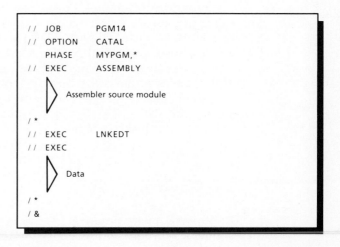

Fig. 11.14   Subroutine names are passed to the linkage editor
                       through INCLUDE statements. The specified
                       subroutines are added to the main program as the
                       linkage editor builds a load module.

```
// JOB         NAME
// OPTION      CATAL
   PHASE       PGMA,*
// EXEC        ASSEMBLY

        > Assembler source module

/*
   INCLUDE     SUBR1
   INCLUDE     SUBR2
// EXEC        LNKEDT
// EXEC

        > Data

/*
/&
```

of the PHASE statement is blank. It isn't a standard job control
statement. Instead, it's an input parameter to the linkage editor
program.

Programs often include subroutines, standard headers, and
other previously written logic. Under VSE, these external references are specified in **INCLUDE statements.** For example, Fig.
11.14 shows an assembly followed by a link edit step that adds
two subroutines to the main program. The subroutines must be
stored on a standard VSE library in object module form. The cataloged phase will include the main program and the two subroutines. The INCLUDE provides input to the linkage editor, so
position 1 (at least) is blank.

I/O Control

Under VSE, every physical I/O device attached to a system is assigned a **symbolic name.** Programmers read input data through

SYSIPT, send print lines to SYSLST, handle tapes through (perhaps) SYS006, and so on. As long as the programmer is willing to accept his or her installation's standard symbolic names, no additional job control language statements are needed.

VSE assembler language programmers code a **DTF** (Define The File) for each file accessed by program. The DTF sets key parameters and specifies an access method. For example, DTFCD defines a card file; DTFPR, a print file; DTFMT, a magnetic tape file; DTFSD, a sequential file on disk; and DTFDA, a direct access file. Many other combinations of device and access method could be cited.

Fig. 11.15 shows an assembler language program containing a DTFCD. The DTF has three parameters. The DEVADDR is the symbolic name of the physical I/O device. IOAREA1 is the label of an 80-character region of memory set aside to hold an input record, and EOFADDR is the address (label) of the instruc-

---

Fig. 11.15   The VSE assembler language programmer defines file linkages by coding DTF instructions. This program segment shows an assembler routine containing a DTF.

```
PGMA      START    0
GO        BALR     12,0          INITIALIZE BASE
          USING    *,12
          OPEN     DATAIN
RUN       GET      DATAIN

                   Other instructions

          B        RUN
QUIT      CLOSE    DATAIN
          EOJ

DATAIN    DTFCD    DEVADDR = SYSIPT, IOAREA1 = INPUT,
                   EOFADDR = QUIT

                   Other data definitions

INPUT     DS       CL80          DATA INPUT AREA

          END      GO
```

tion to be executed when the end-of-file marker (/*) is sensed. In this example, the device address (SYSIPT) is the standard system input device (usually the job stream). This program could be run with no job control references to I/O devices.

Other parameters that might be coded in a DTF include: block size, the name of a second I/O area for dual-buffer I/O, label types, the file type (input or output), record form on devices where this can be a variable, logical record length, information identifying a direct access or indexed sequential key, and many others.

The **ASSGN** Statement

Occasionally, a programmer might wish to change a standard device assignment. Assume, for example, that a DTFMT (magnetic tape) refers to DEVADDR = SYSO10, a particular tape drive. As the programmer enters the computer center, that drive has already been assigned to a two-hour job, but another drive is free. By using an **ASSGN statement** (Fig. 11.16), the programmer can change SYO10 from its standard device assignment to another device *for one job step only.*

To understand the ASSGN statement, it is useful to know how external devices are addressed on an IBM computer. All peripherals are attached to the system through channels. Each channel is assigned a one-digit number; each device is assigned a two-digit hexadecimal number ranging from a minimum of 00 to a maximum of FF (255 in decimal). The system address of any peripheral device is simply its channel number followed by its device number. For example, 008 represents device 08 on chan-

---

Fig. 11.16   A programmer can change a standard device
                   assignment by coding an ASSGN statement.

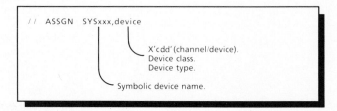

nel 0; OOE is channel 0, device 14 (OE in hex);1 181 is channel 1, device 81; 281 is channel 2, device 81, and so on.

If SYS010 is the symbolic name of device 180, and device 181 is free, the programmer can change to device 181 by placing an ASSGN statement in front of the relevant EXEC (Fig. 11.17). The change in assignment holds for one job step only; for example, in Fig. 11.17 after PROGRAM3 terminates, the standard assignment is once again in effect.

In many batch installations, programmers are not allowed in the computer room. How, then, can they know which tape drive, disk drive, printer, or card reader is free? Perhaps more to the point, do programmers really care which specific drive supports a program? Although some devices are equipped with important special features, generally, all a programmer wants is a device to read input or write output, and one tape drive, or disk drive, or printer is pretty much like any other.

VSE allows a programmer to specify device classes on an ASSGN statement. For example, if any tape drive will do, the programmer might code

// ASSGN SYS005,TAPE

The system will assign logical device SYS005 to the first available tape drive. Likewise,

// ASSGN SYS014,DISK

represents a request for the first available disk drive. Other valid classes include: READER, PRINTER, PUNCH, DISKETTE,

---

Fig. 11.17   These commands show how SYS010 can be changed from its standard device assignment to channel 1, device 81. Note that an ASSGN statement changes a device assignment for a single job step.

```
// JOB      P148
// ASSGN    SYS010,X'181'
// EXEC     PROGRAM3
   .
   .
   .
```

CKD (cylinder/track addressed disk), and FBA (fixed-block architecture disk).

It is not unusual for a computer center to have several different models of tape drives, disk drives, card readers, or printers. The programmer can, of course, always request a device by its channel/device address, but there is a middle-road; the device type can be specified. For example,

// ASSGN SYSLST,3211

assigns logical device SYSLST to the first available 3211 printer, but will not consider a 3203 printer, while

// ASSGN SYS008,3420

assigns the first available 3420 tape drive, and avoids the 3410 tape drive. Using device class or device type assignments can save the programmer work.

VSE/Power and the Job Stream

Most user jobs enter the job stream under control of a spooling routine called **VSE/POWER.** The user tells VSE/POWER what to do by coding **Job Entry Control Language** (JECL) commands.

The basic form of a JECL command is outlined in Fig. 11.18. Position 1 holds an asterisk. Next comes a blank followed by two dollar signs and another blank. The operation is coded in posi-

Figure 11.18   The basic format of a Job Entry Control Language (JECL) command.

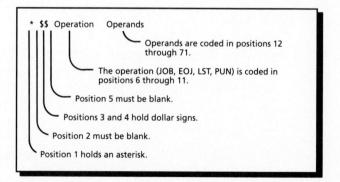

tions 6 through 11, and operands being in position 12. The two most frequently used JECL commands are *JOB*, which marks the start of a user job stream, and *EOJ*, which marks its end. Figure 11.19 shows a typical JECL user job stream.

A single JECL submission to VSE/POWER can include several VSE jobs; note that the JECL *JOB* and *EOJ* commands sandwich the JCL statements. You can specify a job's disposition, scheduling priority, class, and several other attributes by coding parameters on the JECL JOB statement. Two other JECL commands, *LST* and *PUN*, allow you to control printer output and card image output. Do not confuse JECL and JCL; they perform different functions.

The process of submitting work to a VSE system begins with the VSE/ICCF editor (Fig. 11.20). The user types JECL commands, JCL commands, and input data and stores the resulting card images in an ICCF file. When the job is ready to submit to POWER, the user codes a SUBMIT procedure on the ICCF command line, and the contents of the file are transferred to a VSE batch job queue. Eventually, POWER loads and starts the job steps that comprise the job, provides in-stream data, and spools printer and card image output to disk.

Figure 11.19   A typical JECL job stream.

```
* $$ JOB

// JOB   MYJOB

// JOB   SECOND

// JOB   THIRD

* $$ EOJ
```

Figure 11.20   The process of submitting a VSE job.

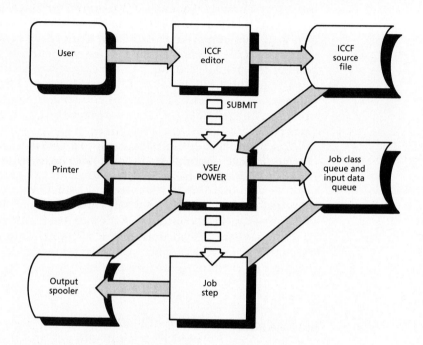

Cataloged Procedures

Once a program has been successfully compiled and tested, it is ready to be placed into production. A final compilation and link edit produces a load module that is assigned a phase name and stored on a library. From this point, the compilation and link edit steps are no longer necessary. Instead, the load module or phase is simply loaded into memory and started.

Earlier in the chapter, you considered a payroll job (Fig. 11.8). It consisted of four programs: a data edit routine, a sort, the payroll program, and an auditing program. As a minimum, this job would require a JOB statement and four EXEC statements. Additionally, several ASSGN statements and, perhaps, other control statements might be needed. The list of job control commands can easily stretch to 20 or more on multiple-step jobs.

Rather than submit scores of control statements every time a production job is run, a programmer can create a **cataloged procedure,** a special library entry consisting of nothing but control statements. Given a cataloged procedure, all the necessary

Figure 11.21   Cataloged procedures containing all the job control
language statements for repetitive jobs can be defined
and stored on a procedure library. When a cataloged
procedure is named on an EXEC statement, its JCL
statements are inserted into the job stream.

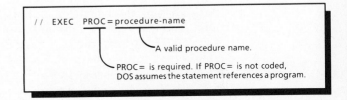

```
/ /   EXEC   PROC = procedure-name
```
A valid procedure name.

PROC= is required. If PROC= is not coded,
DOS assumes the statement references a program.

control statements can be invoked by a single EXEC statement
(Fig. 11.21). For example, assume that a procedure named
PAYSYS holds all the job control for the payroll job. Only three
statements

```
// JOB PAYROLL
// EXEC PROC = PAYSYS
/&
```

are needed to run payroll. When VSE encounters the EXEC statement, it reads PAYSYS from a library and, in effect, inserts the
procedure into the job stream. A single EXEC statement referencing a cataloged procedure might be equivalent to dozens of
job control language statements.

Other Job Control Functions

Most VSE programmers use only a limited subset of job control
language. JOB and EXEC statements are, of course, essential.
An OPTION statement is needed to compile and test a program.
Once testing is completed, load modules must be cataloged, and
that calls for OPTION, PHASE, and possibly one or more IN-
CLUDE statements. Occasionally, an ASSGN statement is
needed to change a standard device assignment. That's about all
the average programmer really needs. Other job control functions are usually left to experts.

Since the purpose of this chapter is to cover some of the more
commonly used features of VSE job control language, little time
will be spent discussing the lesser used statements, but there
are a few the average programmer might occasionally encoun-

ter. Most magnetic tape and direct access files are created with labels. The DLBL statement provides information for writing and/or checking direct access labels; the TLBL statement performs the same functions for magnetic tape labels. The LBLTYP statement tells the linkage editor how much memory is to be set aside for label processing.

A single direct access volume (one disk pack, for example), can hold numerous files. To prevent the accidental destruction of data, the physical location of a new file must be carefully controlled. Often, a system manager allocates space for a file by coding an EXTENT statement. Creating a file on a direct access device often requires both an EXTENT and a DLBL statement.

Current VSE releases support a very flexible library structure. To define a library search chain, insert a LIBDEF statement before the appropriate EXEC statement. A member type operand allows the programmer to limit the search to load modules (phases), object modules, source books, or procedures. A SEARCH operand can specify as many as 15 sublibraries.

Summary

This chapter covered many of the basic features of IBM's VSE job control language. A job is a single unit of work consisting of one or more related programs. JOB statements separate and identify jobs. EXEC statements specify the load modules to be loaded and executed. A single JOB statement might be followed by more than one EXEC, each of which marks a single job step.

To compile and test a program, the programmer must inform the system that the load module produced by the linkage editor is to be loaded and executed. This is done through an OPTION statement. Given a LINK option, the assembler or compiler writes the object module to a system file. The linkage editor reads the object module and prepares a load module. Following an EXEC with no program name, the load module is loaded and executed. The programmer can achieve the same result by coding a GO option on the EXEC statement for the compiler.

In a production environment, programs are usually run by loading and executing a load module directly from a library, bypassing the lengthy assemble (or compile) and link edit steps. Under VSE, these library load modules are called phases. To catalog a phase, the programmer codes a CATAL option. CATAL implies LINK. Each cataloged phase must be given a unique name through a PHASE statement. Additional subroutines and other precoded modules can be specified through INCLUDE statements. The PHASE and INCLUDE statements provide information to the linkage editor; their first position must be blank. The other job control statements—JOB, EXEC, ASSGN, and OPTION—must begin with two slashes (//) in positions 1 and 2. Position 3 (at least) must be blank.

Each peripheral device on a VSE system is assigned a symbolic name. Each combination of a physical device and an access method has its own DTF (Define The File). A program's physical device assignments are specified in its DTFs. A programmer can change a physical device assignment for the current job step by coding an ASSGN statement. Often, programmers specify a device type or a device class rather than a specific physical device.

A cataloged procedure is a set of precoded job control language statements stored on a library and accessed by name through a single EXEC statement. Cataloged procedures are commonly used on production systems.

For the average programmer, these few control statements are enough. In most VSE installations, other less commonly used features are left to specialists. A detailed summary of VSE JCL can be found in Appendix E.

Key Words

ASSGN statement	job control	OPTION statement
cataloged	language	phase
procedure	job entry control	PHASE statement
DTF	language	program name
editor	job name	symbolic name
EXEC statement	JOB statement	VSE/POWER
GO option	job step	/* statement
ICCF	job stream	/& statement
INCLUDE	LINK	
statement	operand	
job	operation	

References

1. Eckols, Steve, and Milnes, Michele (1989). *DOS/VSE JCL*, second edition. Fresno, California: Mike Murach & Associates, Inc.
2. IBM Corporation (1989). *VSE/Advanced Functions System Control Statements.* Mechanicsburg, Pennsylvania: International Business Machines Corporation. Publication Number SC33-6354-01.

Exercises

1. What functions are performed by a JOB statement?

2. Distinguish between a job and a job step.

3. What functions are performed by an EXEC statement?

4. Explain the purpose of the GO option on a VSE EXEC statement.

5. Explain the process of cataloging a load module. Start with a source module.

6. What is the purpose of a DTF?

7. What function is performed by an ASSGN statement?

8. What is a cataloged procedure?

9. Use VSE JCL statements to compile, link edit, and execute a program written in the language of your choice.

10. Catalog the program you wrote for Exercise 9. Then, run it.

11. Briefly explain the difference between ICCF commands, JECL commands, and JCL commands.

12. Explain how a job is submitted to VSE.

13. Write, in the language of your choice, a series of programs to perform the following functions:
    a. Read data from the standard input device and create a sequential file on disk.
    b. Read the sequential disk file, sort the records into sequence, and create a new file of sorted data on disk.
    c. Read the sorted records and print them.

    Use a sort utility or a language sort feature, or write your sort routine. Catalog all three programs. Then, prepare a series of JCL statements to run the three programs.

12

IBM MVS/JCL: JOB and EXEC Statements

MVS/JCL is the command language for IBM's larger mainframe operating systems. This chapter introduces the JOB and EXEC statements. Key topics include:

MVS/JCL
  Jobs and job steps
  Cataloged procedures
  JCL statement format

JOB statements
  Accounting information
  The programmer name
  The CLASS parameter
  The TIME parameter
  The REGION parameter
  The MSGLEVEL parameter
  Defaults
  Other JOB parameters
  Continuing a JCL statement

EXEC statements
  The COND parameter
  Other EXEC parameters

Those statements and parameters that might be used by a typical application programmer are emphasized.

MVS/JCL

IBM's VSE operating system was designed for relatively small computers. IBM's full operating systems support larger, more complex computers, so IBM's MVS/JCL is considerably more complex than VSE/JCL.

There are three basic job control language statements:

1. **JOB statements** separate and identify jobs. Secondary functions include passing the system accounting and priority information.
2. **EXEC,** or execute, **statements** identify the programs to be executed.
3. **DD,** or data definition, **statements** define, in detail, the characteristics of each peripheral device used by the job.

Chapter 12 will discuss the JOB and EXEC statements; DD statements will be covered in Chapter 13. Additionally, Chapter 14 will describe the MVS/JCL statements that support the program development process.

Jobs and Job Steps

Consider the compile, link edit, and execute sequence diagrammed in Fig. 12.1. To the programmer, all these steps constitute a single **job** and produce a single set of output. To the system, however, three distinct programs must be executed. The programmer sees a job consisting of several programs. The computer sees a series of programs, each of which represents a single **job step.**

A job must begin with a JOB statement and can contain almost any number of job steps. Each job step requires one EXEC statement. Within a job step, one DD statement must be coded for each peripheral device accessed by the program.

A compile, link edit, and execute job involves three steps. The compiler reads source statements from a terminal and a macro library, prints a listing, and writes an object module to disk. The linkage editor gets its input from the object file created by the first job step and, perhaps, from a subroutine library. Output goes to the printer and to a disk file where a copy of the load module is stored. This load module is the program for the third job step. The program reads data from a disk file and sends its output to the printer and to another disk file.

Fig. 12.1   An apparently simple compile, link edit, and execute job involves all these peripheral devices and programs.

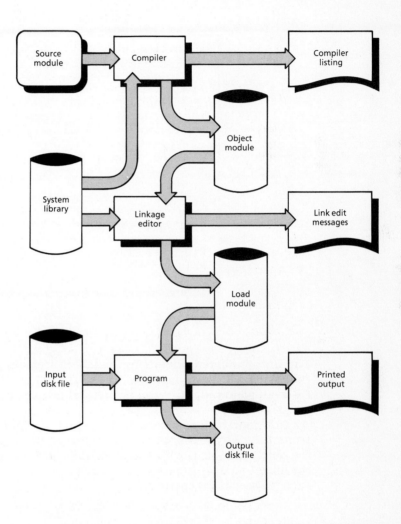

The JCL needed to support this job is outlined in Fig. 12.2. As you read the outline, remember two points:

1. To the computer, each job step is independent.
2. One DD statement must be provided for each input and output device.

Fig. 12.2   A compile, link edit, and execute job calls for all these
                                 job control language statements.

```
 1.  A JOB statement.
 2.  An EXEC statement for the compiler.
 3.  A DD statement for the object module file.
 4.  A DD statement for the printer.
 5.  A DD statement for the source module.
 6.  An EXEC statement for the linkage editor.
 7.  A DD statement for the object module file. This is the same
     file described in statement 3, but, because this is a different job step
     a separate DD statement is needed.
 8.  A DD statement for the load module.
 9.  A DD statement for the printer.
10.  An EXEC statement for the load module.
11.  A DD statement for the load module. This is the same file created
     in the previous job step (statement 8), but, once again, this is a
     new step.
12.  A DD statement for the disk input file.
13.  A DD statement for the disk output file.
14.  A DD statement for the printer.
```

The first statement identifies the job. Statements 2, 6, and 10,
the three EXEC statements, mark the start of the three job steps.
DD statements identify the peripheral devices needed by each
job step.

    Note particularly statements 3 and 7. They describe the
same file. Why are both DDs necessary? Statement 3 defines
the object module file for the first job step. Statement 7 defines
the object module file for the second job step. To the computer,
each job step is independent.

Cataloged Procedures

One compile, link edit, and execute job is much like any other, so
each time a program is tested, the programmer must repeat the
same commands. Typing the same commands again and again is
tedious and error prone. An option is to reference a **cataloged
procedure.**

A cataloged procedure is a set of precoded JCL statements, stored on a library and added to the job stream by the operating system. Figure 12.3 outlines the JCL for a compile, link edit, and execute job using a cataloged procedure. When it reads the EXEC statement, the operating system searches the procedure library, obtains a copy of the procedure's JCL, and inserts the statements into the job stream. The programmer can focus on JCL unique to the job; all the repetitive code is in the procedure.

JCL Statement Format

When IBM's job control language was first released, punched cards were the standard input medium. Cards are prepared on a keypunch. A keypunch can record capital letters, the digits 0-9, and several punctuation marks. Today, JCL statements are prepared using an editor such as CMS XEDIT or CICS, but they still use this limited character set.

The basic format of a JCL statement is shown in Figure 12.4. Job names, step names, and DD names are chosen by the programmer. They consist of from 1 to 8 letters, digits, or national characters (@,$,#), and the first character may not be a digit. The operation field must be JOB, EXEC, or DD. The operands consist of a series of **parameters** separated by commas. Numerous parameters will be discussed in this and the next chapter. Comments are optional.

Fig. 12.3   A cataloged procedure is a library file containing precoded JCL statements. Given a cataloged procedure, a compile, link edit, and execute job calls for only a few JCL statements.

1. A JOB statement.
2. An EXEC COBOL, or EXEC FORTRAN, or some other EXEC statement referencing the appropriate cataloged procedure.
3. A DD statement for disk input.
4. A DD statement for disk output.
5. A DD statement for printer output.

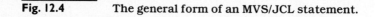

Fig. I2.4   The general form of an MVS/JCL statement.

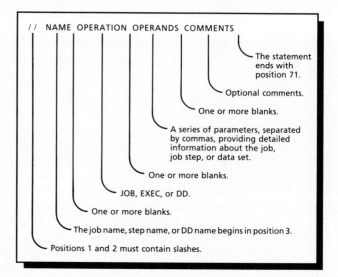

Note carefully that blanks are used to separate fields. Stray blanks are perhaps the most common JCL error. They are interpreted as field separators. For example, coding

// STEP2 EXEC COBOL

will result in a strange error message—there is no such operation as STEP2 (only JOB, EXEC, and DD are valid). You know what you mean, but the computer doesn't. Try

//STEP2 EXEC COBOL

with no blanks between the // and the name field.

Job Statements

The function of a JOB statement (Fig. 12.5) is to identify and mark the beginning of a job, thus separating it from the other

Fig. 12.5   The general form of a JOB statement.

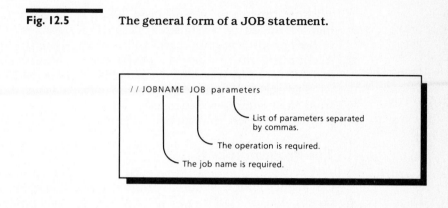

jobs. A unique **job name** is required. It must start with a letter or a national character; otherwise, any combination of from 1 to 8 letters, digits, and national characters is legal. In many computer centers, job names are assigned by the operating system to eliminate the risk that two or more jobs might have the same name.

Accounting Information

The job name and the operation (JOB) are the only required fields. One important secondary function is to pass information to an accounting routine. **Accounting information** is coded as the first parameter in the operands field. For example, the statement

//JOB396 JOB 1234

indicates that the cost of running job JOB396 is to be charged against account 1234. Often, multiple **accounting subparameters** are coded. For example,

//MU435 JOB (1234,875)

might mean that job MU435 is to be charged against account number 1234, user number 875. Subparameters are separated by commas.

Note the use of parentheses. When more than one subparameter is coded, parentheses are required. Also, note the position of the accounting information—it's always the first parameter. Accounting information is a **positional parameter.** Its meaning is determined by its relative position in the operands field.

The exact content of the accounting field is up to the installation; each computer center can define its own accounting subparameters. Note that the subparameters are also positional.

The Programmer Name

On a pure batch system, programmers assemble JCL statements, source statements, and data to form a complete job, submit it to the system, and come back for the results later. To simplify programmer identification, the **programmer's name** is coded in second positional parameter; for example,

```
//MU098 JOB (2987,235),DAVIS
```

or

```
//MU1735 JOB (2195,235),'W.S. DAVIS'
```

Code up to 20 letters or digits. You can also include a single period. The apostrophes are needed when special characters, such as commas, blanks, or additional periods, are part of the programmer's name. Your computer center may have a preferred format. Note that the programmer's name is separated from the accounting information by a comma.

The CLASS Parameter

One way to improve the efficiency of a batch system is to carefully schedule the work by grouping jobs with similar resource needs. Often, the task of grouping jobs is simplified by assigning them to classes. For example, a class A job might need only the standard input and output devices, while jobs calling for multiple-part paper might be assigned to class B, and those needing magnetic tape might fall into class C. A programmer indicates a job's class by coding a **CLASS parameter;** for example,

```
//MU741 JOB (3984,444),SMITH,CLASS=A
```

CLASS is a **keyword parameter.** It derives its meaning not from its position, but from the key word CLASS.

The TIME Parameter

Most multiprogramming systems automatically cancel a program caught in an endless loop after a reasonable time has passed. The data for setting the timer must come from somewhere. Often, the source is a **TIME parameter** (Fig. 12.6). For example,

TIME = (1,30)

asks for 1 minutes and 30 seconds of processor time, while

TIME = (1) or TIME = 1 or TIME = (1,0)

request exactly one minute. Note the parentheses. When the first subparameter alone is coded, they can be skipped but when more than one subparameter is coded, parentheses must be used.

Minutes and seconds are positional subparameters; in other words, they are defined by their relative positions. Minutes come first; seconds come second. For example, to request exactly 10 seconds, code

TIME = (,10)

The comma indicates the absence of the positional subparameter for minutes.

CLASS and TIME are themselves keyword parameters. The keywords CLASS and TIME give them meaning independent of

---

Fig. 12.6   The TIME parameter sets a run-time limit on the job.

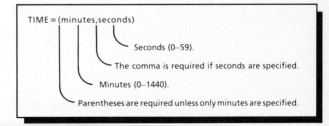

their position. For example, the following JOB statements are both legal:

```
//X14 JOB (345,86),JONES,CLASS=C,TIME=2
//Z135 JOB (296,25),'A. SMITH',TIME=(,30),CLASS=B
```

The accounting information must come first, followed by the programmer name. They are positional parameters, deriving their meaning from their relative positions. Because CLASS and TIME are key word parameters, they can be coded in any order.

The REGION Parameter

On some systems, a job's priority is determined, in part, by the amount of space it requires. The programmer can request space by coding a **REGION parameter**, for example,

```
REGION=512K
```

The MSGLEVEL Parameter

Programmer-coded JCL statements, the JCL statements included in a cataloged procedure, and messages indicating the operating system's actions are valuable to the programmer, but once the program is released, they are meaningless to users. The **MSGLEVEL** (message level) **parameter** (Fig. 12.7) allows the programmer to select which JCL and device allocation messages are to be printed. For example,

```
MSGLEVEL=(1,1)
```

means to print everything, while

```
MSGLEVEL=(0,0)
```

means print only the JOB statement unless the job fails, and

```
MSGLEVEL=(1,0)
```

instructs the system to print all JCL statements but to skip allocation messages.

Fig. 12.7   The MSGLEVEL parameter specifies which JCL
statements and operating system messages are to be
printed.

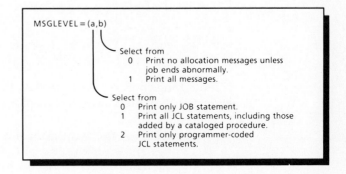

```
MSGLEVEL = (a,b)

              Select from
                 0   Print no allocation messages unless
                     job ends abnormally.
                 1   Print all messages.

            Select from
               0   Print only JOB statement.
               1   Print all JCL statements, including those
                   added by a cataloged procedure.
               2   Print only programmer-coded
                   JCL statements.
```

Note that parentheses were included in all three examples.
Why? How many subparameters were coded? In each case, two.
You must use parentheses any time more than one subpara-
meter is coded.

Defaults

Instead of requiring numerous parameters each time a job is
submitted, most computer centers rely on **defaults.** If the programmer fails, for any reason, to code a particular parameter,
the system assumes a value. Often, only accounting information, the programmer's name, and the job class are required. Defaults are based on the job class with, for example, all CLASS-A
jobs assigned a 640K region and a 3-second time limit, while
CLASS-B jobs get 1024K and 10 seconds. To override a default,
simply code the appropriate parameter.

Other JOB Parameters

Other parameters, all keyword in nature, allow the programmer
to specify such things as job priority, run type, condition code

limits, and restart options. When a need arises, check with a system programmer or look them up in a JCL manual.

Continuing a JCL Statement

Consider the following JOB statement:

```
//C1234567 JOB (3998,659),'A.B. Jones',CLASS=A,
//               TIME=(1,30),REGION=512K
```

It's too long to fit on a single line, so it must be continued. The rules for continuing a JCL statement are:

1. Interrupt the field after a complete parameter or subparameter, including the trailing comma, has been coded. (In other words, stop after any comma.)
2. Optionally code any nonblank character in position 72. Position 72 can be left blank; the continuation character is optional.
3. Code slashes (//) in positions 1 and 2 of the continuation line.
4. Continue coding in any position from 4 through 16. Position 3 must be blank and coding must be resumed no later than position 16.

In other words, just break after a comma and resume coding on the next line. The same rules hold for any type of JCL statement.

EXEC Statements

An EXEC statement (Fig. 12.8) marks the beginning of a job step. Its purpose is to identify the program (or cataloged procedure) to be executed. The **step name** is optional; the rules for coding a step name are the same as the rules for coding a job name. The first parameter must be a program or procedure name; for example,

```
// EXEC PGM=SORT6
```

or

```
// EXEC PROC=COBOL
```

Fig. 12.8   The general form of an EXEC statement.

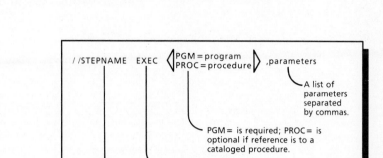

The keyword **PROC** can be skipped; for example,

// EXEC COBOL

If a program is referenced, **PGM** must be coded.

When a cataloged procedure is referenced, the operating system searches the procedure library and replaces the programmer's EXEC statement with a set of precoded JCL; for example, Fig. 12.9 shows the JCL added to the job stream to replace

// EXEC FORTRAN

The final EXEC statement's program name

PGM = *.LKED.SYSLMOD

looks a bit confusing. The asterisk (*) is a **backward reference.** It tells the operating system to look at a previous JCL statement. Find the step named LKED. Then, find the DD statement in that step named SYSLMOD. This reference tells the operating system to "execute the program created in job step LKED and stored on data set SYSLMOD."

The programmer coded a cataloged procedure. The procedure itself contained, in this case, three EXEC statements, each calling for a specific program. References to specific programs contain the keyword PGM.

Fig. 12.9   The cataloged procedure FORTRAN inserts a number
of JCL statements into the job stream.

//FORT	EXEC	PGM = IEYFORT
//SYSPRINT	DD	parameters (printed output)
//SYSGO	DD	parameters (object module output)
//LKED	EXEC	PGM = IEWL, other parameters
//SYSLIB	DD	parameters (system library)
//SYSLMOD	DD	parameters (load module output)
//SYSPRINT	DD	parameters (printed output)
//SYSUT1	DD	parameters (work space)
//SYSLIN	DD	parameters (object module input)
//GO	EXEC	PGM = *.LKED.SYSLMOD,...

Often, the program or cataloged procedure name is the only
parameter coded on an EXEC statement. There are other EXEC
parameters, however.

The COND Parameter

When you submit a job containing compiler errors, the result is
usually a listing followed by a message indicating that the link
edit and go steps were skipped. This makes sense—why bother
with subsequent steps if the first one is wrong? But how does the
operating system know that the last two steps should be
skipped?

You may have noticed something called a severity code on
your compiler listing. Warnings are worth 4 points; simple errors, 8; severe errors, 12 points. A program containing severe
errors will almost certainly not run. The compiler passes the
highest severity code to the system by placing a condition code
in a register. The operating system can check this condition code
prior to loading and executing a job step, skipping the step if the
condition code is not acceptable.

The programmer sets the limits for this comparison through
a **COND** (condition) **parameter** (Fig. 12.10). For example,

COND = (12,LE,Fort)

Fig. 12.10   The COND parameter allows a programmer to specify
run-time conditions under which a job step is to be
skipped.

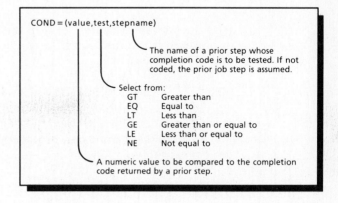

says that if 12 is less than or equal to the actual condition code
returned by job step FORT, the present step is to be skipped.

Run through that logic again. Assume the COND parameter
appears in the following EXEC statement:

```
//LKED  EXEC  PGM=IEWL,COND=(12,LE,FORT)
```

The step named LKED will be *bypassed* if 12 is less than or equal
to the actual condition code returned by job step FORT. The logic
is a bit unusual, so be careful. When comparing a variable and a
constant, most programmers code the variable first. On the
COND parameter, the *constant* is coded first, making the logic
seem to read backward. The fact that a match leads to a negative
decision, skipping a step, adds to the confusion.

The safest way to handle COND logic is to read it as it's
coded, from left to right—the step is skipped if some constant
meets a certain condition with respect to the actual condition
code returned by a prior job step. Incidentally, the third positional subparameter (the step name of the prior job step) is optional; if a step name is not coded, the most recently completed
step is assumed.

The legal comparisons are summarized in Fig. 12.10. In the FORTRAN cataloged procedure (Fig. 12.9), COND parameters are normally added to the EXEC statements for both the link edit and go steps. The statement

```
//LKED EXEC PGM=IEWL,COND=(8,LE,FORT)
```

tells the operating system to skip the LKED step if 8 is less than or equal to the actual condition code returned by the FORT job step. The statement

```
//GO EXEC PGM=*.LKED.SYSLMOD,COND=(4,LT,FORT)
```

places a similar restriction on the GO step.

Multiple conditions can be coded in a single COND parameter; for example,

```
COND=((8,LE,FORT),(4,LT,LKED))
```

means that this step is to be skipped if 8 is less than or equal to the actual condition code returned by FORT *or* if 4 is less than the actual condition code returned by LKED. Note the parentheses; JCL punctuation can be tedious.

You can take advantage of the COND parameter in your own programs, too. For example, imagine a series of programs that screen input data, process those data, and report the bad data found by the first program. If there are no bad data, there is no point running the third program. Why not count errors in that first program, and pass the count to the operating system through a return code? Then, the parameter

```
COND=(0,EQ,SCREEN)
```

on the final program's EXEC statement would cause the step to be skipped if 0 is equal to the condition code returned by SCREEN.

Other EXEC Parameters

Other EXEC parameters allow the programmer to pass accounting information to a job step or set a dispatching priority for the step. Some parameters can be coded on the JOB statement or on an EXEC statement. For example, the programmer has the option of specifying a time limit, a region size, restart options, and other conditions for the complete job or for each job step independently.

Programmers often encounter a **PARM parameter** in a cataloged procedure. For example, in the FORTRAN procedure,

```
// EXEC FORTRAN,PARM.FORT = 'NODECK,LIST'
```

the PARM parameter informs the FORT job step (the compiler) that no object deck is to be output and that a listing is to be printed. Detailed information on the meaning of parameters for any compiler language can be found in the programmer's guide to that language.

A detailed summary of the JOB and EXEC statement parameters is found in Appendix F. Coverage of MVS/JCL will continue in Chapter 13.

Summary

The chapter began with an overview of the three MVS/JCL statements: JOB, EXEC, and DD. The basic format of any JCL statement was described. Each job submitted to the system must begin with a JOB statement. A job consists of one or more job steps, each of which begins with an EXEC statement. Each EXEC statement references a single program or a cataloged procedure. Within a job step, one DD statement is coded for each input or output device accessed by the program. A cataloged procedure is a set of precoded JCL statements stored on a library and added to the job stream when the procedure name is referenced.

On a JOB statement, the job name must be coded. In the operands field, the first two positional parameters are, respectively, accounting information and the programmer's name. Key word parameters include CLASS, TIME, REGION, and MSGLEVEL. Often the programmer codes only accounting information, a programmer name, and a CLASS parameter; default values are used for the other parameters.

The step name field on an EXEC statement is optional. Following the operation, either a PGM or a PROC parameter must be coded. (If a procedure is referenced, the key work PROC can be skipped.) By coding a COND parameter, a programmer can instruct the operating system to skip a job step depending on the return code from a previous job step. A PARM parameter can be used to pass run-time information to a program. Certain parameters, such as TIME and REGION, can be coded on the JOB statement or on an EXEC statement. If coded on the JOB statement, they affect every job step; if coded on an EXEC statement, they affect only that step.

Key Words

accounting information	EXEC statement	PGM parameter
backward reference	job	positional parameter
cataloged procedure	job name	PROC parameter
CLASS parameter	JOB statement	programmer name
COND parameter	job step	REGION parameter
DD statement	keyword parameter	step name
default	MSGLEVEL parameter	subparameters
	PARM parameter	TIME parameter

References

1. Brown, Gary DeWard (1990). *System 370/390 JCL*, third edition. New York: John Wiley & Sons.
2. IBM Corporation (1987). *MVS/370 JCL Reference*, fourth edition. Poughkeepsie, New York: International Business Machines Corporation. Publication number GC28–1350.
3. Janossy, James G. (1987). *Practical MVS JCL for Today's Programmer.* New York: John Wiley & Sons.
4. Trombetta, Michael, and Finkelstein, Sue Carolyn (1989). *OS JCL and Utilities, A Comprehensive Treatment*, second edition. Reading, Massachusetts: Addison-Wesley Publishing Company.

Exercises

1. Distinguish between a job and a job step. How are JOB and EXEC statements related to jobs and job steps?

2. What is a positional parameter? Give some examples.

3. What is a keyword parameter? Give some examples.

4. What does MSGLEVEL = (1,1) mean?

5. What is a cataloged procedure? Why are cataloged procedures used?

6. Explain default options.

7. Code a JOB statement. Use the job name of your choice, your course number as an accounting information parameter, and your own name. Request 256K of memory, 1 minute and 30 seconds of processor time, and job class Q. Don't print any allocation messages. Print only the JCL you code.

8. Code an EXEC statement referencing cataloged procedure COBOL. Skip this step if STEP1 returned a condition code of 100.

9. Compile, link edit, and execute a program written in the language of your choice. Use a cataloged procedure, and print all JCL statements, including those added by the procedure. Read through the JCL, and determine the purpose of each statement. In the exercises following Chapter 13, you will be asked to interpret each DD statement parameter.

10. Write, in the language of your choice, a series of three programs to perform the following functions:
    a. Read data from the standard input device and create a sequential file on disk.
    b. Read the sequential file, sort the records, and create a new disk file to hold the sorted data.
    c. Read and print the sorted records.

    Use a sort utility or a language sort feature, or write your own sort routine. At this point, obtain a clean compilation for each program. The JCL needed to run them will be added at the end of Chapter 13.

13

IBM MVS/JCL: DD Statements

This chapter introduces the MVS/JCL DD
statement. Key topics include:

External device linkage
  Data control blocks
  DD statements

Unit record hardware
  The UNIT parameter
  The DCB parameter

Magnetic disk
  UNIT and DCB
  The DISP parameter
  The DSNAME parameter
  The VOLUME parameter
  The SPACE parameter
  Some examples

Magnetic tape
  UNIT and DCB
  DISP and DSNAME
  VOLUME
  The LABEL parameter
  The DUMMY parameter
  Some examples

System input and output

Job step qualification

Libraries

Other JCL statements

Once again, those parameters that might be
used by a typical programmer are
emphasized.

External Device Linkage

Many second-generation programs were designed to communicate with specific input and output devices. When software is device dependent, changing hardware often means reprogramming, and that's expensive, so device independence became an important part of IBM's System/360-370 design philosophy.

Device independence means a programmer can change peripherals with minimum effort and minimum program revision. On an IBM mainframe, the keys are data control blocks and DD statements. Data control blocks are coded inside a program and contain only those parameters that must be known before the program is loaded. Physical devices are defined outside the program in DD statement. Programs and their peripherals are not linked until load time.

Data Control Blocks

In assembler language, a **data control block** (DCB) is coded for each file accessed by a program. The DCB sets up a series of constants and addresses describing the characteristics of the physical and logical records. For example,

```
INPUT  DCB  MACRF = GM,DSORG = PS,DDNAME = LINES,                    C
            other-parameters
```

defines a sequential file. The MACRF (macro form) and DSORG (data set organization) parameters, taken together, specify an access method. The DDNAME is the link to a DD statement. Other possible parameters include the logical record length, block size, record form, buffering technique, recording density, and many others. The MACRF, DSORG, and DDNAME must be coded within the program; other parameters can appear either in the program DCB or on the DD statement.

Figure 13.1 shows a simple read and print program. The DCBs are highlighted. The DSORG and MACRF parameters define the access methods. The EODAD (end-of-data address) parameter specifies the address of the end-of-data routine. The DDNAME parameters provide a link to a DD statement.

The EXEC statement references a cataloged procedure—ASMFCLG (assemble, link edit, and go). The assembler creates an object module containing two data control blocks. The access methods are added to the load module (Fig. 13.2) by the linkage editor *before* the program is executed.

Fig. 13.1   One data control block is coded for each file accessed by a program. The physical device is specified outside the program in a DD statement.

```
//JOB121   JOB          (2398,34),DAVIS, CLASS = A
//         EXEC         ASMFCLG
//SYSIN    DD           *

          STARTUP       MACRO FOR REGISTER CONVENTIONS
          B       GO    BRANCH TO EXECUTABLE CODE

LINEOUT   DC      CL1'' SPACE FOR INPUT AND OUTPUT DATA
LINEIN    DS      CL80
          DC      CL40

*                       DATA CONTROL BLOCKS
*
SCREEN    DCB     MACRF = GM,DSORG = PS,
                  DDNAME = DATAIN,EODAD = QUIT

PRINTER   DCB     MACRF = GM,DSORG = PS,DDNAME = LINE

*                       START OF PROGRAM -- FILE OPEN
*
GO        OPEN (SCREEN, INPUT)
          OPEN (PRINTER, OUTPUT)

*                       READ AND PRINT LOOP
*
RUN       GET     SCREEN, LINEIN
          PUT     PRINTER, LINEOUT
          B       RUN

*                       END OF PROGRAM ROUTINE
*
QUIT      CLOSE   (SCREEN, PRINTER)
          STOP          END OF PROGRAM MACRO
/*

//LINE     DD      parameters
//DATAIN   DD      parameters
/*
//
```

Fig. 13.2   Based on the data control block MACRF and DSORG
parameters, the linkage editor selects an access
method and links it to the program load module.

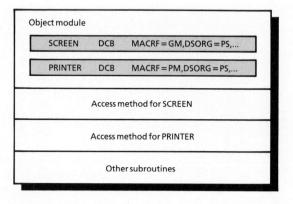

DD Statements

Once the load module is complete, the program can be executed.
The instruction

OPEN (SCREEN,INPUT)

references a data control block labeled SCREEN (Fig. 13.3). The
DCB's **DDNAME** parameter points to a DD statement named
DATAIN, which specifies a physical device. Likewise, the in-
struction

OPEN (PRINTER,OUTPUT)

establishes linkage to a specific physical output device via the
DDNAME parameter coded in the DCB named PRINTER.

Note carefully the timing of major events in this sequence.
The program data control block is written by the programmer
before compilation. It is input to the compiler and included in the
object module. The linkage editor uses DCB parameters to select
an access method. Actual linkage to a physical device is postponed until *run time,* when the OPEN instruction is executed, so

Fig. 13.3   The link to a specific physical device is established at
                       OPEN time.

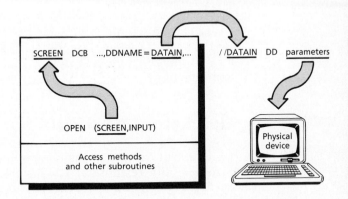

switching physical devices can be accomplished by changing a
job control language statement. Because JCL statements are *not*
part of the load module, devices can be changed without recompiling the program.

In COBOL, a data control block is built from a SELECT . . .
ASSIGN clause in the ENVIRONMENT DIVISION and from sev-
eral DATA DIVISION clauses such as BLOCK CONTAINS,
LABELS ARE, and others. The DDNAME is part of the SELECT
. . . ASSIGN clause, with

SELECT DATAIN ASSIGN TO UT-S-SCREEN.

pointing to

//SCREEN DD parameters

In FORTRAN, a DCB is created for each device number referenced in a READ or WRITE statement. Sequential access is assumed unless a FILE statement specifies otherwise. The
DDNAME is built from the device number, with, for example,

WRITE (6, 15) A,B,C

pointing to data control block

label DCB DDNAME = FT06F001

which references

//FT06F001 DD parameters

In languages such as Pascal and PL/1, the DDNAME is specified in a DECLARE statement. A DD statement's parameters define a specific physical device. The balance of this chapter explains how.

Unit Record Hardware

Unit record hardware includes such devices as card readers, printers, and terminals. They work with unit records—lines, cards, screens, and so on. there is no blocking, all records are the same length, and there is no distinction between logical and physical records. Providing input or dealing with output is the programmer's responsibility; no special operator instructions are necessary. Printers and terminals display different line lengths, and not all card readers are restricted to standard 80-column cards, but, aside from record length, the only variable is the physical device.

The UNIT Parameter

The **UNIT parameter** (Fig. 13.4) specifies the input or output device. One option is coding an actual unit address. Every peripheral attached to an IBM system is identified by a three-digit hex

Fig. 13.4   The UNIT parameter defines a physical device.

```
UNIT = device
        └── Select from:
             Unit or device address (channel/device address)
             Device type (2501, 3330, etc.)
             Group name (READER, PRINTER, etc.)
```

number. For example, if a printer is device 8 on channel 0, its unit address is 008, and the DD statement

```
//PRINTER DD UNIT=008
```

references it. The unit address form implies that no other device will do; given the DD statement illustrated above, if device 008 is busy, or for some other reason not available, the program must wait to be loaded. This form of the UNIT parameter is rarely used.

If a programmer wants a 3211 printer, and any 3211 printer will do, a device type can be specified; for example,

```
//OUTS DD UNIT=3211
```

The program can be loaded and run as soon as *any* 3211 printer is free. A 3178 display can be requested by coding UNIT=3178. A 3278 display is requested by coding UNIT=3278. If a system has more than one of a particular device, specifying a device type is less restrictive than specifying a unit address.

A third choice is referencing a group name. For example, the DD statement

```
//XYZ DD UNIT=PRINTER
```

might be a request for any available printer, be it a 3203, a 3211, or a 3287. It's the most general form of the UNIT parameter, and thus the most frequently used. An installation can define its own group names, although PUNCH, READER, CONSOLE, and PRINTER are almost standard.

Note that there are no blanks in "UNIT=PRINTER." Blanks, remember, are field separators.

The DCB Parameter

Generally, because a unit record's length rarely, if ever, changes, the logical record length is defined in the program DCB. However, some variation is possible. For example, many screens can be switched from an 80-character to a 40-character line. If 80-character logical records are defined inside the program, switching to 40 characters means recompilation.

There is an alternative: **DCB parameters** can be coded on the DD statement (Fig. 13.5). For example, replacing

```
//SCREEN DD UNIT=CONSOLE,DCB=LRECL=80
```

Fig. 13.5   DSORG, MACRF, and DDNAME must be coded in the
                      program data control block. Other DCB
                      subparameters can be coded on the DD statement.

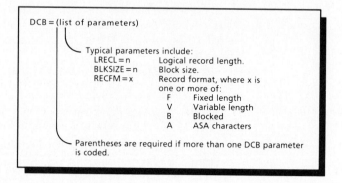

with

//SCREEN DD UNIT = CONSOLE,DCB = LRECL = 40

changes the logical record length without recompiling the program. DCB subparameters can be coded within the program data
control block or on the DD statement.

Note that LRECL = 40 is not enclosed in parentheses. Why
not? Because it's a *single* subparameter, and when only one is
coded, parentheses are not needed.

Data control block subparameters are merged into the program DCB at open time. Parameters coded in the program will
not be changed even if the DD's version is different—hard-coded
information takes precedence. If a programmer anticipates
changing the basic record format, the volatile parameters
should be coded in the DD statement.

Both UNIT and DCB are keyword parameters; they can be
coded in any order.

Magnetic Disk

Magnetic disk is the most common secondary storage medium.
Some disks store data in sectors or fixed-length blocks. Others

allocate space a track at a time and allow the programmer to vary the record format to fit the application. Logical records can be almost any length, and can even vary within a file. Additionally, they can be blocked or unblocked. Also, disk space is a limited resource. On an IBM mainframe, the programmer must estimate the amount of space needed before creating a file.

People can't read the data stored on disk. A human operator is unlikely to load already-punched cards into a card punch, or used paper onto a printer, and the image on a screen is only temporary, but it's quite possible that disk space previously allocated to one program might be reused by another, thus destroying the old data. Rather than trusting to chance, a programmer must carefully specify the disposition of a disk file.

Disk is a shared resource, with numerous files and programs stored on a single pack (or volume). Since disk can only be read electronically, directory entries identifying the individual files must be recorded on the surface. Also, packs can be dismounted and stored off-line. Thus, volumes must be clearly identified, both visually and electronically, if an operator is to mount the right one.

UNIT and DCB

As with unit-record equipment, a disk drive is referenced through a UNIT parameter; for example, UNIT = 181 means channel 1, device 81. The device-address form is rarely used. Direct access devices are most often requested by device type (2314, 3330, 3340, 3370, and so on). For example,

UNIT = 3330

is a request for any 3330 disk drive.

Disk is frequently used to store intermediate results. To simplify requesting temporary work files, many installations set aside some direct access space that a programmer can reference with a group name such as SYSDA or WORK1.

A disk data control block is just like a unit record data control block. On disk, records can be fixed or variable in length and blocked or unblocked, so additional DCB subparameters are needed. A few are summarized in Fig. 13.5.

The DISP Parameter

The **DISP,** or disposition, **parameter** (Fig. 13.6) tells the system what to do with a disk file. The first positional subparameter

Fig. 13.6   The disposition (DISP) parameter specifies the file's
                          status both before and after the program runs.

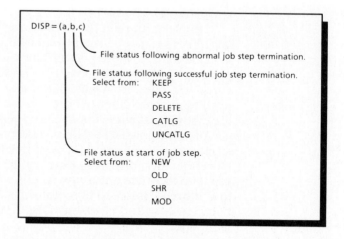

```
DISP = (a,b,c)
          │ │ │
          │ │ └─ File status following abnormal job step termination.
          │ │
          │ └─ File status following successful job step termination.
          │    Select from:    KEEP
          │                    PASS
          │                    DELETE
          │                    CATLG
          │                    UNCATLG
          │
          └─ File status at start of job step.
             Select from:    NEW
                             OLD
                             SHR
                             MOD
```

describes the file's status before the job step is executed. If a file
is to be created, it's NEW. An existing file is OLD. Some, a library
for example, might be concurrently accessed (but not modified)
by more than one program. Such files are shared (SHR). Disposition MOD allows a program to add more data to an existing file.

The second subparameter specifies system action following
normal job step completion. If there is no further need for the
data, the programmer can DELETE them. KEEP means that the
file will be retained. If the data are needed by a subsequent step
within the same job, the programmer can PASS them. The file
can be entered on a catalog (CATLG) and retained, or removed
from a catalog (UNCATLG) and deleted.

The proper disposition might be different following *abnormal* job termination; the third DISP subparameter can be DE-
LETE, KEEP, CATLG, or UNCATLG. If the third subparameter is
not coded, the normal termination disposition is assumed.

To create a file, pass it to another job step, and delete it in the
event of serious error, code

DISP = (NEW,PASS,DELETE)

If a file is to be created and, normally, cataloged but in the event
of an error kept for study or possible restart, code

DISP = (NEW,CATLG,KEEP)

A temporary work file needed only for the life of the job step would have, as part of its DD statement,

DISP = (NEW,DELETE)

which is equivalent to

DISP = (NEW,DELETE,DELETE)

The DSNAME Parameter

To simplify retrieving a cataloged or passed data set, the programmer can give a file a unique name by coding a **DSNAME**, or DSN, **parameter.** A valid data set name consists of from one to eight letters, numbers, or national symbols, and must begin with a letter or a national symbol. Data set names can be qualified; for example,

DSNAME = MU.USERDATA.SAN1

indicates that a data set named SAN1 appears on an index named USERDATA, and that this index can be located by referring to a master index named MU. Each level of qualification must exist as an index in the system catalog.

     Temporary life-of-job files are assigned data set names beginning with an ampersand (&); for example,

DSNAME = &&TEMP

To avoid confusing them with assembler language macro parameters, temporary data set names normally begin with a double ampersand. Incidentally, the term **data set** was coined by IBM to encompass both traditional files and libraries.

The VOLUME Parameter

The **VOLUME,** or **VOL, parameter** specifies a particular disk volume (or pack). Each volume has a unique serial number. To request pack number MU1234, a programmer would code

VOL = SER = MU1234

The VOLUME parameter is coded only if the application demands a specific disk volume.

Note carefully the difference between UNIT and VOLUME. The UNIT parameter specifies a disk *drive*. The VOLUME parameter identifies the *pack* that is to be mounted on that drive.

The SPACE Parameter

It makes little sense to load and execute a program when adequate direct access space is not available, so programmers are required to estimate their space requirements through a **space parameter** (Fig. 13.7). Space can be requested in tracks, cylinders, or blocks. The first positional subparameter identifies the unit; the second indicates the number of units. For example,

SPACE = (TRK,20)

is a request for 20 tracks, while

SPACE = (CYL,14)

Fig. 13.7   A SPACE parameter indicates the amount of direct access space a file will need.

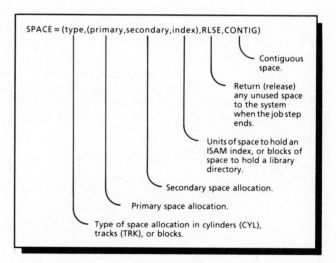

SPACE = (type,(primary,secondary,index),RLSE,CONTIG)

Contiguous space.

Return (release) any unused space to the system when the job step ends.

Units of space to hold an ISAM index, or blocks of space to hold a library directory.

Secondary space allocation.

Primary space allocation.

Type of space allocation in cylinders (CYL), tracks (TRK), or blocks.

asks for 14 cylinders, and

SPACE = (200,10)

asks for ten 200-byte blocks.

Estimating space requirements is not always easy. To ensure sufficient space, a programmer might be tempted to request more than the program needs, thus tying up a limited resource. Fortunately, another option is available. The parameter

SPACE = (TRK,(10,2))

requests a *primary* allocation of 10 tracks, and a *secondary* allocation of 2 tracks. Should the initial 10 tracks be filled, an additional 2 will be allocated, if available. If those 2 are filled, 2 more are allocated. The system will make a maximum of 15 secondary allocations, so the parameter coded above could represent as many as 40 tracks (10, plus 2 times 15).

The primary space allocation is made before the program is loaded. The secondary allocation if filled on an as-needed, if-available basis *after* the job step begins executing. A job step may be canceled for insufficient direct access space, even though its primary and secondary requests are more than adequate, if space is not available at the time of the secondary request. It is to the programmer's advantage to make the primary space estimate as accurate as possible.

Note that the primary and secondary subparameters are enclosed in parentheses. Both deal with the number of units of direct access space, and thus should be treated as a single entity. (In effect, the primary and secondary allocations are *sub*-subparameters. When two or more sub-subparameters are coded, a set of inner parentheses is needed.)

Requesting too much space can tie up a limited resource. The programmer can return unused space to the system at the end of a job step by coding a RLSE (release) subparameter; for example,

SPACE = (CYL,(5,1),RLSE)

It's a positional subparameter that must follow the primary and secondary allocations.

To optimize disk input and output, space is sometimes requested in contiguous units. The parameter

SPACE = (TRK,(5,2),RLSE,CONTIG)

asks for five contiguous tracks, with a secondary request for two
more, and returns unused space to the system at the conclusion
of the job step. Without RLSE, this parameter would be coded

SPACE = (TRK,(5,2),,CONTIG)

Fig. 13.8   This figure shows some examples of complete DD
                      statements to create and retrieve disk files.

```
1.   Creating a temporary data set on the system work pack.

//DISK        DD  DSNAME = &&TEMP,UNIT = SYSDA,
//                DISP = (NEW,PASS),SPACE = (CYL,5),
//                DCB = (LRECL = 120,BLKSIZE = 2400,
//                RECFM = FB)


2.   Creating a cataloged data set on a specific volume.
//RECS        DD  DSN = MU.USERDATA.SAN4,UNIT = 3330,
//                VOL = SER = MIAMI3,DISP = (NEW,CATLG),
//                SPACE = (TRK,(20,5),RLSE,CONTIG),
//                DCB = (LRECL = 155,RECFM = FB,
//                BLKSIZE = 1550)


3.   Creating a kept data set.

//KEEPIT      DD  SPACE = (CYL,(10,2),RLSE),
//                DCB = (RECFM = FB,LRECL = 72,BLKSIZE = 720),
//                VOL = SER = MYPACK,DISP = (NEW,KEEP),
//                DSNAME = MYDATA,UNIT = 3330


4.   Retrieving a passed data set.

//DATA        DD  DSNAME = &&TEMP,DISP = (OLD,DELETE)


5.   Retrieving a cataloged data set.

//STUFF       DD  DSN = MU.USERDATA.SAN4,DISP = OLD


6.   Retrieving a kept data set that has not been cataloged requires UNIT
     and VOLUME parameters in addition to DSNAME and DISP.

//DDNAME      DD  DSNAME = MYDATA,UNIT = 3330,
//                VOL = SER = MYPACK,DISP = (OLD,KEEP)
```

Note the extra comma indicating the absence of a positional sub-parameter.

Some Examples

Figure 13.8 shows several examples of DD statements to create and retrieve disk data sets. If a data set has been cataloged or passed by a prior step, it can normally be retrieved by coding only the DDNAME and DISP parameters. Other parameters, including the data control block parameters, can be found in the directory entry for cataloged data sets and the operating system tables for passed data sets; thus they need not be recoded.

Magnetic Tape

Once the most common secondary storage medium, magnetic tape is now used largely for backup and to transmit data or programs between computer centers. Tape and disk have a great deal in common. Both support a variety of record lengths and record formats. Neither is human-readable, so both require careful labeling, cataloging, and attention to post-job disposition.

There are also some important differences. On disk, a typical volume holds a number of files or data sets. On tape, one volume per file is the general rule, but it is not unusual for a large file to spill over onto a second or third tape. Thus, the programmer must be able to request multiple volumes and (perhaps) multiple drives to mount those volumes.

Disk is generally an in-house medium, with all the drives and packs under control of the computer center. Tape, on the other hand, is often used to transfer data between centers. This "foreign interface" can create problems because not all computer centers use the same tape. Some record data on seven tracks; some use nine tracks; others use ten. The recording density can vary, too. Finally, there are many different types of tape labels.

The programmer must communicate to the system, through DD parameters, the unique characteristics of a given tape file before the system can access that tape.

UNIT and DCB

The UNIT parameter defines the physical device. A programmer can choose to specify a drive's channel/device address, but this is rarely done. Many computer centers define one or more device classes, such as TAPE, TAPE9, or TAPE7. For example,

UNIT = TAPE9

might represent a request for a tape drive able to handle nine-track tapes, while

UNIT = TAPE7

might be a request for a drive that can work with seven-track tapes.

The device type is the most commonly used form for magnetic tape. For example, to request a single 3420 tape drive, code

UNIT = 3420

Occasionally, a multiple volume data set may require more than one tape drive. The unit count subparameter follows the device type; for example,

UNIT = (3420,3)

asks for three 3420 drives. Both subparameters are positional; the device type must be coded first, the unit count second. The parameter

UNIT = (3,3420)

which is *incorrect*, is a request for 3420 model-3 tape drives. Positional parameters derive their meaning from their relative positions. If the unit count subparameter is not coded, a single unit is assumed.

To save system time and eliminate lengthy waits by a program already in memory, tape mount messages are normally given to the operator as the job step is about to be loaded. Occasionally, when probable errors or other special processing characteristics make the tape's use questionable, it makes sense to postpone tape mounting until OPEN time. Coding

UNIT = (3420,2,DEFER)

requests two drives and postpones mounting. The DEFER option is a third positional subparameter. To postpone mounting a single tape, code

UNIT = (3420,,DEFER)

The extra comma indicates a missing positional subparameter. Positional subparameters, to belabor a point, derive their meaning from their relative positions. DEFER is the *third* positional subparameter.

Tape and disk have similar DCB parameters; LRECL, BLKSIZE, and RECFM are most common. Additionally, because magnetic tape can be recorded at several different densities, the DEN (density) subparameter specifies the tape's recording density (Fig. 13.9). For example,

DCB = (BLKSIZE-750,DEN = 3,LRECL = 75,RECFM = FB)

defines fixed-length, blocked records, 75 bytes in length, stored in 750-byte blocks (ten logical records) on 1600-bpi tape.

DISP and DSNAME

Disk and tape dispositions are, for all practical purposes, identical. The DSNAME parameter provides a convenient mechanism for retrieving a cataloged or passed data set.

VOLUME

Changing a disk pack is time-consuming, so in many computer centers disks are permanently mounted. Magnetic tape is different. Tape volumes are stored off-line and mounted only when needed. Consequently, the volume serial number is almost always specified; for example,

VOL = SER = MIAMI5

Fig. 13.9   Because magnetic tape can be recorded at several different densities, the DCB sometimes contains a DEN subparameter.

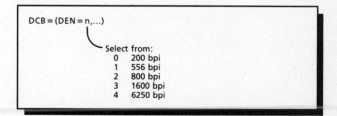

Note that SER is a keyword subparameter.

To request multiple tape volumes, code a list of serial numbers; for example,

VOL = SER = (M01,M02,M03,M04)

asks for four different tapes. A request for four volumes might be accompanied by a UNIT parameter requesting four drives

UNIT = (TAPE,4)

On the other hand, if the tape volumes are to be accessed one after another, a single drive might do.

The programmer can request a scratch or work tape by omitting the VOLUME parameter. Some installations prefer a more specific request, such as

//TAPE DD UNIT = 3420,VOL = SER = SCRTCH, . . .

The VOLUME parameter is used to generate tape mount messages. The message

MOUNT TAPE SCRTCH ON DEVICE 182

is an obvious request for a scratch tape.

The LABEL Parameter

The **LABEL parameter** (Fig. 13.10) specifies both the label type and the relative position of the file on the volume. Normally, one file is stored on each tape, but a volume can hold more than one. The sequence number is the desired file's relative position on the tape—1 for the first file, 2 for the second, and so on. Valid label types are summarized in Fig. 13.10. Standard labels are created and checked by the operating system; user labels and nonstandard labels must be checked by a programmer routine (if they are checked at all). The "bypass label processing" option implies that labels are present, but for some reason, they are not to be processed.

To create a new, single-volume tape file with standard labels, code

LABEL = (1,SL)

Fig. 13.10   Magnetic tape is used to transfer data between
computer centers. Because different computer
centers sometimes follow different labeling
standards, the LABEL parameter might be needed.

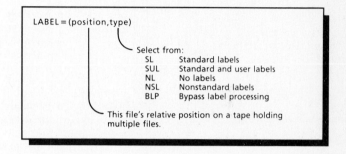

```
LABEL = (position,type)

              Select from:
                  SL      Standard labels
                  SUL     Standard and user labels
                  NL      No labels
                  NSL     Nonstandard labels
                  BLP     Bypass label processing

              This file's relative position on a tape holding
              multiple files.
```

or

LABEL = (,SL)

The lone comma indicates the absence of the first positional parameter, which is assumed to be 1. On a new tape data set, the OPEN macro creates a label; on an existing data set, the OPEN checks the label to determine if the proper file has been mounted.

Standard labels are a typical default, so the LABEL parameter can often be skipped. Remember, however, that magnetic tape is used to transfer data or programs between computer centers, and not all centers follow the same standard, so programmers should be familiar with the LABEL parameter.

The DUMMY Parameter

Loading tapes is time-consuming. Often, particularly during program testing, a programmer may choose to bypass tape mounting by coding a **DUMMY parameter.**

//DATA DD DUMMY,UNIT = 3420

DUMMY must be the first parameter in the operands field. Later, the job can be resubmitted without the DUMMY parameter.

Fig. 13.11   This figure shows some examples of complete DD
                      statements to create magnetic tape files.

```
1.  Create and pass a temporary data set.

//TAPE          DD  UNIT = 3420, VOL = SER = WX2453,
//                  DCB = (LRECL = 145,BLKSIZE = 2900,
//                  RECFM = FB),LABEL = (,SL),
//                  DISP = (NEW,PASS),DSN = &&T


2.  Create and catalog a permanent data set.

//MAG1          DD  UNIT = 3420, LABEL = (,SL),DSN = TT,
//                  VOL = SER = A572,DCB = (RECFM = FB,
//                  BLKSIZE = 1200,LRECL = 120,DEN = 3),
//                  DISP = (NEW,CATLG)


3.  Use a scratch tape.

//SCRATCH       DD  DISP = (NEW,DELETE),DSNAME = &&WORK,
//                  DCB = (BLKSIZE = 104,LRECL = 52,RECFM = FB),
//                  LABEL = (,SL),UNIT = 3420
//                  VOL = SER = SCRTCH
```

Some Examples

Figure 13.11 shows several examples of DD statements for creating files on magnetic tape.

System Input and Output

A great deal of I/O takes place through relatively few devices. On
some systems, a terminal keyboard and screen are the standards. On others, spooling routines create temporary disk files
to insulate application programs from such slow devices as keyboards, card readers, and printers. Default parameters are often
used to access these standard system input and output devices.

For example, the **system input** device is normally accessed
by a statement such as

```
//SYSIN DD
```

The asterisk indicates that the data follows "this" DD statement in the job stream. There is nothing sacred about SYSIN; it's just a DDNAME. The programmer can use any DDNAME for the system input device, as long as it matches the name coded in the program's internal data control block. However, many compilers and utilities use SYSIN to reference the system input device.

To spool data to the **system output** device, code

```
//SYSOUT DD SYSOUT = A
```

or

```
//SYSPRINT DD SYSOUT = A
```

Device A generally implies eventual printer output. For punched card (or card image) output, code

```
//SYSPUNCH DD SYSOUT = B
```

SYSOUT, SYSPRINT, and SYSPUNCH are common DDNAMEs; you can use any name you wish. An installation can choose its own symbols to indicate the various system devices.

Many installations limit the amount of system output space available to a program. You can override this limit by coding a SPACE parameter

```
//SYSPRINT DD SYSOUT = A,SPACE = (CYL,(5,2))
```

Job Step Qualification

Often, two or more DD statements, each in a different job step but still within the same job, are assigned the same DDNAME. For example, on a compile, link edit, and go job, both the compiler and the go step often get input from the system input device, so both can contain a

```
//SYSIN DD
```

statement. To distinguish these two statements, the DDNAMEs are often qualified (Fig. 13.12). The FORTRAN procedure contains three job steps: FORT (the compiler), LKED (the linkage editor), and GO (the program load module). FORT.SYSIN is the name of a DD statement attached to the first job step. GO.SYSIN

Fig. 13.12   When the same DDNAME occurs more than once in a
cataloged procedure, qualify the DDNAMEs by
preceding them with their step names.

```
//JOBNAME       JOB      (9824,18),DAVIS,CLASS=A
//              EXEC            FORTRAN

//FORT.SYSIN    DD       *

      FORTRAN  source module

/*

//GO.SYSIN      DD       *

      Data

/*
```

is attached to the GO step. Qualified DDNAMES can be used only
within a cataloged procedure.

Libraries

A library can contain numerous programs and data files. Each
program or file is a member of the library. To access a given
member, code a member name as part of the DSNAME (Fig.
13.13). For example, to access a file named TIME from the
PAYROLL library, code

DSNAME = PAYROLL(TIME),DISP = OLD

Turn your attention to loading programs. For such system
software as compilers, the linkage editor, and utilities, no library reference is needed. Private libraries, however, must be
identified by the programmer. For example, assume that
MYPGM is stored on MYLIB. The two statements

```
//         EXEC PGM=MYPGM
//STEPLIB DD    DSNAME=MYLIB,DISP=SHR
```

Fig. 13.13   To access a single library member, code the member name as part of the DSNAME.

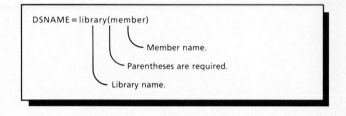

tell the system to "load and execute MYPGM, which is found on MYLIB."

The DDNAME *must be* STEPLIB and the STEPLIB DD statement must *immediately* follow the EXEC statement. The DSNAME defines the library name. DISP = SHR indicates that the contents of the library will not be modified. Note that the member name is not specified; the EXEC statement defines it.

Code a **STEPLIB statement** following each EXEC that references a program on a private library. If a multistep job calls for several programs from the same library, a single JOBLIB statement can replace several STEPLIBs. The JOBLIB statement follows the JOB statement and precedes the first EXEC. A JOBLIB statement defines a library for all steps in the job.

Other JCL Statements

A PROC statement is used to assign default values to symbolic parameters in a cataloged procedure. A null statement (//) is sometimes used to mark the end of a job. A comment starts with //*, followed by anything at all. Comments can be inserted at any point in the job stream.

Summary

Perhaps the best way to summarize what you have learned about IBM MVS/JCL is to work through an example. Figure 13.14 shows a flowchart for a multistep job. The first job step

Fig. 13.14   This flowchart shows the job steps and physical
devices needed to support a four-step master file
update application.

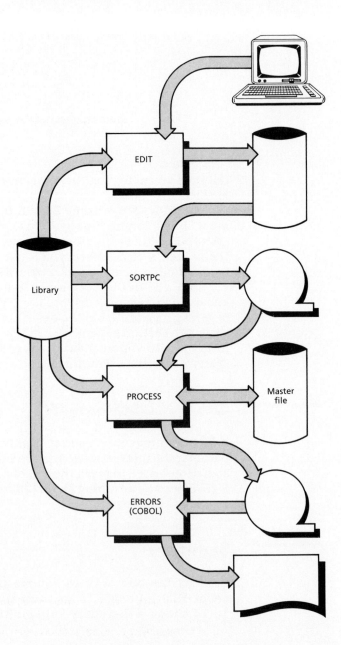

Fig. 13.15   Read through the JCL in this complete example, making sure you understand what each parameter means.

```
//MYJOB      JOB      (9182,222),'W.S. DAVIS',CLASS = A

//STEP1      EXEC     PGM = EDIT
//STEPLIB    DD       DSN = MU.USERPGM.SAN,DISP = SHR
//OUTS       DD       DSNAME = &&TEMP,
//                    UNIT = SYSDA,DISP = (NEW,PASS),
//                    SPACE = (TRK,(10,2,RLSE),
//                    DCB = (LRECL = 80,
//                    BLKSIZE = 800,RECFM = FB)
//SYSIN      DD    *

           ▷ Data

/*

//SECOND     EXEC     SORTPC
//SORTIN     DD       DSN = &&TEMP,DISP = (OLD,DELETE)
//SORTOUT    DD       DSNAME = MYOUTS,UNIT = 2400 − 3,
//                    VOL = SER = R712,
//                    LABEL = (,SL),DISP = (NEW,PASS),
//                    DCB = (LRECL = 80,
//                    BLKSIZE = 800,RECFM = FB)
//* THE NEXT TWO STATEMENTS DEFINE THE SORT FIELDS.
//SYSIN      DD    *
      SORT FIELDS = (1,5,CH,A)
/*        THE FIELD STARTS IN POSITION 1, IS 5 POSITIONS LONG,
//*       AND HOLDS CHARACTER DATA WHICH ARE TO BE SORTED
//*       INTO ASCENDING ORDER.

//THIRD      EXEC     PGM = PROCESS
//STEPLIB    DD       DSN = MU.USERPGM.SAN,DISP = SHR
//TAPEIN     DD       DSN = MYOUTS, DISP = (OLD,CATLG)
//MASTER     DD       DSN = MU.USERDATA.SAN5,
//                    DISP = (OLD,KEEP)
//TAPEOUT    DD       DSN = MYERRS,UNIT = 2400 − 3,
//                    VOL = SER = E712,LABEL = (,SL),
//                    DISP = (NEW,CATLG),DISP = (LRECL = 80,
//                    BLKSIZE = 1200,RECFM = FB)

//LAST       EXEC     COBOL
//COB.SYSIN      DD    *

           ▷ COBOL source module

/*
//TAPEIN     DD       DSN = MYERRS,DISP = (OLD,KEEP)
//
```

303

reads data through the system input device and edits them. The output is written to a temporary disk file. The edit program is stored on a private library. Step two sorts the data to tape. In the third job step, the tape file is merged with a master file on disk; errors are written to another tape, and, at the end of the job step, both tapes are cataloged. Finally, an error processing routine is compiled, link edited, and executed. The JCL to support this job is shown in Fig. 13.15. Incidentally, all of the STEPLIB statements could have been replaced by

```
//JOBLIB  DD  DSN = MU.USERPGM.SAN,DISP = SHR
```

Read through the statements one by one and be sure you understand what each parameter means. If you can do that, you'll have a solid understanding of MVS/JCL. See Appendix F for a summary of the parameters.

Key Words

data control block	DSNAME parameter	STEPLIB statement
data set	DUMMY parameter	system input
DCB parameter		system output
DD statement	JOBLIB statement	UNIT parameter
DDNAME	LABEL parameter	VOLUME parameter
DISP parameter	SPACE parameter	

References

1. Brown, Gary DeWard (1990). *System 370/390 JCL*, third edition. New York: John Wiley & Sons.
2. IBM Corporation (1987). *MVS/370 JCL Reference*, fourth edition. Poughkeepsie, New York: International Business Machines Corporation. Publication Number GC28-1350.
3. Janossy, James G. (1987). *Practical MVS JCL for Today's Programmer.* New York: John Wiley & Sons.
4. Trombetta, Michael, and Finkelstein, Sue Carolyn (1989). *OS JCL and Utilities, A Comprehensive Treatment*, second edition. Reading, Massachusetts: Addison-Wesley Publishing Company.

Exercises

1. Explain how a program is linked to a physical I/O device under operating system/360–370.

2. Explain the relationship between a program DCB and the DCB parameter on a DD statement.

3. Code a UNIT parameter to reserve three 3420 tape drives. Don't mount the tapes until open time.

4. Code a DD statement DCB parameter for a disk file holding fixed-length, blocked records. Logical records are 50 characters long, and the blocking factor is 50.

5. Code a space parameter to reserve 20 contiguous cylinders. Allow for additional cylinders, requesting two at a time. Return unused cylinders to the system at the end of the job step.

6. Code a DD statement to create a 3420-series tape, serial number MYTAPE. Catalog the tape if the job step ends normally; otherwise, keep the tape for analysis. For simplicity, the tape's serial number and catalog name should be the same. Records are 125 characters each, blocked in groups of 20; all records are the same length. Use standard labels.

7. Code a DD statement for a temporary work data set on the system direct access device (SYSDA). Get ten tracks. Request secondary tracks in groups of two. They do not have to be contiguous, but do return unused tracks to the system at the end of the job step. Logical records are 100 bytes each and should be blocked in groups of 30. The data set is to be passed to a subsequent job step.

8. Explain why a JOBLIB or STEPLIB statement is necessary when executing a program stored on a private library.

9. Exercise 9 in Chapter 12 asked you to compile, link edit, and execute a program. Refer to the JCL generated by that cataloged procedure, and interpret each DD statement parameter.

10. Exercise 10 in Chapter 12 asked you to write and test a series of three programs. Add the JCL needed to run those three programs as a single job.

11. Briefly explain the difference between compilation time, link edit time, and run time. Why is this difference significant?

12. Why is it valuable to postpone physical device assignments until run time?

Your instructor might assign additional JCL exercises.

14

Libraries and the Linkage Editor

This chapter illustrates MVS/JCL use by explaining the JCL statements that create and maintain program libraries and access the linkage editor. Key topics include:

Program libraries
  Compile, link edit, and execute

Compilers and source statement libraries
  Creating a library
  Adding members to a library
  Using private source statement libraries

Object modules
  Creating an object module library
  Adding object modules to a library

Load modules
  The linkage editor
  The primary object module
  System libraries
  Private libraries
  Load module libraries

The loader

Program Libraries

Once you learn the essentials of a job control or command language, your next major interface with the operating system often involves libraries. During program development, code may be maintained on a source statement library. Common subroutines are found on object module libraries. Production programs are stored on load module libraries.

This chapter explains the differences between source, object, and load modules, and illustrates (using IBM MVS/JCL) the basics of library management. The key is understanding what happens. Given a sense of the underlying concepts, it is relatively easy to determine how to create and access libraries on almost any system.

Much of the material in this chapter is general and, with a few changes in terminology, can be applied to almost any computer system. Other material is IBM-specific. Those who do not use an IBM computer should read the material following each major topic header.

Compile, Link Edit, and Execute

A programer's source statements are translated into object form by a compiler or an assembler. A linkage editor then converts the object module into a load module. This compile, link edit, and execute sequence (Fig. 14.1) is basic; you probably memorized it in your first computer course. But, what exactly is a source module? an object module? a load module? And, *why* is this sequence necessary?

Generally, a **source module** is a set of program statements written in a source language such as COBOL, FORTRAN, Pascal, or assembler. No computer can directly execute source statements; they must first be translated into machine-level code by a compiler or an interpreter. A compiler accepts a complete source program, and generates a complete object module. An interpreter accepts a single source statement, translates it to machine level, executes the resulting code, and then turns to the next source statement. Interpreters are popular on microcomputers and time-shared systems, and are often used by casual programmers. Professionals are more likely to use compilers.

An **object module** is pure binary, machine-level code. Most are incomplete, however, containing references to other object modules such as access methods and subroutines, so they cannot be loaded and executed. Instead, several object modules

Fig. 14.1   Programs typically pass through a compiler and the
linkage editor before they are ready to execute.

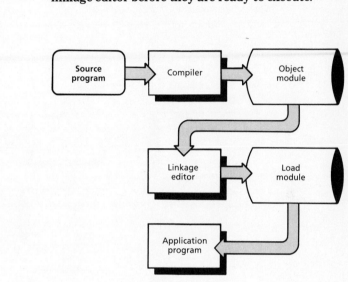

must first be linked to form a complete **load module.** The program that links object modules to form a load module is called
(at least by IBM) the **linkage editor.**

The program flow illustrated in Fig. 14.1 is oversimplified,
because the process of compiling and link editing a program involves several **libraries** (Fig. 14.2). Let's analyze the compile,
link edit, and execute steps one by one, and consider the nature
of each of these libraries.

Compilers and Source Statement Libraries

Source modules are written by programmers in a source language. The statements might be keypunched, creating a source
deck. More often, they are entered through a terminal under control of an editor and stored in electronic form on disk.

The source code as prepared by the programmer is normally
incomplete; for example, an assembler language program might
contain **macros.** Before the program can be assembled, each
macro must be expanded into one or more source statements.
System macros, such as OPEN, CLOSE, GET, and PUT, are

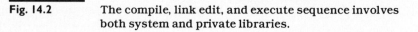

Fig. 14.2   The compile, link edit, and execute sequence involves
                       both system and private libraries.

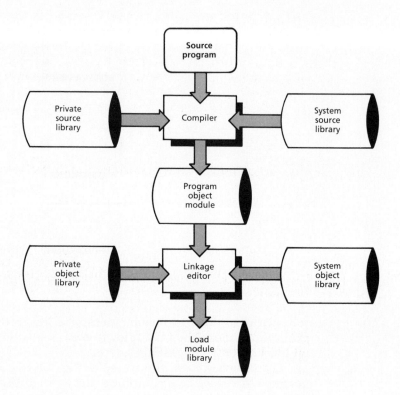

stored on a system **source statement library** (Fig. 14.2). Private
macros are stored on private source statement libraries.

Most languages support source statement libraries. For
example, to merge prewritten code into a program, a COBOL
programmer can code a COPY statement; in PL/1, the command
is INCLUDE. The compiler builds a complete source module,
combining the programmer's source code with other code from
system and/or private source statement libraries, before compiling the code.

For example, imagine that a systems analyst working on a
payroll application has defined the employee time record as a
COBOL data structure and, using a utility program or an editor,
has stored the source code on a COBOL source statement library

(Fig. 14.3). Once it's on the library, a programmer can access it by inserting a COPY statement at the appropriate spot in the source program. As the COBOL compiler scans the source code, it replaces COPY statements with library code (Fig. 14.4). Once all the COPY statements have been expanded, the source module is complete, and compilation can begin. An assembler program expands macros in precisely the same way.

A private source statement library contains "home-grown" macros and customized source code. A system source statement library contains more widely used source code (I/O macros, for example). The compiler combines source statement library en-

Fig. 14.3   Source code is placed on a source statement library by a utility program or an editor.

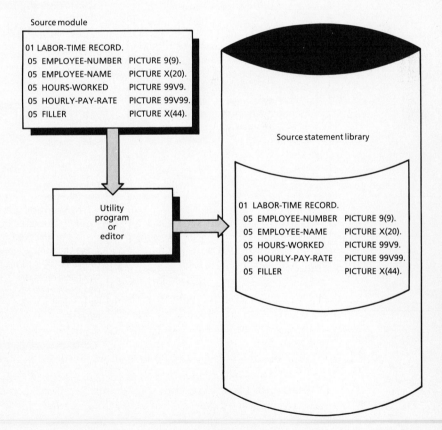

Fig. 14.4   When a compiler encounters a reference to a source
statement library, it replaces the reference with the
library code.

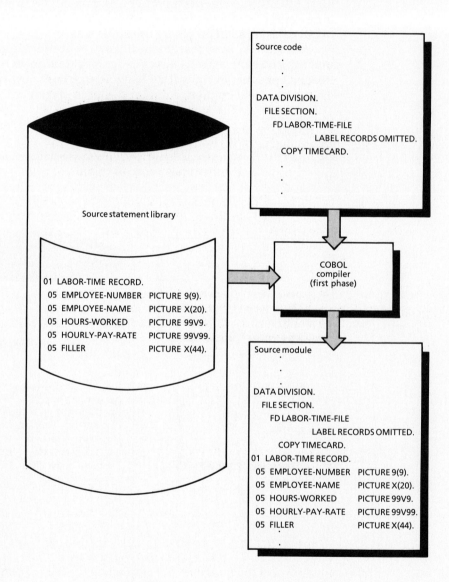

tries with the programmer's source code to produce a source module, which is translated to machine-level object code.

Creating a Library

A library is a special type of file consisting of a **directory** and several **members** (Fig. 14.5). The members can be source modules, object modules, load modules, or data. The members' names and absolute disk addresses are listed in the directory. If, for example, a programmer requests member TAX on a library named PAYROLL, the operating system will find the library, read the directory, search it, and access the requested member. IBM calls this library structure a **partitioned data set** (PDS).

The basic difference between a regular data set (a file) and a partitioned data set is the PDS directory. When creating a library, the programmer must tell the system how much space to allocate to the directory by coding a positional subparameter on the SPACE parameter (Fig. 14.6). The directory subparameter defines the number of 256-byte blocks that are allocated to the directory; each block identifies five (at most six) members.

For example, assume you are about to create a library. You have estimated that ten cylinders will be needed to store about sixty programs. Because each directory block can list, conservatively, five programs, you'll need twelve blocks. To create the library, code

```
//PDS     DD      DSNAME=MYLIB,DISP=(NEW,CATLG),UNIT=3330,
//                VOL=SER=MYPACK,SPACE=(CYL,(10,,12)),
//                DCB=(LRECL=80,BLKSIZE=400,RECFM=FB)
```

Twelve directory blocks are specified; space for them is taken from the ten primary cylinders. There is no secondary space allocation.

Note that the logical record length (LRECL) is set to 80 bytes. Compilers and linkage editors originated when punched cards were the standard input medium. Even today, many installations maintain old program decks, and some continue to use punched cards as a source of library members or as a library backup. Because disk can support any logical record length, it makes sense to accommodate the less flexible medium. Additionally, most workstation screens display an 80-character line, so an 80-byte logical record length makes sense even on modern peripherals.

Fig. 14.5   A library is a type of file that consists of a directory
and several members. IBM calls this library structure
a partitioned data set.

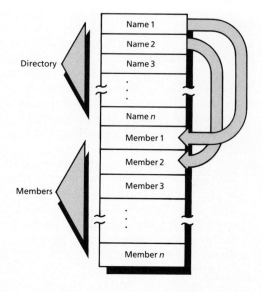

Fig. 14.6   To indicate the amount of space to be allocated to a
partitioned data set's directory, code a positional
subparameter on the SPACE parameter.

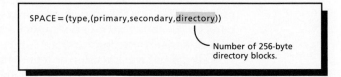

On an IBM computer, a DD statement cannot stand on its own; as a minimum, a JOB statement and a single EXEC must accompany the DD that defines the library. One way to create an empty library is to run a dummy program named **IEFBR14**. A system utility, it consists of a single instruction, a branch to register 14. (In COBOL terms, that branch is equivalent to STOP RUN; in FORTRAN, it's STOP; in BASIC, END.) Figure 14.7 illustrates a job that creates an empty partitioned data set using IEFBR14. When the "program" is loaded, the operating system allocates space for the PDS and starts the program. IEFBR14 immediately quits. In effect, this utility fools the system into creating the partitioned data set.

Adding Members to a Library

Once the library exists, adding members to it is relatively easy. If source statements are entered through a text editor, the output can be written to a designated source statement library. An option is to prepare a source deck (or an electronic source module on disk or tape), and then use a utility program to copy it to the library.

The utility program most often used to add members to a source statement library on an IBM mainframe computer is called **IEBGENER**. It's also used to copy disk files for system backup and to display the contents of a file as a debugging aid. The utility has options that allow a programmer to copy records selectively and to reformat output.

Assume a programmer wants to add a source module named MASTFILE to MYLIB. Figure 14.8 shows the JCL statements

---

Figure 14.7   To create an empty partitioned data set, run a program named IEFBR14.

```
/ /           JOB         ....
/ /           EXEC        PGM = IEFBR14
/ /PDS        DD          DSNAME = MYLIB,DISP = (NEW,CATLG),
/ /                       UNIT = 3330, VOL = SER = MYPACK,
/ /                       SPACE = (CYL,(10,,12)),
/ /                       DCB = (LRECL = 80,RECFM = FB,BLKSIZE = 400)
/ *
```

needed to run the IEBGENER utility. The program requires certain DDNAMEs. The input data set must be called SYSUT1. Output must go to SYSUT2. A SYSPRINT DD statement allows the
program to write messages to the printer; it is required. Finally,
SYSIN allows optional parameters to be passed to the program.
Because this application calls for no optional features, the only
parameter is DUMMY.

Look carefully at the SYSUT2 DD statement. Note the
DSNAME

DSNAME = MYLIB(MASTFILE)

MYLIB is the name of a partitioned data set. MASTFILE is a
member name. Remember the directory at the beginning of the
PDS? When the member is added to the library, an entry under
the name MASTFILE is made in the directory. In the future, the
member can be retrieved by this name. The member name must
be enclosed in parentheses and must immediately follow the
DSNAME. The rules for defining a member name are the same as
the rules for defining a data set name. Note: Assuming that DCB
parameters were defined when the library was created, the DCB
on the SYSUT2 statement in Fig. 14.8 would not be needed.

Fig. 14.8   Use a utility, such as IEBGENER, to add a source
                    module to a library.

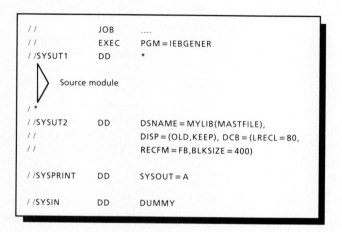

```
/ /              JOB        ....
/ /              EXEC       PGM = IEBGENER
/ /SYSUT1        DD         *

         Source module

/ *
/ /SYSUT2        DD         DSNAME = MYLIB(MASTFILE),
/ /                         DISP = (OLD,KEEP), DCB = (LRECL = 80,
/ /                         RECFM = FB,BLKSIZE = 400)

/ /SYSPRINT      DD         SYSOUT = A

/ /SYSIN         DD         DUMMY
```

Using Private Source Statement Libraries

Compiling or assembling a program involves several input and output data sets that are normally defined in a cataloged procedure. For example, Fig. 14.9 shows the JCL statements generated by the compile-only cataloged procedure ASMFC. One statement is of particular interest:

XXSYSLIB   DD   DSNAME = SYS1.MACLIB,DISP = SHR

It defines the system macro library, SYS1.MACLIB, and thus tells the assembler where to find such system macros as GET, PUT, OPEN, CLOSE, DCB, and so on. To use a private library simply change this statement; for example,

Fig. 14.9   The cataloged procedure for the assembler program, ASMFC. Statements preceded by // are coded by the programmer. Those beginning with XX are part of the cataloged procedure.

```
/ /            JOB      ...
/ /            EXEC     ASMFC
XXASM          EXEC     PGM = IEUASM
XXSYSLIB       DD       DSNAME = SYS1.MACLIB,DISP = SHR
XXSYSUT1       DD       ...
XXSYSUT2       DD       ...
XXSYSUT3       DD       ...
XXSYSPRINT     DD       SYSOUT = A
XXSYSPUNCH     DD       SYSOUT = B
XXSYSGO        DD       DSNAME = &&LOADSET,
XX                      SPACE = (400,(100,20)),
XX                      DISP = (OLD,PASS),UNIT = SYSDA,
XX                      DCB = (LRECL = 80,
XX                      BLKSIZE = 400,RECFM = FB)
/ /ASM.SYSIN   DD       *
               Source code
/ *
```

```
//                     EXEC  ASMFC
//ASM.SYSLIB           DD    DSN = MYLIB,DISP = SHR
```

Coding an explicit **SYSLIB** statement overrides the cataloged procedure, replacing the standard SYSLIB statement with the one provided by the programmer.

To identify two (or more) source statement libraries, concatenate them; for example,

```
//                     EXEC  ASMFC
//ASM.SYSLIB           DD    DSN = SYS1.MACLIB,DISP = SHR
//                     DD    DSN = MYLIB,DISP = SHR
```

Note that the second DD statement has no DDNAME, so the last name encountered, SYSLIB, still holds. When it encounters a macro, the assembler will search SYS1.MACLIB. If the macro is not found, the assembler will search MYLIB. Additional libraries can be concatenated by attaching additional unnamed DD statements; the order of the DD statements determines the order in which the libraries will be searched.

Object Modules

Compilers and assemblers generate object modules. An object module contains machine-level code, but is normally incomplete and thus cannot be loaded and executed. For example, most input and output operations involve calling an access method. A given access method might appear in hundreds of different programs, and recompiling the same code again and again is a waste of time. Instead, access methods are stored in object module form and added to the application program *after* compilation.

To cite another example, consider a subroutine such as the FORTRAN SQRT function. The programmer codes

```
X = SQRT(Y)
```

and, after the instruction is executed, expects to find the square root of Y in the field called X. It isn't quite that simple; the square root is actually estimated in a fairly complex subroutine. The subroutine could be stored as a FORTRAN source module, copied into each program that references SQRT, and recompiled, but that would be very inefficient. Instead, the SQRT function is stored as an object module.

A compiler works with source code. Certain key logical elements, such as access methods and standard subroutines, do not exist at the source level, so there is no way for the *compiler* to incorporate this essential logic into an object module. Consequently, the object module will refer to logic that simply is not there—an unresolved **external reference**. As it builds an object module, the compiler generates a table of unresolved external references and places it at the beginning of the object module (Fig. 14.10). This **external symbol dictionary** (the **ESD**) is used by the linkage editor as it builds a load module.

Creating an Object Module Library

Physically, there is no difference between a source statement library and an **object module library** (or linkage library); in fact, on some systems, you can mix source and object modules on the same library. It is possible to have both private and system ob-

Fig. 14.10   An object module's external references are listed in its external symbol dictionary.

External symbol dictionary	
Symbol	Location
MAIN	Known
SEQAM	?
SUBR1	?

Object code

MAIN _____

    .
    .
    .

    CALL SEQAM
    .
    .
    .

    CALL SUBR1
    .
    .
    .

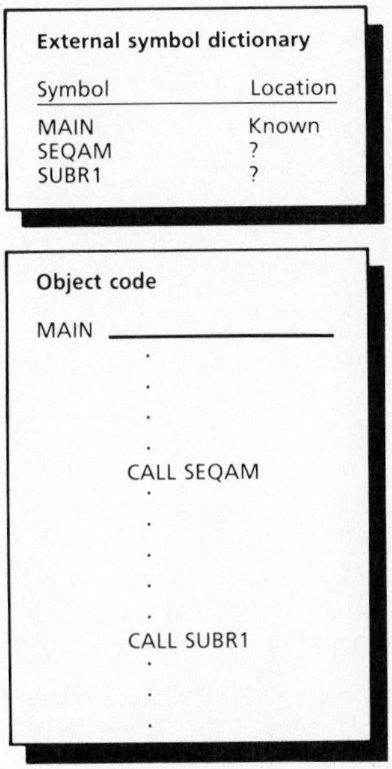

ject module libraries (Fig. 14.11), with the "most recently compiled" object module perhaps being viewed as a special case.

Adding Object Modules to a Library

Object modules are generated by compilers. To add an object module to a library, you must control the compiler's output. For example, Fig. 14.9 shows the JCL statements generated by the cataloged procedure ASMFC (compile only). Earlier, you considered the SYSLIB DD statement, which identified system and private macro libraries. The assembler sends its output to the physical device described in the **SYSGO** DD statement:

```
XXSYSGO  DD  DSNAME=&&LOADSET,SPACE=(400,(100,20)),
XX            DISP=(OLD,PASS),UNIT=SYSDA,
XX            DCB=(LRECL=80,BLKSIZE=400,RECFM=FB)
```

It defines a temporary data set named &&LOADSET; the object module produced by the assembler program will be its only member. The secret to placing an object module on a private library is simple: change this statement.

For example, assume that the program being assembled is called MYPGM. You have already created a library named MYLIB. The following JCL assembles the program and places the object module on the library:

Fig. 14.11   The linkage editor can access both system and private object module libraries.

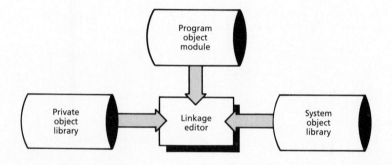

```
//              EXEC  ASMFC
//ASM.SYSGO  DD     DSNAME = MYLIB(MYPGM),DISP = (OLD, KEEP),
//                       DCB = (RECFM = FB,LRECL = 80,BLKSIZE = 400)
//ASM.SYSIN  DD       .
      }source program
/˙
```

Coding a SYSGO DD statement in the job stream overrides the cataloged procedure. The object module will no longer go to a temporary data set named &&LOADSET; instead it will be stored in MYLIB, under the name MYPGM. Note: Once again, given an existing library, you could skip the DCB parameter. If coded, the logical record length, blocksize, and record format must match the library.

Load Modules

An object module containing unresolved external references cannot be loaded and executed. External references are resolved by the linkage editor.

Figure 14.10 pictures an object module. The main program is MAIN. It references two subroutines, an access method (SEQAM) and a private subroutine (SUBR1). The linkage editor faces the situation pictured in Fig. 14.12. SEQAM resides on a

Fig. 14.12   As the linkage editor begins its work, the object modules it must link may be stored on several different libraries.

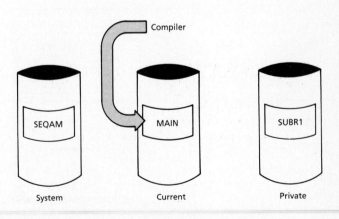

system object module library. SUBR1 is on a private library. The just compiled object module, MAIN, is on another private library (or, perhaps, on a temporary data set).

The linkage editor begins by reading the primary object module, MAIN. The external symbol dictionary is separated from the object code, and the beginning of MAIN is established as the base address or reference point for the load module (Fig. 14.13).

Next, the linkage editor scans the external symbol dictionary. An object module named SEQAM is referenced. The system library is searched, SEQAM is found, the access method is read into main memory, its ESD is separated from the object code, and the object module is placed just after MAIN (Fig. 14.13).

SEQAM's external symbol dictionary is then scanned. (To simplify this example, assume that the access method does not call a lower level subroutine.) Once the reference to SEQAM has been fully resolved, the linkage editor can return to the main program's external symbol dictionary.

MAIN also calls SUBR1. The system library is searched, but SUBR1 is not found. Thus, the private subroutine library is searched, and SUBR1 is there. The object module is read into memory, the ESD and the object code are separated, and the code is placed after SEQAM in the load module (Fig. 14.13). Now the

Fig. 14.13   The linkage editor combines object modules to form a load module. The start of the primary object module is the load module's base address.

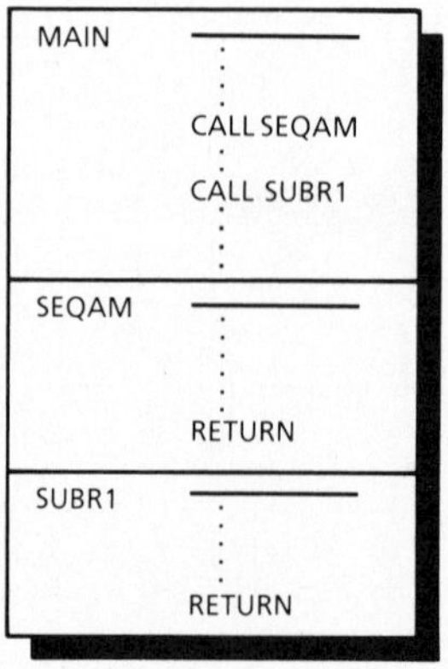

external symbol dictionary for SUBR1 is scanned for unresolved external references; once again assume there are none.

Returning to the main program's external symbol dictionary, the linkage editor finds no more unresolved external references. Thus the load module is complete, referring only to locations that are contained within itself. It is ready to be loaded and executed.

Imagine a somewhat more complex program. The primary module is named CONTROL. It calls four subroutines: A, B, C, and D. Routines A, C, and D are relatively simple, performing a computation and returning to CONTROL, but routine B contains subsequent calls to X, Y, and Z. When the linkage editor reads module B and scans its external symbol dictionary, three lower level unresolved external references will be encountered. These references must be resolved before the linkage editor returns to the main program, so subroutines X, Y, and Z will follow B in the load module (Fig. 14.14).

Fig. 14.14   In a more complex program, the linkage editor might resolve a chain of secondary external references before returning to the primary object module.

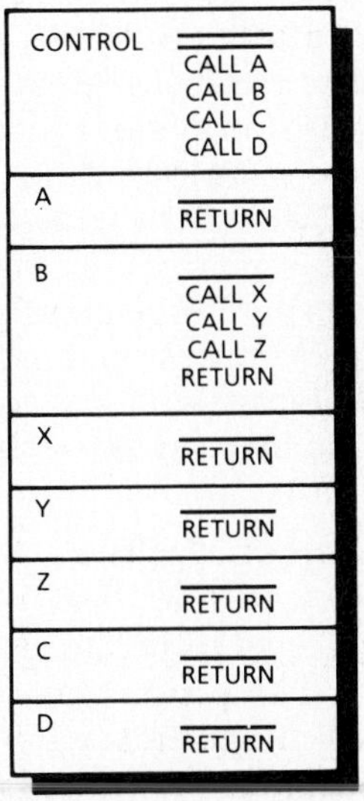

The Linkage Editor

The linkage editor is a program. Its input consists of one or more object modules. It produces a load module. If you have ever programmed an IBM System/360-370 computer, you have almost certainly used the linkage editor, but you have probably never looked at the JCL that supports it. Figure 14.15 shows an expansion of the cataloged procedure ASMFCL (compile and link edit).

The first statement in the LKED step

```
//    EXEC    PGM=IEWL
```

names the linkage editor program. The input data set is SYSLIN. Note the DSNAME, &&LOADSET. It's the same name the assembler used to store the object module—look at the SYSGO DD statement.

A few lines below SYSLIN is a DD statement with no DDNAME

```
//    DD    DDNAME=SYSIN
```

This another source of linkage editor input; it is concatenated to SYSLIN.

The parameter, DDNAME=SYSIN, is a bit unusual. It postpones the data definition. Essentially, the DDNAME parameter tells the operating system to look ahead in the job stream for a DD statement with the specified DDNAME (in this example, SYSIN). The programmer can code a SYSIN DD statement to pass object modules and control statements to the linkage editor.

The **SYSLMOD** (for system load module) statement defines the linkage editor's output data set (the load module). The DSNAME is &&GOSET(GO). It defines a temporary partitioned data set on the system direct access device (SYSDA); this particular load module is given the member name GO. Note the SPACE parameter. Space is requested in 1024-byte blocks. The primary request is for 50 blocks, with a secondary request for 20 more; a single 256-byte block is set aside to hold the directory.

The Primary Object Module

If the linkage editor is to produce a valid load module, it must start somewhere. The primary object module is input through **SYSLIN** (system linkage editor input). Typically, it is the most

Fig. 14.15   The ASMFCL cataloged procedure. Statements that
begin with // are coded by the programmer. Those that
begin with XX are part of the procedure.

```
//              JOB        ...
//              EXEC       ASMFCL
XXASM           EXEC       PGM = IEUASM
XXSYSLIB        DD         ...
XXSYSUT1        DD         ...
XXSYSUT2        DD         ...
XXSYSUT3        DD         ...
XXSYSPRINT      DD         ...
XXSYSPUNCH      DD         ...
XXSYSGO         DD         DSNAME = &&LOADSET,...

//ASM.SYSIN     DD         *

                    Source program

/ *

XXLKED          EXEC       PGM = IEWL
XXSYSLIN        DD         DSNAME = &&LOADSET,
XX                         DISP = (OLD,DELETE),
XX                         DCB = (LRECL = 80,
XX                         BLKSIZE = 400,RECFM = FB)
XX              DD         DDNAME = SYSIN
XXSYSLMOD       DD         DSNAME = &&GOSET(GO),
XX                         SPACE = (1024,(50,20,1)),
XX                         DISP = (NEW,PASS),UNIT = SYSDA
XXSYSUT1        DD         ...
XXSYSPRINT      DD         SYSOUT = A
/ *
```

recently compiled object module; in the compile, link edit, execute sequence, it's the one that started as source code. Figure
14.15 shows the output from the assembler going to SYSGO,
where it is stored under data set name &&LOADSET. This
DSNAME also appears on the SYSLIN statement as input to the
linkage editor. If the object module is stored on a private library,
both SYSGO and SYSLIN must be overridden (Fig. 14.16).

Programmers tend to view the compile, link edit, and execute sequence almost as a single operation—compilelinkeditgo. In reality, three distinct programs must be run. They are usually separated by just a few seconds (or even microseconds). However, it is possible to run the compile on Monday, the link edit on Tuesday, and the execute step on Wednesday (substitute January, February, and March, if you wish). Once a source, object, or load module is written to a nontemporary file, it is captured for later use, and can be accessed at virtually any time.

Fig. 14.16   If the primary object module is stored on a private library, both SYSGO (compile or assemble step) and SYSLIN (link edit step) must be overridden.

```
//              EXEC    ASMFCL
XXASM           EXEC    PGM = IEUASM
XXSYSLIB        DD      ...
XXSYSUT1        DD      ...
XXSYSUT2        DD      ...
XXSYSUT3        DD      ...
XXSYSPRINT      DD      ...
XXSYSPUNCH      DD      ...

//ASM.SYSGO     DD      DSNAME = MYLIB(MYPGM),
//                      DISP = (OLD,KEEP),
//                      DCB = (RECFM = FB,LRECL = 80,
//                      BLKSIZE = 400)

//ASM.SYSIN     DD      *

        ▷    Source program

/*

XXLKED          EXEC    PGM = IEWL

//LKED.SYSLIN   DD      DSNAME = MYLIB(MYPGM),
//                      DISP = (OLD,KEEP)
//              DD      DDNAME = SYSIN

XXSYSLMOD       DD      ...
XXSYSUT1        DD      ...
XXSYSPRINT      DD      ...
```

System Libraries

There are several different types of system libraries. One, a true system library, contains such object modules as the standard access methods that are used by almost every program. The operating system knows where to find them.

Other system libraries are language dependent. FORTRAN, for example, supports a number of scientific subroutines. The programmer who wants to use one of these scientific subroutines must clearly specify to the linkage editor where the subroutine library can be found, so the FORTRAN compile, link edit, and execute procedure normally references one additional DD statement

```
XXSYSLIB   DD   DSNAME = SYS1.FORTLIB,DISP = SHR
```

Other subroutine libraries can be identified by concatenating additional DD statements to SYSLIB. Similar language-dependent functions are supported in COBOL, PL/1, and most other languages.

Note the difference between these two types of system libraries. The first is language independent—almost every program will require one or more of these object modules. System pointers allow the linkage editor to locate a system library; no programmer-generated DD statement is required. The other libraries are language dependent. FORTRAN programs access FORTLIB; COBOL programs request object modules from COBLIB. The programmer (or cataloged procedure) must identify such language-dependent libraries through a SYSLIB DD statement.

Private Libraries

Unless the programmer provides a complete description of a private library, the linkage editor will be unable to find it. The cataloged procedure for the link edit step normally contains an unnamed DD statement concatenated to SYSLIN. This statement, in turn, points to DDNAME = SYSIN. The programmer can take advantage of the SYSIN statement to pass private library information to the linkage editor.

For example, assume that a subroutine named SURB1 resides on a private library named MYLIB. You have just compiled a program that references SUBR1. You can tell the linkage editor

Fig. 14.17   Control statements are passed to the linkage editor
                       through SYSIN.

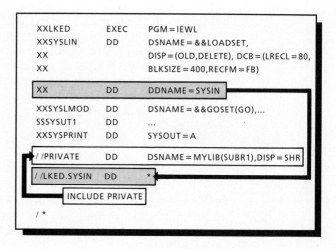

```
XXLKED        EXEC     PGM = IEWL
XXSYSLIN      DD       DSNAME = &&LOADSET,
XX                     DISP = (OLD,DELETE), DCB = (LRECL = 80,
XX                     BLKSIZE = 400,RECFM = FB)

XX            DD       DDNAME = SYSIN

XXSYSLMOD     DD       DSNAME = &&GOSET(GO),...
SSSYSUT1      DD       ...
XXSYSPRINT    DD       SYSOUT = A

//PRIVATE     DD       DSNAME = MYLIB(SUBR1),DISP = SHR
//LKED.SYSIN  DD       *
      INCLUDE PRIVATE

/*
```

to include the subroutine in the load module by passing it a control statement via SYSIN (Fig. 14.17).

Follow the code carefully. Start with the "normal" JCL as it
exists in the cataloged procedure, with the SYSLIN DD statement concatenated to an unnamed DD statement that points to
SYSIN. Following SYSPRINT is a new statement—the // in the
first two positions shows it was coded by the programmer. This
statement, named PRIVATE, describes the private library. Next
comes the SYSIN statement (LKED. is a step qualifier). It precedes the linkage editor control statements. In this example,
only one control statement has been coded:

INCLUDE PRIVATE

It tells the linkage editor to look for a DD statement named PRI-
VATE for a detailed description of one or more object modules
that are to be included in the load module.

Go through the process one more time. The SYSIN statement
passes a series of control statements to the linkage editor. An
INCLUDE statement identifies one or more DD statements. Each

Fig. 14.18 This example shows how the linkage editor can be given the names of two private libraries, each containing multiple object modules.

```
//              EXEC    ASMFCL
//ASM.SYSIN     DD      *

      Source program

/*
//LIBRA         DD      DSNAME = ALIBRARY(A,B,C,D),
//                      DISP = SHR
//LIBRX         DD      DSNAME = XLIBRARY(X,Y,Z),
//                      DISP = SHR
//LKED.SYSIN    DD      *
     INCLUDE LIBRA
     INCLUDE LIBRX
/*
```

DD statement defines, in turn, one or more object modules that are to be included in the load module. The skeleton of another, more complex, example is shown in Fig. 14.18.

This is only one example of how the programmer might use the linkage editor. There are several ways to identify private object modules, and numerous other commands can be coded. It is not our intent to cover all the features of this most useful program, however.

Load Modules Libraries

A **load module library** is a partitioned data set. Load modules are output by the linkage editor. The output is sent to the partitioned data set defined by

```
XXSYSLMOD   DD   DSNAME = &&GOSET(GO) ,SPACE = (1024,(50,20,1)),
XX                         DISP = (NEW,PASS),UNIT = SYSDA
```

Fig. 14.19   To place a load module on a private library, change the
SYSLMOD DD statement.

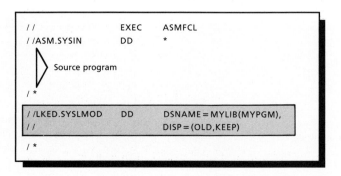

```
//                        EXEC      ASMFCL
//ASM.SYSIN               DD        *

          Source program

/*
//LKED.SYSLMOD    DD           DSNAME = MYLIB(MYPGM),
//                             DISP = (OLD,KEEP)

/*
```

To place a load module on a private library, simply change the
SYSLMOD DD statement (Fig. 14.19).

Load modules can be loaded and executed by the system in
response to an EXEC statement. The system can find load modules that are stored on a system program library. The programmer must identify a private library through a JOBLIB or
STEPLIB statement; for example,

```
//          EXEC    PGM = MYPGM
//STEPLIB    DD      DSNAME = MYLIB,DISP = SHR
```

The Loader

The **loader** does everything the linkage editor does, except output a load module. Instead, it builds a load module in memory,
and then starts it. With the linkage editor, the load module is
written to disk and then reloaded. With the loader, these two I/O
operations are dropped, saving considerable time. Because the
loader outputs no load module, there is no SYSLMOD DD statement. To access the loader, the programmer codes cataloged procedures such as ASMFCG or COBVCG; the CG stands for compile
and go.

Some advanced linkage editor functions (for example, generating overlay structures) are not supported by the loader. Still,

for the compile and test activities common to program development, the loader is usually more than adequate.

Summary

The chapter began with a brief discussion of the compile, link edit, and execute sequence. Source modules, object modules, and load modules were defined and the functions of the compiler, interpreter, and linkage editor were briefly described. Libraries can be maintained at the source, object, or load level.

Assembler macro instructions and COBOL COPY statements refer to a source statement library. The difference between private and system libraries was explored, and an example illustrating the expansion of source code into a source module prior to compilation was developed using COBOL.

On an IBM computer, a library is called a partitioned data set or PDS. The creation of a PDS was illustrated, and a utility program named IEBGENER was used to add members to a source statement library. Most object modules contain unresolved external references, and so must be link edited before execution. A member is placed on an object module library by controlling the destination of the compiler output.

Load modules are built from a set of object modules by the linkage editor. The link edit process was discussed in general terms, and then a specific example using the IBM linkage editor was developed. Because a load module is output by the linkage editor, the secret to placing a load module on a library is to control the destination of the linkage editor's output. The chapter ended with a brief discussion of the loader program.

Key Words

directory	load module	partitioned data
external reference	load module	set
external symbol	library	source module
dictionary	loader	source statement
IEBGENER	macro	library
IEFBR14	member	SYSGO
INCLUDE	object module	SYSLIB
library	object module	SYSLIN
linkage editor	library	SYSLMOD

References

1. IBM Corporation (1985). *MVS/370 Linkage Editor and Loader User's Guide.* International Business Machines Corporation. Publication Number GC26-4061-1.

Exercises

1. Distinguish between a source module, an object module, and a load module. Don't simply say that a source module is produced by a programmer, an object module is produced by a compiler, and a load module is produced by a linkage editor; listing the sources doesn't answer the question. How do these modules differ from each other?

2. Briefly explain how a compiler or an assembler incorporates source statement library members into a source module.

3. Explain the difference between a system library and a private library.

4. Describe the structure of a typical library.

5. Explain how a partitioned data set is created on an IBM System/370.

6. How can a programmer add a member to a source statement library?

7. Why do most object modules contain unresolved external references?

8. What is an external symbol dictionary?

9. Explain how a member is added to an object module library.

10. What does the linkage editor do?

11. What is a concatenated data set?

12. Explain how the linkage editor follows a chain of unresolved external references as it builds a load module.

13. How is a load module placed on a private library? How is this load module eventually executed?

14. What is the loader program?

The following exercises are intended for readers who have access to an IBM System 370 computer. Users of other systems might consider parallel assignments.

15. Submit a program (any program) using a cataloged procedure such as ASMFCLG, COBVCLG, or one you have used in class. Include MSGLEVEL = (1,1) on the EXEC statement. Read and explain each generated job control statement.

16. For this exercise you will need a main program and a subroutine written in any language (or even in two different languages). Use source code from a previous class. If you don't have the source code, write a main program to read two values, call a subroutine that adds them, and print their sum. Don't spend too much time on the code—this is a library manipulation exercise. Do the following:
    a. Compile the subroutine and store it on a private library.
    b. Independently compile the main program and store it on a private library.
    c. Link edit the two object modules and store the load module on a private library.
    d. Execute the load module.

PART FOUR

Operating System Internals

15
MS-DOS

MS-DOS (or simply DOS) is almost the de facto standard microcomputer operating system. This chapter introduces DOS internals. Key topics include:

Evaluating an operating system
  Measures of effectiveness
  System objectives

Microcomputer operating systems
  The microcomputer environment
  Basic operating system functions

DOS internals
  The shell
  Accessing peripherals
  The file system
  Interrupt processing
  Booting DOS
  Running DOS

Several of the topics introduced in this chapter are common to most operating systems.

Evaluating an Operating System

Most people begin seriously studying computers by learning an application programming language. Part III took you a step closer to the hardware by investigating command languages. The hardware itself is directly controlled by its microcode. In between, serving as a hardware/software interface, is the operating system (Fig. 15.1). To the application programmer or user, most of what happens below the command language level is transparent. You are about to drop below that level and turn your attention to operating system internals.

Measures of Effectiveness

If an operating system is to be a hardware/software interface, it makes sense to design an *efficient* interface. On most modern computers, the operating system serves as the primary resource manager, responsible for processor time, main memory space, registers, input and output devices, secondary storage space, and data and program libraries. A well-designed operating system attempts to optimize the utilization of all the system resources.

That objective seems obvious, but it isn't. Consider an analogy. What is the optimum engine for an automobile? The answer depends on your definition of effective performance. Are you primarily interested in speed? safety? fuel efficiency? space? a comfortable ride? cost? status? or some combination? In other

Fig. 15.1   The operating system acts as a hardware/software interface.

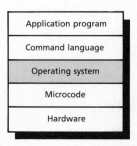

words, what are your measures of effectiveness, and how do you weight them? Identify the characteristics you consider important. Then you can *begin* to discuss the precise meaning of the word optimum. "Best" is a relative term.

A number of criteria are used to measure a computer system's performance, including:

1. Throughput. Generally, total execution time (for all programs) divided by total elapsed time.
2. Turnaround. The elapsed time between job submission and job completion.
3. Response time. The elapsed time between a request for the computer's attention and the computer's response.
4. Availability.
5. Security.
6. Reliability.
7. Cost.
8. Ease of use.

The perfect operating system would maximize throughput while minimizing both turnaround and response time. The system would be available to any programmer or user on demand, and would be remarkably easy to use. Security would, of course, be absolute, and system reliability would approach 100 percent. All this would be accomplished at very low cost.

System Objectives

Unfortunately, such a perfect operating system is impossible to achieve because the measures of effectiveness conflict. For example, throughput can be increased by overloading a system, but overloading negatively impacts turnaround and response time. Conversely, turnaround and response time can be helped by underloading a system which, of course, destroys throughput, since an underloaded system is bound to be idle at times.

Does this imply that turnaround and response time are compatible? Not always. Consider a time-sharing system designed to minimize response time. To prevent any single user from monopolizing the processor, programs are limited to brief time slices. Imagine a ten-second program. If that program is limited to one-tenth second of actual run time each second, it would need 100 seconds of elapsed time. Emphasizing response time can hurt turnaround.

System availability and throughput obviously conflict; how can a busy system be available? Security involves various controls and checks, and time spent on security cannot be used for production. Reliability is gained by duplicating key components, and that's expensive; reliability and cost are conflicting objectives.

Recognizing that the criteria conflict, system objectives are often stated as targets; for example, "Maintain a minimum of 75 percent throughput while keeping turnaround under one hour," or "Maintain response time at a maximum of three seconds for at least 95 percent of system requests," or "Keep average response time below two seconds." The ideal operating system for a particular installation is a function of its application mix. For example, a large time-sharing computer concurrently accessed by hundreds of users will probably stress response time, security, and reliability. An equally large business system might be more concerned with generating massive, end-of-period accounting reports in a timely fashion and at reasonable cost, so throughput and turnaround become crucial. The operating systems for these two machines will be quite different.

When studying an operating system, it is useful to begin with two questions:

1. What hardware is it designed to support?
2. What is the typical (or assumed) application mix?

The answers are essential if you are to understand *why* a particular operating system works as it does.

Microcomputer Operating Systems

The Microcomputer Environment

Start with a microcomputer. Most contain limited memory and support a limited number of peripheral devices (often, a keyboard, a screen, a printer, two diskette drives, and, perhaps, a hard disk). Basic systems cost less than $1000; a typical configuration might cost $2000 to $5000.

Many early users were hackers, who enjoyed "fooling around" with the machine. Such people require (and probably desire) very little support. While hackers still exist, today's typical owner wants a microcomputer for a specific purpose such as analyzing spreadsheets, playing games, writing papers, or supporting research, and doesn't want the hardware to get in the way. Most programs are small and process a limited amount of data. On a given day, relatively few programs will be run. (In fact, the computer is likely to be unused most of the time.) These are, of course, assumptions, but they are reasonable.

For a machine used perhaps two to three hours a day, throughput is not relevant. Given small programs processing limited data, turnaround is not a problem. Even a slow computer is much faster than any human user, so response time is generally not a factor. Forget availability. Modern microcomputers are so inexpensive that almost anyone who needs one can afford one. Given the limited number of users, security it is not a major concern, either.

The typical microcomputer user's criteria for measuring effectiveness include cost, reliability, and ease of use. Cost is the big one. People are drawn to microcomputers because they are inexpensive. Each operating system function increases development cost, and hence selling price. An operation system occupies memory, and the larger the system, the more memory it needs, so microcomputer operating systems generally contain only essential functions.

Reliability and ease of use vie closely for second place. Reliability, unfortunately, is difficult to measure, and tends to be viewed in a negative light: the ABC model 50 is always going down. From an operating system perspective, reliability is largely a function of complexity. Put simply, on a micro it is better to do a few things well than many things badly. Once again, the argument favors simplicity.

Finally, consider ease of use. Must users are uninterested in the subtle nuances of I/O device control or diskette track configurations. As a minimum, they require a simple command language (perhaps even a point-and-click interface such as *Windows*) and the ability to store and retrieve data and programs by name. Application programs may provide more sophisticated interfaces, but commands and file names are needed before an application program can even be loaded.

Basic Operating System Functions

Microcomputer operating systems are generally small. The resident operating system, sometimes called the **nucleus,** the **kernel,** or the **supervisor**, typically contains a **command processor,** or **shell,** an **input/output control system,** or **IOCS,** a **file system,** and interrupt handler routines (Fig. 15.2). Another region holds system constants, parameters, and control fields. These modules reside in memory and provide real-time support to the application programs.

Not all operating system modules must be **resident.** Consider, for example, formatting a disk. The routine that performs this task is needed only when a disk is being formatted, so it is stored on disk and loaded into memory on demand. The free or **transient area** of memory (Fig. 15.2), containing all the space not allocated to the resident operating system, can hold one of these **transient** modules or an application program.

Where in memory is the operating system found? That depends on the system. The architecture of many computers requires that key control information be stored at specific memory locations, thus defining the address of at least the system parameters. Other systems assume a standard load address for a

Fig. 15.2   Microcomputer operating systems typically contain a command processor, an input/output control system, a file system, and interrupt handler routines. Other transient operating system modules are stored on disk and read into memory on demand.

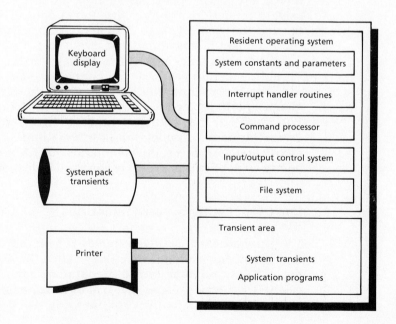

primary control program. Figure 15.2 shows the components of an operating system in a general sense, without regard for their placement.

Few microcomputers operate 24 hours a day. Main memory is volatile, so the resident operating system must be reloaded each time the system is restarted. Normally, a copy of the operating system is kept on disk and loaded into memory by a boot routine each time the system is activated. The boot is another essential microcomputer operating system module.

DOS Internals

MS-DOS is the world's most commonly used microcomputer operating system. Developed for the IBM Personal Computer by Microsoft Corporation, versions of DOS are available on all IBM and IBM-compatible machines. (The IBM-PC version is called **PC-DOS**.)

The original IBM PC was constructed around an Intel 8088 microprocessor, a 16-bit processor with an 8-bit I/O bus. PC/AT and smaller PS/2 machines use the newer 80286 processor, while more powerful PS/2 computers use the 32-bit Intel 80386 and the Intel 80486. Competitive, functionally compatible non-IBM machines, sometimes called clones, are able to run virtually all IBM/PC and PS/2 software because the operating system, DOS, provides a common platform.

The Shell

DOS is command driven. Users request support by typing commands in response to a system prompt (Fig. 15.3). When the return key is pressed, the shell, called **COMMAND.COM,** interprets the command and calls the appropriate lower level routine or program. COMMAND.COM consists of a command interpreter and a number of resident (or internal) operating system routines that remain in memory at all times (Fig. 15.3). Other routines are transient (or external) and are read into memory on demand. Generally, those routines needed to support an active program are resident.

Accessing Peripherals

The task of accessing peripheral devices is divided between two of the operating system modules (Fig. 15.4). **IO.SYS** (called

Fig. 15.3   DOS is command-driven. To request support, a user
                       types a command in response to a system prompt. The
                       operation system then reads and interprets the
                       command and calls the routine that carries out the
                       command.

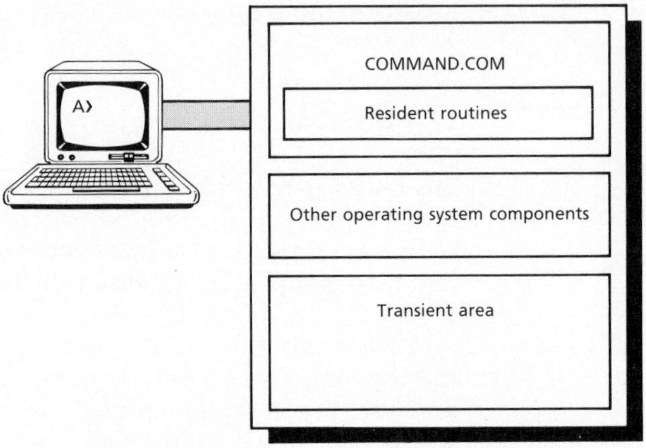

Resident commands

BREAK	PATH
CALL	PAUSE
CHDIR	PROMPT
CLS	REM
COPY	REN
CTTY	RMDIR
DATE	SET
DEL	SHIFT
DIR	TIME
ECHO	TYPE
ERASE	VER
EXIT	VERIFY
FOR	VOL
GOTO	d:
IF	
MKDIR	

Transient commands

APPEND	LIB
APPLY	LINK
ASSIGN	MACHINE
ATTRIB	MAP
BACKUP	MODE
BOOTF	MORE
CHCP	NLSFUNC
CHKDSK	NOSTACK
COMMAND	PART
COMP	PREP
COMPACT	PRINT
CONFIGUR	RDCPM
DEBUG	RECOVER
DETECT	REPLACE
DISKCOMP	RESTORE
DISKCOPY	SEARCH
DSKSETUP	SELECT
EDLIN	SHARE
EXE2BIN	SHIP
FC	SORT
FIND	SUBST
FORMAT	SYS
GDU	TREE
GDUSTR	XCOPY
GRAFTABL	ZCOM
GRAPHICS	ZSPOOL
JOIN	
KEYB	
LABEL	

Fig. 15.4   Two modules, IO.SYS and MSDOS.SYS, share
                       responsibility for accessing peripheral devices.

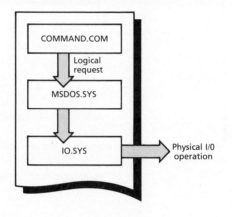

IBMBIO.COM under PC-DOS) is a hardware-dependent module
that issues *physical* data transfer commands. On an IBM PC,
this module interacts with a proprietary, basic input/output system, or BIOS, implemented in read-only memory. This ROM
BIOS distinguishes an IBM PC from compatible computers made
by other manufacturers.

Logical I/O and other file system functions are implemented
by a hardware-independent module called **MSDOS.SYS** (IBM-
DOS.COM under PC-DOS). MSDOS.SYS accepts logical I/O requests from application programs or other operating system
modules, translates them into physical I/O commands, and
passes the physical commands to IO.SYS. Note that only IO.SYS,
the machine-dependent module, deals directly with peripheral
devices. A version of MS-DOS written for a COMPAQ computer
and one written for a Zenith computer will differ only in their
IO.SYS; other operating system modules will be the same.

Each physical device attached to the computer is described
in a special file called a **device driver** (Fig. 15.5). Character drivers control such devices as the keyboard, the screen, and the
printer. Block drivers control disk and similar block-oriented devices, and transfer data in 512-byte blocks. The device driver is
used by MSDOS.SYS to translate logical I/O requests to physical
form. Certain standard device drivers are built into the operat-

Fig. 15.5   MSDOS.SYS uses a device driver to translate logical
I/O requests to physical form.

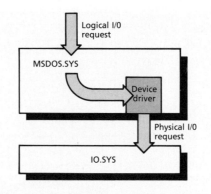

Standard character device drivers	
Name	**Description**
AUX	First serial printer or modem
COM1	Same as AUX
CLOCK$	Real-time clock
COM2	Second serial device (printer or modem)
CON	Console—keyboard/display
LPT2	Second parallel device (usually, printer)
LPT3	Third parallel device
NUL	"Null" device—output discarded
PRN	First parallel printer
LPT1	Same as PRN

ing system (Fig. 15.5). Additional devices can be defined by adding a description to a special file called CONFIG.SYS.

The File System

MSDOS.SYS converts logical I/O requests to physical form. One
of its responsibilities is directory management. Chapter 8 introduced the DOS directory structure; if you completed the chapter
tutorial, you know how to create and delete directories with operating system commands. For example, when a make directory
command, such as

MKDIR LETTERS

is read by COMMAND.COM, the shell calls MSDOS.SYS (Fig.
15.6a), which, in turn, asks IO.SYS to read the directory (Fig.
15.6b). MSDOS.SYS then adds the new directory entry
(Fig. 15.6c), and asks IO.SYS to write the modified directory
back to disk (Fig. 15.6d). MSDOS.SYS creates, deletes, and modifies directory entries in response to requests from COM-
MAND.COM (or an application routine), and relies on IO.SYS to
perform the actual data transfer operations.

MSDOS.SYS also supports application programs. When a
disk file is first opened, MSDOS.SYS asks IO.SYS to read the directory. It then extracts the location of an existing file or creates
a directory entry for a new one and, if necessary, asks IO.SYS to
rewrite the directory. As the program runs, logical input and
output operations result in a transfer of control to MSDOS.SYS.
Using the start-of-file address from open, the operating system
computes the physical address of the data, and then passes the
address to IO.SYS. Additionally, MSDOS.SYS blocks and
deblocks data.

Fig. 15.6   MSDOS.SYS is responsible for directory management.

a. Commands are read and interpreted by COMMAND.COM. Following
   a make directory (MKDIR) command, COMMAND.COM calls
   MSDOS.SYS.

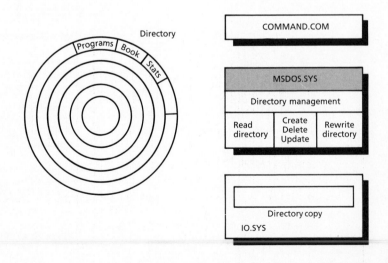

b. **MSDOS.SYS then asks IO.SYS to read the directory.**

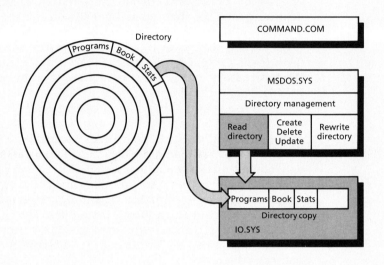

c. **Once the directory is in memory, MSDOS.SYS can modify it. In this example, a new directory entry is added.**

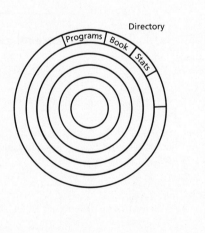
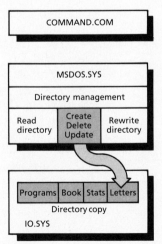

d. Finally, MSDOS.SYS asks IO.SYS to rewrite the directory to disk.

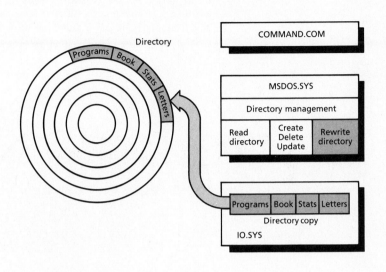

Another MSDOS.SYS responsibility is allocating space on disk. Start with an overview of a disk's format (Fig. 15.7). The first sector holds the boot routine. Next come two copies of the file allocation table (FAT) followed by the root directory. On system disks, the various components of the operating system follow the root directory. Figure 15.7 shows a system disk; on disks that do not contain a copy of the system, this space (and the rest of the disk) is used for data storage.

Disk space is allocated in **clusters**. On a single-sided disk, each cluster holds 512 bytes (one sector); on a double-sided disk, each cluster holds 1024 bytes (two sectors). The clusters are numbered sequentially, and the **file allocation table** contains an entry for each cluster on the disk.

When a file is created, the number of its first cluster is stored in the directory. As data are added to the file, the second cluster is assigned dynamically by recording its number in the first cluster's FAT entry, so the first cluster points to the second one (Fig. 15.8). As additional data are added, the third cluster's number is recorded in the second cluster's FAT entry, and so on; by following a chain of pointers from the directory through the file allocation table until an end-of-file marker is reached, it is possible to step, cluster by cluster, through a file. Note that the clusters belonging to a file need not be contiguous.

Fig. 15.7   This diagram shows the format of a typical DOS disk.
                     If the disk does not contain a copy of the operating
                     system, the space set aside for IO.SYS, MSDOS.SYS,
                     and COMMAND.COM is used for data.

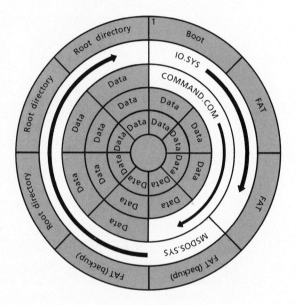

DOS views the data stored in a disk file as a continuous
stream of bytes. Logical I/O operations request data by relative
byte (rather than by relative record or relative sector). Assuming
a double-sided disk, a file's first cluster holds relative bytes 0
through 1023, its second cluster holds relative bytes 1024
through 4095, and so on. As part of its blocking and deblocking
functions, MSDOS.SYS calls IO.SYS to perform whatever physical I/O operations are necessary to access the requested string.
Logically, data on disk are addressed just like data in memory.

Interrupt Processing

The Intel 8086 family relies on **interrupts** to establish communication with peripheral devices. Consequently, processing interrupts is an important DOS function.

The key to interrupt processing is an **interrupt vector table**
that occupies the first 1K bytes of memory (Fig. 15.9). This table
holds the addresses (interrupt vectors) of up to 256 different in-

Fig. 15.8   A file's first cluster number is recorded in the disk
directory. To locate the clusters that comprise a file,
follow the chain of pointers through the file allocation
table.

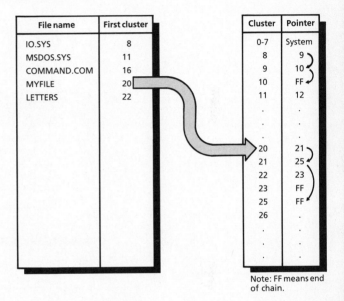

File name	First cluster		Cluster	Pointer
IO.SYS	8		0-7	System
MSDOS.SYS	11		8	9
COMMAND.COM	16		9	10
MYFILE	20		10	FF
LETTERS	22		11	12
			.	.
			.	.
			.	.
			20	21
			21	25
			22	23
			23	FF
			25	FF
			26	.
			.	.
			.	.
			.	.

Note: FF means end
of chain.

terrupt processing modules, most of which are found in
MSDOS.SYS or IO.SYS. Two special registers are also crucial.
The instruction counter is found in the IP, or instruction pointer
register, also called the IC, or instruction counter register. Another register points to a memory stack.

The interrupt itself consists of an electronic pulse and the
address of an interrupt vector. When an interrupt occurs, hardware copies the contents of the IP register (along with a few
other registers) to the stack (Fig. 15.9a), and loads the specified
interrupt vector into the IP register (Fig. 15.9b). As the next machine cycle begins, the first instruction in the interrupt processing routine is fetched (Fig. 15.9c). Once the interrupt is
processed, the contents of the stack are copied back into the IP
register, and the original program resumes processing (Fig.
15.9d).

Interrupts are much more common than you might imagine.
For example, each time you press a key on the keyboard, an interrupt is generated. In response, the operating system copies a

Fig. 15.9 DOS contains modules to process interrupts.

a. When an interrupt occurs, the contents of the instruction pointer register are copied to the stack.

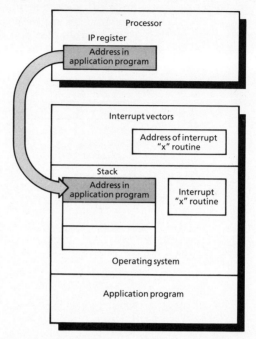

b. Next, the specified interrupt vector is loaded into the instruction pointer.

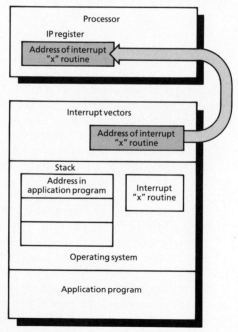

c. With the next machine cycle, the first instruction in the interrupt processing routine is fetched.

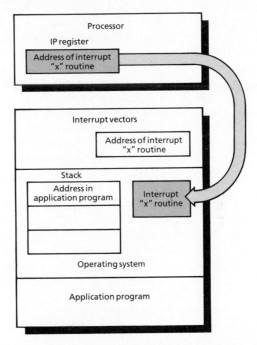

d. Finally, the contents of the stack are loaded back into the instruction pointer register, and the application program resumes processing.

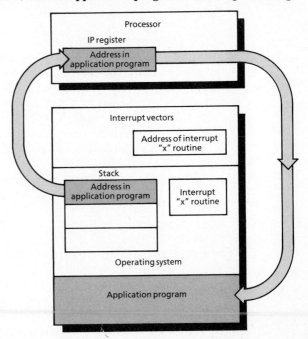

single character into memory, and then waits for the next interrupt to herald the arrival of the next character. A few keys, such as return and escape, signal the operating system to take a different action. Interrupts also allow the printer, a disk drive, and other peripherals to communicate with the main processor.

Not all interrupts originate with hardware, however. Although it is legal for an application program to communicate directly with IO.SYS, most rely on MSDOS.SYS to translate their logical I/O requests to physical form. Branching to or calling an operating system module implies a knowledge of DOS internals that few people possess, so by convention, an assembler language programmer who wants to perform I/O loads descriptive information into a few registers and then executes an interrupt instruction referencing vector 33 (21 hex).[1]

Hardware responds to a software-generated interrupt exactly as if the source had been hardware, copying the IP register to the stack and loading the contents of the specified vector into the IP register. The address in vector 33 points to an MSDOS. SYS module that analyzes register contents and determines the requested I/O operation. In compiler languages, the instructions to set registers and interrupt the operating system are generated for you.

Booting DOS

Main memory is volatile. Consequently, the operating-system must be read into memory each time the computer is switched on. Under DOS, the boot routine is stored on the first sector of each disk. Flipping the power switch (or simultaneously pressing the control, alt, and delete keys) causes hardware to read into memory the first sector from the disk in the system drive (Fig. 15.10). The boot then reads IO.SYS, which, in turn, initializes key system tables, reads MSDOS.SYS, and, finally, reads COMMAND.COM (Fig. 15.11).

The COMMAND.COM modules that immediately follow MSDOS.SYS are resident. Other COMMAND.COM modules are stored at the high end of memory, following the transient area. While technically resident, this second group of routines can be overlaid, if necessary, by a large application program. If they are overlaid, they must be restored after the program is finished.

---

[1]There is nothing special about vector 33. It's just a widely accepted coding standard adopted by Microsoft and used by most software developers.

Fig. 15.10   When you turn on the computer, hardware reads the
boot routine from the first sector on the system disk.

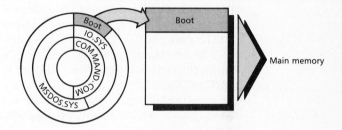

Main memory

Running DOS

Once loaded, DOS controls literally everything that happens on
the computer. First, COMMAND.COM gets control and, by calling IO.SYS, displays a system prompt on the screen. As the user
types a command, each character generates an interrupt.
Responding to the interrupt, the operating system reads the

Fig. 15.11   After the system is booted, the operating system's
resident components occupy memory.

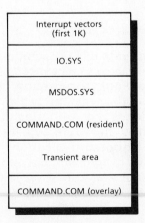

character, stores it in memory, and, again using IO.SYS, echoes it to the screen.

Eventually, the user presses enter. Like any other key, it generates an interrupt. Sensing that this key is different, the operating system transfers control to the COMMAND.COM module that interprets commands. This module, in turn, either displays an error message or takes whatever action is necessary to carry out the command.

For example, imagine the user has typed a resident command. Since the appropriate routine is already in memory, COMMAND.COM simply calls it. When it finishes carrying out the command, the resident module returns control to COMMAND.COM, which displays a prompt and waits for the next command.

If the command refers to a transient module or to an application program, COMMAND.COM calls MSDOS.SYS, passing it the module name. MSDOS.SYS, in turn, reads (by calling IO.SYS) the disk directory, searches it, finds the referenced module, and instructs IO.SYS to read it into the transient area. Once the requested module is in memory, control is returned to COMMAND.COM. At this point, with the transient module in memory, there is no real difference between calling it and calling a resident module.

The basic work flow is simple. A prompt is displayed. The user types a command or a program name. The appropriate operating system module or application program gets control. As the program runs, the operating system supports it by processing interrupts. Eventually, it returns control to COMMAND.COM, and the process is repeated, again and again, until the machine is shut down. DOS is command driven.

Summary

The operating system is the computer's resource manager. Several criteria are used to measure a computer's effectiveness, including throughput, turnaround, response time, availability, security, reliability, cost, and ease of use. Unfortunately these criteria conflict. When evaluating the effectiveness of an operating system, it is important to consider the hardware environment and the expected application mix.

The hardware environment and application mix of a microcomputer system suggests three key measures of effectiveness: cost, reliability, and ease of use. Most microcomputer operating systems include a command processor, an input/output control system, and a file system. Because memory is volatile, a boot routine is needed to load the system.

The DOS command processor is called COMMAND.COM. Physical I/O is controlled by IO.SYS; logical I/O is the responsibility of MSDOS.SYS. The boot occupies the first sector of a disk. Next come two copies of the file allocation table, the root directory, the operating system (on a system disk), and, finally, data storage.

Space on disk is allocated in clusters. The clusters are numbered sequentially, and an entry for each one is recorded in the file allocation table (FAT). The number of a file's first cluster is recorded in the directory. The clusters making up a file are linked by a series of pointers through the file allocation table.

Interrupts control communications between the main processor and its peripherals. The first 1K bytes of memory hold up to 256 interrupt vectors. When an interrupt occurs, the contents of the instruction pointer are copied to the stack, and the contents of the designated interrupt vector are loaded into the instruction pointer. Thus, the interrupt processing routine gets control. After the interrupt is processed, the contents of the stack are loaded back into the instruction pointer, and the original program resumes processing. Some interrupts originate with hardware; others originate with software.

The DOS boot is stored on the first sector of each disk. When the computer is turned on, hardware reads the boot, which loads the rest of the operating system.

The chapter's last section, "Running DOS," summarizes the operating system's primary features.

Key Words

boot	input/output	MSDOS.SYS
cluster	control system	nucleus
command	interrupt	PC-DOS
processor	interrupt vector	resident
COMMAND.COM	table	shell
device driver	IOCS	supervisor
file allocation	IO.SYS	transient
table (FAT)	kernel	transient area
file system	MS-DOS	

References

1. Dvorak, John C., and Anis, Nick (1991). *Dvorak's Guide to DOS and PC Performance.* Berkeley, California: Osborne McGraw-Hill.
2. Norton, Peter (1990). *Inside the IBM PC and PS/2.* New York: Bradley Division of Simon & Schuster, Inc.
3. Shanley, Tom (1991). *The IBM PS/2 from the Inside Out.* Reading, Massachusetts: Addison-Wesley Publishing Company.

Exercises

1. Why does it make sense to use the operating system as a resource manager?

2. Briefly define several common measures of computer performance.

3. A computer's measures of performance often conflict. Explain.

4. When evaluating an operating system, it makes sense to consider the hardware environment and the application mix. Why?

5. Briefly describe the hardware environment of a typical microcomputer system.

6. Briefly describe the assumed application mix of a typical microcomputer system. Does this mix seem reasonable to you? Why, or why not? Can you think of any exceptions?

7. What criteria are typically used to measure a microcomputer system's effectiveness? Why?

8. Microcomputer operating systems generally contain a command processor, an input/output control system, and a file system. Why *these* components?

9. Distinguish between an input/output control system and a file system. Relate your answer to the difference between physical and logical I/O.

10. Distinguish between resident and transient modules. Why does it make sense to have some modules transient? Why must other operating system modules be resident?

11. Why is a boot routine necessary?

12. Relate the functions of COMMAND.COM to the general functions of a command processor or shell as described in Chapter 5.

13. The task of accessing physical devices is divided between IO.SYS and MSDOS.SYS. Briefly explain the functions performed by these two modules. Why does it make sense to split these sets of functions?

14. What is a device driver?

15. Relate the functions performed by IO.SYS and MSDOS.SYS to the basic concepts of logical and physical I/O.

16. Sketch the contents of a DOS disk.

17. Briefly explain how the clusters making up a disk file are linked through the file allocation table.

18. What is an interrupt? Explain how DOS processes interrupts.

19. Some interrupts originate with hardware; others, with software. Why?

20. Sketch the contents of memory immediately after DOS has been booted.

16

Segmentation, Paging, and Virtual Memory

Most current mainframe systems utilize virtual memory management. This chapter discusses segmentation, paging, and virtual memory. Key topics include:

Memory utilization

Address translation

Segmentation
  Translating segment addresses
  Addressing the operating system
  Segmentation and memory management

Paging
  Paging and memory management

Segmentation and paging

Virtual memory
  Addressing virtual memory
  Virtual-equals-real area
  Thrashing
  Implementing virtual memory

These concepts are crucial to understanding Chapters 17 through 22.

Memory Utilization

Multiprogramming implies several programs sharing memory and executing concurrently. Generally, adding another program to memory means improving system utilization. As the number of programs increases, interference eventually overwhelms gains in efficiency, but the limiting factor is usually memory space, not processor time.

Fixed-partition memory management wastes space. Dynamic memory management is more efficient, but tends to leave small fragments of unused space spread throughout memory. More of this space can be utilized if programs are broken into independently addressed segments or pages and loaded into noncontiguous memory. With virtual memory, programs are stored on a secondary device, and only active pages or segments are loaded. Each technique represents an improvement in memory, hence, processor utilization. However, moving from simple fixed-partition to virtual memory management does have a price—increased complexity.

Address Translation

Each memory location in a computer is assigned a unique **absolute address**. Usually, the bytes or words are numbered sequentially, starting with zero. Hardware fetches and stores data by absolute address.

While absolute addresses are essential to hardware, they are inconvenient for software. For one thing, referencing absolute addresses can restrict a program to a fixed load point. That might be acceptable on a single-user system, but on a multiple-user system, specifying an absolute address can force a program to wait until a particular region of memory is available (and that might *never* happen).

Relative addressing is a common solution. Programs are written as though they begin at address 0, and every location in the program is addressed relative to its **entry point.** When the program is loaded into memory, the absolute address of its entry point is loaded into a base register. As the program runs and instructions are fetched, the addresses found in the operands are expressed in relative terms. Before an instruction executes the processor computes the absolute address of any referenced location by adding its displacement to the **base address** (Fig. 16.1).

Figure 16.1   As a program runs, the absolute address of any
referenced memory location is computed by adding a
displacement to the contents of a base register.

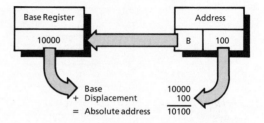

With base-plus-displacement addressing, a program can be
relocated in memory each time it is loaded. For example, if a program is loaded at absolute address 10000, its 100th byte (**displacement** 100 from the beginning of the program) is absolute
address 10100. If, next time the program runs, it is loaded at
20000, its 100th byte will be 20100. In either case, a reference
to the base address plus 100 will get the program's 100th byte.

While it makes sense for software to record and manipulate
relative addresses, *hardware* still requires *absolute* addresses.
Before an instruction can be executed, the addresses specified in
its operands must be translated, and that takes time. **Address
translation** is performed by hardware during I-time, immediately before the instruction is executed.

Segmentation

With **segmentation** programs are divided into independently addressed segments and stored in noncontiguous memory (Fig.
16.2). Structured programming stresses independent modules
and subroutines, so segmentation requires little additional effort on the programmer's part. Individual segments are smaller
than complete programs, and thus better fit into small openings
in memory, yielding improved memory utilization. There are additional costs, however. If a program is loaded as a set of independently addressed segments, the operating system must keep
track of each segment's entry point, and that complicates address translation.

Figure 16.2   Segmentation complicates address translation
because programs are broken into independent
segments and stored in noncontiguous memory.

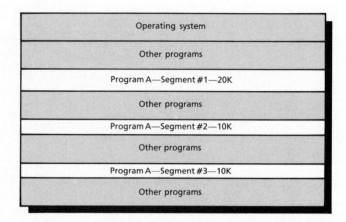

| Operating system |
| Other programs |
| Program A—Segment #1—20K |
| Other programs |
| Program A—Segment #2—10K |
| Other programs |
| Program A—Segment #3—10K |
| Other programs |

Translating Segment Addresses

Often, the solution is adding a step to the address translation
process. Programmers still write the same code, and compilers
still generate base-plus-displacement addresses. After fetching
an instruction, the instruction control unit still expands each
operand address by adding the base register and the displacement. Up to this point, there is no apparent difference between a
segmented system and a contiguous program system.

Traditionally, the expanded address was an absolute address. On a segmented system, however, the expanded address
consists of two parts: a segment number and a displacement
within the segment (Fig. 16.3). To compute the absolute address,
hardware extracts the segment number, uses that number to
search a **segment table,** finds the segment's entry point address, and, finally, adds the displacement to it, yielding an absolute address.

When a program is loaded, the operating system builds a segment table listing the entry points of each of its segments. Later,
when the program gets control of the processor, the address of
its segment table is loaded into the **segment table location register.** During program execution, this register and the segment

Figure 16.3   To compute an absolute address using segmentation, break the address into segment and displacement portions, use the segment number to find the segment's entry point address in a segment table, and add the displacement to the entry point address.

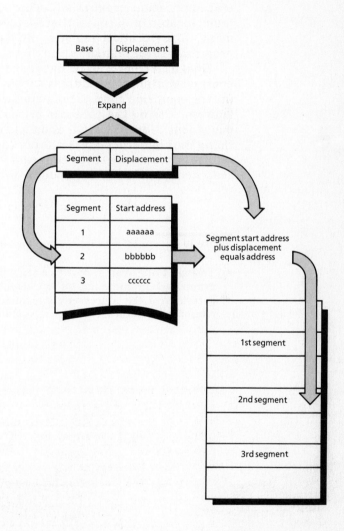

table are used by the processor to dynamically translate addresses.

For example, step through the **dynamic address translation** process on a computer that uses a 16-bit address consisting of a 4-bit segment number and a 12-bit displacement (Fig. 16.4). The first program in memory is the operating system. Next come several application programs. Focus on program A. Its segment table, located in the operating system and pointed to by the segment table location register, holds the entry points of the program's three segments (Fig 16.4a).

Imagine the processor has just fetched an instruction. One operand contains the address shown in Fig. 16.4b. After checking the operation code, the instruction control unit expands this address, adding the contents of the base register and the displacement. Now, the final address translation process begins. Using the high-order 4 bits, the program's segment table (which, remember, is pointed to by the segment table location register) is searched, yielding the segment's entry point address. The last

Figure 16.4   An example of dynamic address translation.

a. The operating system creates a segment table when it loads a program. Each program has its own segment table. When a program gets control, the address of its segment table is loaded into the segment table location register.

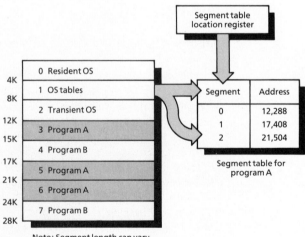

Note: Segment length can vary.

b. As the program runs, the segment table provides a base address for computing absolute addresses.

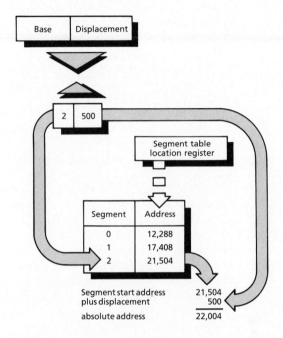

12 bits are then added to this base address, giving an absolute address in memory.

Addressing the Operating System

Look back at Fig. 16.4, and note the relative positions of the operating system's segments. Generally, the resident operating system occupies low memory beginning with address 0, so the operating system's segment table has a rather unusual property; its segment/displacement and absolute addresses are identical (Fig. 16.5). Except by chance, this happens only in low memory and, since the operating system occupies low memory can be assumed only in the operating system.

The operating system is the one place where machine-dependent programs must be written and absolute addressing must be used. When the operating system is running, once the instruction control unit completes its initial base-plus-displacement

Figure 16.5   Because the operating system begins at memory address 0, its segment/displacement and absolute addresses are identical.

| Address | | Absolute | Binary address | | Absolute |
Seg.	Disp.	address	Seg.	Disp.	binary address
0	000	0	0000	000000000000	0000000000000000
0	FFF	4095	0000	111111111111	0000111111111111
1	000	4096	0001	000000000000	0001000000000000
1	FFF	8191	0001	111111111111	0001111111111111
2	000	8192	0010	000000000000	0010000000000000
2	FFF	12,287	0010	111111111111	0010111111111111

computation, no additional address translation is needed. Generally, a special flag that tells hardware to skip dynamic address translation is turned on when a resident operating system module has control.

Segmentation and Memory Management

The operating system maintains a table (something like the one pictured in Fig. 16.6) listing regions of memory that are in use and regions that are free. Before it loads a new program, the operating system searches this table to locate free space. Note that the table has nothing to do with programs already in memory; it is used to determine where *new* programs can be loaded.

Segmentation allows efficient program loading simply because segments are smaller than complete programs and will therefore fit into smaller spaces. Note, however, that segment size can vary. If, for example, the maximum segment size is 64K, a given segment might hold 1 byte, 64K bytes, or any number in between. From a software perspective, that is good; segment break points can be matched to the program's logic. However, if no segment is small enough to fit into an available memory fragment, that space will be wasted. Also, because memory management involves tracking numerous, variable-length units of storage, segmentation adds to the operating system's complexity.

Fig. 16.6   The operating system manages memory space by
maintaining a table of free space. Before loading a
program, the operating system searches this table.
Note that segment size can vary.

Start address	Length	Status
0K	16K	In Use
16K	8K	Free
24K	16K	In Use
40K	4K	Free
44K	12K	In Use
66K	10K	Free

Note: Status
is usually
represented by
a simple bit flag.

Paging

Under **paging** a program is broken into *fixed-length* pages. Page
size is generally small (2K to 4K), and chosen with hardware efficiency in mind. Given small, fixed-length pages, fragmentation

Figure 16.7   A program's pages can be loaded into noncontiguous
memory.

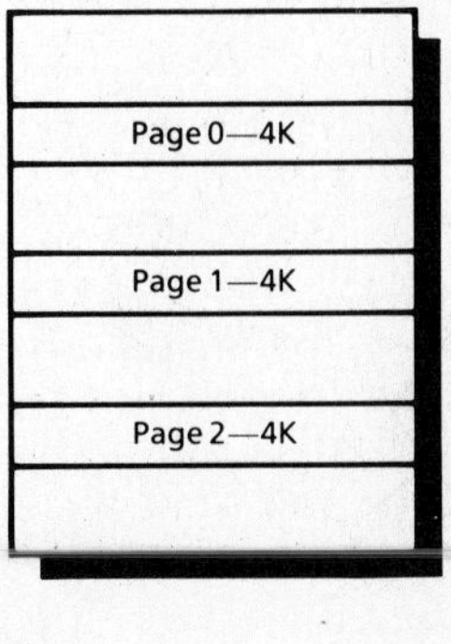

Page 0—4K

Page 1—4K

Page 2—4K

Figure 16.8   To compute an absolute address under paging, break
the address into page and displacement portions, use
the page number to find the page's entry point
address in a page table, and add the displacement to
this entry point address.

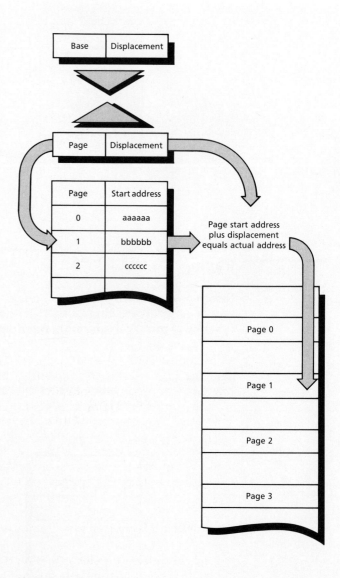

Figure 16.9   A paging operating system maintains a page frame
table to track the status of each main memory page.

Page frame number	Program ID	Page number	Status
0	Operating system	1	1
1	Operating system	2	1
2	Operating system	3	1
3	Operating system	4	1
4	Program A	1	1
5	Program B	1	1
6	Program A	2	1
7	Program C	1	1
8			0
9			0
10	Program A	3	1
11	Program C	2	1
.			0
.			

is no longer a problem, and memory management is relatively
easy to implement.

A program's pages can be loaded into noncontiguous memory (Fig. 16.7). Addresses consist of two parts (Fig. 16.8), a page
number and a displacement. Addresses are dynamically translated as the program runs. When an instruction is fetched, its
base-plus-displacement addresses are expanded by hardware.
Then, an absolute address is computed by looking up the page's
base address in a program **page table** and adding the displacement. What was called a segment table location register becomes
a **page table location register**.

Paging and Memory Management

Paging simplifies memory management because all pages are
the *same* length, so the system never has to check size. The operating system maintains a **page frame table** (Fig. 16.9) holding

flags that indicate each page's status (free or in use). For example, to locate a free page, the operating system might search the page frame table for a "0" status bit, assign the first free page to the program, and then change the status bit to a "1."

Note the difference between this page frame table and the program page table described earlier. The page frame table is used by the operating system to allocate memory space. The program page table supports dynamic address translation for programs already in memory.

Some wasted space is inevitable with *any* memory allocation scheme, and paging is no exception. Programmers do not code in fixed-length increments, so almost every program will have at least one page that is only partially filled. In effect, *any* fixed-length page is bound to be the wrong length.

Segmentation and Paging

Segmentation complements actual program logic. Paging is more hardware oriented, with page sizes geared to a system's memory allocation scheme; consequently, it's a bit easier to manage loading pages. Why not combine segmentation and paging? Programs could then be broken into logical segments, and the segments subdivided into fixed-length pages. Thus, a programmer could plan a segment structure, while the system loads pages.

With **segmentation *and* paging,** addresses are divided into a segment number, a page number within that segment, and a displacement within that page (Fig. 16.10). After the instruction control unit expands the relative address, dynamic address translation begins. First, the program's segment table is found (through the segment table location register) and searched for the segment number. This table, in turn, gives the address of the segment's page table. The page table is then searched for the page's base address, which is added to the displacement to get an absolute address.

Dynamic address translation under segmentation and paging involves a great deal of overhead. Fortunately, there are shortcuts. When a well-designed program references an address on a particular page, the chances are very good that the next instruction will reference the same page. Most segmentation and paging systems take advantage of this relationship to boost dynamic address translation.

Figure 16.10   A segment *and* paging address is divided into three
parts: a segment, a page, and a displacement. Thus,
dynamic address translation involves two table
look-up operations.

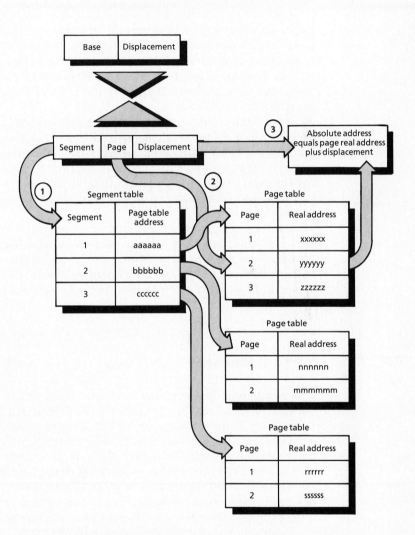

When an address is translated, its page base address is
stored in one of several **page address registers.** As dynamic address translation begins for subsequent instructions, these registers are checked in parallel. If the desired base address is in a
register, the relatively slow address translation process is

skipped. However, if the page's base address is not in a register, it must be computed through the segment and page tables. It then replaces the "least currently accessed" entry in the page address registers. Consequently, these registers always list the most currently referenced page base addresses.

Consider, for example, a small program consisting of a single page. As the program begins, its first instruction references a data field on that page, so the entry point address is dynamically translated through the tables and stored in a page address register. As additional instructions reference data fields on the same page, the base address is already in the registers, so addresses are quickly translated.

Eventually, the program finishes processing. The computer, however, continues working with other programs, dynamically translating their addresses. Given time, all other entries in the page address registers will be more current than the reference to the original program's page, so its page address will be the next one dropped from the array to make room for a new page address.

Under segmentation and paging, memory is managed much as it is in a pure paging system, with the operating system maintaining a page frame table. Once again, remember that the page frame table is used by the operating system to allocate memory space and has nothing to do with the actual execution of already loaded programs.

Virtual Memory

If a processor can execute only one instruction at a time, it should not be necessary for *every* instruction in a program to be in memory before that program can begin executing. Chapter 5 briefly discussed overlay structures in which only portions of a program are in memory at any given time. Those early overlay structures were precursors of modern **virtual memory** systems.

The word virtual means "not in actual fact." Virtual memory *seems* like **real memory,** but it isn't. On a traditional system, programs are loaded from a library directly into memory. On a virtual memory system, programs are loaded from a library into *virtual* memory (Fig. 16.11). Selected portions are then paged into real memory for execution.

To the programmer, virtual memory looks just like real memory. Normally, disk space is used to physically simulate virtual memory. The disk space is broken into fixed-length parti-

Figure 16.11 On a virtual memory system, programs are loaded into partitions or regions on secondary *virtual* memory, and then paged into *real* memory for execution.

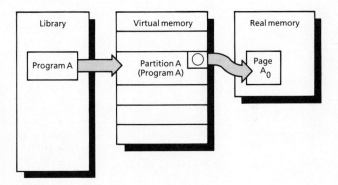

tions or variable-length regions, and one program is loaded into each one. Pages or segments are then transferred between virtual and real memory; the programmer has no control over the physical paging process.

Addressing Virtual Memory

Figure 16.12 shows an example of virtual memory. The programs are physically stored on disk. Visualize the disk space as a series of segments and pages. Granted a disk's contents are *really* addressed by track and sector, but because both addressing schemes are sequential, it's easy to convert between a track/sector address and a segment/page address.

Now, move inside real memory. The operating system maintains a real page frame table to help it allocate real memory pages (Fig. 16.13). Segment and page tables (Fig. 16.14) describe all the pages associated with any active program, no matter where they may be physically stored.

To read a page from virtual into real memory, the operating system searches the page frame table for a free page. Once it finds one, the page's status is changed to "busy," and the page-

Figure 16.12   The contents of virtual memory can be assigned segment and page addresses.

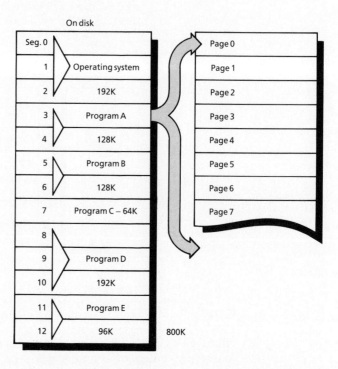

On disk

Seg. 0	
1	Operating system
2	192K
3	Program A
4	128K
5	Program B
6	128K
7	Program C – 64K
8	
9	Program D
10	192K
11	Program E
12	96K

800K

| Page 0 |
| Page 1 |
| Page 2 |
| Page 3 |
| Page 4 |
| Page 5 |
| Page 6 |
| Page 7 |

Figure 16.13   A virtual memory operating system allocates *real* memory by maintaining a page frame table.

Page	Program	Program segment and page		Status
0	OS	0	0	1
1	OS	0	1	1
2	OS	0	2	1
3	OS	0	3	1
4	OS	0	4	1
5	OS	0	5	1
6	OS	0	6	1
7	A	3	5	1
8	B	2	9	0	← Free page
9	E	1	1	1
10	B	2	1	0
11	D	5	12	1

Figure 16.14   A virtual memory operating system keeps track of
active programs by maintaining segment and page
tables for all program pages, no matter where they are
physically stored.

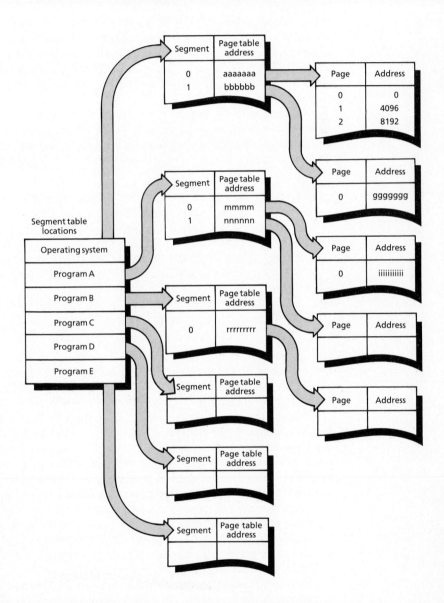

in operation begins. Finally, the physical address of the selected page frame is recorded in the segment and page tables.

The instructions that run on a virtual memory system are identical to the instructions that run on a regular system. The operands hold relative (base-plus-displacement) addresses. Immediately after an instruction is fetched, the instruction control unit expands the address by adding the displacement to the contents of a base register. On a regular system, the base register holds the program's load point in real memory. On a virtual system, the base register holds the program's load point in *virtual* memory, so the computed address reflects the page's *virtual* memory location.

Unfortunately, the real processor can't work with virtual addresses, so additional address translation is necessary. Assume segment/page addressing. To convert a virtual address to a real address, hardware

1. accesses the segment table using the high-order bits of the virtual address as a key,
2. locates the proper page table using the pointer in the segment table,
3. accesses the page table to find the page's base address, using the virtual address's middle bits as a key, and, finally,
4. adds the displacement found in the low-order bits of the virtual address to the base address.

On most systems, the translation process is streamlined through the use of page address registers. (In other words, virtual address translation is just like segment/page/displacement address translation.)

What happens when a virtual address points to a page that is not in real storage? Each page table entry contains a flag called (by IBM, at least) the invalid bit. Imagine that 0 bit indicates the page is in real storage and a 1 bit means the page is in virtual memory. When hardware encounters a 1 bit at the end of the translation process, a **page fault** is recognized and an interrupt generated, causing a link to the operating system's page-in module. If a survey of the page frame table shows no real memory available for the new page, some other page must be paged-out. While many different schemes have been implemented, most are based on a least currently accessed algorithm.

Bringing pages into memory only when they are referenced is called **demand paging.** An option called prepaging involves predicting the demand for a new page and bring it into memory before it is actually needed. Many prepaging algorithms assume that segments hold logically related code; for example, if instructions on page 1 are currently executing, the chances are that instructions on page 2 will be executed next. While far from perfect, such techniques can significantly speed up a program.

Virtual-Equals-Real Area

You may have noticed that the operating system, as pictured in Figs. 16.12 and 16.13, occupies the same locations in both real and virtual memory. Operating system routines perform such tasks as dynamically modifying channel programs and often refer to absolute addresses, so it makes sense to load the operating system in such a way that the virtual, real, and absolute addresses for key control fields and resident modules are identical. This is possible only in low memory, so the operating system begins at address 0 both in virtual and real. The region of memory where virtual, real, and absolute addresses match is called the **virtual-equals-real area.**

Thrashing

When real memory is full, a demand for a new page means that another must be paged-out. If this happens frequently, the system can find itself doing so much paging that little time is left for useful work. This is called **thrashing**, and it can seriously degrade system performance. The solution is to remove a program or two from real memory until the system settles down.

One possible cause is poor program design. For example, a program that branches frequently to widely separated modules or references data fields spread haphazardly throughout memory can be a disaster on a virtual memory system. Top-down or structured programming can help.

Implementing Virtual Memory

In a traditional multiprogramming system, the operating system and several application programs are loaded into memory. On a virtual memory system, programs are loaded into secondary storage, and then paged into real memory as necessary. Think of virtual memory as a staging area. Visualize it holding the operating system and application programs. Then visualize selected, active pages moving into real memory, and you'll have a good mental picture of how virtual memory systems work. The only problem with this visual image is that much of the operating system must be stored in real memory. Consequently, it appears twice, once in real and once in virtual.

Figure 16.15 illustrates a more common approach. It shows three levels of storage—virtual memory, the **external paging device**, and real memory. Virtual memory contains the operating system and all the application programs; it matches the visual image described in the prior paragraph. But it does not physically exist anywhere; it is just a model. Virtual memory's contents are physically stored in real memory and on the external paging device. Real memory is good, old-fashioned main memory, directly addressable by the processor. The paging device is usually disk.

Virtual memory is divided into two components. The first is exactly equal to the amount of real memory on the system, and its contents are physically stored in real. It contains the resident operating system and the transient program area (called the **page pool**). The second component consists of space over and

---

Figure 16.15   Virtual memory is a model that holds space for the operating system and several application programs. The operating system and selected pages occupy real memory. Application programs are physically stored on an external paging device.

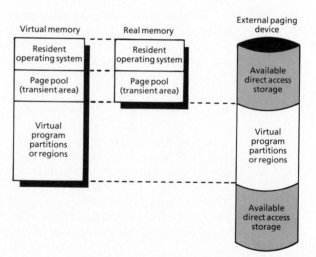

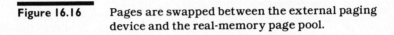

Figure 16.16 Pages are swapped between the external paging device and the real-memory page pool.

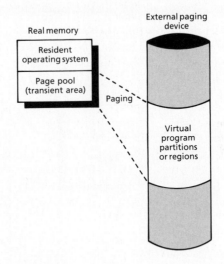

Figure 16.17 In this example, 4 megabytes of virtual memory will be supported by a computer containing only 1 megabyte of real memory.

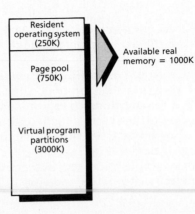

Figure 16.18   The operating system and the page pool are in real
                     memory. The external paging device holds contents of
                     virtual memory over and above real memory's
                     capacity (the application programs). Selected pages
                     move between the external paging device and the page
                     pool.

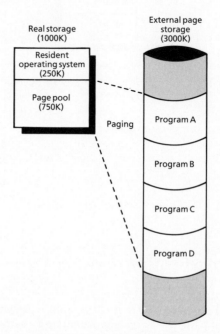

above real memory capacity. This second part is physically
stored on the external paging device. It contains the application
programs.

The resident operating system is loaded into real memory at
initial program load or boot time. Application programs are
loaded into partitions or regions on the external paging device
by the operating system's scheduling routine. Selected pages are
then swapped between the real memory page pool and the external paging device (Fig. 16.16).

For example, picture a system with 1000K (1 megabyte) of
real memory. Its virtual memory might hold 4 megabytes—four

times as much. Visualize virtual memory's contents. Start with a 250K operating system and a 750K page pool. Those two components alone match the available real memory space. The remaining 3 megabytes represent space over and above real memory's capacity (Fig. 16.17). The first megabyte, containing the operating system and the page pool, is stored in real memory (Fig. 16.18). The second 3 megabytes are stored on the external paging device, and pages are swapped back and forth between it and the page pool.

Traditionally, the operating system's memory management module was concerned with allocating space in main memory. On a virtual system, an equivalent module allocates space on the external paging device. This space can be divided into fixed-length partitions, variable-length regions, segments, pages, or any other convenient unit. Transferring pages between the external paging device and real memory is a system function that is transparent to the programmer. It is reasonable to view the act of paging much as you view the transfer of an instruction from memory into the instruction register for execution.

Summary

Hardware deals with absolute memory addresses. Software normally works with relative addresses. When an instruction is fetched, the instruction control unit translates its relative addresses to absolute form before executing it.

Under segmentation, a program is broken into variable-size segments that can be independently loaded into noncontiguous memory, thus improving memory utilization. Because the segments must be independently addressed, the addressed translation process is a bit more complex. Once an address is expanded, its high-order bits are used to look up a base address in a segment table. The base address is then added to the displacement to get an absolute address. Paging is similar except that pages are fixed in length. A segmentation *and* paging system enjoys many of the best features of both, with programs broken into logical segments and the segments subdivided into pages.

On a virtual memory system, programs are loaded, in segment or page form, on a direct access device, and individual pages are paged-in to real memory as needed. Virtual memory is a logical model that contains everything traditionally stored in main memory, including the operating system and application programs. Real memory holds the operating system and a page pool. Virtual memory space above and beyond the available real memory contains the application programs; physically, they are stored on an external paging device, which is divided into partitions or regions. Pages are swapped between real memory and the external paging device.

Key Words

absolute address	page fault	segment table
address translation	page frame table	segment table
base address	page pool	location register
demand paging	page table	segmentation
displacement	page table location	segmentation and
dynamic address	register	paging
translation	paging	thrashing
entry point	prepaging	virtual-equals-real
external paging	real memory	area
device	relative address	virtual memory
page address		
registers		

Exercises

1. Explain the difference between an absolute address and a relative address. Why are both types needed?

2. The instruction control unit translates the addresses it finds in an instruction's operands before that instruction is executed. Why?

3. Explain how a program's segments can be loaded into non-contiguous memory and independently addressed. How are the segment table and segment table location register involved?

4. Why is segmentation more difficult to implement than fixed-partition memory management?

5. Distinguish between segmentation and paging.

6. Why is a page-oriented memory management system easier to implement than a segment-oriented memory management system?

7. Explain segmentation *and* paging.

8. Explain dynamic address translation. Why are associative array registers or page address registers necessary?

9. How does a virtual memory system work? Distinguish between virtual memory and real memory.

10. What is a page fault? If a virtual memory system finds it necessary to page-out a page to free some space, how is this page selected?

11. Distinguish between demand paging and prepaging.

12. Why is something like a virtual-equals-real feature needed on a virtual memory system?

13. What are the advantages of virtual memory? What are the disadvantages?

14. Virtual memory does not make a computer faster—just more efficient. Explain.

15. Virtual memory does not physically exist. Explain.

16. If virtual memory is a logical model of memory's contents, where are those contents physically stored?

17
UNIX

UNIX is a multiple-user operating system that, at least on larger systems, utilizes virtual memory management. This chapter introduces UNIX internals. Key topics include:

The UNIX system

Images and processes
  Process creation
  Initialization
  Process management

The shell

Time-slicing and interrupts

Memory management
  Swapping (or paging)
  Memory space and reentrant code

The file system
  Accessing disk files
  Managing disk space
  Buffering

UNIX internals

The UNIX System

When Thompson and Ritchie developed UNIX, their primary objective was creating a friendly working environment for writing programs. Because program development is an interactive task, response time was an important measure of effectiveness, so UNIX became a time-sharing system. Simplicity, ease of use, and elegance were key design criteria; hardware efficiency and throughput were not.

A UNIX user communicates with the system through a **shell** (Fig. 17.1). Essentially a command interpreter, the shell is treated much like an application program and is technically not part of the operating system. This is an important UNIX innovation, because it allows a user to replace the standard shell with a custom shell. For example, a professional programmer might consider the rather terse commands associated with the Bourne shell (see Chapter 9) easy to use, while a nontechnical user might find the same commands intimidating. The solution is a custom shell for that nontechnical user, with, perhaps, a graphic user interface (GUI) with icons or menus replacing traditional commands.

It is even possible to bypass the shell. For example, imagine a user who, day after day, performs a single application such as data entry. Instead of forcing this user to learn shell commands, the appropriate application program can be loaded and the user allowed to communicate directly with it. Another advantage is security. Since this user is limited to a single application, he or she cannot poke around in other parts of the system by typing shell commands.

Among its resident modules, UNIX contains an input/output control system, a file system, and routines to swap segments, handle interrupts, schedule the processor's time, manage memory space, and allocate peripheral devices. Additionally, the operating system maintains several tables to track the system's status. Routines that communicate directly with the hardware are concentrated in a relatively small **kernel** (Fig. 17.1). The kernel is hardware dependent and varies from system to system. However, the interface to the kernel is generally consistent across implementations.

Because most operating systems are written in assembler language, they are limited to a single family of computers. UNIX, on the other hand, was written primarily in a high-level language (C), making it highly portable (only a small portion of the kernel is written in assembler). Today, UNIX is a standard, particularly

Fig. 17.1   A UNIX user communicates with the operating system
through a shell. Hardware-dependent logic is
concentrated in the kernel.

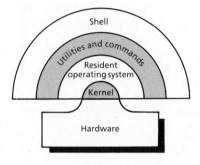

in the academic world, and is available on a variety of machines.
More important, however, is the impact UNIX has had on the design of other operating systems. For example, the current versions of DOS (see Chapter 16) clearly reflect the UNIX influence.

UNIX is a time-sharing system, with program segments
swapped in and out of memory as required. To ensure reasonable response time, processor access is limited by time-slicing.
Segmentation is the most common addressing scheme, and most
UNIX systems implement virtual memory techniques.

Images and Processes

The pseudocomputer concept is another important UNIX innovation. A user's routine is viewed as an **image,** defined by
Ritchie and Thompson as an "execution environment" that consists of program and data storage, the contents of general-
purpose registers, the status of open files, the current directory,
and other key elements. To the user, it *appears* that this image
is executed on a private **pseudocomputer** under control of a
command-driven operating system. In reality, UNIX is a
multiple-user, time-sharing system.

An image consists of three segments (Fig. 17.2). First, starting at virtual address 0, is a program **text segment,** followed by

Fig. 17.2   An image consists of a program text segment, a data
                 segment, and a stack segment.

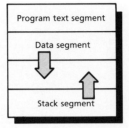

a **data segment.** The image ends with a **stack segment.** Between
the data and the stack segments is a free area. As the program
runs, the data segment grows toward high memory (down in Fig.
17.2), and the stack segment grows toward low memory.

The execution of an image is called a **process.** As a process
executes, the image's text, data, and stack segments must be in
memory. (Note: they need not occupy contiguous memory.)
Thus, the image is not *really* executed on a pseudocomputer. Instead, the image and the pseudocomputer serve as virtual models of the user's environment.

The program text segment is reentrant; it can be shared.
UNIX, remember, is a multiple-user system. If two or more users
access the same program, only one text segment is physically
stored in memory. Both users will have their independent images. Both will *imagine* that they, and they alone, have access to
their program code. Physically, however, they will share a single
text segment (Fig. 17.3).

The data and stack segments, on the other hand, are private;
for example, if two users are executing the same code, memory
will hold one text segment, two data segments, and two stack
segments. Additionally, each process has its own **system data
segment** containing data needed by the operating system when
the process is active. This system data segment is not part of the
user's image; the user cannot access it. When the user calls the
system (for example, to request I/O), the process switches from a
user state to a system state, making the system data segment
available to UNIX.

Fig. 17.3   The text segment is reentrant. If two or more processes are executing the same code, only a single shared text segment is physically stored in real memory. The data and stack segments, however, are private.

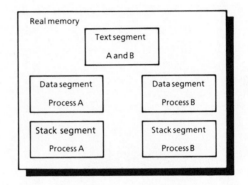

Process Creation

A process is created by a system call named *fork.* The *fork* system call, part of the operating system, is called by an executing process. In response, UNIX duplicates that process, creating two identical copies. Because both copies contain the system data segment, they share open files and other key data. The operating system distinguishes between the **parent** and the **child** by giving them different return codes from the *fork* call. Thus, although the parent and the child are identical, they can check the return code and take different actions.

The parent starts the operation by calling *fork.* It's a system call, so a return address is stored in the process's system data area and UNIX gets control. After the duplicate process is created, control returns to the parent, which checks the return code. By convention, the parent gets the process number (called the **process id,** or **pid**) of the child (a positive integer), while the child gets a return code of 0 (a negative return code indicates an error). Because the return code is positive, the parent normally calls *wait,* and waits for the child to die[1] (Fig. 17.4a).

---

[1] Or to finish processing. UNIX terminology can be a bit morbid.

Fig. 17.4   UNIX process creation.

a. The parent calls *fork*. In response, the operating system creates a
    duplicate process (the child), and returns control to the parent.
    Since the return code is a positive integer, the parent drops into a
    wait state.

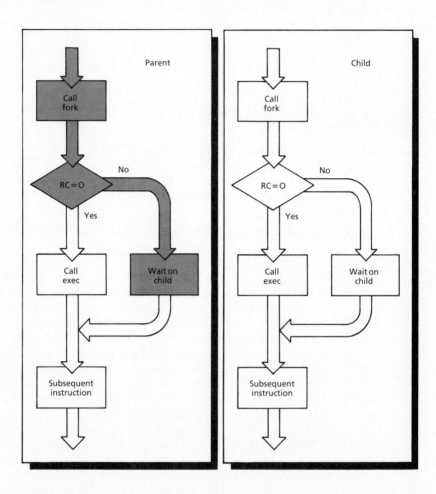

Eventually, the child begins to execute. Because it is a duplicate of the parent, the return address in its system data area
points to the instruction immediately following *fork* (addresses
are virtual). The child begins by checking the return code (Fig.
17.4b). It's 0, so the child calls another system call, **exec.** The

Fig. I7.4   (continued)

b. The child begins by checking the return code. Because it's 0, the
    child calls *exec*.

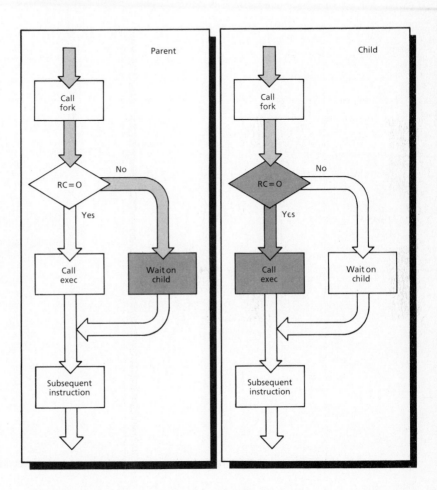

exec routine responds by overlaying the child's text and data
segments with the contents of a new file (Fig. 17.4c). Technically, the resulting image is still the same process, but its contents are different, and UNIX might have to rearrange memory
to accommodate the new segment. Later, when the child dies,
the parent can resume processing (Fig. 17.4d).

Fig. 17.4   (continued)

c. The *exec* routine overlays the child's text and data segments with the contents of a new file.

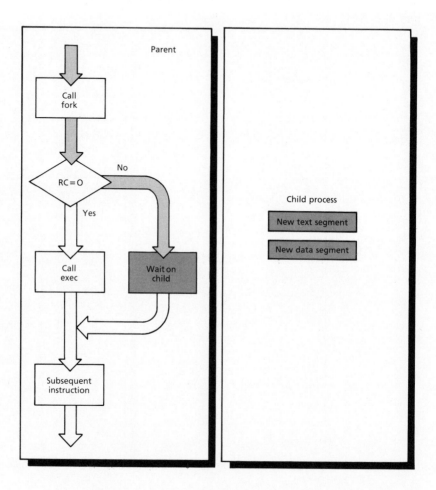

Briefly review the process creation sequence, because it's important. The parent calls *fork*. In response, UNIX duplicates the process, and returns control to the parent. Because the return code is a positive integer (the child's process number), the parent calls *wait*, and "goes to sleep" until the child dies.

Eventually, the child gets control. It is a duplicate of the parent. When the parent called *fork*, the address of its next instruc-

Fig. 17.4   (continued)

d. When the child dies, the parent resumes processing. Note that the child process no longer exists.

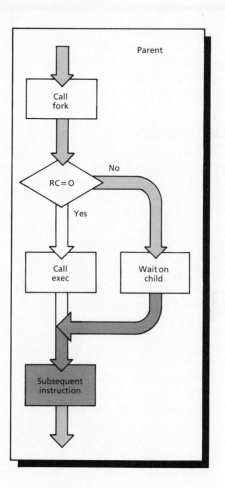

tion was recorded in the system data area. The child's system data area contains the same (virtual) return address, so when the child gets control, the instruction following fork is executed. Typically, this instruction checks the return code. Because the return code is 0, *exec* is called, and a new program overlays the child. Following *exec,* the first instruction in this new program gets control. Eventually, the new program calls *exit,* and thus the child dies. Consequently, the parent is awakened, and, eventually, resumes processing.

Some applications call for parallel parent and child processes. The child is created when the parent calls *fork.* But, instead of calling *wait,* the parent executes regular instructions, so both the parent and the child are active. With most operating systems, radically different commands or parameters are used to define parallel and serial processes. UNIX is remarkably consistent; in fact, its consistency is one reason why professional programmers find it so elegant.

Initialization

When UNIX is booted, a process named *init* is activated. This "original ancestor" creates one system process for each terminal line; for example, if the system supports eight concurrent terminals, eight processes are created. A user logs on to one of these processes. The logon process then (normally) executes (*exec*) the shell, and thus is overlayed. Later, when the shell dies (in other words, when the user logs off), *init* creates a new logon process.

When a user logs on, the logon process scans a table of login names, verifies the password, identifies the user's default shell, and, typically, executes either the Bourne shell or the C shell. Because the shell is treated as a process, it's relatively easy to substitute a custom shell. Another option is no shell. In response to a particular login name, the logon process can start an *application* routine, effectively placing the user inside a restricted shell, thus limiting that user to commands and responses appropriate to that application routine. The logon process overlays itself with the user's primary system interface. When that interface dies, *init* spawns another logon process, which waits for another user to log on.

The image described earlier allows a user to visualize a program. Real memory is a bit more complex, however. Imagine a UNIX system supporting four concurrent users (Fig. 17.5). Three are active, so memory holds three shells. Running under each shell are user processes; note that two or more parallel processes can be associated with a single shell. A fourth potential user has not yet logged on, so the logon process is still active.

The user sees the image of a *single process,* and can imagine that process running, all by itself, on a private pseudocomputer. The details associated with time-slicing, swapping, real-memory

Fig. 17.5   This diagram shows the possible contents of real
                       memory on a UNIX system supporting four
                       concurrent users.

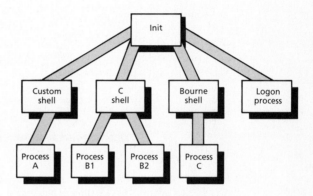

allocation, and physical device access are buried in UNIX, and
thus are transparent to the user.

Process Management

UNIX is a multiple-user operating system, with several concurrent programs occupying memory. It is inevitable that two or
more programs will want the processor at the same time, so the
operating system must carefully schedule them. Thus, UNIX
contains a dispatcher.

The UNIX dispatcher relies on a **process table** that contains
one entry for each process (Fig. 17.6). The entry is allocated
when the process is created (*fork*) and freed when the process
dies. Each entry contains all the data needed by UNIX when the
process is *not* active. Among other things, the process table
entry indicates whether the process is ready (awake) or waiting
(asleep).

For example, imagine the shell (the parent) has just received
a command that requires a new process; and thus has called
fork. In response, UNIX creates the new process, assigns it a process id (a positive integer), adds a new entity to the process table,
and returns control to the shell. The shell then (typically) calls
wait, and goes to sleep until the newly created child dies.

Fig. 17.6   UNIX maintains a process table with one entry per
                       process. The dispatcher uses this information to
                       schedule processes.

One entry per process.

Each entry contains:

    Process number
    Process state (ready, waiting)
    Process priority
    Event number process is waiting on
    Text table address
    Data segment address
    Stack segment address
    System data segment address

Meanwhile, the child gets control, calls *exec*, and carries out
the command. As it finishes processing, it calls *exit* and dies.
The death of a process generates an **event** that produces a **signal.** The event is reported to the operating system's *event-wait*
routine as a positive integer—the event number or process number. UNIX responds by searching the process table and waking
(setting to a ready state) every process waiting for that event.

Each user process has a priority. Priorities are recomputed
frequently by dividing execution time by elapsed real time; the
smaller the number, the higher the priority. When an event signal is sensed, the operating system's *event-wait* routine gets
control. First, it awakens all processes waiting for that event.
Then, it searches the process table, selects the highest priority
ready process, and starts it.

Events occupy no memory. They are represented by a signal.
When a signal is sensed, *event-wait* scans the process table and
awakens all processes waiting for the associated event. Then the
system forgets the event ever happened. What if some time
passes between the decision to wait and the implementation of
the wait state? For example, imagine a process calls *fork*, performs some calculations, and *then* calls *wait*. What if, between
fork and *wait*, the new process gets control and dies? By the time
the parent calls *wait*, the event it plans to wait for has already
happened.

Because the child process has already died, it will not appear
in the process table. When the UNIX *wait* routine gets control, it
checks the process table, and, if the calling routine has no chil-

dren, returns an error code. A programmer should be prepared for this sequence of events any time parallel processes are activated.

The Shell

The UNIX shell is a customized command line interpreter. As you learned earlier in the chapter, UNIX sees the shell as simply another process, so it is subject to change. The idea of a custom shell was an important UNIX innovation.

When *init* creates a logon process, it opens the standard input, output, and error files, so the logon process can accept user input from the terminal and display both normal output and error messages. When a user logs on, the shell overlays the logon process's text and data segments, but the system data segment is not affected. Thus the shell's standard input, output, and error files are open. Consequently, the user can begin issuing commands without opening these standard files.

In response to a command, the shell sets up an *exec*, calls *fork*, and then waits for the child process to carry out the command. If the command is followed by an ampersand (&), the shell does not wait. Instead, it spawns a new process to carry out the command in parallel, and immediately displays a prompt for the next command.

Incidentally, pipes (see Chapter 9) are implemented in the shell. For example, the *cat* command in

```
cat file1  | sort
```

normally reads the contents of *file1* and sends them to its standard output device, the console. The *sort* command accepts data from its standard input device, the console, sorts them, and sends the output to its standard output device, the console, again. In response to the pipe operator, the shell closes the standard output device for *cat*, reassigns it to a pipe, closes the standard input device for *sort*, and reassigns it to the same pipe. Thus, *cat* sends its output to *sort*'s standard input device. The pipeline is transparent to the child processes.

Time-slicing and Interrupts

Under UNIX, the operating system schedules processes by responding to event signals. An event occurs when a process dies or when an interrupt occurs. If the process is compute-bound, considerable time can pass between events, and that, in turn, can negatively impact response time. To minimize the risk that a single process will monopolize the system's time, time-slicing is imposed.

For example, programs might be limited to a single second of processor time. If, during that second, the process voluntarily surrenders control, fine; normal dispatching rules are adequate. If, however, a process exceeds one second, a special event (perhaps, a timer interrupt) is signaled. As a result, *event-wait* is called. After recomputing priorities (thus lowering the offending process's priority), *event-wait* searches the process table and selects the highest priority ready process.

UNIX is supported on a variety of computers, each of which might implement interrupts differently. Interrupt handling routines are located in the UNIX kernel. When an interrupt occurs, control is transferred to the kernel. Once the interrupt is handled, *event-wait* awakens any processes waiting for the interrupt, and then schedules the next process.

Memory Management

UNIX relies on virtual memory and segmentation techniques to manage memory space. The user's image is a virtual model of a pseudocomputer. The text, data, and stack segments making up that image are independently loaded into real memory. As necessary, segments (and even complete images) are swapped out to secondary storage to free space for active processes.

Swapping (or Paging)

When a process first enters real memory, the entire image is loaded. As the process grows, new primary memory is allocated, the process is copied to the new space, and the process table is updated. If sufficient memory is not available, the growing process is allocated space on secondary memory and swapped out. At this point, the process is ready to be swapped back in. Over time, several processes can reside on secondary memory.

The **swapping** process is part of the kernel (Fig. 17.7), so it can be activated each time UNIX gets control. It scans the process table, looking for a ready process that has been swapped out. If it finds one, it allocates primary memory and swaps in the process. If insufficient memory space is available, the swapping

Fig. 17.7   The swapping process is part of the kernel. It scans
the process table, locates a process ready to be
swapped in, allocates memory, and reads the process.
If insufficient primary memory space is available, it
looks for a waiting process to swap out.

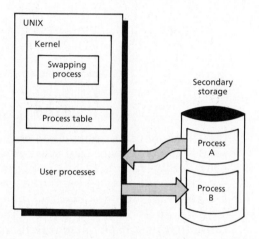

routine selects a process to be swapped out, copies the selected
process to secondary storage, frees the memory space, and then
swaps in the ready process.

   The swap-in decision is based on secondary storage residency time—the longer a process resides on disk, the higher its
priority. Generally, processes waiting for slow events are primary swap-out candidates; if there are several such processes,
age in primary memory is a secondary criterion. A slight penalty
is imposed on large programs. To help minimize thrashing, processes do not become candidates for swapping out until they
have achieved at least a minimum age in primary memory.

   Early versions of UNIX swapped segments. Newer versions
designed to run on page-oriented hardware subdivide segments
into pages and swap pages.

Memory Space and Reentrant Code

The fact that text segments contain reentrant code has memory
management implications. On the one hand, because a single

Fig. 17.8   To keep track of active segments, UNIX maintains a
text table. Note that a single text segment can be
shared by several processes. Each process table entry
points to the text table.

Each text table entry contains:

    The text segment's identification
    The text segment's primary memory address
    Its secondary memory address
    A count of the number of processes using this text segment

text segment can be physically shared by several processes, the
total amount of space that must be allocated to support all those
processes is reduced. On the other hand, if several processes
share the same text segment, that segment's space cannot be released until *all* processes using it have died.

To keep trace of active text segments, UNIX maintains a **text
table** that lists each current text segment, its primary and secondary addresses, and a count of the number of processes sharing it (Fig. 17.8). As a process dies, the count is decremented.
Although the space associated with the data, stack, and system
data segments can immediately be freed, the text segment must
remain in memory until its count reaches zero.

The File System

According to its designers, the **file system** is the key to UNIX. It
offers compatible device, file, and interprocess I/O; in essence,
the user simply sends and receives data. All data are treated as
strings of bytes, and no physical structure is imposed by the system. Instead, the user's program overlays its own structure on
the data. The result is considerable freedom from any concern
for physical I/O.

Block (structured) **devices** (normally, disk) hold files. A hierarchical directory structure (see Chapter 9) maps the entire file
system, and allows the operating system to create, retrieve, and
update data files by name. The information associated with a directory is itself kept in a file (another important UNIX innovation).

Character devices include printers, terminals, and other nonblock peripherals. They operate through a simple queuing process. For example, to output data to a printer, UNIX places bytes, one by one, on the printer's output queue, and the printer's controller subsequently retrieves them, one by one.

Character devices, block devices, and data files are accessed by a common set of system calls (*open, read, write,* and so on); all three are treated as files. Data files are called ordinary files. Files that represent a block or character device are called special files. Once again, consistency makes the operating system easier to use.

Inside the operating system, each physical device is controlled by a **device driver** (Fig. 17.9). All devices attached to the system are listed in a **configuration table** and identified by a major **device number** and a minor device number. When UNIX receives a request to start I/O, it uses the major device number to search the configuration table, finds the address of the appropriate device driver, and then activates the device driver. The minor device number is passed to the device driver. It might designate a specific disk drive on a multiple drive system, a specific

Fig. 17.9   Each physical device is controlled by a device driver. A configuration table lists all the device drivers. When a program requests I/O, UNIX uses the device number to search the configuration table, finds the address of the appropriate device driver, and activates it.

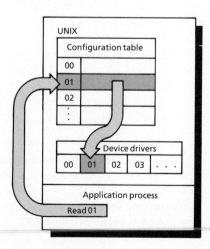

peripheral on a multiplexer channel, or, depending on the device, some other detail. As a system changes, device drivers and configuration table entries can be added or deleted, usually by the system's super user.

Accessing Disk Files

Disk is the standard block device. The disk surface is divided into four regions (Fig. 17.10). The boot block, as the name implies, holds a boot routine. It is followed by a **super block** that identifies the disk, defines the sizes of the disk's regions, and tracks free blocks. The third region holds the **i-list.** Each entry on the i-list is an **i-node,** a 64-byte file definition that lists the disk addresses of blocks associated with a single ordinary file.[2] The i-nodes are numbered sequentially. An i-node's offset from the beginning of the i-list to its **i-number;** the combination of a device number and an i-number defines a specific file. Following the i-list, the remaining space on disk is divided into 512-byte blocks that hold data and/or directories.

A known i-node (often, i-number 2) points to the root directory. When a user logs on, UNIX reads the root directory, finds the user's home directory, and records the home directory's i-number in the process's system data area. In response to a change directory command, UNIX replaces the recorded i-number with the new directory's i-number.

When a program opens an ordinary file (Fig. 17.11), UNIX

Fig. 17.10   A UNIX disk is divided into four regions.

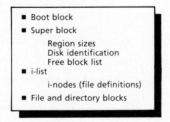

- Boot block
- Super block
     Region sizes
     Disk identification
     Free block list
- i-list
     i-nodes (file definitions)
- File and directory blocks

---

[2]A special file describes a physical device. A special file's i-node holds the device's major and minor device numbers.

Fig. 17.11   When a file is opened, the disk directory is read and
searched for the file name. Associated with the file
name is an i-number that points to a specific i-node.
Recorded in that i-node is the file's disk address.

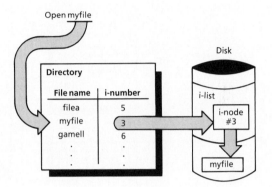

uses the working directory's i-number to begin its search for the
requested file. Each directory entry consists of a file name and
an i-number. Once the file name is found, the associated i-
number points to the file's i-node. That i-node, in turn, contains
a list of block numbers that, directly or indirectly, link all the
file's blocks.

UNIX, remember, is a multiple-user system. Thus, at any
given time, numerous devices and files will be open, and it is
likely that two or more processes will concurrently access the
same disk (or even the same file). To avoid conflicts, the operating system maintains a **system file table,** sometimes called the
i-node table (Fig. 17.12). When the file is opened, its i-node is
copied into the system file table.

To the user's process, the open file is identified by a small,
nonnegative integer number called a **file descriptor.** Within the
process's system data area, the file is listed in a **process file
table.** The process file table entry points, in turn, to an i-node in
the system file table. Thus, the process is aware only of its own
open files. UNIX, on the other hand, can track every open file, no
matter what process it might be associated with.

Later, when the user process calls read or write, UNIX uses
the *process* file table's pointer to locate the file's i-node in the
system file table. That i-node, in turn, provides a start-of-file

Fig. 17.12   UNIX maintains a system file table of the i-nodes of all
open files. Each process maintains a table of its own
open files. A process file table entry points to a
system file table entry which, in turn, points to the
file's location on disk.

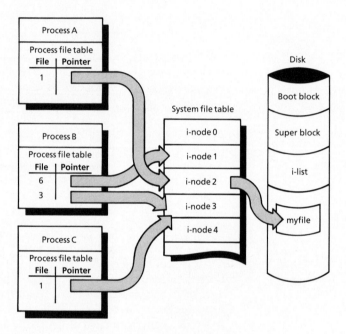

address. Because the file is viewed as a simple string of bytes,
data can be accessed by using relative byte numbers. The UNIX
file system assumes responsibility for converting relative byte
addresses into physical disk addresses and reading or writing
the appropriate block or blocks. The application program makes
sense of these data by overlaying its own data structure.

Managing Disk Space

UNIX is also responsible for managing disk space. When a file is
created or an existing file grows, the operating system scans the
free block list in the super block and allocates space to the file.
The free block list is a series of pointers that link unused disk
blocks. After allocating space, UNIX updates the pointers.

Note that space is allocated dynamically. When a file is first created, it might be assigned several contiguous blocks. Subsequent requests for space might be filled by allocating blocks located anywhere on the disk's surface, however. In addition to pointing to the start-of-file address, the i-node starts a list of pointers that link a file's blocks.

Buffering

All block I/O takes place through a **buffer pool** located in the operating system (no system buffers are found in the user's image). A read command implies a buffer search. If the requested block is already in memory, no physical input operation is needed. If physical I/O is necessary, the least currently accessed buffer is reused, and the block is read into it. Additionally, whenever UNIX must physically read a block, it automatically prereads the next one. Consequently, the data are often already in memory when the next read command is issued.

Normally, when UNIX selects the least currently accessed buffer and renames it, the contents of that buffer are lost. To avoid destroying valid output data residing in a buffer, UNIX responds to a write command by marking the appropriate buffer "dirty" (basically, the operating system sets a switch). No physical output occurs at write time, however. Instead, when the buffer is later identified as least currently accessed, its contents are physically copied to disk before the buffer space is reassigned. Delaying the physical data transfer until a buffer is no longer active also tends to reduce physical I/O.

UNIX implements pipes by taking advantage of its buffering scheme. When data are sent to the standard output device, they are first copied to a buffer, and then output. Likewise, when data are read from the standard input device, they flow from the device, into a buffer, and are subsequently made available to the process. With pipes, the standard output is transferred to a buffer and simply held. The next process then gets its input directly from the first process's output buffer.

By reducing physical I/O operations, UNIX dramatically improves system efficiency. There are, however, disadvantages to the dynamic buffering approach. For one thing, although physical I/O may *appear* synchronous, it is really asynchronous (in other words, physical data transfers and logical read or write commands do not necessarily occur in a predictable time sequence). This makes real-time error reporting or user error handling difficult to implement. Because of the delayed write described earlier, valid output data can be lost if UNIX goes down unexpectedly. Finally, the sequence of logical and physical I/O operations can differ, and this can cause serious problems for applications that rely on data sequence.[3] In spite of these problems, however, the UNIX I/O model has been adopted by a number of modern operating systems.

Fig. 17.13   This diagram summarizes key UNIX system tables.

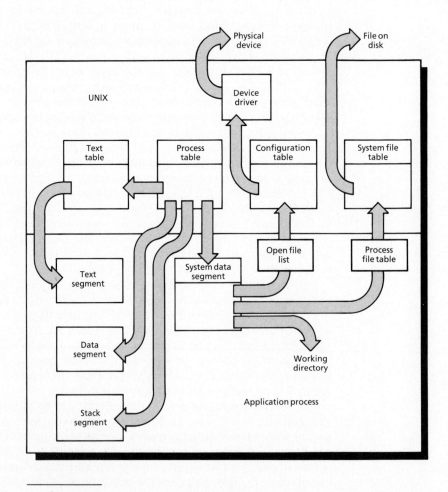

_____

[3]UNIX does allow a user to open a file in raw mode. Such files maintain a logical/physical correspondence.

UNIX Internals

One of the best ways to get an overview of an operating system is to follow the pointers that link the system's components. Figure 17.13 summarizes the key UNIX tables. Start with the process table. For each process, it holds pointers to the process's data segment, stack segment, and system data segment. Additionally, the process table entry points to a text table entry which, in turn, points to the process's text segment. Together, the process table and the text table link all the process's segments.

Each process has a system data segment. The i-number of the user's working directory is stored here. Physical devices are linked to the process through a list of open files. Each open file reference points to a configuration table entry that, in turn, points to a device driver. The files themselves are identified through pointers (in the process file table) to the system file table. Each system file table entry is an i-node that holds a file's disk address.

At first glance, Fig. 17.13 appears complex, but, compared to other operating systems, its use of tables and pointers to link a system's components is remarkably elegant. Indeed, that's one reason why UNIX is so often studied and used as a model for other operating systems.

Summary

UNIX was created as a pleasant working environment for developing programs. Users communicate with the system through a shell. Process management, scheduling, interrupt handling, and memory management routines, as well as device drivers, are concentrated in a relatively small, memory-resident kernel.

To a user, an executing program image appears to be running on a personal pseudocomputer. The image consists of a text segment, a data segment, and a stack segment. To run, the image must be loaded on a real computer; the execution of an image is called a process. The shell is treated as a process. When a user logs on, a default shell is assigned, but the shall can be changed.

Processes are created by the *fork* system primitive. The parent requests a child process by calling *fork*. In response, the operating system creates a child process, an exact duplicate of the parent, and enters the new process in the process table.

Because the child and the parent are passed different return codes, they can take different actions. Normally, the parent calls *wait* and goes to sleep until the child dies. The child routine calls *exec*. UNIX responds by overlaying the process with the contents of a new file. When the new image has finished processing, it calls *exit*, and dies. The death of a process creates an event signal. The operating system's *event-wait* routine then awakens those processes waiting for that event, selects the highest priority ready process, and starts it.

UNIX manages memory space by swapping or paging processes between primary and secondary memory. The process table contains pointers that link the segments making up each process. The text segment is reentrant and might be shared by two or more processes, so text segments are tracked in a separate system text table.

UNIX supports both block and character devices. Files that represent devices are called special files; data files are called ordinary files; both special and ordinary files are accessed by a common set of system calls. Physical I/O operations are controlled by device drivers (one per device). A system's device drivers are listed in a configuration table. An I/O operation references a device umber that is used to search the configuration table for the address of the appropriate device driver. A table of open devices is maintained in each process's system data segment.

A UNIX disk is divided into four regions: a boot block, a super block that identifies the disk and links free blocks, an i-list, and a data area. The i-list contains a series of i-nodes, each of which defines the disk address of a file. A given i-node's relative position on the i-list is its i-number; the combination of a device number and an i-number uniquely defines a file. A special file's i-node holds its major and minor device numbers.

A list of open file i-nodes, called the system file table, is maintained by the operating system. Each process's system data segment holds a process file table with a pointer to a system file table entry for each open file. UNIX manages disk space by maintaining a list of free block pointers in the super block. The i-node starts a series of pointers that link a file's blocks, so the blocks need not be contiguous.

Block I/O takes place through a system buffer pool. When an application process calls read, UNIX searches the buffer pool. If the data are already in memory, no physical input is necessary. If a physical read is necessary, UNIX reads not only the requested block, but the next one as well. If all buffers are full, the least currently accessed buffer is renamed and overlayed. On output, a buffer's contents are not physically transferred following each logical write. Instead, the buffer is marked "dirty." Subsequently, when the buffer becomes the least currently accessed, its contents are physically written before the space is renamed and reused. Because of its dynamic buffering technique, pipes are relatively easy to implement on UNIX. Although this approach efficiently minimizes physical I/O, the fact that logical and physical I/O operations are asynchronous can cause problems.

The chapter ended with a summary of UNIX tables and pointers. Take the time to understand Fig. 17.13.

Key Words

block device	file system	process table
buffer pool	*fork*	pseudocomputer
character device	i-list	shell
child	image	signal
configuration table	*init*	stack segment
data segment	i-node	super block
device driver	i-node table	swapping
device number	i-number	system data
event	kernel	segment
event-wait	parent	system file table
exec	process	text segment
exit	process id	text table
file descriptor	process file table	*wait*

References

1. American Telephone and Telegraph Company (1978). *The Bell System Technical Journal*, July/August, Vol. 57, No. 6, Part 2. Several articles, including: Ritchie, D.M. and Thompson, K., "The UNIX Time-Sharing System"; Thompson, K., "UNIX Implementation"; Ritchie, D.M., "A Retrospective"; and Bourne, S.R., "The UNIX Shell."
2. Bourne, S.R. (1983). *The UNIX System*. Reading, Massachusetts: Addison-Wesley Publishing Company.

3. Deitel, Harvey M. (1989). *An Introduction to Operating Systems,* second edition. Reading, Massachusetts: Addison-Wesley Publishing Company.
4. Foxley, Eric (1985). *UNIX for Super-users.* Reading, Massachusetts: Addison-Wesley Publishing Company.
5. Sobell, Mark G. (1989). *A Practical Guide to the UNIX System,* second edition. Menlo Park, California: The Benjamin/Cummings Publishing Company.

Exercises

1. What is the shell? What is the kernel?

2. UNIX is highly portable. What is portability? What makes UNIX so portable? Why is portability important?

3. Briefly explain the pseudocomputer concept. Relate the pseudocomputer concept to the ease-of-use criterion.

4. Describe (or sketch) a UNIX user's program image.

5. Distinguish an image from a process.

6. A user's text segment is reentrant; it can be shared. Data and stack segments, on the other hand, are private. What does this mean? Why is it significant?

7. Why is the system data segment necessary? It isn't part of the user's image. Why?

8. Briefly explain how processes are created under UNIX.

9. The *fork* primitive creates two *identical* processes. Yet, those processes can yield very different results. Explain.

10. Briefly explain UNIX dispatching.

11. Distinguish between an event and a process.

12. Briefly explain the UNIX swapping process.

13. Why does UNIX need a text table?

14. Explain how UNIX links a peripheral device and an application process.

15. Sketch the contents of a UNIX disk.

16. Briefly explain how UNIX converts a file name to the file's location on disk. Why is the system file table necessary?

17. All block I/O takes place through a buffer pool. Explain.

18. The UNIX buffering scheme makes pipes easy to implement. Explain.

19. Under UNIX, logical and physical I/O are asynchronous. What does this mean? Why is it significant?

20. Briefly explain how UNIX links the various segments that comprise a process. Explain how that process is linked to its physical devices and files.

18

OS/400

This chapter discusses OS/400, the
operating system for IBM's AS/400
computer series. Key concepts include:

The IBM AS/400
  Hardware
  Systems Applications Architecture

OS/400 architecture

System start-up

Memory addressing and memory management
  Virtual memory
  Single-level storage
  Shared objects

Work management
  Jobs
  Subsystems and job queuing
  Spooling

Dispatching

Object management
  Objects
  Libraries

Data management
  File types
  Common data management
  File-specific data management

Software migration

The IBM AS/400

Hardware

The IBM AS/400 is a *multiprocessing* computer system (Fig. 18.1), with several processors sharing the workload. The system processor coordinates the other system components and executes instructions. I/O operations are controlled by **I/O processors** that are linked to the system processor by high-speed bus lines. A system can have several busses, several I/O processors can be attached to each bus, and several devices can be attached to each I/O processor, so an AS/400 can support numerous peripherals. Additionally, a **service processor** provides initial program load (IPL) support and monitors system performance.

The AS/400 uses a heavily microcoded, layered architecture (Fig. 18.2). At the bottom is the hardware. Insulating the hardware from the application software are two layers of microcode that together form IBM's proprietary **licensed internal code,** or LIC. The lower level, called the internal microcode, communicates directly with the hardware. Object-level software deals

Fig. 18.1   The IBM AS/400 is a multiprocessing computer system.

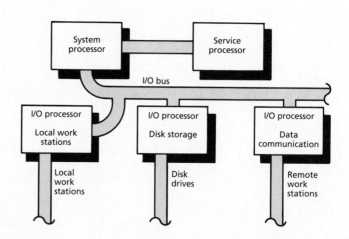

Fig. 18.2   The AS/400 uses a layered architecture.

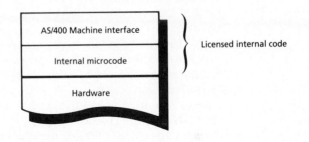

with the top microcode layer, the high-level machine interface (MI). Because of this interface, AS/400 object code is comparable to compiler-level instructions on traditional systems. (Hence the "high-level" interface.) Consequently, the programmer writes fewer instructions to accomplish the same task.

Systems Applications Architecture

The AS/400 is designed to be compatible with IBM's **Systems Applications Architecture**, or SAA, a set of standards and guidelines that define a common interface for the PS/2, AS/400, and System/370 computing environments. The idea is to give applications on each of these platforms a standard "look and feel." One long-term objective is to develop application programs that run with little or no change on all three systems.

A key aspect of Systems Applications Architecture is called the common programming interface, or CPI. It suggests a set of consistent coding standards for database, database query, I/O, and dialogue in several programming languages. On the AS/400 system, this common programming interface is implemented in the various language compilers. A set of guidelines for screen design, function keys, dialogue design, user aids, message and help formats, user options, national languages, and terminology is called the common user access (CUA). Additionally, SAA defines a set of standards for common communications support (CCS).

OS/400 Architecture

The AS/400's operating system, **OS/400** (Fig. 18.3), is object-oriented. Programs, files, libraries, queues, and any other entities that can be stored and/or retrieved are treated as **objects.** The operating system rests on the microcode described earlier. Several functions, such as dispatching, multitasking, virtual address translation, swapping, security, program loading, database management, and I/O management are performed by the licensed internal code.

OS/400's object code includes numerous higher-level routines. Comparable to the DOS file system, object management creates, maintains, and deletes objects by name. Work management provides support for multiprogramming and deals with contention problems. It allows jobs to be submitted by the user and, subsequently, presented to the machine for processing. Control language functions and those data management functions not implemented in microcode are also performed at the object code level.

Application programs include such IBM-licensed software as the *Programming Development Manager, OfficeVision/400, AS/400 Query,* and several compilers. Custom programs are

Fig. 18.3   OS/400 architecture.

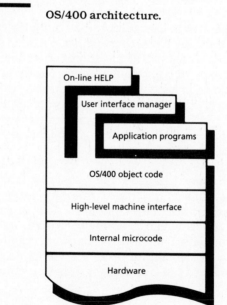

also supported, of course, and many firms sell third-party AS/400 software.

The **user interface manager** (UIM) is the OS/400 command processor or shell. (The OS/400 control language was introduced in Chapter 10.) Commands can be issued by selecting choices from a series of menus or by typing them (the fast path). They can be entered interactively, through the batch job stream, or as part of a control language program. An extensive contextual help facility is also available. Note that a user can communicate with an AS/400 system through an application program, by issuing control language commands, or by requesting help.

OS/400 is a **closed architecture** operating system. Every AS/400 installation gets the same version, and, except for defining the peripheral device configuration and establishing operating environments, the operating system is not custom tuned. One advantage of this approach is that few AS/400 installations need system programmers because so little technical expertise is needed to maintain the system. Also, because the closed architecture is proprietary, it is relatively difficult to copy or to clone, and IBM sees that as a significant competitive advantage. Some technical experts argue that a closed architecture negatively impacts flexibility, but that is not a significant issue for most midrange computer system users.

Adding database management and data communication to a traditional system means purchasing independent database, data communication, and network software. In addition to the initial cost of the software, each package has its own interface, and that complicates program development. Software maintenance is another problem; it is not unusual for a large mainframe installation to employ a small army of expensive system programmers, database specialists, and network managers.

Database management and data communication are integrated into OS/400, so there is no need to purchase additional software or to employ specialists. The system's architecture presents the programmer with a consistent interface to the database, local and remote workstations, and all other peripheral devices, and that simplifies program development. The AS/400 is marketed as a complete, ready-to-use, easy-to-maintain computing environment.

System Start-up

Before you begin to use an AS/400 computer, the operating system must be loaded into memory. System start-up, or **initial**

program load (IPL), procedures are implemented by the service processor whenever the system is turned on. Alternatively, the system can be started from a remote site or by a timer. (For example, the computer can be set to turn itself on fifteen minutes before the office opens.)

Initial program load involves several distinct steps. First, the service processor is tested. The service processor then takes over, tests the I/O bus, accesses the disk or tape drive on which the operating system is stored, and loads its own microcode. That microcode then performs some diagnostics on the system processor and loads the licensed internal code. The system processor then starts the operating system, which initializes the remaining I/O busses in preparation for user access.

Memory Addressing and Memory Management

Virtual Memory

The AS/400 is a virtual memory machine. Hardware uses a 48-bit address that yields up to 281 trillion bytes of virtual memory. The necessary address translation tables are maintained in real memory. Each object is assigned to its own segment. Segments are divided into pages, and physical paging is handled by the microcode. Virtual address translation is another hardware function; a set of translation look-aside buffers helps to improve efficiency.

Real memory not needed by the operating system is divided into one or more noncontiguous storage pools. Each of these pools is then assigned to a subsystem and used by a single group or class of jobs. (You will learn more about subsystems later.) A user can assign a job to a subsystem by specifying the appropriate control language command parameters. Application routines are paged into a pool as they execute.

Single-level Storage

On an AS/400 system, primary and secondary storage are treated as a single, contiguous level of virtual memory (**single-level storage**). Addressing starts with the first byte of real memory, increments sequentially to the last byte in real memory, and then continues, without interruption, from the first to the last byte of secondary storage (Fig. 18.4).

Fig. 18.4   The AS/400 treats main and secondary memory as a
single, contiguous level of storage.

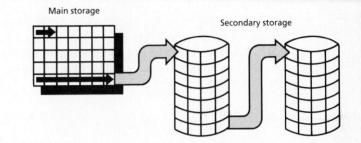

Programs, files, and other entities are all stored as AS/400
objects. An object's location is defined by its virtual address.
Programs are started by calling them by name. The system directory and the various libraries reference virtual addresses, so
the name is converted to a virtual address through the library.
Data are also accessed by virtual address. Consequently, I/O operations are transparent to the user; to find an object, you sim-

Fig. 18.5   AS/400 users often share reentrant software and
access a common database.

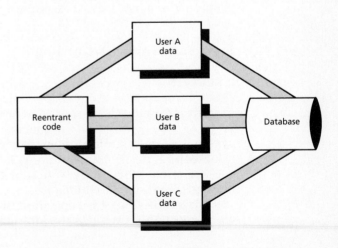

ply reference its virtual address. Objects move into real storage when requested, but the user can ignore the physical details.

Shared Objects

To more efficiently utilize real memory space, AS/400 users often share reentrant software (Fig. 18.5). Obviously, different users need different data, so each user has an independent data area. The AS/400 architecture makes it easy to share common database files, too.

Work Management

Jobs

An AS/400 **job** can consist of any number of related or unrelated functions such as commands or programs. For example, an interactive job is defined as all the tasks the user performs between sign-on and sign-off. User jobs are submitted through local workstations, remote workstations, and the batch job queue. Autostart jobs and prestart jobs are initiated automatically by the system.

An AS/400 is a multiple-user system, so several different jobs can be active concurrently. Additionally, a program can call other programs and users can submit work to a batch queue, so it is possible that any given job can represent several concurrently active programs. The OS/400 **work management** functions support multiprogramming, deal with resource contention problems, and initiate and terminate jobs.

Subsystems and Job Queuing

A **subsystem** is a predefined operating environment that specifies (for a particular group of jobs) the maximum number of concurrent jobs and the amount of available storage pool space. A given AS/400 installation can concurrently support several subsystems; the maximum number is theoretically unlimited. When a job enters an AS/400 system, it is placed on a subsystem's **routing queue** (Fig. 18.6). Note that the subsystem serves as a method for grouping related jobs.

A job's attributes are specified in a job description called a **work entry** that provides the job-related information recorded

Fig. 18.6   When a job enters an AS/400 system, it is placed on a
subsystem routing queue. Work management
subsequently starts the job by entering it on the
active dispatching queue.

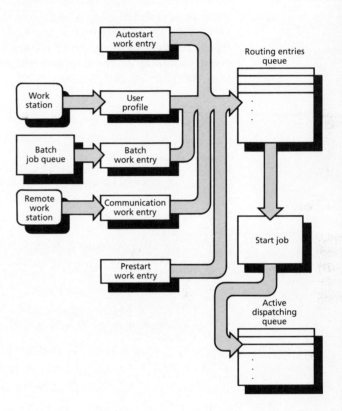

on the routing queue (Fig. 18.6). The routing entries, in turn, define the job's operating requirements.

When a user signs on to a local or remote workstation, the
user ID identifies a **user profile** that identifies his or her password and initial program, menu, and library list. The user profile also specifies work entry routing information, such as the
job's subsystem, scheduling priority, output spooling queue,
spooling priority, processing priority, time slice, and maximum
processor time. When a batch job is submitted, the *submit job*
command creates a work entry from subsystem defaults and

command parameters. Prestart work entries are defined within
the operating system. Autostart jobs are activated when a subsystem is started; their work entries are part of the subsystem
definition.

When real memory space becomes available, work management starts the job associated with the routing queue entry that
has the best scheduling priority. At this point, the job is removed
from the routing queue and added to the subsystem's **active** (or
dispatching) **queue** (Fig. 18.6). By issuing a *work with active
jobs* command, a user can view the contents of the active queue
(Fig. 18.7).

Fig. 18.7   By issuing a *work with active jobs* command, a user
can view the contents of the active queue.

```
                          Work with Active Jobs                      SYS00001
                                                        03/15/91    10:55:23
 CPU %:    19.8      Elapsed time:    00:04:13    Active jobs:   61

 Type options, press Enter.
   2=Change      3=Hold       4=End       5=Work with    6=Release    8=Spooled files
   9=Exclude    10=Program stack         11=Locks          13=Disconnect

                                                  ----------Elapsed----------

 Opt   Subsystem/Job   Type   Pool   Pty   CPU   Int   RSP   AUXIO   CPU %

  -    QBATCH          SBS    2      0     3.8                  0      .0
  -    QCMN            SBS    2      0     6.9                  0      .0
  -      PC60602       EVK    2      50    .2                   0      .0
  -      PC60604       EVK    2      50    .3                   0      .0
  -      PC60605       EVK    2      50    .2                   0      .0
  -      PC60606       EVK    2      50    .2                   0      .0
  -      PC60607       EVK    2      50    .2                   0      .0
  -      PC60608       EVK    2      50    .2                   0      .0
  -      PC60609       EVK    2      20    6.6                  0      .0
                                                                    More...
 Parameters or Command
 ===>
 F3=Exit    F5=Refresh     F10=Restart statistics    F11=Display status
```

IBM supplies two standard configurations. The default, QBASE, supports interactive, batch, and communication subsystems plus QSPL, the spooling subsystem. An alternate configuration, QCTL, serves as a convenient starting point for building a custom subsystem configuration. For example, an installation might want to modify the standard pattern to create one or more new subsystems for weekend, long-running, time-activated, or high-priority batch jobs. Subsystems can be started and ended by system action or by the system operator; for example, the weekend batch subsystem might be activated only on Saturday.

Spooling

Both input and output spooling are supported at the subsystem level. A job's spooling queue and spooling priority are defined in its routing entry.

Dispatching

The AS/400 dispatcher is part of the system microcode. The dispatching algorithm utilizes the active dispatching queue described earlier (Fig. 18.7). Each job is assigned a time slice. Whenever a job exceeds its time slice or issues an interrupt requesting system support, the operating system performs the requested function and then calls the dispatcher. The dispatcher, in turn, calls the highest priority ready-state program on the active queue. Note that each subsystem has its own dispatching queue. OS/400 uses time-sharing techniques to switch from subsystem to subsystem.

A keyboard interrupt provides a good example of OS/400 interrupt handling and dispatching. Imagine that your job has already started and your active program is waiting for input data from the keyboard. (In other words, it is in a wait state.) As characters are typed, they are stored in a buffer. Eventually, the enter key is pressed, and that generates an interrupt. The operating system responds by transferring the data to the appropriate program, setting the program's active queue entry to a ready state, and calling the dispatcher.

Eventually, your program is called and the data are processed. (Because interactive jobs have priority, this usually happens quickly.) After executing for less than a single time slice, the program notifies the operating system that it needs more data. Consequently, OS/400 resets the program's active queue entry to a wait state, starts another keyboard input operation, and calls the dispatcher again. While you type, other jobs are executed.

A job's priority and the length of its time slice are specified in the job's routing entry. Normally, system default priorities and time slices are adequate, but a user can change both parameters. The operating system is assigned priority 0, interactive jobs get a higher number (often 20), and batch jobs get an even higher number (such as 50); the lower the value, the better the priority.

Object Management

Objects

OS/400 is object-oriented. Programs, files, libraries, queues, folders, commands, user profiles, and other entities are stored as objects. Access and security are implemented at the object level. OS/400's **object management** functions allow the user to allocate, manage, change, clear, copy, create, delete, display, move, rename, save, and restore objects, no matter what their type.

Every object has a common header that specifies such attributes as its name, type, size, creation date, description, library, owner, and authority (Fig. 18.8). Of course, different types of objects have different contents; for example, programs hold code,

---

Fig. 18.8   Every object, no matter what its type, has a common header.

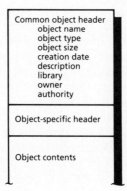

Common object header
  object name
  object type
  object size
  creation date
  description
  library
  owner
  authority

Object-specific header

Object contents

files hold data, and the batch queue lists job requests. Consequently, each object has a functional header that varies by object type.

Objects can be combined to form **composite objects.** For example, a physical file consists of a data space object, a cursor object (for addressability), and (optionally) an index object. Because objects can be combined, it is possible to independently define data descriptions, screen dialogue, and source code and then merge them in an application program. That simplifies program development.

Libraries

A **library** is an object that groups related objects. Every user has access to a **library list** that identifies the libraries containing objects he or she can access (Fig. 18.9). Objects are requested by name. When an object is requested, the system searches through the appropriate library or libraries until it finds the target object name and then extracts its virtual address from the library.

If no library is specified, the system libraries are searched first, followed by the product libraries, the current library, and, finally, the user libraries. An option is to identify the target library by coding the appropriate control language command parameters or by qualifying the object name. For example, imagine that two files named *RESULT* are stored respectively on libraries named *MYLIB* and *YOURLIB*. You can distinguish them by referring to *MYLIB/RESULT* and *YOURLIB/RESULT*. If a library name is specified, the system searches only that library.

Fig. 18.9   A typical library list.

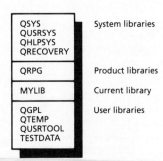

Data Management

File Types

OS/400 data management is file based. Several different types of files are supported. **Database files** (as the name suggests) hold data and are part of the database. A **device file** holds a device description that specifies how the device can be used. Distributed data management files are stored on a remote system. Save files are intended primarily for backup and recovery.

Common Data Management

OS/400 data management begins at compilation time when a **user file control block,** or UFCB (one for each referenced file), is created by the compiler. Later, at open time, an **open data path** (ODP) is defined and information to access this data path is recorded in the user file control block (Fig. 18.10).

The open data path is the link between the application program and the operating system's file-specific data management routines; note that this link is not established until the program runs. The file is subsequently accessed by read and write (or get and put) operations and released by a close operation. These

---

Fig. 18.10   The open operations defines an open data path that
                    links the application program to file-specific data
                    management routines. The open data path is then
                    recorded in the program's user-file control block.

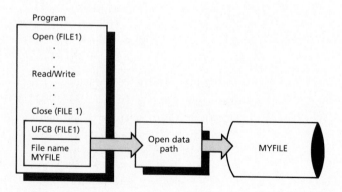

common data management routines are applied to all types of files; in other words, file processing looks the same to the user no matter what kind of file is involved.

File-specific Data Management

An important AS/400 feature is the integration of relational database support into the operating system. There are two types of database files. A physical file (or table) holds data, while a logical file (or view) describes how the data in one or more physical files are to be presented to a program.

Each file has a **file description** that summarizes the file's characteristics at the field, record, and file levels. File descriptions are defined when the file is created through control language commands, data description specifications (DDS), the interactive data definition utility (IDDU), or the structured query language (SQL). The file description is the key to accessing a database file.

Device files describe physical peripheral devices to the system. They are similar to DOS and UNIX device drivers. Display data management routines control display station input and output. Access to remote devices is managed by the inter-systems communications function (ICF). Physically, these devices are quite different, but, because of the common data management interface, the differences are transparent to the user.

Software Migration

The initial version of a software routine might reasonably be viewed as a prototype. Because source code is relatively easy to change, it makes sense to debug, fine-tune, and generalize the logic at the application program level. Only when the routine is stable does it make sense to move it to the operating system and, eventually, to the microcode level. Consequently, much of what we now call system software evolved from application software.

For example, consider access methods. Back in the 1950s when the first computers became available, some enterprising programmer wrote a subroutine to access data. Rather than reinvent the wheel, other programmers copied that subroutine into their own programs. Soon, the subroutine found its way to a system library where it was stored as an object module and added to application routines by the linkage editor. Eventually, the best of those access methods formed the basis for the operating system's resident, default data management routines. Finally, some of those functions were implemented in microcode.

There are good reasons for this software migration. The most obvious one is efficiency; executing common routines at the microcode level saves processor time and memory space and minimizes the need for software maintenance. A second reason is software compatibility. With a layer of microcode insulating the hardware from the software, hardware modifications can be absorbed in the microcode without affecting the software.

Finally, implementing system software in microcode gives the system supplier a real competitive advantage. Software is easy to duplicate. Copying or cloning microcode, on the other hand, requires expensive equipment and the microcode enjoys legal protections that do not apply to software. Simply put, given a successful product, moving operating system functions into the microcode reduces the risk that a low-cost competitor will take away your customers. With its licensed internal code and integrated database and data communication support, the AS/400 is an excellent example of this phenomenon.

Summary

The AS/400 is a multiprocessing system. In addition to the main system processor, I/O processors handle input and output operations and a service processor supports initial program loading and monitors the system. The AS/400 is compatible with IBM's Systems Applications Architecture.

OS/400 is a layered, closed-architecture operating system. Many system functions are implemented in microcode as part of IBM's licensed internal code. The command processor is called the user interface manager. IPL procedures can be initiated at system start-up, from a remote location, or by a timer. The available real and secondary storage space is treated as a single level of virtual memory. To save real memory, users share reentrant code.

OS/400 work management is responsible for accepting user jobs and submitting them to the system for processing. Several subsystems can be supported concurrently. When a job enters the system, its work entry provides routing information that is placed on a subsystem's routing queue. Routing information for an interactive job is found in the user profile. Work management subsequently starts the job by moving it from the routing queue to the active dispatching queue. The dispatcher calls the highest priority job on the active queue.

OS/400 is object-oriented. Files, programs, libraries, and other entities are treated as objects and are accessed by a set of common object management routines no matter what their type. Each object is composed of a common header, a type-specific header, and the object's contents. Objects can be combined to form composite objects. Related objects are grouped through libraries. Each user has a library list that defines the search order when an object is accessed.

Data management is file oriented. There are several different types of files, including database files and device files, but they are all accessed using a set of common data management routines. When a program is compiled, a user file control block (one per file) is added to the object code. At open time, an open data path is established and recorded in the user file control block. A file description that summarizes the file's field-, record-, and file-level characteristics is the key to accessing a database file.

Much current system software evolved from application software. Modern architectures often implement key elements of system software in microcode.

Key Words

active queue	library list	single-level storage
closed	licensed	subsystem
architecture	internal	Systems
common data	code	Applications
management	multiprocessing	Architecture
composite object	object	user file control
database file	object	block
device file	management	user interface
file description	open data path	manager
initial program	OS/400	user profile
load	routing queue	work entry
I/O processor	service	work
job	processor	management
library		

References

1. Hoskins, Jim (1990). *IBM AS/400, A Business Perspective,* second edition. New York: John Wiley & Sons, Inc.
2. IBM Corporation (1989). *Application System/400. System Concepts.* Rochester, Minnesota: International Business Machines Corporation. Publication Number GC21-9802.
3. IBM Corporation (1989). *Application System/400. System Introduction,* second edition. Rochester, Minnesota: International Business Machines Corporation. Publication Number GC21-9766.
4. IBM Corporation (1988). *Application System/400. Technology: Advantage AS/400.* Rochester, Minnesota: International Business Machines Corporation. Publication number SA21-9540.

Exercises

1. The AS/400 is a multiprocessing system. What does that mean?

2. Briefly describe the objectives of IBM's Systems Application Architecture (SAA).

3. Sketch a diagram showing OS/400's components.

4. OS/400 is a closed architecture operating system. What does that mean?

5. Briefly explain what happens during OS/400 IPL. How is IPL initiated?

6. Briefly explain the single-level storage concept. Cite some advantages.

7. Under OS/400 input and output operations are transparent to the user. What does that mean? Why is it important?

8. What is an OS/400 subsystem?

9. Briefly explain how OS/400 work management prepares a job for execution.

10. Distinguish between work management and dispatching.

11. OS/400 is object-oriented. What does that mean? Why is it significant?

12. Briefly explain how an object is located if no library is specified.

13. Distinguish between common data management and file-specific data management.

14. Distinguish between a database file and a device file.

15. Most system software evolved from application software. Why?

16. What advantages are associated with implementing key operating system functions in microcode? What disadvantages?

19

Operating Principles of the IBM System/370 Family

This chapter introduces the operating principles of the IBM System/370 family of computers. Key topics include:

The hardware environment

Addressing memory

The program status word
  Executing instructions
  Instruction length
  The condition code
  Memory protection

Controlling physical I/O
  Privileged instructions

Interrupts
  Interrupt types
  Permanent storage assignments
  Masking interrupts
  Interrupt priority

Program states

An example

These concepts are necessary for understanding Chapters 20, 21, and 22.

The Hardware Environment

An operating system functions within a specific hardware environment; the hardware both limits and supports the software. Initially established with the release of System/360 in 1964, IBM's System/370 architecture remains the foundation of the company's latest mainframes, including the 4300 series, the 3090 series, the 9370, and the 9000 family. This chapter introduces IBM System/370 principles of operation. Chapters 20, 21, and 22 describe three operating systems designed to work within that environment.

Addressing Memory

The IBM System/370 is a byte-addressed machine. The bytes are numbered sequentially starting with 0 (Fig. 19.1), and grouped to form 16-bit halfwords, 32-bit fullwords, and 64-bit doublewords. The first fullword occupies bytes 0 through 3; the second, bytes 4 through 7; and so on. A fullword's address is simply the address of its first byte—0, 4, 8, . . . ; note that fullword addresses are evenly divisible by 4.

In addition to main memory, a programmer also has access to 16 general-purpose registers numbered 0 through 15 (0

Fig. 19.1   An IBM System/370 computer is a byte-addressed machine. The bytes are numbered sequentially, starting with 0. Bytes are grouped to form halfwords, fullwords, and doublewords.

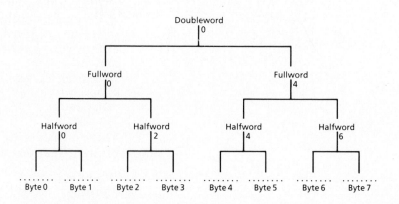

through F in hexadecimal). Because 15 is 1111 in binary, 4 bits are enough to identify a register.

Relative memory addresses can appear as operands in an instruction. Programs are written as though they begin at location zero, and the address of any byte in the program is expressed as a **displacement** from this **base.** When the program is loaded, its absolute entry point address is stored in a base register. As it executes, the instruction control unit converts relative base-plus-displacement addresses to absolute (virtual) form by adding the displacement to the contents of the base register.

Displacements are 12 bits long. Because the largest possible 12-bit number is equivalent to decimal 4095, programs exceeding 4096 bytes (displacements 0 through 4095) require multiple base registers. To specify a base register (4 bits) and a displacement (12 bits) requires 16 bits or 2 bytes, so a relative base-plus-displacement address occupies 2 bytes.

Translating relative addresses to absolute form is a hardware function performed by the processor. Current IBM mainframes incorporate additional dynamic address translation hardware to translate segment/page virtual addresses.

The Program Status Word

A computer executes one instruction during each machine cycle. The instruction control unit looks to the instruction counter for the address of its next instruction. An IBM System/370's instruction counter is called the **program status word,** or **PSW.**

The program status word has three different forms (Fig. 19.2). The **basic control (BC) mode** is compatible with the original System/360 architecture, and is used only when the dynamic address translation feature is disabled. The **extended control (EC) mode** implies virtual memory; in other words, adding a base register and a displacement yields a virtual address that must be translated through segment and page tables. Bit 12 is set to 0 for the basic control mode, and 1 for extended control. The **extended architecture (XA) mode** format resembles EC mode. The primary difference is that the last 31 bits of an XA mode PSW hold the instruction address. Bit 32 is set to 0 in BC and EC modes (indicating a 24-bit address) and 1 in XA mode (indicating a 31-bit address).

Executing Instructions

The program status word (actually, a doubleword) occupies a system register. Its key function is program control. For exam-

Fig. 19.2   The program status word (PSW) has three forms:

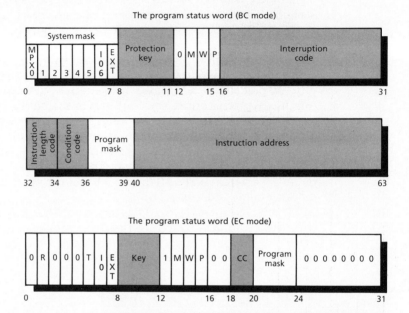

The program status word (BC mode)

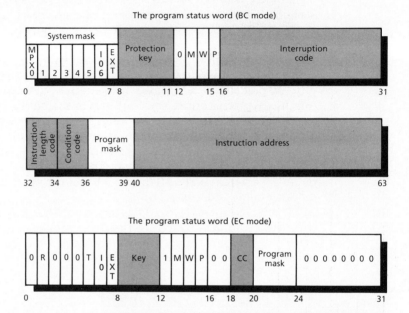

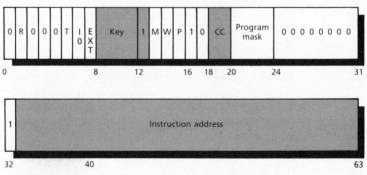

ple, consider the assembler language program segment shown in Fig. 19.3. It loads binary numbers into registers 3 and 4, adds the numbers, and stores their sum, eventually repeating the instructions. Variables X, Y, and Z are symbolic addresses. The numbers to the left in Fig. 19.3 are absolute addresses expressed in decimal.

The PSW's last three bytes (Fig. 19.2) contain the address of the instruction to be executed next. As this program segment begins, the instruction address holds the binary equivalent of the decimal number 1000. The processor looks at the PSW, gets the address of the next instruction, and fetches it, so the machine-language equivalent of

GO L 3,X

is fetched into the instruction register. While the instruction is moving from memory to the processor, the instruction control

Fig. 19.3   An assembler language program segment.

Address	Instruction		
1000	GO	L	3,X
1004		L	4,Y
1008		AR	3,4
1010		ST	3,Z

Several more instructions

1050	B	GO

Balance of program

1100	X	DS	F
1104	Y	DS	F
1108	Z	DS	F

Other data storage areas

unit has plenty of time to increment the PSW's **instruction address** field by 4 (the length of the load instruction), so the PSW points to 1004, the address of the *next* instruction.

The load instruction's first operand references register 3. The second operand, X, is a memory address expressed as a base register and a displacement. Before the instruction can be executed, this relative address must be converted to absolute form, so the instruction control unit adds the base register and the displacement. If PSW bit 12 is 0, the result is the absolute address. If PSW bit 12 is 1, the dynamic address translation feature is activated, and segment and page tables are used to compute an absolute address.

Note carefully the difference between the instruction address in the PSW and the instruction's operand addresses. The PSW holds the absolute address of the instruction. The operands, on the other hand, point to the memory locations that are to participate in the operation. The operand addresses are relative (and, perhaps, virtual), and must be translated to absolute form before the instruction can be executed.

Once its operand addresses have been translated, the first instruction is executed and the value stored at location X is copied into register 3. Now, another instruction cycle begins. As before, the processor

1. finds the instruction address in the PSW,
2. fetches the instruction stored at that address,
3. increments the instruction address so it points to the "next" instruction,
4. translates the instruction's operands, and
5. executes the instruction.

Thus the second load is fetched, the instruction address is incremented to 1008, and the contents of memory location Y are copied into register 4.

During the next cycle, the instruction stored at location 1008 is fetched, the instruction address is incremented to 1010, and the contents of registers 3 and 4 are added. Note that the instruction address was incremented by 2 instead of 4 this time. The "AR" instruction is only 2 bytes long.

The PSW points to address 1010, so during the next cycle the store instruction is fetched and executed and the instruction address is incremented by 4. Continuing in its single-minded way, the processor executes several other instructions until, finally, the instruction address is 1050 and the instruction

B GO

is fetched. It's an unconditional branch (a GOTO). The single operand, GO, is a relative (base-plus-displacement) address that must be translated to absolute. When the processor executes an unconditional branch, it replaces the contents of the PSW's instruction address with the address specified in the operand—in this case, with 1000, so the next instruction to be fetched is the one labeled GO. Thus the loop repeats.

Instruction Length

In the just-completed example (Fig. 19.3), most of the instructions occupied 4 bytes, but one (the AR) needed only 2. Actually, an IBM System/370 computer supports three different instruction lengths (Fig. 19.4). Each instruction contains an operation code and two operands. The key to the instruction's length is the number of bytes needed to represent operand addresses. The sixteen general-purpose registers are numbered 0 through 15, so a register can be uniquely identified by a 4-bit number. Main memory addresses are represented as a base register (4 bits) and a 12-bit displacement, yielding a 16-bit or 2-byte relative address.

Some instructions involve two registers. Combining a 1-byte operation code with two half-byte register numbers yields a 2-byte (halfword) instruction. Other instructions move data between memory and a register. The 1-byte operation code, combined with a half-byte register address, a half-byte index register, and a 2-byte memory address, totals 4 bytes. Storage-to-storage instructions include an operation code, two memory addresses, and, frequently, a 1-byte length field, for a total of 6 bytes.

The operation code of every 2-byte, register-to-register instruction begins with bit values 00. Instructions referencing a register and a storage location start with 01 or 10; those involving two storage locations all start with 11. The processor can determine an instruction's length by checking its operation code.

Bits 32 and 33 of a BC mode PSW indicate the length of the instruction currently being executed (Fig. 19.2); they are set when the instruction address is incremented. The program status word points to the "next" instruction, not the current one. Should an error occur, it is possible to use the **instruction length code** to compute the address of the current instruction. The instruction length code does not appear in an EC or XA mode PSW.

Fig. 19.4   An IBM System/370 computer can execute 2-, 4-, and 6-byte instructions.

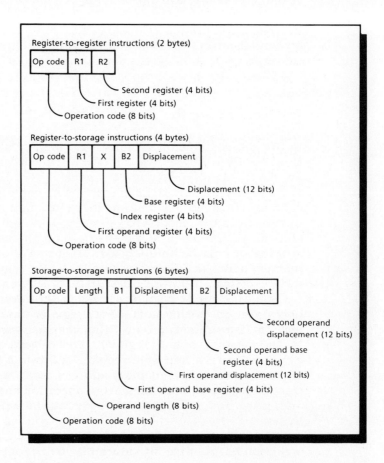

The Condition Code

The key to decision logic on an IBM System/370 computer is a 2-bit **condition code** in the program status word (bits 34 and 35 in BC mode; bits 18 and 19 in EC and XA modes; see Fig. 19.2). Comparison instructions and certain arithmetic instructions set the condition code. When a conditional branch is executed, the processor checks the condition code and, if its value is correct, replaces the PSW's instruction address with an operand address.

Memory Protection

On a multiprogramming system, it is possible for one program to destroy the contents of memory belonging to another, so most systems include a memory protection feature. On an IBM System/370 computer, each active program is assigned a 4-bit **protection key**. The operating system uses 0000; the first program in memory gets 0001, and so on; each program has a different key. A program's protection key is associated with each block of memory space assigned to it. Later, during program execution, the protection key is stored in PSW bits 8 through 12 (Fig. 19.2, all three modes). Access to any block whose protection key does not match the one in the PSW is a protection exception, and can cause program termination.

Controlling Physical I/O

One of the most important elements of a computer's architecture is its link to peripheral devices. External devices are attached to an IBM System/370 computer through channels. A channel is a special-purpose computer. Because it has its own, independent processor, it can function in parallel with the main processor, and thus free the computer to do other work.

Like any computer, a channel executes instructions. Its function is to transfer a certain number of bytes from a peripheral device into memory (or vice versa), so it must be given a byte count and a memory address. The channel program and key control data are stored in the computer's memory and passed to the channel when the I/O operation begins.

A **channel program** consists of one or more **channel command words** (Fig. 19.5). Each **CCW** contains a command code that specifies the operation to be performed (read, write, seek), a data address, a byte count, and several flags. For example, near the bottom of Fig. 19.5 is a channel program that tells an IBM 3211 printer to skip one line and then write a line of data. Programmers can write their own channel programs, but they rarely do. Instead, the channel program is typically part of an access method.

Just before the main processor sends the channel a start I/O command, the operating system places the address of the first

Fig. 19.5   A channel program consists of one or more channel command words (CCWs). The sample channel program tells an IBM 3211 printer to skip one line and then print a line of data.

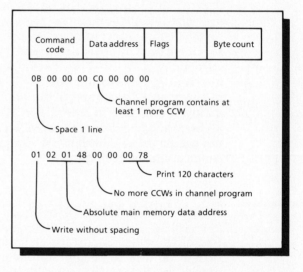

CCW in the **channel address word** (Fig. 19.6). The **CAW** is always found at memory address 72. When the channel's processor receives a start I/O command, it copies the channel address word into its own instruction counter (Fig. 19.7). Then the channel fetches and executes its first channel command (CCW).

The channel passes status information to the computer through the **channel status word** (Fig. 19.8) (memory address 64). The **CSW** contains the channel program address, a data address, a byte count, and several flags that indicate the I/O operation's status. The program's protection key is found in both the channel address word and the channel status word, so the channel can recognize protection exceptions. Following completion of the I/O operation, the operating system uses the protection key in the CSW to identify the program waiting for I/O.

Most channel programs are found in access methods. The linkage editor creates a load module by grafting access methods and other subroutines onto the main object module. The main program requests a logical I/O operation by calling the access

Fig. 19.6   The address of the first channel command word in the channel program is passed to the channel through the channel address word (CAW).

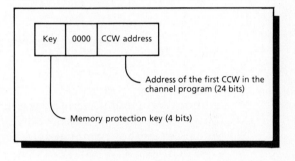

Fig. 19.7   The main processor sends the channel's processor a start I/O command. The channel responds by copying the channel address word from memory (address 72) into its own instruction counter. Then it fetches its first channel command word.

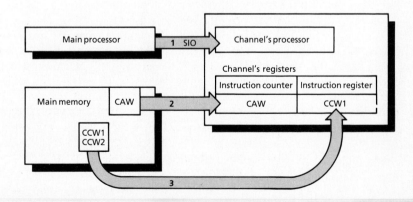

Fig. 19.8   The channel passes status information to the main
                       computer through the channel status word (CSW).

method (Fig. 19.9a). Using parameters passed to it by the calling
routine (for example, a data address and a logical record length),
the access method completes the channel program and transfers
control to the operating system.

    The operating system stores the address of the channel
program's first CCW in the channel address word (memory address 72), and executes a start I/O instruction (Fig. 19.9b). The
channel responds by copying the channel address word and then
fetching the first CCW (Fig. 19.9c). At this point, the channel has

Fig. 19.9   Controlling I/O on an IBM System/370 computer.

a. The application program calls the access method, which completes
    the channel program and transfers control to the operating system.

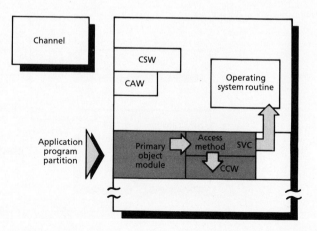

b. The operating system stores the address of the channel program in the channel address word and executes a start I/O instruction.

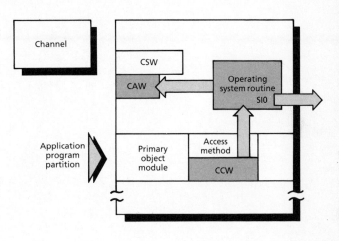

c. The channel copies the contents of the channel address word and then fetches its first channel command word.

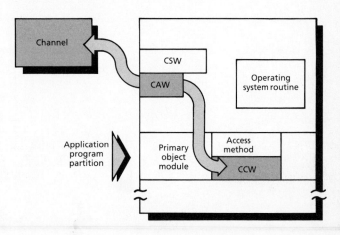

d. When the I/O operation is complete, the channel signals the main processor.

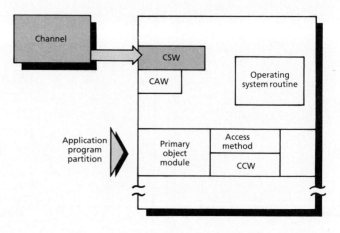

e. After checking the channel status word, the operating system returns control to the application program.

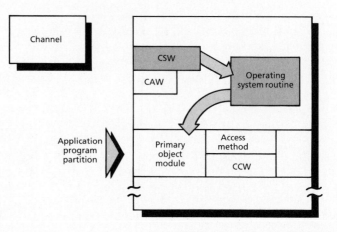

assumed full responsibility for the I/O operation, and the main computer can process instructions in some other program.

The channel and the computer are asynchronous; in other words, they function independently. Consequently, the main processor has no way of knowing when the channel has completed its work unless the channel tells it. When the I/O operation is finished, the channel signals the main processor by issuing an interrupt and reports its status to the operating system through the channel status word (Fig. 19.9d). Assuming the CSW indicates successful completion, the operating system can return control to the application program (Fig. 19.9e).

Privileged Instructions

On a computer running multiple concurrent programs, it is essential that all input and output operations be funneled through the operating system. To prevent cheating, the instructions that communicate directly with a channel are privileged; in other words, they can be executed only by an operating system routine. PSW bit 15 (all three modes) holds the problem state bit. This bit is set to 0 when the operating system is running. Before executing a privileged instruction, the process checks bit 15. If it's not 0, a privileged instruction exception is recognized, and the application program is usually terminated. Consequently, the programmer must transfer control to the operating system to start an I/O operation.

Interrupts

Because the operating system and an application program have different protection keys, it is illegal to branch to or call an operating system module. The only way for an application program to transfer control to the operating system is by issuing an **interrupt**. Application programs are not the only source of interrupts; they can originate in hardware or software.

An IBM System/370 computer responds to an interrupt signal by switching PSWs. Three fields are involved: the **current PSW**, an **old PSW**, and a **new PSW**. The current PSW is the system register that holds the address of the next instruction. The old PSW is located in memory. The new PSW, also found in memory, holds the address of an interrupt handling routine in the operating system.

When an interrupt occurs, hardware stores the current program status word in the old PSW field and then loads the new PSW into the current PSW register (Fig. 19.10). When the processor begins its next cycle, it fetches the instruction whose address in the program status word—the operating system's interrupt handling routine. Note that the old PSW holds the address of the next instruction in the original application program, so after the interrupt has been processed, the application program can be resumed.

Consider an example (Fig. 19.11a). Imagine a program loaded at memory location 50000. The operating system's interrupt handling routine starts at address 1000. The new PSW has protection key 0000 and points to instruction address 1000. The contents of the old PSW are unknown. The current PSW points to memory location 50500 (an address in the application program). The program's protection key is 0010.

When an interrupt occurs, hardware stores the current PSW in the old PSW (Fig. 19.11b). A fraction of a nanosecond later, the new PSW is copied into the current PSW (Fig. 19.11c). This completes the interrupt.

Interrupt processing begins with the next machine cycle. The address in the current PSW is 1000, so the processor fetches the first instruction in the interrupt handling routine (Fig. 19.11d). Since the operating system is in control, privileged instructions are legal. Eventually, the old PSW is loaded back into the current PSW, and the application program resumes processing (Fig. 19.11e).

Interrupt Types

IBM System/370 computers recognize six different interrupt types. Sources include application programs, peripheral devices, the operator's console, the computer's self-checking error circuitry, and other processors.

External interrupts come from the operator's console, another processor, or the timer. When an external interrupt is sensed, hardware stores the current program status word at memory address 24 (the old external PSW), and then loads the contents of the doubleword beginning at address 88 (the new external PSW) into the current PSW register (Fig. 19.12). If the interrupt arrives while the processor is executing an instruction, it is ignored until the instruction is completed; in other words, external interrupts are recognized between instructions.

Fig. 19.10   An IBM System/370 responds to an interrupt by switching PSWs. First, the current PSW is stored in the old PSW field. Then, the new PSW is loaded into the current PSW register.

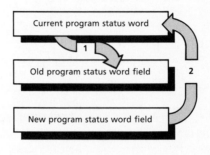

In BC mode, PSW bits 16 through 31 contain an **interruption code** (Fig. 19.2). By checking these 16 bits, the external interruption handler routine can determine the exact cause of the interrupt. Under EC and XA modes, the interruption code is stored in a special register.

Fig. 19.11   An example of PSW switching.

a. The current PSW points to an instruction in the application program.

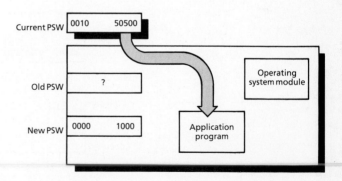

b. When an interrupt occurs, the current PSW is stored in the old PSW
    field.

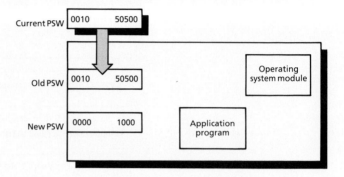

c. Then, the new PSW is loaded into current PSW register.

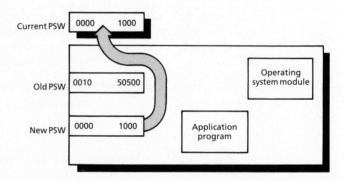

d. Because the new PSW now points to an operating system routine,
    the first instruction in the interrupt handler is fetched.

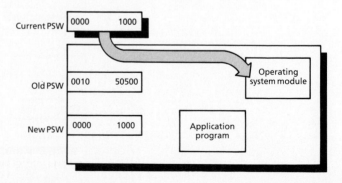

e. Eventually, the old PSW's contents are loaded back into the current PSW, and the application program resumes processing.

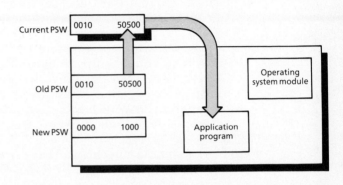

A supervisor call or **SVC interrupt** starts when a program executes an SVC instruction, such as

SVC 17

The operand requests a particular supervisor module. In response to an SVC instruction, the processor generates an

Fig. 19.12   When an external interrupt occurs, hardware stores the current PSW at memory address 24, and then loads the contents of address 88 into the current PSW.

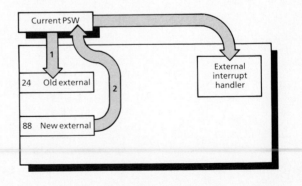

interrupt. Hardware reacts by storing the current program status word at memory address 32 (the old SVC PSW), loading the doubleword beginning at address 96 (the new SVC PSW) into the current PSW, and copying the operand field (the 17 in the instruction illustrated) into the interruption code (Fig. 19.13).

An SVC interrupt is generated by a valid instruction. A **program interrupt** results from an illegal or invalid instruction. The processor recognizes errors as they occur and generates the interrupt. In response, hardware stores the current PSW into the old program PSW field (address 40), loads the new program PSW (address 104) into the current PSW, and stores the interruption code (Fig. 19.14).

A **machine check interrupt** occurs when the computer's self-checking circuitry detects a hardware failure. If an instruction is executing, it is terminated—no sense performing computations or logical operations on a computer known to be malfunctioning. Hardware responds to a machine check interrupt by storing the current PSW in the old machine check PSW (address 48), loading the new machine check PSW (address 112) into the current PSW, and dumping the contents of key control fields into the next few hundred bytes of memory (Fig. 19.15).

Because the channels and the main processor work independently, the channel must signal the processor when an I/O operation is completed by sending it an input/output or **I/O interrupt**

Fig. 19.13   When an SVC interrupt occurs, hardware stores the current PSW in the old SVC field, and then loads the new SVC into the current PSW.

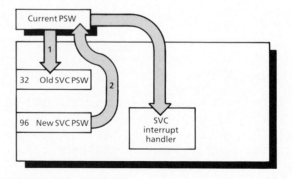

Fig. 19.14   When a program interrupt occurs, hardware stores
the current PSW in the old program PSW field, and
then loads the new program PSW into the current
PSW. Listed below the diagram are the valid program
interrupt codes.

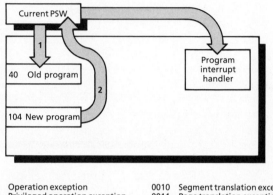

0001	Operation exception	0010	Segment translation exception
0002	Privileged operation exception	0011	Page translation exception
0003	Execute exception	0012	Translation specification exception
0004	Protection exception	0013	Special operation exception
0005	Addressing exception	0017	ASN-translation spec exception
0006	Specification exception	001C	Space-switch event
0007	Data exception	001F	PC-translation spec exception
0008	Fixed-point overflow exception	0020	AFX translation exception
0009	Fixed-point divide exception	0021	ASX translation exception
000A	Decimal overflow exception	0022	LX translation exception
000B	Decimal divide exception	0023	EX translation exception
000C	Exponent overflow exception	0024	Primary authority exception
000D	Exponent underflow exception	0025	Secondary authority exception
000E	Significance exception	0040	Monitor event
000F	Floating-point divide exception	0080	PER event (code may be combined with another code)

(Fig. 19.16). Hardware responds by storing the current PSW in
the old I/O PSW (address 56), loading the new I/O PSW (address
120) into the current PSW, and storing the channel/device address of the unit causing the interrupt in the interruption code.
If the processor is executing an instruction when an I/O interrupt occurs, the instruction is completed before the interrupt is
recognized.

A **restart interrupt** allows an operator or another processor
to start a program. This interrupt type was not available on the
original IBM System/360 computers; it was added after the basic
architecture was established. The new restart PSW is found at
memory location 0; the old restart PSW is at memory location 8.

Fig. 19.15

When a machine check interrupt occurs, hardware stores the current PSW in the old machine check PSW field, and then loads the new machine check PSW into the current PSW.

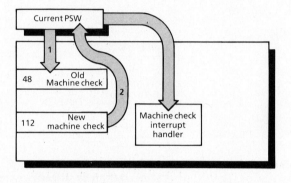

Permanent Storage Assignments

The old and new PSWs, the channel status word, and the channel address word are stored in fixed memory locations (Fig. 19.17); in other words, these key fields are found at the same addresses on every IBM System/370 computer. Along with the computer's

Fig. 19.16

When an I/O interrupt occurs, hardware stores the current PSW in the old I/O PSW field, and then loads the new I/O PSW into the current PSW.

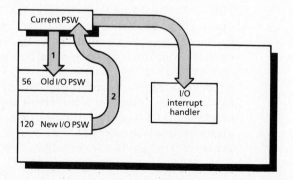

Fig. 19.17 The old and new PSWs, the channel address word, the channel status word, and other key control fields are stored at fixed memory locations.

Address			
Decimal	Hexadecimal	Length	Purpose
0	0	Doubleword	Restart new PSW
8	8	Doubleword	Restart old PSW
16	10	Doubleword	Unused
24	18	Doubleword	External old PSW
32	20	Doubleword	Supervisor call old PSW
40	28	Doubleword	Program old PSW
48	30	Doubleword	Machine check old PSW
56	38	Doubleword	Input/output old PSW
65	40	Doubleword	Channel status word
72	48	Word	Channel address word
76	4C	Word	Unused
80	50	Word	Timer
84	54	Word	Unused
88	58	Doubleword	External new PSW
96	60	Doubleword	Supervisor call new PSW
104	68	Doubleword	Program new PSW
112	70	Doubleword	Machine check new PSW
120	78	Doubleword	Input/output new PSW

control registers, they represent the primary interface between hardware and software.

Masking Interrupts

A typical mainframe computer supports several channels. The channels operate independently, so it is possible that two or more I/O interrupts might be generated by different channels in a very brief time span, perhaps even simultaneously. Consider what might happen if two I/O interrupts were to occur within a few nanoseconds.

An application program is executing. In response to the first I/O interrupt, hardware copies the current program status word to the old I/O PSW, and loads the new I/O PSW into the current PSW (Fig. 19.18a). Within a single machine cycle, a second interrupt arrives. Clearly, the first interrupt is still being processed, but that makes no difference to hardware, which, in its automatic way, drops the current PSW into the old I/O PSW and loads the new I/O PSW (Fig. 19.18b). As a result, the link back to the application program is destroyed. Consequently, the operating system will be unable to restart the application program, and that is unacceptable.

Fig. 19.18   Two or more interrupts occurring in a brief time span can destroy the trail back to the original program.

a. When the first interrupt occurs, the link back to the application program is stored in the old PSW.

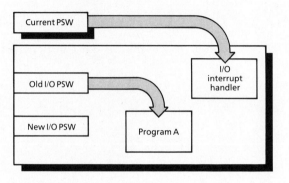

b. The second interrupt overlays the link and thus destroys it.

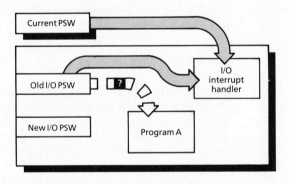

The solution is **masking** interrupts. The first 8 bits of the BC mode program status word hold a **system mask** (Fig. 19.19). The first bit is associated with channel 0. If it's 1, the processor can accept an interrupt from the channel; if it's 0, the interrupt is ignored. (The channel will continue to send the interrupt signal, again and again, until the processor acknowledges it.) Bits 1 through 5 control channels 1 through 5; again, a 1-bit permits

Fig. 19.19   Several program status word bits are used to mask interrupts.

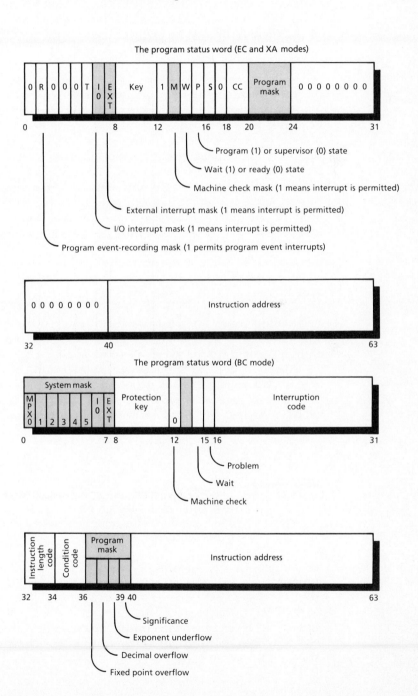

an interrupt from the associated channel, and a 0-bit means the processor will ignore interrupts from that channel. Bit 6 controls channels 6 through 255. In the EC and XA mode PSWs, a single bit (bit 6) serves to mask I/O interrupts from *all* channels.

Normally, the system mask or the I/O interrupt bit is set to 1, so I/O interrupts can be accepted. In the new I/O PSW, however, these key mask bits are set to 0 (Fig. 19.20), so once again an I/O interrupt is accepted, subsequent I/O interrupts are ignored until the operating system changes the PSW.

Bit 7 masks external interrupts in all three PSW modes. Like I/O interrupts, external interrupts are generated asynchronously, so they can occur, unexpectedly, at any time. Picture an I/O interrupt, followed closely by an external interrupt, followed closely by another I/O interrupt. That sequence could destroy the original program's PSW in the old I/O PSW field. The same thing could happen with an external, I/O, external sequence, so both I/O and external interrupts are masked when either type is processed.

Machine checks can be masked by turning off PSW bit 13 (all three modes). Once a hardware failure is detected, the error checking circuitry sends an interrupt signal and continues to send signals until the problem is fixed or the machine is shut down. If machine check interrupts were not masked, hardware, responding to an unending series of interrupt signals, would simply load the new machine-check PSW over and over again, and the system would be unable to respond to the interrupt.

Closely spaced SVC and program interrupts are not a problem. Both are generated by program instructions, and since the processor can execute only one instruction at a time, simultaneous SVC and program interrupts are impossible. An SVC transfers control to the operating system, which has no need to

Fig. 19.20   In the new I/O PSW, the I/O interrupt mask bits are set to 0, so when the new I/O PSW is loaded, all subsequent I/O interrupts are masked while the first one is processed.

issue a subsequent SVC. (Why call the supervisor when you're already there?) A program interrupt also transfers control to the operating system, which is assumed to be bug free. (In fact, operating system bugs usually lead to a system crash.)

Following a program interrupt, normal system action is to terminate the offending program and generate a dump. At times, a programmer might choose to override the standard procedure, trapping and handling such potential problems as overflows or underflows in a program subroutine. Bits 36 through 39 (BC mode) or bits 20 through 23 (EC and XA modes) allow the programmer to suppress fixed-point overflows, decimal overflows, exponent underflows, and significance exceptions.

Interrupt Priority

"If it can possibly happen, it will." Engineers and programmers recognize the essential truth behind that old cliché. Given time, it is almost inevitable that every possible type of interrupt will hit the processor at the same instant. Which one goes first? A well-designed system anticipates such problems and has procedures for dealing with them.

On an IBM System/370 computer, machine checks are serviced first—no sense trying to do anything else on a malfunctioning machine. Once the machine check is out of the way, here's what happens (Fig. 19.21):

1. The program (or SVC) interrupt is accepted, dropping the application program's PSW into the old program PSW.
2. The external interrupt is accepted, dropping the current PSW (which by now points to the program interrupt handling routine) into the old external PSW.
3. The I/O interrupt is accepted, dropping the external interrupt's program status word into the old I/O PSW.

Note that the current PSW points to the I/O interrupt handler. Additional I/O or external interrupts will be ignored because they are masked. Additional SVC or program interrupts can't possible happen until another instruction is executed. Thus, the I/O interrupt handler begins processing. When it finishes, the old I/O PSW is made current, and the external interrupt handler takes over. Finally, the program interrupt handler gets control.

Fig. 19.21   When simultaneous interrupts occur, hardware
accepts the program (or SVC) interrupts first, then the
external interrupt, and, finally, the I/O interrupt.
Because of their relative positions on the old PSW
queue, they are processed in reverse order.

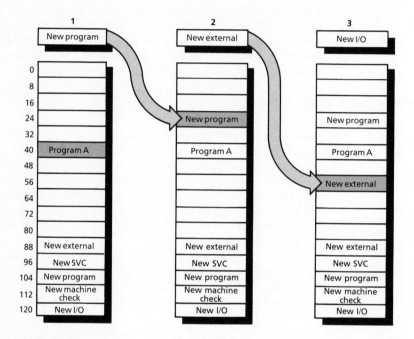

Program States

The computer, at any given time, is either executing an application program or a supervisor routine; in other words, it is either
in the **problem state** or the **supervisory state.** PSW bit 15 (all
three modes, Fig. 19.19) indicates the computer's state—1
means problem and 0 means supervisory. Privileged instructions can be executed only in supervisory state. Protection exceptions are ignored when the system is in supervisory state.

Additionally, a given program is either ready to resume processing or waiting for the completion of some event such as an
I/O operation; in other words, it's either in a **ready state** or a
wait state. A 0 is PSW bit 14 means ready; 1 means wait. As

you'll see in subsequent chapters, this bit is crucial on a multi-programming system.

Three other EC and XA mode bits deserve mention. Bit 1 is associated with program event recording (a System/370 facility we won't cover in detail). Bit 5 controls dynamic address translation. If it's set to 0, addresses are not dynamically translated (which makes sense for operating system routines in the virtual-equals-real area). If bit 5 is set to 1, addresses are dynamically translated through the segment and page tables. Finally, bit 16 affects the way addresses are dynamically translated. It must be set to 0 in EC mode and to 1 in XA mode.

An Example

Perhaps the best way to pull together all these concepts is through an example. Start with a single program in memory (Fig. 19.22a). The program needs data, so it executes an SVC. The result is an SVC interrupt (Fig. 19.22b), which transfers control to the SVC interrupt handler (Fig. 19.22c). Note that the old SVC PSW points to the application program.

The SVC interrupt handler starts the physical I/O operation (Fig. 19.22d) by

1. storing the address of the first channel command word in the channel address word, and
2. executing a start I/O instruction, thus signaling the channel.

Before returning control to the initial program, the operating system repeatedly checks the channel status word (CSW) until the channel reports either a successful or unsuccessful start (Fig. 19.22e). Assuming success, the channel is now responsible for the I/O operation. The program cannot resume processing until the I/O operation is completed, so the interrupt handler places the application program in a wait state by turning on bit 14.

Next, the operating system tries to start another program. Since there is only one application program in memory, its old PSW is loaded (Fig. 19.22f). Because PSW bit 14 is set to 1, the computer is in a wait state, so the processor does nothing for a while.

Eventually, the channel completes the input operation and sends an I/O interrupt. Consequently, the current PSW is copied

Fig. 19.22 An example.

a. Memory holds a single application program.

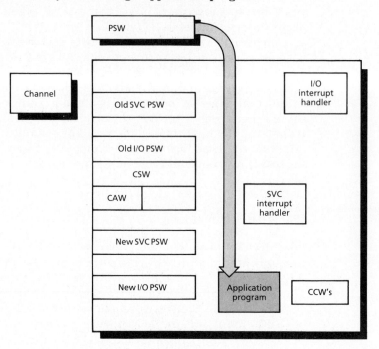

b. The program issues an SVC.

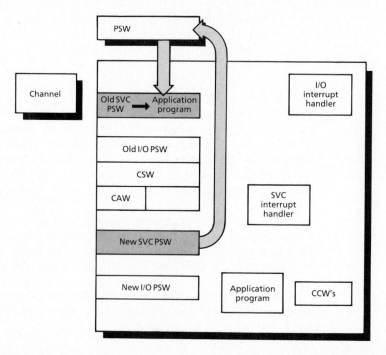

c. **The SVC interrupt handler gets control.**

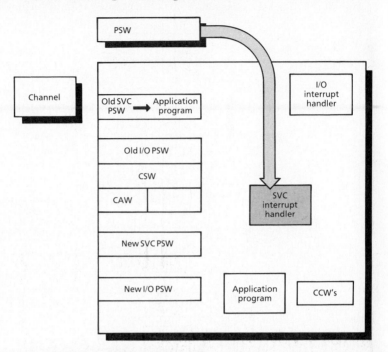

d. **The interrupt handler starts the physical I/O operation by storing the channel program address in the channel address word and executing a start I/O instruction.**

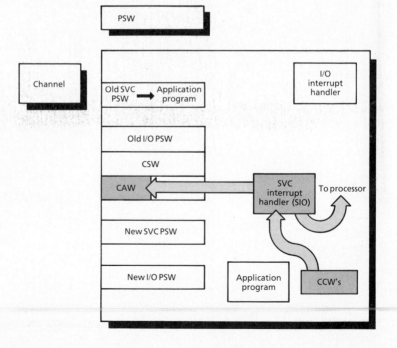

e. The SVC interrupt handler then checks the channel status word until the channel reports the I/O operation's status.

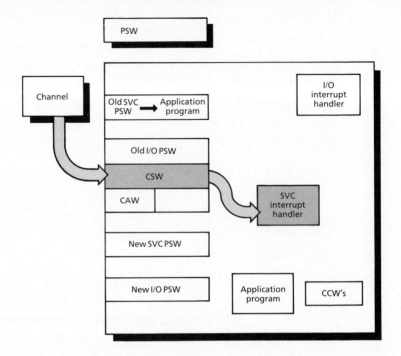

f. The original PSW is loaded, dropping the computer into a wait state.

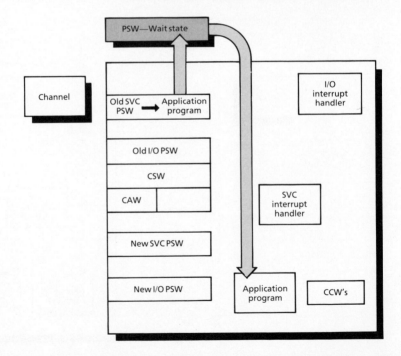

g. Following an I/O interrupt, the I/O interrupt handler gets control.

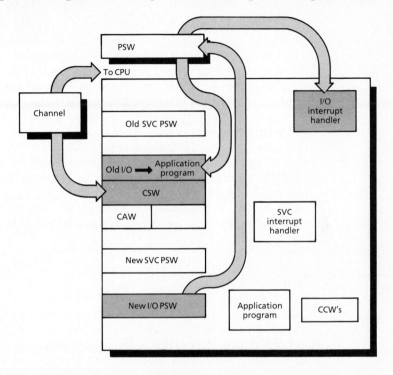

h. Eventually, the application program resumes prcessing.

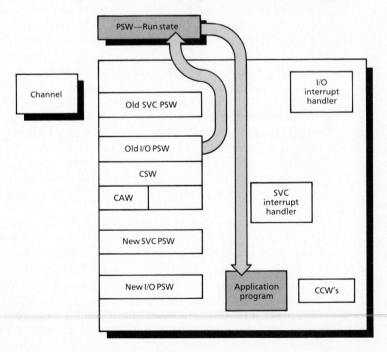

to the old I/O PSW, and the new I/O PSW is loaded (Fig. 19.22g). The current PSW's bit 14 is now 0, so the processor can execute instructions. The first instruction in the I/O interrupt handler routine is fetched. The channel status word is checked, and the application program's PSW is set to a ready state. Eventually, the application program resumes processing (Fig. 19.22h).

With multiprogramming, of course, the problem is a bit more complex. If a program drops into a wait state, the operating system will attempt to start a different one, and the new program is likely to generate its own interrupts. Because there is only one old PSW for each interrupt type, the original program's PSW must be saved if a return trail is to be preserved. Solutions to this problem will be explored in the next two chapters.

Summary

IBM System/370 computers are byte addressed. The bytes are grouped to form halfwords, fullwords, and doublewords. Memory addresses appearing in instruction operands are expressed in relative, base-plus-displacement form, and must be translated to absolute form before the instruction can be executed.

A System/370's instruction counter is called the program status word. It holds the address of the next instruction to be executed. Three forms—the basic control (BC) mode, the extended control (EC) mode, and the extended architecture (XA) mode—are used. The instruction length code (BC mode only), condition code, and protection key are all found in the PSW.

An application starts an I/O operation by calling an access method. The access method completes a channel program (one or more channel command words), and transfers control to the operating system. The operating system, in turn, stores the address of the first CCW in the channel address word (CAW), and issues a privileged start I/O instruction. When the I/O operation is completed, the channel notifies the processor by sending an interrupt and reporting its status through the channel status word (CSW).

An IBM System/370 computer responds to an interrupt by storing the current PSW in the old PSW field, and loading the new PSW into the current PSW. Six types of interrupts are supported—external, I/O, program, SVC, machine check, and restart. Each type has its own old and new PSW fields. To avoid losing the trail back to the original program, I/O and external interrupts are masked. Machine-check interrupts and selected program interrupts can be masked, too. Given simultaneous interrupts, the program (or SVC) interrupt is accepted first, then the external interrupt, and, finally, the I/O interrupt. They are processed in reverse order.

Other PSW bits identify a program's state, activate the dynamic address translation feature, and control program event recording.

The chapter ended with an example. If you have not already done so, take the time to read and understand the example.

Key Words

base	extended	privileged
basic control	architecture mode	instruction
mode PSW	extended control	problem state
CAW	mode	program interrupt
CCW	external interrupt	program status
channel address	instruction address	word
word	instruction length	protection key
channel command	code	PSW
word	interrupt	ready state
channel program	interruption code	restart interrupt
channel status	I/O interrupt	supervisory state
word	machine check	SVC interrupt
condition code	interrupt	system mask
current PSW	masking	wait state
CSW	new PSW	
displacement	old PSW	

References

1. IBM Corporation (1987). *IBM System/370 Extended Architecture Principles of Operation*, second edition. Poughkeepsie, New York: International Business Machines Corporation. Publication Number SA22-7085.
2. IBM Corporation (1983). *IBM System/370 Principles of Operation*, tenth edition. Poughkeepsie, New York: International Business Machines Corporation. Publication Number GA22-7000.

Exercises

1. The IBM System/370 is a byte-addressed machine. Explain.

2. Distinguish between an absolute address and a relative address. Briefly explain the structure of both address types on an IBM System/370 computer.

3. Explain how the PSW determines the order in which instructions are executed.

4. How can an IBM System/370 computer determine the length of its instructions? What distinguishes 2-byte, 4-byte, and 6-byte instructions?

5. Explain how I/O is controlled on an IBM System/370. What functions are performed by
   a. the access method?
   b. the channel program?
   c. the channel command word?
   d. the channel address word?
   e. the operating system?
   f. the channel status word?

6. What is a privileged instruction? Why are such instructions important?

7. What is an interrupt? How is the interrupt concept implemented on an IBM System/370?

8. Name the types of interrupts recognized on an IBM System/370. Describe the source of each.

9. What are permanent storage assignments? Why are they necessary on an IBM System/370?

10. Why must certain types of interrupts be masked at certain times? How are they masked?

11. Explain the IBM System/370's interrupt priority.

12. Distinguish between the BC mode and the EC mode. When is each used? How do the PSWs differ?

13. Assume an IBM System/370 is running under basic control mode. The contents of certain fixed locations in main memory are:

Address	Contents in Hexadecimal
0	FF0400000001C000
8	0000000000000720
16	0000000000000000
24	00550082C0026400
32	FF550008C0031424
40	FF55000BC003F340
48	00550000C004A000
56	00550003C00422FA
64	0000000000000000
72	0000000000000000
80	0000000000000000
88	000400000001A000
96	FF0400000017000
104	FF0400000013000
112	0000000000011000
120	0004000000015000

The current PSW holds:

FF04000B0001 3000

Sketch a map of main memory showing the location of each interrupt handling routine. What kind of interrupt has just happened? What is the address of the "bad" instruction? Can an I/O interrupt happen now? How do you know? Can a privileged instruction be executed? How can you tell the computer is in basic control (BC) mode?

20

IBM VSE

This chapter discusses the internals of a
popular midsize mainframe operating
system, IBM's VSE. Key topics include:

The VSE environment

Virtual memory contents
  SYSGEN and IPL

Memory management

Loading application programs
  The job control program
  Spooling and queuing

Multiprogramming and physical I/O

The logical I/O control system

Allocating peripheral devices

Libraries

Before you begin reading, be sure you
understand virtual memory (Chapter 16)
and System/370 principles of operation
(Chapter 19).

The VSE Environment

IBM's VSE (virtual storage extended) is a batch-oriented operating system that includes modules to handle interrupts, coordinate job-to-job transition, communicate with channels, manage I/O operations, maintain libraries, compile and link edit programs, and supervise multiprogramming. All these functions are performed within an IBM System/370 environment, so VSE must deal with the PSW, interrupt handling, and channel communication concepts built into this computer series.

VSE was first released in the mid-1960s as DOS. As virtual memory gained acceptance; it evolved into **DOS/VSE**. For a time, IBM urged its owners to convert to MVS, but customers continued to use DOS/VSE because it met their needs and converting to another operating system would be too costly. Recently, IBM acceded to the wishes of its users and announced continuing support for this venerable operating system, now rechristened simply VSE. Most VSE systems run on intermediate-size mainframes such as the IBM 4300 series and the 9370.

Virtual Memory Contents

VSE is a virtual memory operating system. Virtual memory is divided into two components (Fig. 20.1). The first part, beginning with address 0, exactly equals the available real memory, and is called the **real address area.** Virtual space over and above available real memory is called the **virtual address area.**

The resident operating system, called the **supervisor,** occupies the low-address region of the real address area. Following the supervisor come several **real partitions,** one (potentially) for each application program partition. Certain types of applications (for example, data communication routines) require that key modules not be paged but remain in real memory; such modules are stored in a real partition. The remainder of the real address area contains the **page pool.**

The virtual address area is divided into from one to 12 application program **partitions.** The low-priority **background** partition comes first, followed by up to 11 **foreground** partitions (Fig. 20.1). Following the application program partitions is a **shared virtual area** that holds routines designed to be shared by all partitions (for example, a data base manager).

The contents of the real address area occupy real memory (Fig. 20.2). The partitions in the virtual address area reside on

Fig. 20.1   Virtual memory space is divided into a real address
                     area and a virtual address area.

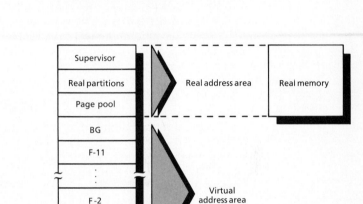

an external paging device, usually disk. Pages are swapped between the external paging device and the real memory page pool.
Because paging is a hardware function, it is transparent to software, so it is reasonable to pretend that programs and the operating system really reside in virtual memory. Focusing on the
virtual memory model makes the operating system much easier
to visualize.

SYSGEN and IPL

An operating system does not simply spring into being; it must
come from somewhere. For VSE, the source is a procedure called
system generation (**SYSGEN**).

   IBM maintains a complete master copy of the operating system. When a customer decides to purchase or lease a computer,
the customer's data processing environment is reviewed and
necessary operating system functions are identified. Key modules are concentrated in the supervisor, while infrequently used
routines are assigned transient status. Tables are created to
support the specific I/O devices and the partition configuration

Fig. 20.2

Fig. 20.2   The contents of the real address area are stored in
real memory. The partitions in the virtual address
area are stored on an external paging device (usually,
disk). Pages are swapped between the external paging
device and the real page pool.

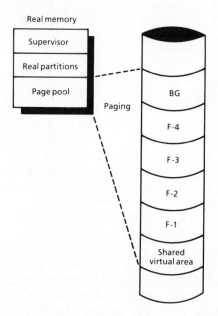

chosen by the customer, and this made-to-order operating system is copied to a system residence device, usually a disk pack.
The **SYSRES** pack then becomes the source of the operating system on the customer's computer.

As long as the operating system, even a disk operating system, remains on disk, it does little or no good. If the operating
system is to perform useful work, it must be copied into memory. The process of copying the resident operating system into
real memory is called initial program load (**IPL**). Generally,
small computers are booted, and mainframes are IPLed.

Memory Management

When memory contains several independent programs, space
must be carefully managed to avoid conflicts. At the virtual

memory level, VSE is a fixed-length partition operating system. At system generation time, virtual memory is divided into from one to 12 application program partitions. The operator, at IPL time, can change the standard configuration, but once the system starts running, virtual memory allocation is fixed and constant.

Memory protection is related to memory allocation. Each partition is assigned a unique protection key. Any attempt to execute an instruction that would destroy the contents of any storage location in another partition generates a protection interrupt. Usually, the offending program is terminated.

Note that application program partitions are defined in virtual memory. How is real memory managed? On an IBM System/370 computer, virtual addresses are broken into segment, page, and displacement portions and are dynamically translated by hardware. Consequently, to support dynamic address translation, VSE maintains program segment and page tables. Additionally, the operating system relies on a page frame table to keep track of available real memory space. However, the tasks associated with swapping pages are transparent to system users.

Loading Application Programs

Data processing applications often call for executing a series of related programs; for example, payroll might involve data entry and verification, a sort, the payroll program, and a check printing routine. Under VSE, such applications form a **job.** The computer, however, does not concurrently load and execute all the programs making up a job; instead, it loads one **task** at a time. A task is a single program or routine. A job is a set of related tasks.

Following IPL, the system is ready to accept application programs. On early versions of DOS, the computer operator directly controlled loading tasks by communicating with the single program initiation (SPI) routine, but SPI is no longer supported. Instead, job control language statements are prepared by the programmer and submitted through the job stream. Generally, the job stream is prepared interactively using an editor such as VSE/ICCF (Interactive Computing and Control Facility), CICS, or VM/CMS XEDIT.

Each job begins with a JOB statement and ends with a /& statement. EXEC statements identify individual job steps. Generally, several jobs are submitted, back to back and processed in sequence, one after another. JOB and /& statements serve to separate jobs; within a job, the EXEC statements serve to identify individual job steps or tasks. Because the control statements can be converted to electronic form, job-to-job and step-to-step transition can be handled by an operating system module, so little or no operator intervention is required.

The Job Control Program

Job steps or tasks are loaded by a **job control program**. When a transition point (such as end-of-job-step) is reached, the supervisor loads the job control program into the newly freed partition. (Note that this routine is *not* part of the resident operating system.) The job control program then reads job control statements, makes device assignments, prepares the partition for the application routine, performs other housekeeping functions, and in response to an EXEC statement, asks the resident supervisor to load the requested program.

For example, consider the sequence of events outlined in Fig. 20.3. A program in the background partition has just reached successful completion and executed a RETURN (Fig. 20.3a). Thus, the supervisor gets control and loads the job control program from the SYSRES pack into the background partition (Fig. 20.3b). The job control program, in turn, reads job control statements for the next job step and performs any requested services. Normally, the job step ends with an EXEC statement. In response, the job control program gives control back to the resident supervisor, which loads the requested program from a library into the background partition (Fig. 20.3c).

Figure 20.3 illustrates how a program is loaded into virtual memory. What *really* happens? First, the supervisor attempts to load all the new task's pages into real memory. However, except for the first few programs following IPL, there simply will not be enough room in real memory, so the incoming application program will immediately be paged-out to the external page device. In effect, the program is copied, page by page, through real memory and onto the external paging device. From there, pages are swapped into the real page pool as needed.

Spooling and Queuing

Under VSE, a separate job stream is maintained for each partition. When a partition becomes free, the job control program is loaded into the partition and reads the partition's job stream. Jobs are processed in sequential order—first come, first served.

Fig. 20.3 An example of program loading.

a. An application routine in the background partition returns control to the supervisor.

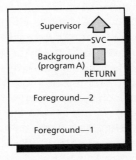

b. The supervisor loads the job control program into the background partition.

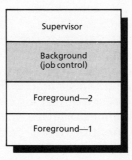

c. The application program then overlays the job control program.

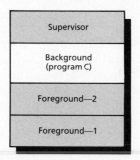

Within a job, the individual job steps are loaded and executed in sequential order.

Job control statements are typically prepared using an editor (such as VSE/ICCF) and stored on a disk file. The file's contents are then inserted into the job stream by issuing commands to a scheduler such as **VSE/POWER** (Priority Output Writers, Execution processors, and input Readers). VSE/POWER interprets those commands, reads the job control statements, separates the jobs, and based on job class, copies each job to the end of the appropriate partition's queue. Subsequently, the job control program gets all its input from high-speed disk.

In addition to enqueuing jobs, VSE/POWER also serves an an output spooler. Program output to the system output device (generally, the printer) is spooled to disk and later sent to the printer by VSE/POWER. Because application programs need not wait for slow printer output, their residency time is decreased. That, in turn, increases the rate of program turnover and means that more application programs can be executed in the same amount of time. VSE/POWER normally occupies the high-priority foreground-1 partition.

Multiprogramming and Physical I/O

VSE is a multiprogramming operating system. The key to multiprogramming is the speed disparity between a computer and its I/O devices. Rather than forcing a high-speed processor to wait for a (relatively) slow I/O device, the processor switches its attention to another program. By executing several programs concurrently, both throughput and turnaround are improved.

If a multiprogramming operating system is to utilize otherwise wasted I/O time, it must take action at the beginning and end of each physical I/O operation. Under VSE, physical I/O is implemented through a **physical I/O control system (PIOCS)**.

To use PIOCS, the programmer first writes a channel program (see Chapter 19). Next, a **CCB** macro creates a **command control block** containing such information as the symbolic name of the actual I/O device, the address of the first CCW in the channel program, and various flags. Both the CCB and the channel program are stored in the program partition (Fig. 20.4a).

To request an I/O operation, the programmer codes an **execute channel program (EXCP)** macro (Fig. 20.4b). The EXCP references the command control block (which, remember, points to the channel program), and generates a supervisor call interrupt. Once it gets control, the supervisor stores the address of the

Fig. 20.4   The physical input/output control system.

a. The programmer codes a channel program and a command control block (CCB).

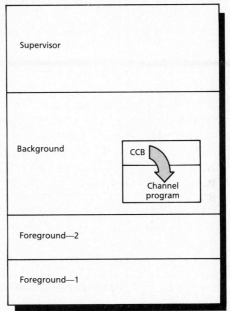

b. The programmer requests an I/O operation by coding an EXCP macro. The resulting supervisor call interrupt transfers control to the supervisor, which stores the channel program address in the channel address word and executes a start I/O instruction.

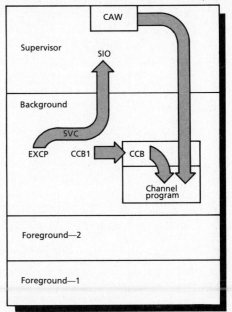

c. Unable to continue until the I/O operation is completed, the program asks the supervisor to put it into a wait state.

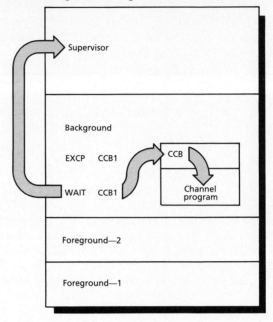

d. The supervisor responds by saving the program's most current PSW, changing the wait state bit (14) to 1, and giving control to another task.

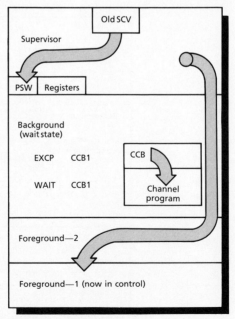

channel program in the channel address word, and executes a start I/O command. The channel then assumes responsibility for the I/O operation and the supervisor returns control to the application program.

In most cases, the program is unable to continue until the requested I/O operation is completed, so it issues a **WAIT** (Fig. 20.4c). The WAIT macro generates another supervisor call. In response, the operating system drops the program into a wait state, saves the old SVC PSW (which points to the application program), and starts another task (Fig. 20.4d). Eventually, when the I/O operation is completed, the program's PSW is reset to a ready state, and the task becomes eligible to resume processing.

Each partition has a **control block** (Fig. 20.5). Following *any* interrupt, the PSW associated with the interrupted program is copied from the old PSW field and stored in the partition's control block. The partition control blocks are established at SYSGEN time and linked in priority order, with F-1 pointing to F-2, F-2 pointing to F-3, and so on down to the background partition. The dispatcher searches the partition control blocks in priority order, checking the PSW stored in each one for a ready task. As

---

Fig. 20.5   Each partition has a control block. The most current PSW associated with the task in that partition is stored in the control block. The dispatcher searches the control blocks in priority order, and starts the first ready program it finds.

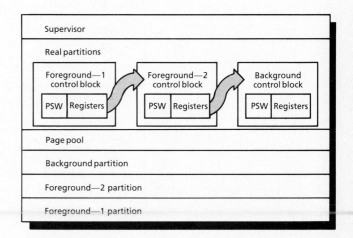

soon as it finds a ready task the supervisor loads the partition's PSW, and the selected program resumes executing with the next machine cycle.

The Logical I/O Control System

Few application programmers are willing (or even able) to write their own channel programs, so few VSE programmers use PIOCS. Instead, they rely on the **logical (I/O) control system (LIOCS)**.

For each file accessed by a program, the programmer codes a **DTF (define the file)** macro. The DTF generates a table that specifies the file's logical record length, block size, record format, and other descriptive information needed by the access

Fig. 20.6
A programmer codes a DTF to define each file. Logical I/O instructions generate calls to the access method which, in addition to a channel program and blocking/deblocking logic, includes the necessary PIOCS commands.

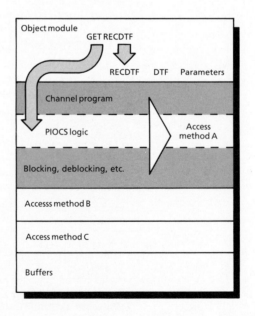

method. (In effect, the DTF defines the access method.) As it builds a load module, the linkage editor grafts a copy of the appropriate access method onto the program object module. Once the resulting load module (or **phase**) is loaded and begins running, the programmer's GET and PUT or READ and WRITE macros reference the DTF table and call the access method (Fig. 20.6).

The access method contains a channel program. A second key component is the PIOCS logic (CCB, EXCP, and WAIT) needed to support physical I/O—LIOCS uses PIOCS. Finally, the access method contains instructions to support blocking, deblocking, and buffering.

Allocating Peripheral Devices

VSE uses three key tables to control I/O device allocation. The **physical unit block,** or **PUB,** table lists the peripheral devices attached to the system (Fig. 20.7). Each device has a single, 8-byte PUB table entry; the first byte identifies the channel number, the second identifies the device number, the other six hold various pointers and flags. This table, stored in the supervisor partition, is created at system generation time and maintained in channel sequence.

Programmers rarely refer to physical I/O devices. Instead, they use symbolic names. The symbolic names are listed in a **logical unit block,** or **LUB,** table. There is one LUB table for each partition. LUB table entries are stored in a fixed sequence (Fig. 20.8). Each entry is 2 bytes long and points to a PUB table entry.

The best way to visualize the relationship between the PUB and LUB tables is through an example (Fig. 20.9). Assume a program in the background partition has just issued an SVC requesting input data from logical device SYSIPT. To find the physical device, the supervisor looks at the background partition's LUB table. SYSIPT is always the second entry in any LUB table (Fig. 20.9a). The first byte of this entry identifies PUB table entry 03 as the one containing information on the physical device assigned to SYSIPT—it's channel 0, device 14 (00 0E in hex, Fig. 20.9b).

A start I/O (SIO) instruction's operands specify the channel and device address of the physical unit. Under VSE, the PUB table is the source of this information (Fig. 20.9c). Assuming the channel is free, the channel/device address is moved into an SIO

Fig. 20.7   Each physical device attached to a VSE system is
                       listed in the PUB table.

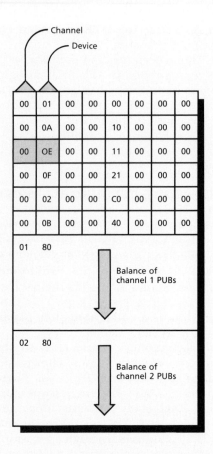

instruction, the instruction is executed, and the channel takes
over.

What if the channel is busy? Rather than keep the system
waiting, an I/O operation that cannot be started because of a
channel-busy condition is placed on a **channel queue** for later
processing. Following any I/O interrupt, the supervisor checks
the channel queue for pending requests before resuming normal
processing. Individual channel queue entries are 4 bytes long.

Fig. 20.8   Each partition has its own LUB table that provides logical names for the physical devices. The logical names are listed in a fixed sequence.

SYSRDR	Input unit for job control statements
SYSIPT	Input unit for application programs
SYSIN	(Optional) System input device for spooling
SYSPCH	Punched card output unit
SYSLST	Printer output unit
SYSOUT	(Optional) System output device for spooling
SYSLOG	Operator messages output unit
SYSLNK	Disk extent for linkage editor input
SYSRES	System residence device (or extent)
SYSVIS	Disk extent for virtual storage support
SYSCAT	Disk extent for VSAM master catalog
SYSREC	Disk extent for error logging
SYS000–	Other units. Exact meaning is
SYSmax	installation dependent

Each one contains the address of a command control block (CCB) and a pointer to the next channel queue entry (Fig. 20.10).

The meaning of a logical device name can vary from partition to partition. For example, assume the standard system input device is a terminal, and that the foreground-1, foreground-2, and background partitions all require terminal input. Each partition has its own LUB table. In F-1, SYSIPT might be assigned to PUB entry 1 and thus, indirectly, to channel 00 device 01 (Fig. 20.11), while in F-2, SYSIPT is linked to PUB entry 2 and channel 00 device 02. Meanwhile, in the background LUB, SYSIPT points to PUB 3 and thus to channel 00 device 03.

Spooling is implemented in much the same way. If, for example, the spooling routine resides in the F-1 partition, this partition's SYSRDR and SYSIPT might refer to actual terminals or to a disk holding VSE/ICFF (editor) files. In all other partition LUB tables, SYSRDR and SYSIPT refer to the disk files created by the spooling program. Under VSE, another logical input device, SYSIN, can be designated as a system input device that contains both control statements and data. On output, SYSOUT can be designated as the spooled system output device.

Fig. 20.9   Each LUB table entry points to a PUB table entry, and
                   thus links the logical name to a physical device.

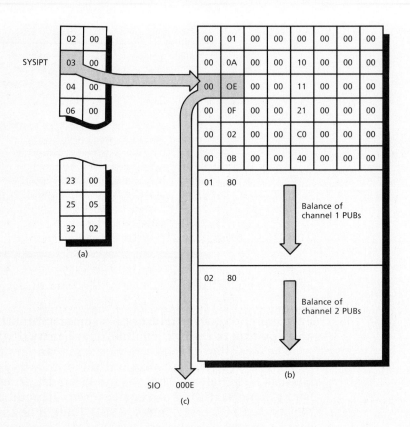

(a)

(b)

(c)

Fig. 20.10   The channel queue holds pending I/O requests. Each
                   channel queue entry holds the address of a command
                   control block and a pointer to the next channel queue
                   entry.

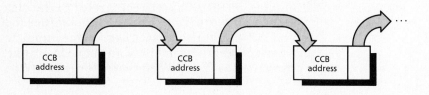

Fig. 20.11   Because each partition has its own LUB table, the same logical name can refer to different physical devices in different partitions.

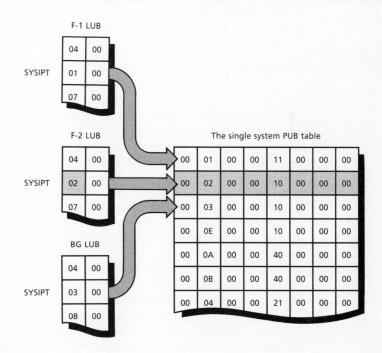

<hr>

Libraries

On early versions of DOS, source statements occupied a source statement library, object modules were stored in a relocatable library, load modules (or phases) resided in a core image library, and cataloged procedures had a separate library of their own. Current releases of VSE support a much more flexible library structure, however.

A VSE **library** is divided into one or more **sublibraries**. Those sublibraries, in turn, hold **members**. A library's **directory** lists its sublibraries, and a sublibrary's directory lists each member's name, type, disk address, and size. Valid member types include phases or load modules, object modules, source books, cataloged procedures, memory dumps, and user-defined members. At the user's option, a library can be limited to a single type, but member types can also be mixed on the same library. Both system and private libraries are supported.

VSE includes programs to maintain, service, and copy library members. These programs allow a programmer to add, delete, or rename members, maintain library directories, list or punch library members, create new private libraries, and reorganize a library.

Summary

VSE is a fixed-partition multiprogramming operating system designed to support small to medium-size IBM mainframe computers. Virtual memory is divided into two regions. The real address area contains the supervisor, optional real partitions, and the page pool; its total size equals the available real memory. The virtual address area holds space in excess of real memory capacity and is divided into a background partition, from one to 11 foreground partitions, and a shared virtual area. The real address area is physically stored in real memory; the virtual address area is stored on an external page device, usually disk. A customer's version of the operating system is created during SYSGEN. The operating system is loaded into primary memory during IPL.

A task is a single program or routine; a job is a set of related tasks. Tasks are loaded into memory under control of the job control program. When a partition becomes free, the supervisor loads the transient job control program, which reads job stream commands and identifies the next program to be loaded. Often, the job stream is spooled or queued; VSE/POWER is a popular spooler.

The key to controlling multiprogramming is I/O. Under VSE, a programmer can code physical input/output control system (PIOCS) macros. The CCB macro creates a command control block that points to a channel program. The command control block is referenced by an execute channel program (EXCP) macro, which generates an SVC interrupt that tells the supervisor to start the I/O operation. A third PIOCS macro, WAIT, generates another SVC; in response, the supervisor drops the program into a wait state and transfers control to another task.

Few programmers code PIOCS macros. Instead, most rely on logical input/output control system (LIOCS) macros, such as DTF, GET, PUT, READ, and WRITE. Under LIOCS, physical I/O is performed by an access method which contains the channel program, necessary PIOCS logic, and blocking/deblocking routines.

I/O device allocation is controlled through system tables. The physical unit block, or PUB, table holds one entry for each I/O device attached to the system. The logical unit block, or LUB, table relates symbolic device assignments to the physical devices listed in the PUB table. If a channel is busy at the time an input or output operation is requested, the request is kept pending by placing it on a channel queue; later, when an I/O interrupt occurs, the supervisor checks for pending I/O requests before starting the next program.

When an interrupt occurs, the PSW associated with the interrupted program is copied from an old PSW field into a partition control block. The supervisor determines internal priority by searching the partition control blocks in fixed sequence, from foreground-1 to background. Each partition has its own job stream. When the partition becomes free, the job control program loads the next program in that partition's job stream.

A VSE library is divided into sublibraries that hold members of various types. A library's directory lists its sublibraries; a sublibrary's directory lists its members. VSE supports both system and private libraries.

Key Words

background	job control	PIOCS
CCB	program	PUB
channel queue	library	real address area
command control	LIOCS	real partition
block	logical I/O	shared virtual area
control block	control system	sublibrary
define the file	logical unit block	supervisor
directory	LUB	SYSGEN
DOS/VSE	member	SYSRES
DTF	page pool	task
EXCP	partition	virtual address area
execute channel	physical I/O	VSE
program	control system	VSE/POWER
foreground	physical unit	WAIT
IPL	block	
job		

References

1. Eckols, Steve, and Milnes, Michele (1989). *DOS/VSE JCL*, second edition. Fresno, California: Mike Murach & Associates, Inc.

Exercises

1. Distinguish between the real address area and the virtual address area.

2. Sketch a map of virtual memory under VSE. Assume four application program partitions.

3. How are the contents of virtual memory physically stored under VSE?

4. Briefly describe memory management under VSE.

5. Distinguish between a job and a task.

6. Explain how application programs are loaded from a core image library under VSE. The job control program is transient. What does this mean?

7. Explain how PIOCS supports multiprogramming under VSE.

8. Explain the difference between PIOCS and LIOCS. Which one does an application programmer use? Why? When LIOCS is used, where is the PIOCS logic normally found?

9. Briefly describe processor management under VSE. In other words, explain how the supervisor selects the next program to be given control.

10. Explain how I/O device access is controlled under VSE. Why is there one LUB table for each partition? Why is there a single PUB table for the entire system?

11. Briefly explain how the external priority decision is made under VSE. In other words, explain how the supervisor selects the next program to be loaded into memory.

12. Briefly describe the VSE library structure.

21

IBM MVS

This chapter explains how IBM's full-size
mainframe operating systems—VS1, VS2,
and MVS—work internally. Key topics
include:

The OS/370 family
  Virtual memory contents

Job and task management
  Jobs and tasks
  The master scheduler
  The job entry subsystem
  The initiator/terminator
  Task management

Control blocks

Dispatching

Allocating peripheral devices
  The unit control block
  The task input/output table
  The DCB and the DEB
  Open
  Linking I/O control blocks

Data management

System generation

Before you begin reading, be sure you
understand virtual memory (Chapter 16)
and System/370 principles of operation
(Chapter 19).

The OS/370 Family

IBM's System/360 computer family was announced in 1964. Initially, it supported three operating systems—DOS, OS/MFT, and OS/MVT. The current version of DOS is called VSE (see Chapter 20). OS/MFT (multiprogramming with a fixed number of tasks) incorporated fixed-partition memory management, and has evolved into **OS/VS1**. OS/MVT (multiprogramming with a variable number of tasks) utilized dynamic memory management. It became **OS/VS2**, and, eventually, MVS. This chapter discusses a number of internal concepts that are common to the operating systems in the OS/370 family.

Virtual Memory Contents

OS/VS1, OS/VS2, and MVS are virtual storage operating systems. Virtual memory is divided into a **real address area** and a **virtual address area** (Fig. 21.1). The resident supervisor begins with real address area byte 0. Next comes space for key system control blocks. The rest of the real address area is called the **vir-**

Fig. 21.1   Under OS/VS1, OS/VS2, and MVS, virtual memory is divided into a real address area and a virtual address area.

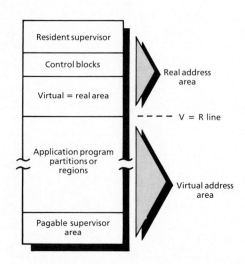

tual-equals-real (or **V** = **R**) area; the line separating the real and virtual address areas is called the V = R line. If necessary, application routines can be loaded into the V = R area. The remaining V = R space forms the page pool.

The virtual address area ends with a pagable supervisor that holds transient supervisor modules. Under VS1, the remaining virtual address area is divided into as many as fifteen fixed-length application program **partitions.** Partition sizes are set at SYSGEN time and can be changed by the operator at IPL time, but once the system begins running, the partition configuration is fixed. Under VS2, this remaining virtual address area is treated as a pool of free space to be dynamically allocated at run time to as many as fifteen variable-length application program **regions.**

The real address area occupies the available real storage (Fig. 21.2), while the virtual address area is stored on an exter-

Fig. 21.2   The contents of the real address area are stored in real memory. The virtual address area is stored on an external paging device.

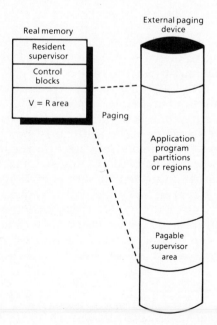

Fig. 21.3   MVS supports multiple virtual address spaces, each of which can hold multiple application programs.

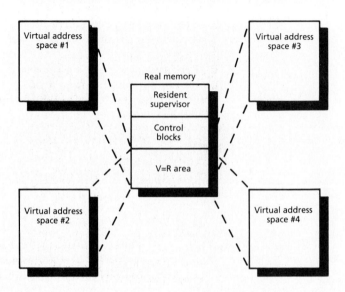

nal paging device. Paging takes place between the external paging device and that portion of the V = R area not allocated to real partitions (the page pool).

MVS supports multiple virtual address spaces, each of which can hold multiple application programs (Fig. 21.3). Consequently, the total amount of virtual memory accessible to an MVS system can significantly exceed the space limitation suggested by the address size[1]. In theory, an MVS system can concurrently execute an almost unlimited number of tasks in an almost unlimited amount of virtual storage, although the available real memory space does set practical limits.

Internally, OS/VS1, OS/VS2, and MVS are similar; the major difference is the way they manage virtual memory space.

Of course, virtual memory is just a model, and paging is transparent to the user. Consequently, it is reasonable to

[1]16 megabytes on a machine with a 24-bit address and roughly 2 gigabytes on a machine with a 31-bit address.

analyze these three operating systems by focusing on the contents of virtual memory.

Since the phrase "partition or region" would become tedious, the chapter generally refers to partitions only.

Job and Task Management

Jobs and Tasks

To a programmer, a test run is a single job that generates a listing and a set of results. To the computer, this job involves three distinct steps or tasks: compile, link edit, and execute. A **task** is a single program or routine that has been loaded on the computer and is ready to run. (Before it is loaded, the routine is called a **job step**.) A **job** consists of one or more related tasks or job steps.

Within the operating system, the routines that dispatch, queue, schedule, load, initiate, and terminate jobs or tasks comprise **job management**. Note that job management is concerned with job-to-job and task-to-task *transitions*. Once a program or routine has been loaded, **task management** supports it as it runs, basically by handling interrupts.

The Master Scheduler

The **master scheduler** (Fig. 21.4), a key job management routine, is the OS/370 dispatcher. With several application tasks sharing memory, it is inevitable that two or more will want the processor at the same time. The master scheduler resolves this conflict by following a scheduling algorithm. The operator can communicate with the master scheduler and override standard system action, perhaps improving the priority of a "hot" routine, or canceling a task locked in an endless loop.

The Job Entry Subsystem

The **job entry subsystem (JES)**, a second job management routine, reads the job stream and assigns jobs to class queues (Fig. 21.5). First, JES scans job control language statements for accuracy and, if errors are encountered, cancels the job before it even enters the system. Assuming valid JCL, cataloged procedures are added to the job stream. A series of tables listing programs by class and, within class, by priority is created and maintained. Additionally, output data are spooled to secondary storage and

Fig. 21.4 Following any interrupt, the master scheduler determines which task gets control of the processor next. The operator can override standard system action by communicating with the master scheduler.

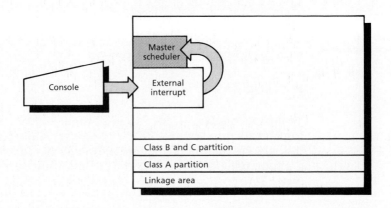

Fig. 21.5 The job entry subsystem (JES) reads the job stream and copies jobs to queues based on their class.

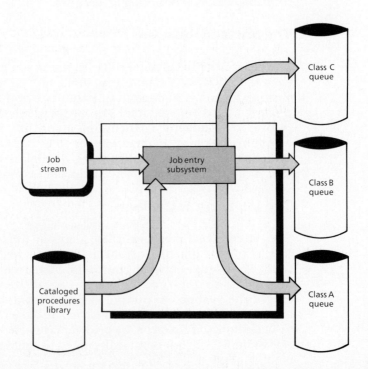

later printed or punched under control of the job entry subsystem (Fig. 21.6).

The Initiator/Terminator

There is one **initiator/terminator** for each partition or region. Like the VSE job control program, the initiator/terminator is a transient module that occupies the partition only when needed. As a partition becomes available, the initiator/terminator reads the next job step from a class queue and loads it into memory (Fig. 21.7). The terminator takes control when the task ends. Because the initiator/terminator starts and ends tasks (two obvious transition points), it, too, is part of job management.

At SYSGEN or IPL time, a specific job class (or classes) is associated with each partition or region. The partition's initiator/terminator considers only the designated job class queue or queues. Note that the job entry subsystem works with the complete job, reading all the job stream statements and enqueueing them, while the initiator/terminator concentrates on individual tasks, reading one at a time from its job class queue, loading it, and, following task completion, cleaning up the partition.

Task Management

Task management supports a program as it runs. A task management interrupt handler routine gets control following an interrupt. After the interrupt has been processed, control

---

Fig. 21.6   The job entry subsystem also acts as an output spooler.

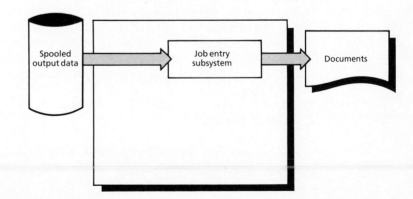

Fig. 21.7   Each partition or region has an initiator/terminator.
                       The initiator/terminator is loaded into the application
                       program partition, and subsequently loads an
                       application routine from a class queue. After the task
                       has finished, the terminator routine prepares the
                       partition for the next task.

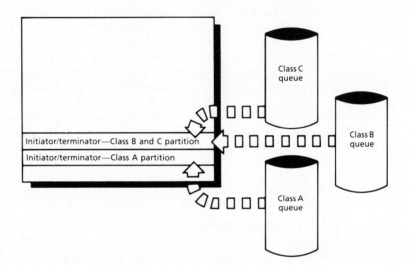

normally passes to job management's master scheduler, which
selects the next task to be executed.

On an IBM System/370 computer, interrupts are implemented by switching program status words and the old PSW
field provides a link back to the task that was executing at the
time the interrupt occurred. Following the interrupt, the master
scheduler will not necessarily return control to the original task.
Thus, the contents of the old PSW must be stored; otherwise, if
another program gains control, the link back to the initial program might be destroyed by a subsequent interrupt of the same
type. Task management is responsible for saving the old PSW.

Control Blocks

Job management, task management, and application program
routines are linked through a series of **control blocks**. The

Fig. 21.8   The communication vector table holds the addresses
of key system control blocks.

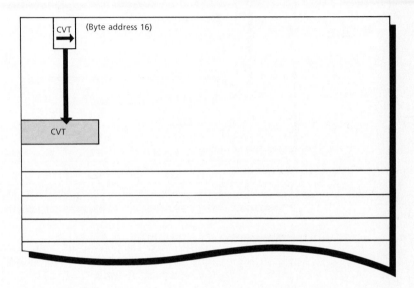

communication vector table, or **CVT** (Fig. 21.8), holds system
constants and pointers to most of the key control blocks.[2] Each
partition or region has its own **task control block,** or **TCB** (Fig.
21.9). The communication vector table points to the first TCB,
which points to the second TCB, which points to the third, and so
on, forming a TCB queue.

The contents of a given partition or region are described by a
series of **request blocks** spun off the task control block (Fig.
21.10). The existence of an active task is indicated by a **program
request block,** or **PRB.** If a supervisor call interrupt is being processed in support of the partition, this fact is indicated by a **supervisor request block,** or **SVRB.** Request blocks identify
active modules executing in (or in support of) a partition; if the
request block queue is empty, so is the partition. The terminator
wipes out these request blocks following task completion.

_____

[2]The CVT's address is stored at absolute address 16.

Fig. 21.9 The contents of a partition or region are defined in a
task control block. The TCBs (one per partition or
region) are linked by pointers.

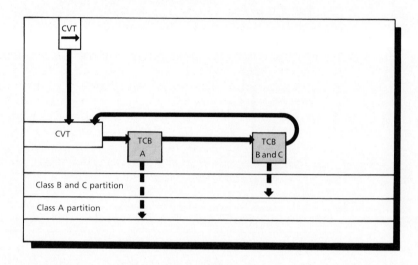

Fig. 21.10 Additional details about the contents of a partition or
region are specified in a request block queue linked to
the task control block.

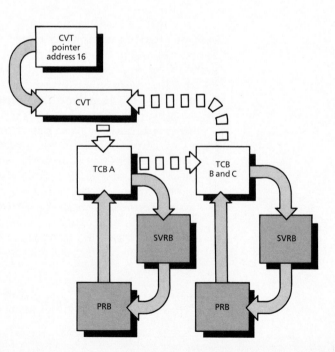

502

Dispatching

The master scheduler gets control of the processor after any interrupt. It selects the next task by following the task control block queue. The communication vector table points to the high-priority partition's task control block. If the task in this first partition is ready to go, the master scheduler looks no further. If the task in the first partition is waiting, however, the master scheduler looks to the second partition's task control block. One by one, it follows the pointers from TCB to TCB, starting the first ready task it finds. Thus, on a system with fifteen active partitions or regions, the task at the end of the TCB queue can get control only if the fourteen higher priority tasks are all in a wait state.

Let's use an example to illustrate OS/370 dispatching. Assume that the computer holds two partitions (Fig. 21.11). Both

Fig. 21.11   The master scheduler is in control. By following the task control block queue, it has discovered that partition A is empty, so it loads the initiator/terminator.

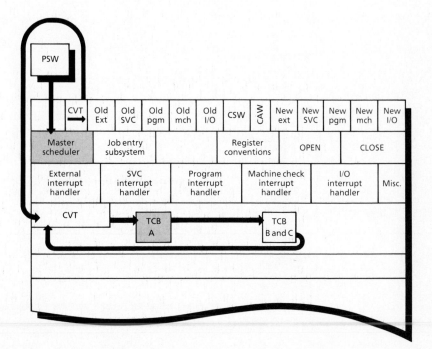

partitions are empty (no request blocks) and a number of programs have already been spooled to the job class queues. The
master scheduler has control.

The master scheduler's job is to start a task, so it searches
the TCB queue (Fig. 21.11). The communication vector table
points to the first task control block, which has no active request
blocks. Because this first partition is empty, the master scheduler creates a program request block, loads the initiator/termi-
nator, and gives it control (Fig. 21.12).

The initiator/terminator reads the first task from the class A
queue and loads it into the partition. (For simplicity, ignore the
time delay inherent in reading a program.) After executing several instructions, the application routine finds itself in need of
data, so it issues a supervisor call (Fig. 21.13). The resulting SVC
interrupt transfers control to the SVC interrupt handler routine
(Fig. 21.14).

Fig. 21.12   The initiator/terminator loads a task from the class A
queue. The program request block shows that the
partition is active.

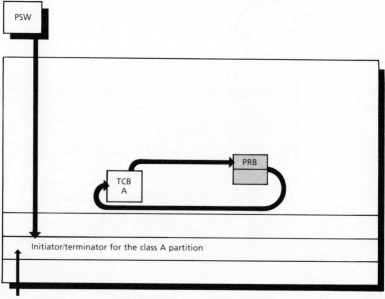

Fig. 21.13   Once the application task is loaded, it's only a matter
of time before it needs input data.

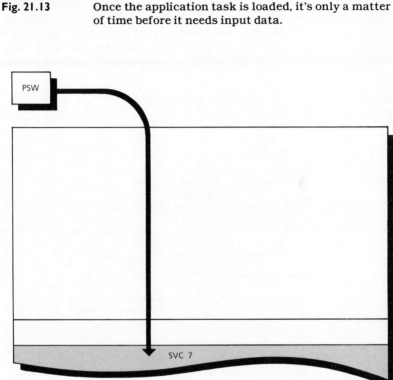

The interrupt handler stores the old SVC PSW in the class A
partition's program request block and attaches a supervisor request block to the queue (Fig. 21.14). After storing the channel
program address in the channel address word, the interrupt handler executes a start I/O instruction, and then waits until the
channel reports its status through the channel status word. Finally, the wait state bit in the original program's PSW (it's
stored in the program request block) is set to 1 (wait state), and
the master scheduler is called.

Once again, the master scheduler searches the TCB queue.
The communication vector table points to the class A partition's
task control block. The partition is active (there are request
blocks), but the PSW field in the program request block indicates
a wait state (Fig. 21.15). Since the first partition's task is waiting, the master scheduler follows the pointer to the second task

Fig. 21.14   Following the SVC interrupt, the interrupt handler
routine saves the application routine's most current
PSW, stores the channel program address in the
channel address word, and starts the I/O operation.

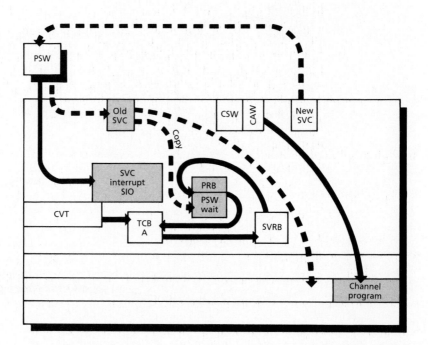

control block. Because there are no request blocks attached to
this second TCB, the master scheduler knows the partition is
empty. Thus, the initiator/terminator is loaded into the partition
(Fig. 21.16), and it loads a task from the class B queue (Fig.
21.17).

Suddenly, an I/O interrupt occurs. After PSWs are switched,
the I/O interrupt handler, a task management routine, takes
over (Fig. 21.18). The old I/O PSW field, don't forget, still points
to the class B program, and this program is in a ready state; even
so, the old PSW is copied to the program request block. The interrupt handler checks the protection key in the channel status
word, and thus identifies the partition that requested the I/O operation. By following the CVT/TCB/PRB chain, the interrupt handler locates the partition's most current program status word
and resets its wait state bit to a ready state (Fig. 21.19).

Fig. 21.15 The master scheduler determines that the program in the class A partition is in a wait state.

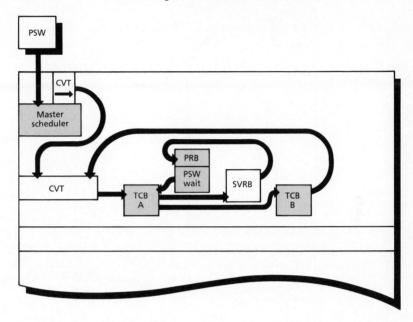

Fig. 21.16 The master scheduler continues following the TCB queue. Discovering that no program occupies the class B partition, the master scheduler creates a program request block and loads the initiator/terminator.

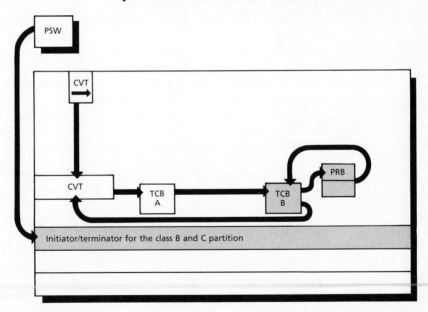

Fig. 21.17 A second application program begins processing.

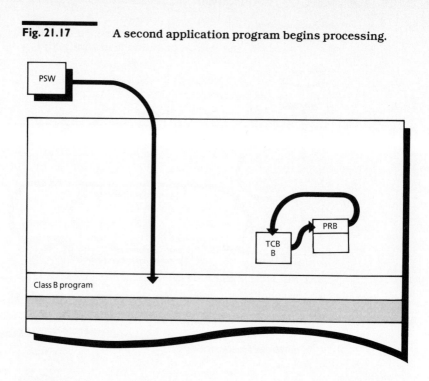

Fig. 21.18 Following an I/O interrupt, the I/O interrupt handler saves the class B program's most current PSW and deals with the interrupt.

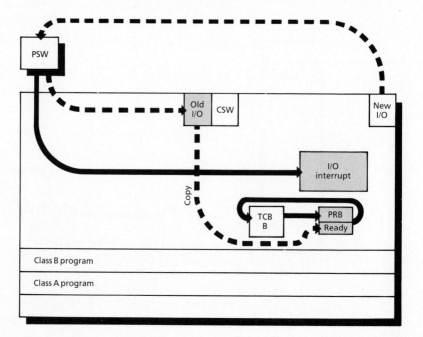

Fig. 21.19   After handling the interrupt, the I/O interrupt routine resets the appropriate program's wait state bit and calls the master scheduler. Following the task control block queue, the master scheduler finds that the class A task is now ready, so the class A routine's PSW is loaded.

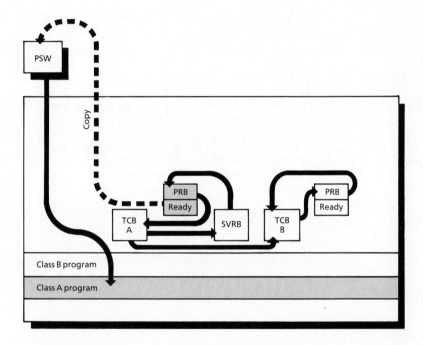

Once again, the master scheduler is called and begins searching the task control block queue. The first TCB is associated with the class A program. Because it's ready, its PSW is loaded, and the class A program resumes processing (Fig. 21.19), even though the class B task is also ready. Note that a supervisor call routine is still actively supporting this partition—you can tell by the presence of an SVRB on the request block queue. This particular I/O operation involved the system input device, and there are a number of unprocessed logical records left in the buffer.

Soon, the class A program is ready to output data to the printer, so it issues an SVC interrupt. As a result, control passes to the SVC interrupt handler (Fig. 21.20), which stores the old

Fig. 21.20   Eventually, another supervisor call returns control to
                   task management.

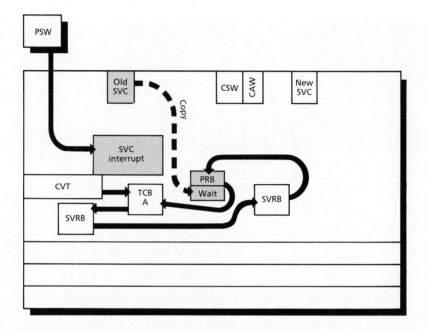

SVC PSW in the program request block, creates another SVRB,
starts the output operation, sets the application task's PSW to a
wait state, and calls the master scheduler (Fig. 21.21).

The master scheduler, once again, searches the TCB queue.
The program in the first partition is in a wait state, so it moves
to the class B partition. The class B task is in a ready state, so its
most current PSW is loaded, and the class B program resumes
processing (Fig. 21.22).

Eventually, the class B task issues an SVC requesting input
data. The SVC interrupt handler takes over, saves the old SVC
PSW, creates an SVRB, starts the input operation, sets the class
B task's PSW to a wait state (Fig. 21.23), and calls the master
scheduler (Fig. 21.24).

This time, as it searches the TCB queue, the master scheduler discovers that the programs in both partitions are in a wait

Fig. 21.21   Once again, the master scheduler gets control. The first ready task on the TCB queue is the class B program, so its PSW is loaded.

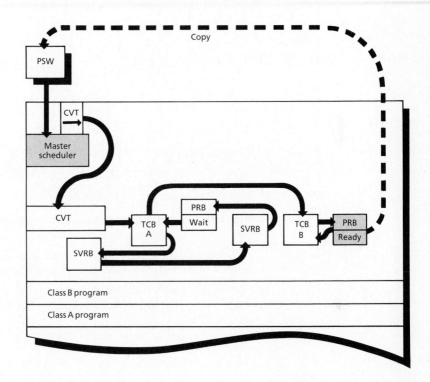

state. Because no application task is ready to go, control is passed to the job entry subsystem (Fig. 21.25), which requests an input operation and calls the master scheduler (Fig. 21.26).

Once again, all active tasks are waiting, so control is passed to the job entry subsystem (Fig. 21.27), which starts an output operation and calls the master scheduler (Fig. 21.28). The application tasks are still waiting, and the job entry subsystem has both input and output operations pending, so the system settles into a hard wait (Fig. 21.29).

Eventually, an I/O interrupt occurs (Fig. 21.30). Assume that the interrupt is for the class A program so its PSW is set to a ready state. Then the master scheduler is called. Because the

Fig. 21.22 The class B task gets control.

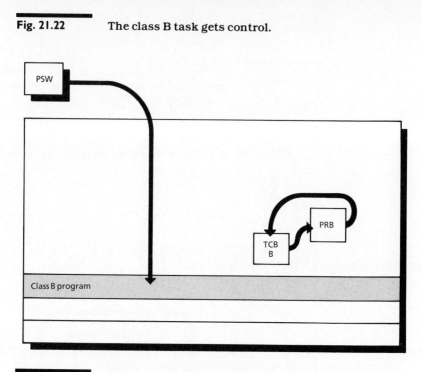

Fig. 21.23 Eventually, the class B task needs data, so it executes an SVC, and the SVC interrupt handler routine gets control.

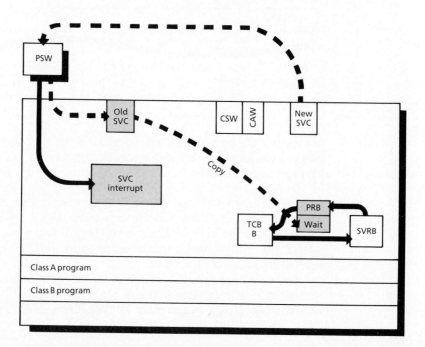

Fig. 21.24

The SVC interrupt handler calls the master scheduler. This time, both application routines are in a wait state.

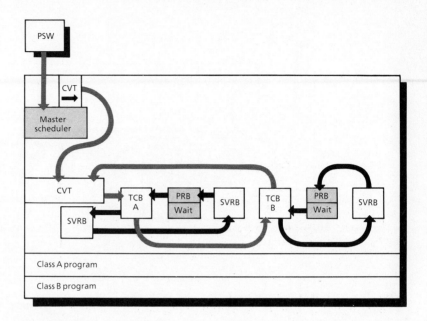

Fig. 21.25

The job entry subsystem starts an I/O operation to spool in one record.

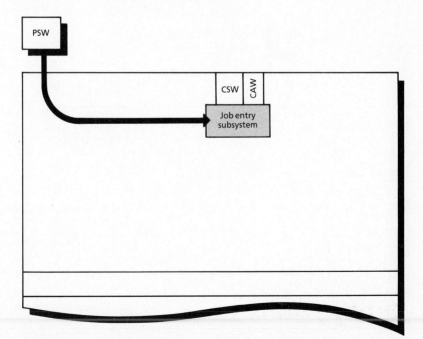

Fig. 21.26

Once again the master scheduler gets control, but both application tasks are still in a wait state.

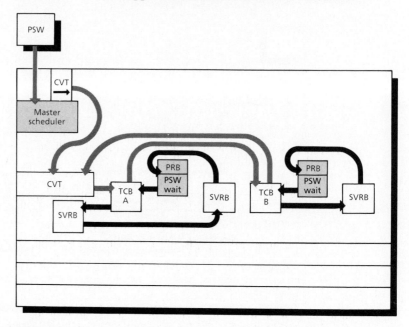

Fig. 21.27

The job entry subsystem is still waiting for the input operation to be completed, so it writes a record from the spooled output data set to the printer.

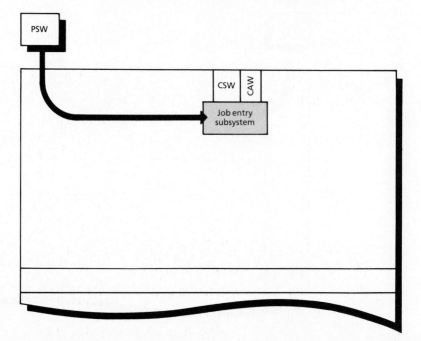

Fig. 21.28   This time, the master scheduler finds both application tasks in a wait state and the job entry subsystem waiting on two I/O operations.

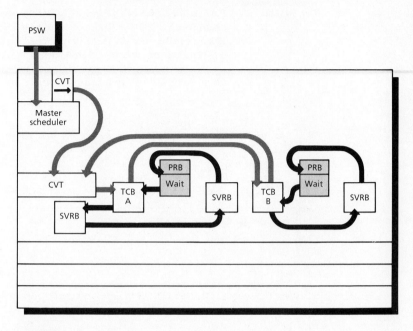

Fig. 21.29   The entire system waits.

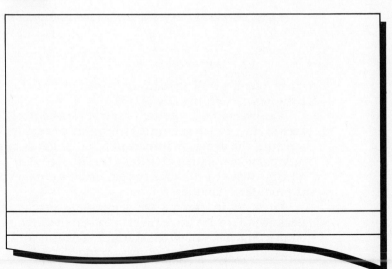

Fig. 21.30   Eventually, one of the pending I/O operations is
completed, and the channel sends an I/O interrupt.
Because the new I/O PSW is in a ready state, the
system begins executing instructions. After handling
the interrupt, the task management routine sets the
class A PSW back to a ready state.

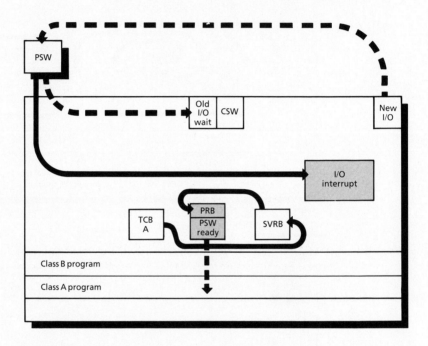

class A task's PSW is ready, it is loaded, and the class A program
resumes processing (Fig. 21.31).

Unfortunately, the two instructions into the program is a
zero divide, which generates a program interrupt (Fig. 21.32). As
a result, the program interrupt handler gets control, prepares a
dump, and calls the partition's terminator. The terminator (Fig.
21.33) erases the links to the partition's request blocks and calls
the master scheduler.

Once again, the master scheduler searches the TCB queue.
Because there are no requests blocks, the first partition must be
empty (Fig. 21.34), so the initiator/terminator is loaded into the
class A partition, and the system moves on to its next task.

Fig. 21.31   The master scheduler finds a ready state PSW and loads it.

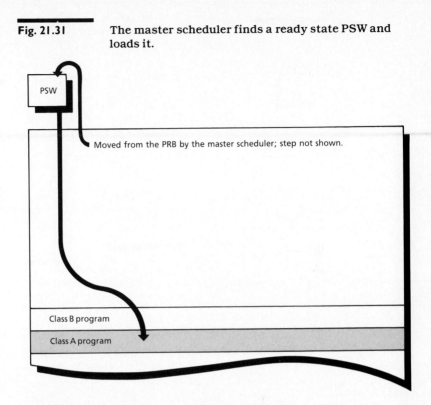

PSW

Moved from the PRB by the master scheduler; step not shown.

Class B program

Class A program

Fig. 21.32   The class A routine executes a zero divide. The resulting program interrupt gives control to the program interrupt handling routine.

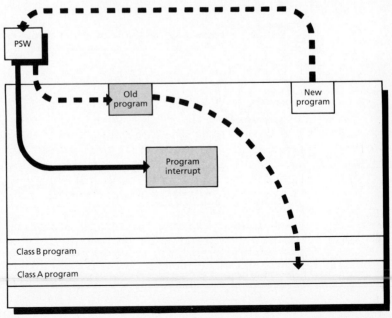

PSW

Old program

New program

Program interrupt

Class B program

Class A program

Fig. 21.33 The terminator prepares the partition from the next program by erasing the link to active request blocks.

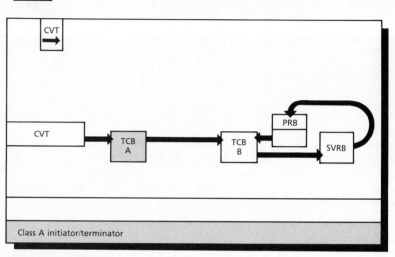

Class A initiator/terminator

Fig. 21.34 The master scheduler notes that the class A partition is empty, so the initiator/terminator is loaded.

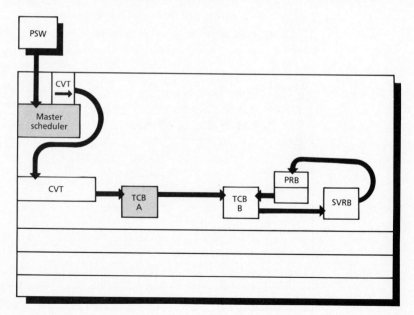

Note how predictable the dispatching process is. Following any interrupt, the master scheduler gets control. It finds the address of the first task control block in the communication vector table. Pointers link the TCBs in a fixed sequence. The master scheduler follows the chain of TCB pointers, assigning control of the processor to the first ready task it finds.

Allocating Peripheral Devices

On a single-user system, an active program has access to all input and output devices. On a multiprogramming system, however, conflicts are inevitable and must be resolved by the operating system. To implement I/O device controls, OS/VS1, OS/VS2, and MVS build and maintain a series of control blocks and pointers.

The Unit Control Block

Each peripheral device attached to a computer is listed in at least one **unit control block,** or **UCB** (Fig. 21.35). The UCB contains such information as the peripheral's channel/device address, its device type, and several sense and status fields. Each UCB points to the next one, forming a table or queue that is created at system generation time. If a DD statement's UNIT parameter (Chapter 13) specifies a device that does not appear in a unit control block, a JCL error is recognized. To the operating system, devices not listed in a UCB do not exist; each valid unit address, device type, or group name must have its own UCB.

Should a job step require exclusive access to a device, a UCB flag informs other initiator/terminators that additional tasks requesting this device should not be loaded. Other flags mark the device busy, thus helping the operating system to avoid illegal concurrent access by two or more tasks.

The Task Input/Output Table

The **task input/output table,** or **TIOT** (Fig. 21.36), is created by job management just before a task is loaded. The TIOT lists all the DDNAMEs from the step's DD statements. Pointers allow the

Fig. 21.35   Each peripheral device attached to the system is listed in a unit control block (UCB). The UCBs are linked by a series of pointers to form a queue.

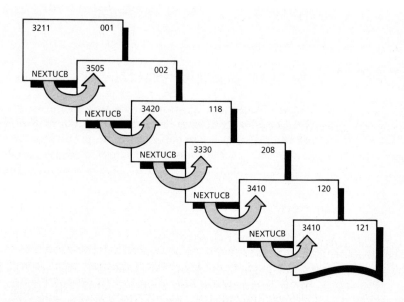

Fig. 21.36   The task input/output (TIOT) lists information from the task's DD Statements and ties each DDNAME to a unit control block entry.

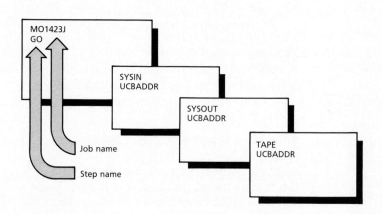

system to find the other DD parameters and to link each DDNAME to a unit control block.

The DCB and the DEB

The **data control block (DCB)** is a series of constants that describe such things as the access method, the logical record length, the block size, the record format, the DDNAME of the associated JCL statement, and other data characteristics. There is one data control block for each device accessed by the task. The **data extent block (DEB)** is an extension of the data control block. The DCB lies entirely within the programmer's own region and thus is subject to programmer modification. The DEB is not accessible to the programmer.

Open

Logically, a program calls open when it is ready to begin requesting input or output on a particular device. Open generates an SVC interrupt that transfers control to a task management routine. A key function of the open logic is completing the data control block. Not all data control block parameters must be coded within the program DCB. Some can be coded in the DD statement's DCB parameter (see Chapter 13); others are found on the data set label. The open routine merges DCB parameters from all three sources.

When the open routine is executed (Fig. 21.37), any parameters coded as zero in the program data control block (uncoded fields are zero fields) are filled from the DCB parameter of the associated DD statement. The DDNAME, remember, must be coded in the program DCB, and the open routine can find the right DD statement by checking the task input/output table. After inserting parameters from the DD statement, the open routine reads and checks the data set label. At this time, any remaining zero-value DCB fields are filled from label information. (Open *creates* a label for a *new* data set.)

Linking I/O Control Blocks

Actual physical I/O operations are controlled by a channel. The channel gets its instructions from a channel program—one or more CCWs. Channel programs are found either in the operating system or in the access method and so cannot normally be modified by the programmer.

Fig. 21.37   The open logic completes the program data control
block by merging DD parameters from the DD
statement and then merging values from the data set
label.

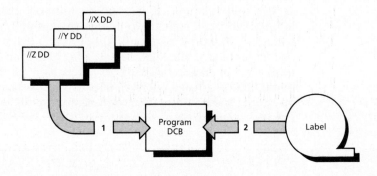

The data extent block is an extension of the data control
block that lies outside the application program partition. It provides a link between the DCB and the unit control block (Fig.
21.38). The DCB and the channel program are linked by an
input/output block, or **IOB.** As a result of these links, the super-

Fig. 21.38   The data control block is found in the user's partition.
Other control blocks outside the partition create a
complete link between the program, the physical
device, and the channel program.

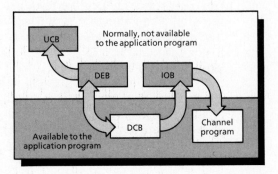

visor is able to find the physical device and its channel program given only the DCB address.

Data Management

Data management consists of routines to access and manage files and libraries. To simplify access to key libraries, pointers to their directories are stored in the communication vector table. For example, SYS1.LINKLIB contains routines used by the linkage editor, and SYS1.SVCLIB holds SVC and other transient operating system routines. Because the operating system can find their directories through the CVT, these critical libraries can be accessed quickly.

The system input and output devices are a part of data management. These two data sets provide an excellent example of the difficulty involved in separating functions into neat, clean categories. Data are placed on the system input device by the job entry subsystem, a job management routine, and moved from the device into memory under the control of task management. Yet, the system input device is part of data management. Direct communication between operating system routines is the rule rather than the exception.

System Generation

System generation is the process of creating an installation's operating system. A key is specifying which modules should be included in the resident supervisor. One possible answer is all of them; after all, it takes time to read a transient module into memory. Unfortunately, operating system routines take up space, and that space is not available for application programs. The other extreme is to keep most of the operating system on disk. Unfortunately, a great deal of time can be wasted while modules are loaded, and that's inefficient.

Somewhere between these two extremes is the best solution. On a large computer running a variety of small programs, the ideal might be close to the all-in-real alternative. A scientific machine running lengthy, compute-bound programs might lean toward a minimum-nucleus operating system. Most systems lie somewhere between these two extremes. OS/VS1, OS/VS2, and

MVS were designed to be general-purpose operating systems, capable of supporting all types of applications.

Modularity is the key to flexibility. Certain routines (the master scheduler and interrupt handlers, for example) and key control blocks must be resident. Other modules can be made resident or transient at the user's option during system generation. In effect, the operating system can be somewhat customized to fit a particular user's needs.

Summary

This chapter introduced three operating systems (VS1, VS2, and MVS) that run in a virtual environment on an IBM System/370 computer. Virtual memory is divided into a real address area containing the resident supervisor and the page pool, and a virtual address area containing the application program partitions or regions and a supervisor transient area. The line dividing the real address area from the virtual address area is called the virtual-equals-real (V = R) line; the real partitions plus the page pool make up what is called the virtual-equals-real area.

A task is a routine loaded on the computer and ready to run. A job is a set of related tasks. (Before it is loaded, a task is called a job step.) Job management is concerned with job-to-job and task-to-task transitions. Task management supports the tasks as they run.

Job management includes the master scheduler, the job entry subsystem (JES), and a transient routine called the initiator/terminator. The master scheduler dispatches tasks, identifies empty or available partitions, loads the initiator/terminator in an empty partition, and communicates with the operator. The initiator/terminator loads tasks from a library, reading and interpreting the job control language statements from the job stream as a guide. The job entry subsystem enqueues jobs and spools both input and output data. Task management is composed of interrupt handler routines.

System constants and pointers to key control areas are recorded in the communication vector table. The contents of a given partition are defined (in general terms) by a task control block. The specific functions active in a given partition are described by a chain of request blocks spun off the task control block. TCBs are linked in a fixed order, with the CVT pointing to the first TCB, the first TCB pointing to the second, and so on.

Internal priority is determined by the master scheduler as it follows this chain. IBM's dispatching scheme was illustrated by an example showing a brief interval of computer time.

The unit control block queue contains at least one entry for each physical device on the system. The task input/output table holds information taken from a job step's DD statements and describes the task's I/O device requirements. The data extent block and the input/output block link the channel program, the data control block, and the unit control block. The OPEN macro establishes this linkage.

Data management was briefly discussed. A customized version of the operating system can be created at system generation time.

Key Words

communication vector table	job management	task
	job step	task control block
control block	master scheduler	task input/output table
CVT	OS/VS1	
data control block	OS/VS2	task management
data extent block	partition	TCB
DCB	PRB	TIOT
DEB	program request block	UCB
initiator/terminator		unit control block
input/output block	real address area	virtual address area
IOB	region	
JES	request block	virtual-equals-real area
job	supervisor request block	V = R area
job entry subsystem	SVRB	

References

1. Johnson, Robert H. (1989). *MVS Concepts and Facilities.* New York: Intertext Publications, McGraw-Hill Book Company.

2. Katzan, Jr., Harry, and Tharayil, Davis (1984). *Invitation to MVS, Logic and Debugging.* New York: Petrocelli Books, Inc.

Exercises

1. Under OS/VS1, what are the contents of the real address area of virtual memory? of the virtual address area?

2. What might be found in the area assigned to the pagable supervisor?

3. What distinguishes OS/VS1, OS/VS2, and MVS?

4. Distinguish between a job, a job step, and a task.

5. Distinguish between job management and task management.

6. What are the functions of job management?

7. What are the functions of task management?

8. What does the job entry subsystem (JES) do? Describe the relationship, if any, between JES and the master scheduler.

9. The initiator/terminator is a transient module. Why? What does this mean?

10. How does the master scheduler discover if a partition is free or busy? Mention all the tables, control blocks, and pointers involved in this process.

11. The master scheduler supports operator/system communication. How? (Hint: refer back to Chapter 19, and review the external interrupt.)

12. Add a third partition (for class D jobs) to the example system developed in the text. Explain how this third partition might change the flow of control through the system.

13. Describe the series of control blocks involved in linking an application program's DCB to a unit control block and a

channel program. What is the function of each of these control blocks?

14. How are DD statement DCB subparameters and label information merged with the program DCB?

15. MVS is designed to be a general-purpose operating system. What does this mean?

22

Virtual Machines

This chapter explains how a single
computer can concurrently support several
virtual machines. Key topics include:

Operating system development
  The virtual machine concept
  VM/SP

VM's structure
  CMS

The control program(CP)
  Processor management
  Memory management
  Managing peripheral devices
  Principles of operation

Advantages

Before you begin reading, be sure you
understand virtual memory (Chapter 16),
System/370 principles of operation
(Chapter 19), and OS/370 internals
(Chapter 21).

Operating System Development

Early first-generation computers did not have operating systems. Primarily scientific machines, they were dedicated to a single user who wrote and tested programs at the console. As a result, response time was excellent, but, given the cost of the equipment, the single-user mode of operation was economically unsound.

The first operating systems supported efficient, serial-batch job-to-job transition. Typically, responsibility for running these early systems was assigned to a professional operator. Instead of working at the console, programmers prepared job decks on punched cards, submitted them to the operator, and returned a few hours later to pick up the results. Most multiprogramming operation systems were designed with such batch processing in mind.

The objective of batch processing is machine efficiency; ideally, there is always at least one job waiting for the computer, so the computer is never idle. Unfortunately, a batch system is not an efficient program development environment. Imagine writing a program on coding sheets, waiting a day or two for the punched cards to come back from the keypunching center, visually checking them, submitting the deck for compilation, waiting several hours (sometimes, a day or more) for the results, correcting a few cards, resubmitting the deck, waiting a few more hours, and so on. Programming requires concentration. With brief bursts of activity separated by lengthy wait times, it's difficult to write a good program on a batch system.

Time-sharing was an alternative. On a time-sharing system, programs are developed interactively, which is far more efficient. Unfortunately, most early time-sharing systems restricted a programmer's access to system resources, and many supported only a few languages such as BASIC and APL, making it difficult adequately to write and test a large program. Consequently, most business applications continued to be developed in a batch environment.

Modern personal computers have brought us full circle. Once again, it is possible to dedicate a complete machine and all its resources to a single programmer. However, although personal computers are at least as powerful as a typical first-generation machine, the definition of computing power has changed. Today's mainframes contain millions of bytes of main storage, execute millions of instructions per second, and support scores of secondary storage devices. Personal computers are simply not powerful enough to support testing and debugging main-frame applications.

The ideal program development environment combines the interactive nature of a personal computer with the power of a mainframe. The programmer has access to a full set of peripherals, megabytes of memory, mainframe computing speed, and a mainframe's full, rich instruction set. Such environments can be supported on a modern virtual machine system.

The Virtual Machine Concept

Start with a full-featured mainframe. Share its resources among several concurrent users. If those users occupy partitions, regions, or work spaces, you have a traditional multiprogramming or time-sharing system. Take the idea a step further. Instead of simply allocating each application routine some memory and running it directly under the operating system, simulate several imaginary computers on that real computer (Fig. 22.1). Assign each **virtual machine** its own virtual operating system and its own virtual peripherals. Traditionally, *application routines* are

Fig. 22.1   The virtual machine concept implies multiprogramming at the operating system level. Each virtual machine has its own virtual operating system and its own virtual peripherals.

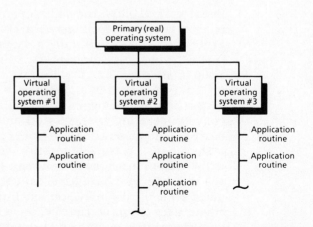

multiprogrammed. The virtual machine concept calls for multi-programming *operating systems.*

Each virtual machine has its own virtual operating system, its own virtual memory, and its own virtual peripherals. Because all the virtual machines run on the same real computer, their access to facilities is limited only by the facilities of the real machine, so each virtual machine has access to megabytes of storage and scores of peripherals, and can execute millions of instructions per second. Because they share a single real computer, program development can take place on one virtual machine in interactive mode, while production applications run on another virtual machine under a traditional multiprogramming operating system.

To the user, the virtual machine is *the* computer; the details associated with the real machine are **transparent,** hidden by the facilities of the real operating system. Consequently, much as a time-sharing user can ignore other concurrent users and imagine that he or she directly controls the computer, a virtual machine user can ignore other virtual machines.

A UNIX user (Chapter 17) can visualize an image running on a personal pseudocomputer. Details, such as the number of users sharing a text segment, dispatching, swapping, and peripheral device linkage, can be ignored because the operating system makes them transparent. The UNIX pseudocomputer is a virtual machine. IBM has implemented the virtual machine concept under **VM/SP** (virtual machine/system product).

VM/SP

In the early 1960s, the computer industry switched from discrete transistors to integrated circuits. As a result, second-generation computers quickly became obsolete. For example, IBM's System/360, announced in 1964, replaced the company's 1400 line.

The change was not entirely positive, however. Third-generation technology was radically different, supporting advanced operating systems and enhanced instruction sets, so most second-generation programs were rendered obsolete. The manager of a second-generation computing center was faced with three almost equally unacceptable choices: keep the old, obsolete, inefficient hardware; emulate a second-generation computer on a third-generation machine, thus losing many of the advantages of the new hardware; or rewrite existing programs.

Several new operating systems were developed to support

the IBM System/360 and its successors (Fig. 22.2). Initially, DOS proved quite popular, but IBM's mainstream operating system was OS. OS/MFT and OS/MVT were released in the 1960s. By the mid-1970s, they had evolved, respectively, to VS1 and VS2; eventually, VS2 became MVS.

While significant improvements were made in DOS (today's VSE), IBM has consistently urged its users to migrate toward its OS products. Many VSE users have been reluctant to change, however. Programs written under VSE and OS are different, particularly when they communicate with an external device. Consequently, converting a VSE program to an equivalent OS program, even in the same source language, means, at a minimum, changing all the input and output routines. A typical business data processing shop might have hundreds of such programs, and converting them is a significant expense. Although IBM dominates the mainframe marketplace, there are competitors who would be more than happy to pick up dissatisfied VSE users. Not even IBM can dictate such a change, so the company has continued to support VSE.

System/360 architecture imposes some limitations on a computer's capacity. Because absolute addresses are only 24 bits long, main memory is limited to 16 megabytes. Because only 4 bits are available for the protection key, only fifteen concurrent application routines can share the processor with the operating system.

In 1964, these limits were irrelevant. In those days, a large computer had perhaps 512K of memory, and running five or six applications concurrently was considered impressive. Today,

---

Fig. 22.2   Since IBM's System/360 was announced, several new operating systems have evolved to support it and its successors.

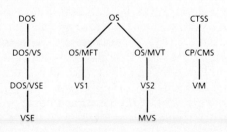

however, a modern mainframe is capable of supporting more memory and more concurrent applications than anyone dreamed possible in 1964. These new, more powerful machines require new, more powerful operating systems. However, the aggregate investment in software is thousands of times what it was in the 1960s, and it is unrealistic to assume that potential customers will willingly convert all those programs just to gain speed or computing power. If a new computer is to sell, it must maintain compatibility with applications written under the old operating systems.

If all IBM applications had been written under OS, upgrading to a new, more powerful operating system would be relatively easy, but VSE has proved surprisingly popular. Consequently, IBM faced a problem. Clearly, a new operating system was needed. Maintaining compatibility with two essentially incompatible operating systems, VSE and OS, was considered essential. VM has emerged as a solution.

Under IBM's VM, the **real computer's** resources are managed by a high-level operating system called the **control program** or **CP** (Fig. 22.3). Normally, application routines run under the operating system. With VM, operating systems are managed by the control program, and application routines run under those **virtual operating systems.**

Fig. 22.3   Under VM, the real computer is managed by a control program. Other virtual operating systems run under CP, managing their own application routines.

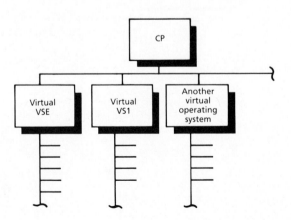

The result is considerable leverage. For example, on a normal VS1 system, up to fifteen application routines share memory with the operating system. With VM, up to fifteen concurrent virtual operating systems can each manage up to fifteen application routines, yielding 225 potential concurrent programs! It is also possible to run a virtual control program under a real control program (Fig. 22.4). Imagine fifteen copies of CP, each of which manages fifteen virtual operating systems. That's 225 operating systems. Now, picture each of them managing fifteen application routines. That's leverage!

Each virtual operating system manages a virtual machine and controls its own virtual memory and virtual peripheral devices. A virtual machine is functionally equivalent to a real machine. The control program simulates a real computer on each virtual machine, so the virtual operating systems can function without change. Any VSE- or OS-based operating system can run under VM.

For example, consider the problem faced by a VSE shop that has outgrown its system. A more powerful computer capable of supporting more concurrent application routines is needed, but hundreds of VSE programs exist, and revising all of them is

Fig. 22.4   It is even possible to run another control program under CP.

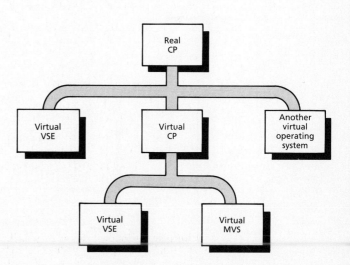

clearly out of the question. With VM, the programs need not be revised. Instead, two virtual copies of VSE can be loaded. Each one can support up to twelve concurrent application routines, thus doubling the system's capacity. Additionally, those routines can run on a larger, faster, more powerful computer.

VM's Structure

Under VM, the real computer's resources are managed by the control program (Fig. 22.5). As with any current IBM mainframe, memory starts with several fixed locations—old PSWs, new PSWs, the channel address word, the channel status word, and so on. Next comes the resident portion of CP, which holds key tables and control blocks plus routines that dispatch virtual machines, manage real memory, control paging, handle interrupts, and so on. Some CP modules are pagable; space for them comes next. Finally, the remaining real memory is divided into real page frames. Pages are swapped between the real page frames and the external paging devices associated with one or more virtual machines.

Visualize each virtual machine as though it were a complete computer in its own right. Its virtual memory begins with a set of virtual fixed memory locations; in other words, each virtual operating system has its own old and new PSWs, its own channel command word, and its own channel status word. Following the fixed locations comes the virtual operating system itself.

Fig. 22.5   The basic structure of a VM system.

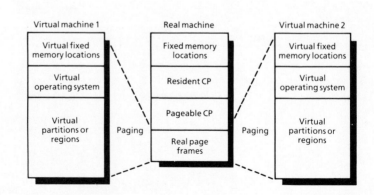

Remaining virtual memory holds virtual program partitions or regions.

On every operating system you've studied to this point, key modules and control fields were stored in fixed real memory locations. Since virtual operating systems are subject to paging (Fig. 22.5), a virtual operating system's modules will *not* occupy the expected, real, absolute addresses. Instead, a virtual operating system runs under the control program in much the same way an application routine runs under a traditional operating system.

For example, consider the fixed memory locations. The real computer has a set of fixed locations that start at *real* address 0. Each virtual machine has its own set of fixed locations that start at its *virtual* address 0. When an interrupt is sensed, which PSWs are switched? The real ones. Interrupts are sensed by hardware, and, as far as hardware is concerned, there is only one real computer. Once PSWs have been switched, the control program's interrupt handler routine is activated. If necessary, CP can then switch (through software) the appropriate virtual machine's PSWs, thus *simulating* the interrupt at the virtual machine level.

The real control program does not concern itself with the application routines. Each virtual operating system is responsible for managing its own processor time, virtual memory space, and virtual peripheral devices. CP communicates with the hardware, simulates the results for the virtual machines, protects the virtual machines from each other, and allows the virtual operating systems to handle the details.

Figure 22.6 lists operating systems that can control a virtual machine. Note that VM can run under VM. RSCS, the remote spooling and communication system, supports remote process-

Fig. 22.6   All these operating systems can run under VM.

DOS	OS/PCP	PS44	MVS/TSO
DOS/VS	OS/MFT	RSCS	VM
DOS/VSE	OS/MVT		CMS
VSE	OS/VS1		
	OS/VS2		
	MVS		
	OS-ASP		

ing. CMS, the conversational monitor system, is an interactive, single-user operating system that supports program development. It is a key part of VM that deserves a more detailed description.

CMS

Traditional operating systems are not very good for program development. Multiprogramming implies batch processing. Time-sharing systems are interactive, but most limit the programmer to a small subset of a mainframe's resources. An ideal program development environment would combine the interactive nature of a personal computer and the resources of a large mainframe. Running as a virtual operating system under CP, CMS does exactly that (Fig. 22.7).

CMS, the **Conversational Monitor System,** simulates a personal computer. The user's terminal acts as a console. Each user has his or her own CMS virtual machine complete with virtual memory, virtual batch devices (a reader, a printer, and a punch), and virtual disk space. Because it runs under CP, a CMS virtual machine's facilities are limited only by the mainframe's facilities. Each user has access to a variety of compilers, a linkage editor, utility routines, and a spooler. Additionally, users can assign work to the CMS batch facility and run two or more

Fig. 22.7   CMS is an interactive, single-user operating system that controls a virtual machine under VM. It supports an interactive program development environment.

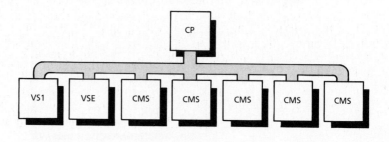

independent tasks in parallel. CMS supports a powerful, interactive program development environment.

The Control Program (CP)

Processor Management

The control program uses a time-slicing algorithm to manage the real processor's time. A virtual machine is given control of the processor for a fixed amount of time. When the time slice expires, CP passes control to another virtual machine. Interactive virtual machines (for example, CMS users) are assigned frequent but brief time slices. Noninteractive virtual machines (for example, a VSE system running accounting applications) are assigned fewer but longer time slices. Each virtual operating system manages its own time, shifting from application routine to application routine by responding to interrupts or by implementing a secondary time-slicing algorithm. Thus, each virtual operating system "thinks" it controls access to the processor.

Memory Management

VM can be implemented only on computers that support dynamic address translation. Memory space is managed using segmentation and paging techniques, with 64K-byte segments divided into 4K pages. A demand paging algorithm controls swapping between real memory and one or more external paging devices. The control program maintains a separate set of page frame tables and a separate set of paging and segmentation tables for each virtual machine.

Paging can be initiated by the control program or by one of the virtual operating systems. If it's initiated by CP, paging is transparent to the virtual machine. As far as the control program is concerned, a paging request coming from a virtual operating system is an I/O operation.

With both virtual and real operating systems initiating paging, a VM system can appear confusing. Sometimes, a simple visualization helps. Imagine a page of data stored on disk. Mentally transfer the page into a virtual machine's virtual memory (Fig. 22.8). Next, move it to the *real* machine's virtual memory. Finally, transfer the page to real memory. Note that a single

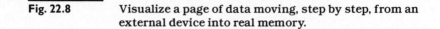

Fig. 22.8   Visualize a page of data moving, step by step, from an
                       external device into real memory.

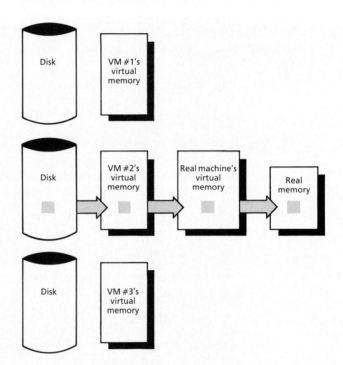

computer's real memory supports a much larger virtual memory, which, in turn, supports several "virtual" virtual memories. That's the source of VM's leverage.

  Of course, no computer actually performs all these data
transfer operations (that would be terribly inefficient). Instead,
pages are swapped between an external paging device and the
real page frames, and an algorithm is used to translate virtual
addresses to real. For example, imagine starting with a relative
address in a virtual machine's virtual memory. Adding the base
register and the displacement yields an absolute virtual address. Passing that virtual address through the virtual machine's segmentation and paging tables yields an absolute
address in the real machine's virtual memory. Finally, passing
that address through the control program's segmentation and
paging tables yields a real absolute address. Various mathemat-

ical techniques and page address registers can help streamline these computations.

Managing Peripheral Devices

Each virtual machine has a set of **virtual peripheral devices.** All *real* peripherals, however, are controlled by the control program, CP. Some devices are nonsharable. For example, the user's terminal, the source of that machine's operator commands, is treated as a console dedicated to a specific virtual machine. Other nonsharable devices, such as a reader, a printer, and a punch (a source of machine-readable output), are simulated through spooling. Magnetic tapes are generally dedicated to a single virtual machine upon request.

One future possibility is running a personal computer as a virtual machine (perhaps with MS-DOS, OS/2, or UNIX as the virtual operating system). On such a system, the personal computer's keyboard, display, printer, diskette drives, and hard disk would be private, dedicated devices; in effect, CP would ignore them. Pages would be swapped between the personal computer's memory and the mainframe's real memory. The personal computer would be able to function as a dedicated, standalone machine or as a virtual machine with access to the storage capacity and computing power of a large mainframe.

Sharable devices, such as disk, are supported through the **minidisk** concept. When a user logs onto CP, the main control program generates the appropriate virtual machine. For each disk file requested, CP allocates several tracks or cylinders to the virtual machine. To the control program, these disk extents are files. The virtual machine, however, sees them as dedicated, independent "mini" disk packs.

Under CMS selected minidisks can be shared by several users. For example, in a university system the instructor and each student might have a private minidisk. An additional minidisk is shared by the instructor and the students. The instructor has read/write access; the students have read-only access; the shared minidisk serves to pass assignments and common code (for example, data structures) to the students.

Principles of Operation

The control program maintains a **system directory** with one entry for each virtual machine (Fig. 22.9). The entry completely describes the virtual machine environment, and includes such

Fig. 22.9   CP maintains a system directory that holds one entry for each virtual machine. When a user logs on to CP, the system directory entry is used to generate a virtual machine environment.

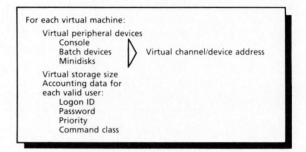

For each virtual machine:
    Virtual peripheral devices
        Console
        Batch devices   Virtual channel/device address
        Minidisks
    Virtual storage size
    Accounting data for
    each valid user:
        Logon ID
        Password
        Priority
        Command class

data as a list of virtual peripherals, the virtual storage size, valid logon IDs and passwords, accounting data, user priorities, and each user's command class. Valid command classes are listed in Fig. 22.10; they limit the commands a given user is authorized to issue.

A user logs onto the control program. CP then checks its system directory, verifies the user number and password, and generates the virtual machine environment. The user can then IPL the appropriate operating system and begin working.

Fig. 22.10   A user's command class indicates the commands he or she is permitted to issue.

Class	User
A	Primary system operator
B	System resource operator
C	System programmer
D	Spooling operator
E	Systems analyst
F	Service representative
G	General user
H	Reserved for IBM use

When an interrupt is sensed, control is passed to an interrupt handling routine in the control program. Interrupts, remember, are sensed by hardware, which switches PSWs stored in fixed memory locations. Since only CP controls real memory, it follows that the addresses of CP's interrupt handling routines are stored in the real new PSW fields. Consequently, a CP routine gets control following any interrupt.

Normally, the control program passes the interrupt to the virtual operating system by copying the appropriate old PSW's contents into the virtual machine's old PSW field, and then loading the virtual machine's new PSW. Other relevant fields, such as the channel status word or channel address word, are also copied if necessary. When the virtual operating system's interrupt handler gets control, its fixed memory locations contain exactly what they would have held had its virtual machine sensed the interrupt. Consequently, the control program's manipulations are transparent to the virtual machine.

Privileged instructions, such as SIO, are used to start or control *physical* I/O operations. Because a virtual machine has no physical peripherals (only virtual, imaginary peripherals), it cannot be allowed to directly control physical I/O. Consequently, the control program traps privileged instructions and performs the requested physical I/O operations itself. It then simulates the results and returns control to the appropriate virtual machine.

Virtual operating systems run under CP in the control program's *problem* state. (Normally, an operating system runs in supervisory state.) Privileged instructions are illegal in problem state; they generate program interrupts. All interrupts, remember, result in a transfer of control to a CP interrupt handler routine. If the interrupt cause code indicates anything but a privileged instruction, CP passes the interrupt to the virtual machine's operating system. Otherwise, it reads the privileged instruction and performs the operation.

Each virtual device assigned to a virtual machine has its own virtual channel/device address. For each virtual machine, the control program maintains a list of virtual devices and their real channel/device equivalents. The virtual peripheral device address can be any valid channel/device address; it need not match the real device address. When an I/O operation is requested, the control program extracts the virtual channel/device address, finds the associated real channel/device address in the table, substitutes it, and performs the operation. Results are then reported back to the virtual operating system using the virtual address.

Does this mean that application programs on a virtual

machine can issue their own privileged instructions? No. Each virtual operating system has its own problem state bit. When it issues a privileged instruction, a program interrupt is generated because the virtual operating system runs in the *real* operating system's problem state. The control program checks the *virtual* machine's problem state bit. If it's 0 (supervisor state), the virtual operating system must have issued the privileged instruction, and that's legal. If, however, the virtual machine's problem state bit is 1, an application routine issued the privileged instruction, and that's illegal. When that happens, the interrupt is passed back to the virtual operating system for handling.

Advantages

The virtual machine concept solves a number of problems. It supports a program development environment that combines access to the full power of a mainframe with the response of a personal computer. It provides an efficient means of increasing the number of levels of multiprogramming while protecting customers' software investments. Compatibility with existing operating systems is a real key, because it allows a customer to move up to more powerful hardware without changing operating environments.

VM is particularly valuable for testing. For example, with VM, it is possible to test an operating system without dedicating a computer to the task (and thus postponing other work). When application routines are modified, the old and new versions can be tested in parallel. Another, related opportunity is running parallel production and development systems.

There are, of course, some disadvantages. Time-dependent code is illegal on a virtual machine, and channel command words can no longer be dynamically modified because the virtual operating system no longer controls real peripherals. However, time-dependent code and dynamically modified CCWs are not considered acceptable programming practice, so these restrictions generally apply only to older programs. More relevant is the fact that VM adds one more level of overhead and thus introduces potential inefficiencies. On a small machine, these inefficiencies could be fatal, but VM is intended for large, fast mainframes.

Traditional operating systems insulate application routines from the hardware. VM's real potential is derived from the fact that the control program insulates the user's *entire operating environment* from the hardware. Consequently, future hardware changes can be implemented without affecting the existing customer base. As long as the control program acts as an interface between the user's operating system and the hardware, even radical changes in architecture will remain transparent. Look for VM to continue as an important operating system for the next several years.

Also, expect more user operating systems to move under the VM umbrella. UNIX (more accurately, IBM's version of UNIX) is a likely candidate. So are PC-DOS (or MS-DOS) and OS/2; the idea of using personal computers as intelligent workstations in a program development network is an intriguing one. VM is remarkably flexible.

Summary

Traditional multiprogramming operating systems emphasize batch processing, not program development. Time-sharing supports interactive program development, but most time-sharing systems limit the programmer to a small subset of the computer's facilities. An ideal program development environment would offer interactive access to the full power of a mainframe. The virtual machine concept is a solution.

On a virtual machine system, a mainframe's resources are managed by a real operating system that simulates one or more virtual machines. Each virtual machine is the functional equivalent of a real computer, with its own virtual memory, virtual operating system, and virtual peripheral devices; in effect, the real operating system multiprograms at the operating system level. UNIX pseudocomputers are one example. This chapter focused on IBM's VM/SP.

Moving from the second to the third generation was a conversion nightmare. Because the new machines were so different, most programs had to be rewritten, and this was expensive. Today, the investment in software is thousands of times what it was in the 1960s, and new technology that does not maintain compatibility with existing software is probably doomed to failure. Again, the virtual machine concept offers a solution.

Under VM, a single control program (CP) manages the real computer's resources. Individual virtual machines run under CP. Because CP simulates a real computer for each virtual machine, a variety of virtual operating systems can be supported, including both DOS and OS derivatives. Multiprogramming at the operating system level gives VM tremendous leverage, and allows a computer to support an impressive number of concurrent application routines. One key VM operating system, CMS, simulates a personal computer and supports an efficient program development environment.

The control program relies on time-slicing to manage the real processor's time. A virtual machine is assigned a slice of time. The virtual operating system manages that time. When a time slice expires, CP assigns the processor to a different virtual machine.

Segmentation and paging techniques are used to manage memory space. Paging initiated by CP is transparent to a virtual machine; CP treats paging requests initiated by a virtual operating system as I/O operations. The control program maintains page frame tables, paging tables, and segmentation tables for each virtual machine. It is possible to visualize a page moving from an external device, to a virtual machine's virtual storage, to the real machine's virtual storage, and finally into real memory.

CP manages all real peripheral devices. Each virtual machine has a set of virtual peripherals. Most nonsharable devices are simulated by spooling. A few, such as the console or a tape drive, are dedicated to a virtual machine. Disk is sharable. When CP generates a virtual machine environment, it assigns disk space to the virtual machine. To CP, each minidisk is a file; to the virtual machine, a minidisk resembles a dedicated drive.

CP maintains a system directory that holds one entry for each virtual machine. A user logs onto CP, which generates the virtual machine environment. The user can then IPL the appropriate operating system and start working.

Interrupts are sensed by hardware, which responds by switching PSWs. Because CP controls real memory, its new PSWs are stored in the real computer's fixed locations, so following any interrupt, a control program interrupt handler routine is activated. Normally, CP software simulates the interrupt on the virtual machine by switching PSWs. The virtual operating system then handles the interrupt.

Virtual operating systems run in CP's problem state. When a virtual operating system issues a privileged instruction, a program interrupt is recognized. If the virtual machine was in supervisory mode when the privileged instruction was issued, CP performs the requested operation and simulates the results for the virtual machine. If the virtual machine was in problem mode, the interrupt is passed to the virtual operating system and treated as a program exception.

VM supports an effective program development environment. It allows users to move up to more powerful hardware while protecting their existing software investments. Although it adds another level of overhead, its impact is generally positive.

Key Words

CMS	real computer	virtual
control program	system directory	peripheral
conversational	transparent	devices
monitor system	virtual machine	VM/SP
CP	virtual operating	
minidisk	system	

Exercises

1. Briefly describe the ideal program development environment. Why are batch processing systems, time-sharing systems, and personal computers less than ideal?

2. Distinguish between virtual and real.

3. Briefly explain the virtual machine concept.

4. Real machine details are transparent to the virtual machine. Explain what this means.

5. The fact that two different operating system families, DOS and OS, support applications on IBM mainframes created a serious conversion problem for the company. Explain. How does VM help solve the problem?

6. System/360 architecture imposes several limitations on a computer's capacity. Describe at least two. Why weren't these restrictions recognized in 1964?

7. The virtual machine concept generates considerable leverage, significantly increasing the potential number of concurrent application routines. How?

8. Sketch the components of a virtual machine.

9. Sketch the contents of real memory on a computer running under VM.

10. On the real machine and each virtual machine, the contents of certain fixed memory locations are considered important. Each set of fixed memory locations begins at address 0. How is this possible? Hardware deals with only one set. Which one? Why?

11. The real control program simulates interrupts for the virtual machine. Explain.

12. What is CMS? Why is CMS considered an important component of IBM's VM/SP?

13. Briefly explain how the control program manages the real processor's time.

14. Explain how memory is managed under VM.

15. Briefly explain paging under VM.

16. Distinguish between a real peripheral and a virtual peripheral. How does VM handle nonsharable devices? Explain the minidisk concept.

17. Explain how the control program keeps track of its various virtual machine environments.

18. Explain how interrupts are handled under VM.

19. Explain how the control program traps privileged instructions. Why is this necessary?

20. Why is the virtual machine concept so useful?

PART FIVE

User Support Software

23

Networks and Distributed Systems

This chapter introduces data
communication, networks, and associated
software. Key concepts include:

Networks
   Why networks?
   Network configurations

Signals
   Modulation and demodulation

Communication systems
   Communication media
   Protocols
   Switching

Network management

Data communication software
   Network operating systems
   Partition management
   Front ends

Network communication is a significant
part of a modern programming
environment.

Networks

Why Networks?

Historically, computers were so expensive that most large organizations did all their data processing on a single, centralized machine. While quite efficient for such tasks as generating payroll and accounting reports, the centralized approach did not allow users to respond quickly to unique, local problems. Centralized data processing is inconvenient because the people who need the information do not necessarily work in the computer center.

During the 1970s, many organizations began to support remote access by linking **terminals** to their mainframes. A terminal is an input/output device that consists of a keyboard, a display screen, and (sometimes) a printer. Terminals allow remote users to access a computer and perform such tasks as data entry, data retrieval, and report generation. A terminal operates under the control of the central computer, responding to commands issued by that central computer.

Given today's low-cost microcomputers, anyone who wants one can have one, but it is difficult to supply consistent software and data to multiple stand-alone machines. The solution is often to link them. Two or more computers linked by communication lines form a **network** (Fig. 23.1). The computers that comprise the network can share data, hardware, and software, and, because they are still computers, can be used independently to solve local problems.

Many networks support a central database. With this central source of data, it is easy to provide up-to-date information to all users. Resource sharing is another advantage. For example, a laser printer produces higher quality output than a dot matrix printer, but at a significantly higher cost. Attaching a laser printer to each user's microcomputer is much too expensive for most organizations, but network users can generate draft quality output on their own inexpensive dot matrix printers and send finished documents over the network to a shared laser printer.

In many organizations, software sharing was the most important reason for implementing a network. Popular commercial packages, such as *dBASE IV*, *WordPerfect*, and *Lotus 1-2-3*, are sold under a license agreement that, essentially, limits use to one machine per copy, and keeping track of hundreds of copies of a program is a management nightmare. Given a network, a

Fig. 23.1   A network consists of two or more computers linked
                       by communication lines.

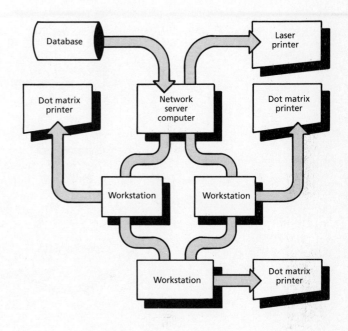

single copy of each program can be stored on the central
database and down-loaded to a user's computer on demand.
Today, most software suppliers offer special network versions
of their programs.

Network Configurations

Figure 23.1 shows a typical microcomputer network configuration. The individual, "end-user" computers are called **workstations.** One computer, the **network server,** controls the
network and houses the central database and other shared resources. The workstations are linked to the network server by
wires or by some other medium. All communication is routed
through the network server.

On a **local area network,** or **LAN,** all the computers are in a
limited area, typically within a single building or on a single

Fig. 23.2   A wide area network covers a large geographic area. Generally, special communication processors control access to the network.

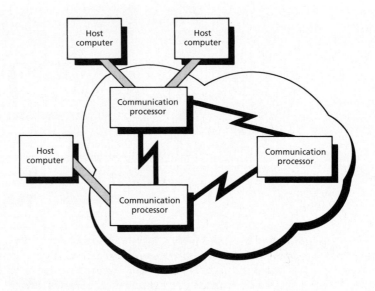

Fig. 23.3   In some networks, the host computers are linked to form a hierarchy.

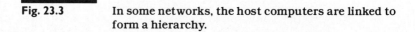

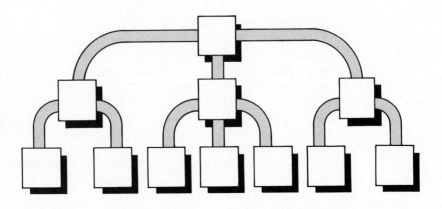

Fig. 23.4   In a star network, all the host computers communicate through a central "star" computer that often houses the organization's central data base.

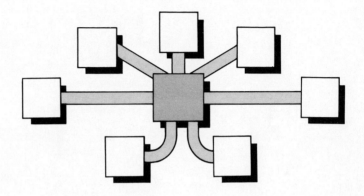

campus. Dedicated wires are sometimes used, but many local area networks rely on existing telephone wires to carry both voice and data. Most LANs link microcomputers, with one micro or a minicomputer acting as the network server. A **wide area network,** or **WAN** (Fig. 23.2), is composed of computers, or **hosts,** that are more widely separated. Generally, at least some

Fig. 23.5   In a ring network, the host computers are linked to form a ring.

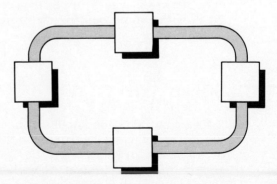

Fig. 23.6   On a multiple-access bus network, host computers are
plugged into a common bus.

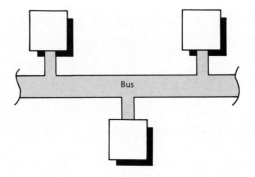

data are transmitted over public or leased communication services, and intermediate computers dedicated to controlling the network might be involved.

Some networks are hierarchical (Fig. 23.3). For example, many supermarkets have computer-controlled checkout systems. Each checkout station has its own microcomputer that is connected to the store's minicomputer. The store minis, in turn, are linked to regional computers, and the regional machines communicate with a central corporate system. Data collection takes place at the bottom of the hierarchy; data analysis takes place at the top.

Another type of network is called a star network (Fig. 23.4), with each host linked to a central "star" machine. In a ring network, the host computers form a ring (Fig. 23.5), and messages are passed from machine to machine around the ring. Many local area networks use a multiple-access bus configuration (Fig. 23.6), with a single bus linking the network controller, the hosts, and shared peripheral devices.

Signals

Data communication implies transmitting data over a distance. When a signal is transmitted, it quickly begins to lose intensity or "die down" (Fig. 23.7). At the same time, it picks up interference or **noise;** the static in the background of a distant radio station is a good example. As it moves away from its source, the

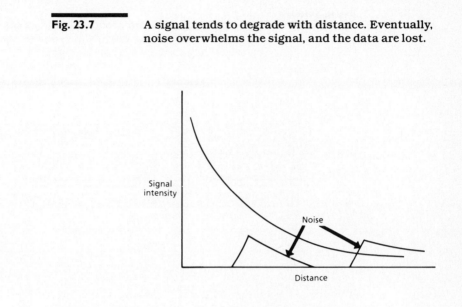

Fig. 23.7   A signal tends to degrade with distance. Eventually, noise overwhelms the signal, and the data are lost.

signal grows steadily weaker and the noise becomes more intense until eventually the signal is overwhelmed.

Signal degradation and noise combine to limit the distance over which data can be transmitted. Special shielded cables help to minimize noise, but **local** data transmission is limited to little more than a mile or two. When the separation is such that data cannot be directly transmitted between two devices, they are considered **remote.** Communication between remote devices is possible only if the signal is boosted (to increase its strength) and/or filtered (to decrease noise).

Modulation and Demodulation

One common technique is to transmit a **carrier signal** such as the sine wave pictured in Fig. 23.8. One complete "S-on-its-side" pattern is called a cycle. The height of the wave is its amplitude; the number of cycles per second is its frequency; data are represented by selectively changing amplitude or frequency. Because the carrier signal is consistent and predictable, several amplification techniques can be used to boost the signal. Because noise rarely follows a standard pattern, the signal can be filtered.

Inside a computer, data are represented as discrete, **digital** electrical pulses. A sine wave is a continuous **analog** that represents the data. Analogs are used every day. The height of a

Fig. 23.8   Data can be transmitted in the context of a carrier
                       signal such as this sine wave. Values are represented
                       by selectively varying the carrier signal.

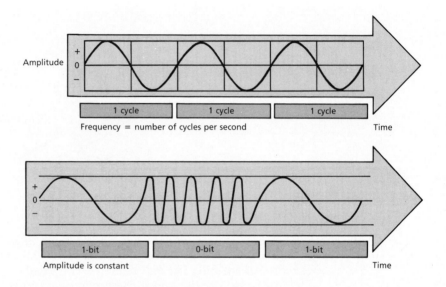

column of mercury in a thermometer isn't the actual temperature; it represents temperature. The position of a needle on your
automobile's control panel isn't speed, but represents speed. A
continuous wave passing over a communication line isn't the
data, but it is analogous to the data.

Analog and digital signals are different, so computers and
analog communication lines are electronically incompatible.
When data move from a computer (or a terminal) to a communication line, they must be changed from digital to analog form, a
process called **modulation.** During modulation, a data signal is
merged with the carrier signal (Fig. 23.9); it is the sum of the carrier and data signals that is transmitted over the line. At the
other end of the line, the carrier signal is subtracted (or filtered)
from the signal (**demodulation**), leaving the data. These functions are performed by a **modem** (modulator/demodulator)
placed at each end of the line (Fig. 23.10).

Radio works on essentially the same principle. The radio station transmits a constant carrier signal at an assigned

Fig. 23.9   A data signal is merged with a carrier signal during
modulation. At the other end of the line the carrier
signal is subtracted, leaving the data.

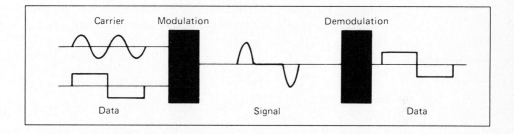

frequency (say, 102.7), and adds music and voice (data) to it. To
tune that station, you set the dial to its frequency. Your receiver
then filters out the carrier signal, leaving the data. If you set the
dial to a different frequency, a different carrier signal is filtered,
leaving different data. The carrier signal allows you to tune the
radio to your favorite station.

Fig. 23.10   A modem placed at each end of a communication line
converts data from digital to analog form and back
again.

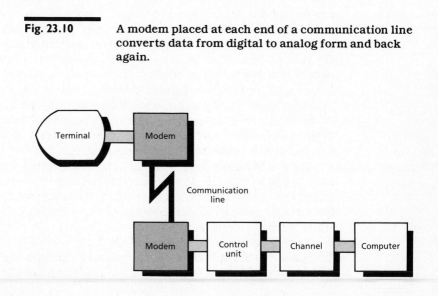

Just as turning up the volume on a tape deck amplifies the hiss as well as the music, amplifying an analog signal boosts the noise along with the data. The result is often poor quality. With modern digital data transmission, the signal is read by a digital repeater, reconstructed, and then retransmitted in almost precisely its original form. The result is much less noise, and that means higher quality. Incidentally, data can be transmitted without a carrier signal on some dedicated digital lines.

Communication Systems

Communication Media

The telephone network is the best known data communication medium. It operates as a public utility. Most people pay a set monthly fee and an additional charge for each long distance call. Leasing private lines is an alternative to dial-up service.

Data are usually transmitted using a binary code such as ASCII or EBCDIC. The transmission speed, or **baud** rate, is a function of the signal's frequency. A voice-grade line has a carrier frequency of roughly 2400 cycles (or signal events) per second, so it is rated at 2400 baud. Typically, one bit is transmitted during each cycle, so a voice-grade line is rated at 2400 bits/second, but special hardware can transmit over the same line at 4800, 7200, or 9600 bits/second. Additionally, wide-band channels with speeds ranging from 19,200 to over one million baud can be leased.

Early telephone lines were analog, and many local lines still are. However, as new lines are installed, most are digital. With a digital line, data can be transmitted as discrete pulses, so modems are not necessary. Today, digital fiber optics lines are beginning to replace traditional copper wires. A fiber optics line transmits laser pulses that are almost unaffected by noise and do not degrade as quickly as electronic signals. Also, the glass fibers have considerably more data transmission capacity than an equivalent cross-section of copper wire.

Microwave data transmission is an alternative. One problem with microwaves is that they are limited to a "line of sight." Because the earth curves, relay stations or communication satellites are necessary if microwaves are to be transmitted over a significant distance (Fig. 23.11).

Trying to distinguish among all these media can be confusing, so the general term **line** will be used throughout the rest of this chapter to mean any data communication medium.

Fig. 23.11   Microwave data transmission is limited to a line of
sight. Long-distance microwave transmission
requires relay stations or satellites.

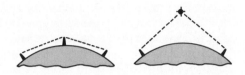

Protocols

At a minimum, data communication involves a transmitter, a
line, and a receiver. One problem is the speed disparity between
those components. For example, consider a terminal linked to a
mainframe by a telephone line. The terminal (at least for input)
is limited to typing speed, a few characters per second. A typical
telephone line can transmit at 2400 baud. Assuming 8-bit characters, that's 300 characters per second. A mainframe can process *millions* of characters per second. The data communication
system must adjust for the relative speeds of its components.

A second problem arises from the fact that the components
operate asynchronously; in other words, they are independent,
and each one is controlled by its own internal clock. With bits
moving at high rates of speed, even minor timing discrepancies
can mean lost data. Because they do not share a common clock,
independent devices must be synchronized before they can
begin communicating.

Additional timing problems are caused by the communication lines themselves. Although electronic communication
seems instantaneous, it isn't; data take a measurable amount of
time to move from point A to point B, and the time varies with
distance. Consequently, if one message is transmitted directly
between New York and Boston, and a second goes by way of Los
Angeles, transmission times will differ. That complicates synchronization.

As if that's not enough, the computers and related hardware
manufactured by different companies are often incompatible.
Two pieces of equipment might use different codes to represent
characters and different internal representations for numeric
data. Parity rules and word sizes can vary, too.

As a result of these (and other) variables, establishing a communication link means following a precise **protocol.** You use a primitive protocol when you answer the telephone. When the phone rings, you pick up the receiver and say "hello." The caller responds with something like "Hello, this is X; may I speak to Y, please." If the desired party is not present or a wrong number has been dialed, the call quickly ends. Otherwise, communication begins. Certain rules govern the conversation, with the participants essentially taking turns. Transmission ends when both parties say "good-bye" and hang up.

Electronic devices do much the same thing when they transmit data. First, an electronic pulse indicates that a signal is coming. Next, the sender and receiver must synchronize their signals and identify each other through a process called handshaking. Data are then exchanged using a common code, message format, and baud rate. Often, the message is checked for accuracy and, if necessary, retransmitted. Finally, the message is acknowledged and the transmission ends. The rules that govern each of these elements comprise the protocol.

Switching

In the simplest form of data communication, a permanent line links points A and B. More realistically, particularly when a public network is used, there are several possible paths between any two points. The act of establishing a link is called **switching.** On circuit switching systems, a fixed connection is made for the life of a task; for example, a physical link might be maintained from the time a user logs on until he or she issues an explicit termination command such as log-off. With message switching, a link is established for each discrete transmission. For example, on a time-sharing system, a new link might be assigned for each transaction.

Another option, packet switching is a good choice for high-volume data communication. Start with a message. Break it into small units called packets. A continuous stream of such packets flows over the line. A network computer monitors the line and, when an opening is sensed, inserts a packet into the message stream until all the packets comprising a single message are flowing over the line. (*Note:* They are probably not contiguous.) Eventually, another computer extracts the packets, reassembles the message, and sends it on its way.

Circuit switching is relatively inefficient because the line's potential for transmitting data is wasted between transactions. Message switching does a better job of utilizing the line's capacity, but the dynamic nature of this technique requires more sophisticated equipment. Packet switching is very efficient, but it relies on special dedicated computers to monitor and manage the line.

Network Management

A network might include numerous terminals, computers, and communication lines. Each terminal or computer might support an independent user accessing an independent program. Data intended for user A are useless to user B, so data must be routed to specific computers or terminals. Also, with multiple users active, it is inevitable that two or more will try to transmit data at the same time. Consequently, it is essential that access to the network be managed.

One way to manage the network is through a process called **polling.** Start with a user workstation. As data are typed, they are stored in the workstation's memory. Eventually, the user issues a command to send the data to the central database, thus making his or her workstation "ready."

Inside the network server, the network operating system has a table listing every active workstation. Referring to this table, the operating system sends a polling signal to the first workstation (Fig. 23.12a), in effect asking if it is ready to transmit data. Assume this user is still typing. Seeing that the workstation is

---

Fig. 23.12   Polling.

a. A polling signal is sent to the first workstation.

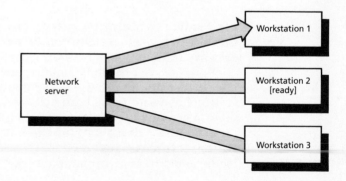

b. Because the first workstation is not ready, a polling signal is sent to the second workstation.

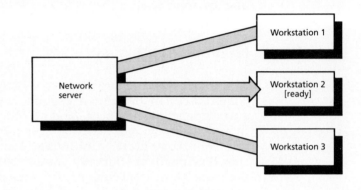

c. Because the second workstation is ready, it transmits its data to the network server.

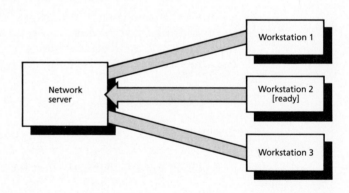

not ready, the operating system issues another polling signal, this time to your workstation. It's ready (Fig. 23.12b), so the data are transmitted across the network (Fig. 23.12c).

Polling is not the only way to manage a network. With **collision detection,** the individual computers, terminals, or workstations contend for access by listening for a carrier signal. If none is present the computer transmits its data and then monitors the line, "listening" for the noise that is generated when two or more messages "collide." If a collision is detected, the affected computers retransmit in turn.

Token passing is a second option. An electronic signal called a token is passed continuously, from component to component, around the network, and a given component is authorized to transmit a message only when it holds the token. In another approach, a set of **message slots** move continuously around the network. When a component has a message to transmit, it waits for an empty slot.

Collision detection is most efficient on a lightly used network because, with relatively few messages, the risk of a collision is slight. As the network's load increases, however, more and more messages will require retransmission, and performance quickly degrades. With token passing or message slot transmission, the risk of a collision (and, thus, the need to retransmit) is eliminated.

In part because of the wide range of available alternatives, data communication can be confusing, but standards do exist. The International Standards Organization's OSI (Open System Interconnection) guidelines and the Comité Consultate Internationale Telegraphique et Telephoniques recommendation X.25 are two good examples. Many organizations have established their own corporate standards; for example, IBM has its System Network Architecture and Digital Equipment Corporation has its Digital Network Architecture. Unfortunately, no universal standard has yet emerged.

Data Communication Software

Network Operating Systems

Because networks are relatively complex, special **network operating systems** have been developed to control access to them. Typically, each host computer has its own, non-network operating system and an **agent process** to link it to the network (Fig. 23.13). Dealing with the host's operating system, the network itself, and, perhaps, incompatible operating systems on other hosts is a complex task. A good network operating system makes the network and the various host operating systems transparent.

One advantage of a network is **resource sharing**, but if a user must know exactly where each resource is physically located, the advantage is largely negated. The network operating system makes all resources, even those attached to remote hosts, appear local. Usually, that implies implementing uniform accounting procedures so that users need not establish accounts on each host computer.

Fig. 23.13   On a typical network, each host computer has its own,
                       non-network operating system and an agent process
                       to link it to the network.

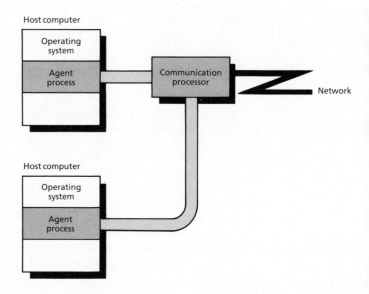

The network operating system also controls the transfer of
complete files or selected data elements between hosts (**data migration**). Shared files might be located on a central computer, or
each host might have both sharable and private files. To further
complicate matters, different computers often store data in different formats. The network operating system performs necessary data transformations.

On some systems, tasks can be transferred between hosts
(**computation migration**), thus allowing a network operating
system to balance its processing load and assign parallel tasks
to independent mainframes to speed up computation. Occasionally, a particular task will call for a preferred hardware or software configuration, and such tasks can be assigned to the most
appropriate host computer. Finally, the ability to assign a task
to an alternate processor can improve the network's reliability
and provide effective backup.

At a more mundane level, the network operating system supports communication between the system, its users, and

between the individual users (electronic mail). Finally, it is the obvious place to screen users, restrict access, encrypt data, and implement other security procedures.

Partition Management

On a time-sharing system, users at workstations (both local and remote) communicate with a central mainframe. Occasionally, the entire computer is dedicated to data communication. More often, time-sharing runs in a single partition or region, with a **data communication monitor** managing the partition and serving as the agent process (Fig. 23.14).

Partition management involves controlling a user's access to processor time, memory space, and peripheral devices. (In effect, the data communication monitor serves as a virtual operating system within its own partition.) Generally, each user is assigned a limited amount of disk space. When the user logs on, the data communication monitor checks his or her user number and password, assigns a workspace, and loads relevant code from disk. Between transactions, the monitor rolls the workspace out to disk and then reloads it when the next transaction arrives.

The processor's time is typically managed through timeslicing. The data communication monitor maintains a queue of ready tasks. The processor is assigned to a particular user task for a single time-slice. Eventually, the task either requests the

Fig. 23.14   On many time-sharing systems, a data communication monitor manages a partition and serves as the agent process.

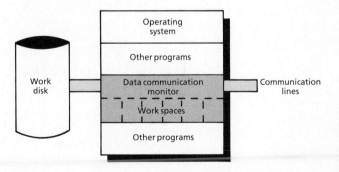

monitor's support or exceeds its time allotment, and control is given to the next user task on the queue. Generally, a user is restricted to his or her own terminal and disk space. The data communication monitor maintains a table of assigned devices and deals with contention problems.

In addition to managing the partition, the data communication monitor serves as the agent process (the link to the network). Additionally, a relationship must be maintained between a user's workspace and a specific terminal. Finally, I/O operations such as spooling and disk access must be supported.

Front Ends

A computer is at its least efficient when performing I/O, and data communication is I/O intensive. Consequently, the responsibility for communicating with terminals and executing protocol

Fig. 23.15   Responsibility for polling terminals and executing protocol logic is often assigned to a front-end device.

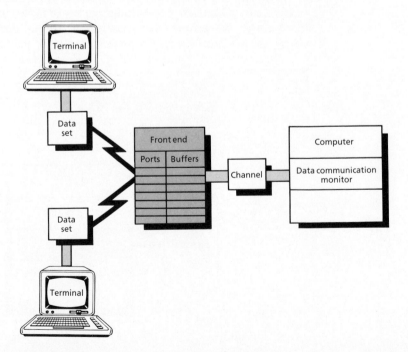

logic is often assigned to a **front-end device** (Fig. 23.15) that consists of a series of ports (complete with necessary modems) and associated buffers.

Typically, the front-end device assumes responsibility for communicating with the terminals and workstations, polling them, transmitting data between its own buffers and the remote devices, and performing necessary protocol functions. Consequently, the computer can deal exclusively with local buffers on the front-end device, and that simplifies I/O. Terminal and protocol management require some intelligence, so the front-end must contain at least a rudimentary processor and the software (or microcode) necessary to control it.

Summary

Data communication is necessary because the people who need the data do not always work in the computer center. A network consists of two or more computers linked by communication lines. Networks allow users to share data, hardware, and software. Typically, one computer, the network server, controls access to the network; the end-user computers are called hosts. The computers that form a local area network are generally quite close to each other. The computers in a wide area network can be widely separated. Common network configurations include hierarchical, star, ring, and multiple-access bus.

When data are transmitted to a remote device, they must be boosted and filtered because the signal tends to degrade and to pick up noise. Often, data are transmitted in the context of a carrier signal. Adding data to the carrier signal is called modulation; extracting the data is called demodulation; these tasks are performed by a modem. With analog data transmission, the entire signal, including noise, is amplified. With digital data transmission, the signal is reconstructed and then retransmitted.

Perhaps the best known data communication medium is the telephone network. Microwave is an alternative. A general term for a data communication medium is line. The speed of a line is its baud rate. The processing speeds of components linked to a communication network can vary. Generally, those components function asynchronously, and their internal data formats can differ. Consequently, a protocol is needed to establish communication.

With circuit switching, a link is established for the life of the task. With message switching, the link is established for each discrete transmission. With packet switching, a message is broken into discrete packets. The packets are then transmitted separately and reassembled at the other end of the line. Because conflicts are possible, access to the network must be managed using a technique such as polling, collision detection, token passing, or message slot transmission. Software is needed to perform these tasks.

Typically, each host has its own non-network operating system and an agent process to link it to the network. The network operating systems makes the network and the various host operating systems transparent to the user. Most support resource sharing, data migration, and computation migration.

Time-sharing often implies numerous users and a single mainframe. On some systems, a data communication monitor runs under the mainframe's operating system and manages a partition. Responsibility for polling and protocols can be transferred to a front-end device.

Key Words

agent process	host	polling
analog	line	protocol
baud	local	remote
carrier signal	local area network	resource
collision detection	(LAN)	sharing
computation	message slot	signal
migration	modem	degradation
data communication	modulation	switching
data communication	network	terminal
monitor	network operating	token passing
data migration	system	wide area
demodulation	network server	network (WAN)
digital	noise	workstation
front-end device	partition	
	management	

Exercises

1. Why is data communication necessary?

2. What is a network? Why are networks used? Distinguish between a local area network and a wide area network.

3. Distinguish among hierarchical, star, ring, and multiple-access bus networks.

4. Signal degradation and noise combine to limit the distance over which data can be transmitted. Explain. How are these problems overcome?

5. Distinguish between local and remote data communication.

6. Distinguish between analog and digital data. Briefly explain modulation and demodulation.

7. Briefly describe several alternative data communication media.

8. What is protocol? Why are protocols necessary?

9. Distinguish among circuit switching, message switching, and packet switching.

10. Briefly explain polling.

11. Distinguish among collision detection, token passing, and message slot transmission.

12. What functions are performed by a network operating system? What is an agent process?

13. Briefly explain resource sharing, data migration, and computation migration.

14. What functions are performed by a data communication monitor? Briefly explain each function.

15. Often, a front-end device serves as a computer's interface to a communication line. Why? What functions does the front-end device perform?

24

Database Systems

This chapter explains a number of
database concepts. Key topics include:

Traditional data management
  Custom files
  Data redundancy
  Data ownership
  Data dependency

The central database approach
  Data integrity
  Data as a resource
  Data-independent software
  Advantages and disadvantages

Implementing a database
  Database organization
  The database management system

Today's application programmers often
  work in a database environment.

Traditional Data Management

Payroll was, for many firms, one of the first computer applications. As an organization grows, the cost of processing payroll grows with it; and, by automating this highly repetitive task and doing it on a computer, these costs can be brought under control. Because the alternative to computerization might be several full-time clerks, the payroll application is easy to cost justify. Add the advantages of speed and accuracy, and it is simply impossible for any organization with a significant number of employees to justify processing payroll any other way.

Other, similar applications—accounts payable, accounts receivable, general ledger, inventory—are equally easy to cost justify on their own merits. The basic argument in each case is cost reduction: It's cheaper to do the job on a computer than by hand. These bread-and-butter applications formed the foundation of the modern computer industry.

Custom Files

Cost justification makes sense, particularly in a business environment. Unfortunately, with each application standing on its own, efficiency tends to be defined at the application level. The ideal program thus becomes one that minimizes processor time and memory space. Because computers are at their least efficient when performing I/O, one of the best ways to achieve program-level optimization is to custom-design the data files to fit the application. Thus, a typical organization has a set of payroll files, an independent set of accounts receivable files, and yet another set of files for each major application. The independence of these files, the lack of integration of all these data, can create problems.

Data Redundancy

Perhaps the most obvious problem is **data redundancy.** With so many independent files, it is almost certain that the same data will appear again and again. For example, consider the files maintained by your school. Information about *you* probably appears in several different places. For billing purposes, the bursar's file contains your name and address. These same data elements also appear in the registrar's file, your major department's file, several social groups' files, housing files, library files, alumni files, automobile registration files, and, probably, many more.

What happens if you change your address or your name? The correction will be made on some of the files, perhaps even most of the files, but it almost certainly will not be made on all the files. Thus, the computer will hold two or more different values for the same data element. With different versions of the truth, **data integrity** is subject to question.

Clearly, if two different values are listed for the same person's address, one of them must be wrong. Why can't the school simply correct the error? Remember that, because the applications are considered independent, the files are independent. Consequently, correcting each file requires independent action. When does the bursar need your name and address? Probably just before the beginning of the term, when bills are mailed. When does the registrar need your name and address? At the end of the term, when grades are mailed. Billing and grade distribution are independent applications with different timing requirements, so the bursar and the registrar will update their files at different times. Thus, at any given time, they might legitimately have different values for a given student's name and address.

How important is your name and address to the bursar? If you don't receive your bill, you won't pay it. The bursar considers your name and address very important, and will make a serious effort to see that they are correct. How important are the same data elements to the registrar? If you don't get your grade report, you will be mildly inconvenienced, but a telephone call or a visit to the administration building will usually solve the problem. It's not that the registrar doesn't care, but the penalty for bad data is not as great as it is for the bursar, so it is not reasonable to expect the registrar to assign the same priority to updating the file.

Your department probably has your name and address on file, too. How often does a department try to contact students at home? Only occasionally. Most departments update their student files during slack periods when the secretary has nothing else to do. If you have moved, your department probably still has your old address. The accuracy of a particular data element depends on the importance the file's owner attaches to it.

When selected data values are clearly wrong, the integrity of the entire file is subject to question. For example, most schools use the number of majors in each discipline as a basis for distributing resources such as teaching positions. When a student changes majors, the new department updates its records as soon as the necessary papers are signed, but the registrar's file might not be corrected until the end of the term. Consequently, the department's and the registrar's counts won't match. Given different versions of the truth, the tendency is to trust neither.

Such problems are not, of course, limited to universities. Whenever files are custom fit to applications, data redundancy is almost inevitable. Given redundant data, different values of the same data element will be found on the computer. With different versions of the truth, how can anyone trust the data?

Data Ownership

Users tend to define data integrity strictly in terms of their own applications. The bursar's office will take steps to ensure the accuracy of financial data. The registrar will carefully verify academic data. Each user group is concerned with the integrity of the data it considers important.

Each time a data element is accessed, its value can be changed. By denying access to untrained individuals, the risk of incorrect data being accidentally introduced is minimized. Thus, given the opportunity, most users will choose to restrict access to key data. As a result, only the bursar's office is allowed to access the bursar's files, and only the registrar's office can use the registrar's files.

Security is another concern. Along with names, addresses, and telephone numbers, the bursar's files contain confidential data that simply cannot be shared. If only authorized personnel are allowed to access the files, confidentiality can be preserved. The result, however, is that access to data is denied to all but a handful of people.

Who owns the data? The answer is not always clear. Operations controls the hardware on which the data are stored, and thus has a claim. Without software to create, maintain, and manipulate the data, there would be no files, so systems and programming might claim ownership. The user, on the other hand, is responsible for data integrity, and has a right to define conditions for accessing them. All three groups can claim ownership.

To access a given file, it is often necessary to first get permission from operations, programming, and a user group. The result is red tape and bureaucracy. The bursar might have the most accurate list of student names and addresses, but because the bursar's file holds other confidential data, no other group is allowed to access these records. Custom files tend to limit **data accessibility.**

Data Dependency

Programs designed to access custom files are, almost by definition, **data dependent.** Consider, for example, a sequential master file update program. A master file and a transactions file are sorted into sequence. The program then reads transactions, matches them with master file records, and generates a new master file.

Much of the program's logic is concerned with input and output—first-record processing, last-record processing, matching records, sequence errors, and so on. To the user, who simply wants results in the form of valid paychecks or bills, I/O is irrelevant. In addition to solving the user's problem, the programmer is concerned with efficiently controlling data movement between the processor and two or more peripherals. If the data's structure or organization changes, the program will not work. Clearly, it is data dependent.

Often, data dependency is more subtle. For example, imagine a program that ages accounts receivable, applying no carrying charge to bills less than 30 days old, adding 5 percent to bills between 30 and 60 days old, and flagging as overdue bills over 60 days in arrears. Clearly, the program's logic will include a comparison to the current date. To save space, the year is often stored as a two-digit number (91 instead of 1991). What happens on January 1, 2000? The current date will include year 00. Does 91 mean 9 years in the past, or 91 years in the future? Beginning on January 1, 2000, the program simply will not work!

Why not change the date field to hold a four-digit year? Changing the length of the date field means changing the logical record length. Changing the logical record length means changing every program that accesses the file (even those that don't use the date). Clearly, all these programs are data dependent.

Whenever a data file is customized to meet the needs of a particular program, that program becomes data dependent. Any change in the data structure requires a change in the program. As a result, management is faced with three equally unacceptable choices: (1) patch the existing programs, (2) rewrite those programs, or (3) risk falling behind the competition. Simple maintenance is almost impossible. Although the precise cost of data dependency is difficult to quantify, it is substantial.

The Central Database Approach

Instead of creating independent files for each application, why not combine all the data to form an integrated **database?** Clearly, a single database would reduce the problems associated with data redundancy and data integrity. Centralized data implies centralized control, and that clarifies ownership. With all programs sharing data, access can be managed by a "super access method" called a **database management system** (Fig. 24.1). Future changes in the data's physical structure would affect only the database management system, making application routines independent of their physical data.

Data Integrity

A database contains a single value for each data element. On custom files, redundant data are replicated in two or more places, but with a database, only one copy is stored, so a central database almost eliminates data redundancy. For example, imagine that student names and addresses are stored on a database. If your name or address changes, the data are corrected once, on the database. Subsequently, every program has access to the correct version.

Fig. 24.1   If an organization's data are collected in a central database, all application routines can access the data through a common database management system.

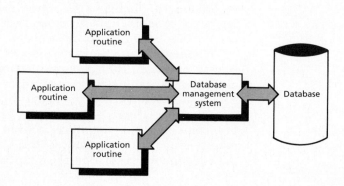

With custom files, data are generally edited or verified at a *record* level, with the responsible department carefully scrutinizing critical fields. All too often, however, secondary fields are checked haphazardly, if at all. With a database, data can be verified at the *element* level, so responsibility for each data element can be assigned to the department or individual most concerned about its accuracy. Reducing data redundancy and clearly defining responsibility for the accuracy of each data element both help to dramatically improve data integrity.

With custom files, the existence of a single confidential data element is often cited as sufficient reason to deny access to the entire file. With a database, a database management system sits between the application routines and the data, and all access is routed through this common module. Typically, security is implemented at the data element level, so a given application routine can be denied access to unauthorized data without affecting its access to other data. Consequently, data accessability is improved without risking data integrity.

Data as a Resource

The central database approach clearly defines data ownership. With all data stored in a central database, the data become an organizational resource, not the property of any single department. In today's increasingly complex world, information may well be the organization's most valuable resource.

Traditionally, the organizational structure of Management Information Systems, or MIS, resembles Fig. 24.2. The

---

Fig. 24.2   Management Information Systems traditionally includes two departments: Operations, and Systems and Programming.

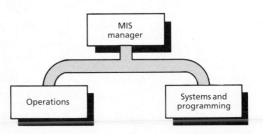

Operations Department runs the computer, maintains equipment, and enters the data. The Systems and Programming Department plans, implements, and maintains software. Who is responsible for the data? *Physical* responsibility rests with the department that controls the hardware on which the data are stored—Operations. *Logical* responsibility rests with the group that writes the programs that create and maintain the data—Systems and Programming. Often, the user, who is not even represented on the organizational chart, is responsible for data integrity. Thus, responsibility is split among three groups.

With a database, centralized control becomes possible. Many organizations have added a new function to their MIS group, the **database administrator** (Fig. 24.3). Operations is still responsible for hardware, and Systems and Programming still controls software, but the responsibility for data is now clearly and unambiguously defined.

Lying between application software and the database is a database management system. It implements the organization's rules for accessing the data. The database administrator maintains the database management system, ensuring that it accurately reflects the rules, as defined by company policy.

Data-independent Software

The problems associated with poor data integrity and unclear data ownership are well known to application programmers, but data dependency is more subtle. The programmer accessing

---

Fig. 24.3   With a database, a database administrator is often
                   assigned responsibility for the data.

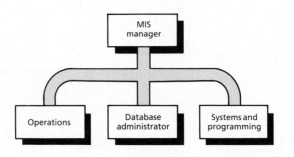

custom files is often concerned both with the user's application and with data access, rarely seeing them as independent problems. Instead, data manipulation and the user's application are so tightly linked that they become a single problem in the programmer's mind and in the code. Thus, a relatively minor change in the data structure can mean a major program revision.

For example, if a change in the tax laws renders the payroll system obsolete, programming sees a need for a new system development project. Management, on the other hand, sees considerable money being spent to allow the organization to continue doing what it already was doing—generating valid paychecks. Management considers such projects maintenance and sees the need to redesign and recode significant parts of the payroll system as highly inefficient. The argument that an apparently simple change in the data structure can render program logic obsolete does not impress nontechnical management. All too often, computer professionals are too close to the data dependency problem to see it.

When accessing a traditional file, a programmer requests logical I/O by calling an access method (Fig. 24.4). The access method converts the logical I/O request to physical form and passes it to the operating system, which issues the necessary physical I/O commands. Except for extracting logical records from a physical block, the access method does not manipulate the data. Thus, the programmer's logical data structure must match a physical data structure; in other words, the programmer must know the exact physical format of the data before he or she can access them. This is why a change in the data's physical structure means a change in the program.

Fig. 24.4   When accessing a traditional file, a programmer requests logical I/O by calling an access method.

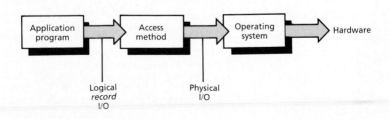

Now, place a database management system between the application program and the access method (Fig. 24.5). Although the database management system still uses traditional access methods to read and write physical records, the application routine is insulated from this physical interface, so the application program can request true logical I/O at a *data element* level.

For example, imagine an application program needs an employee's name and address. It asks the database management system for a new set of values for these two data elements. The database manager accepts the program's logical request, performs whatever physical I/O operations are necessary to get the two values, extracts the name and address from whatever physical records or blocks it reads, and passes only the requested values back to the original program. As far as the application routine is concerned, it requested and got values for two data elements. The physical operations needed to find them are transparent. The application program is data independent.

Consider carefully the difference between true logical I/O and traditional logical I/O. When a program reads a traditional record from a traditional file, that record must physically exist. It might be part of a larger block, or it might span two or more physical records, but every byte, every element in the data structure, must physically exist in the prescribed order. Using the traditional approach, the programmer must accept the entire logical record, as it is physically stored, or accept none of it.

A database management system supports true logical I/O. If a program needs only certain data elements, the programmer can create a logical data structure containing only those data

---

Fig. 24.5   The database management system insulates the
                       application routine from the physical data, and thus
                       supports true logical I/O at a data element level.

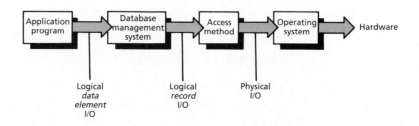

elements. The database management system accepts the programmer's logical requests, issues the necessary physical I/O commands, and assembles the requested data elements. It is possible that the logical data structure might match a physical data structure. More often, however, the requested logical data structure does not exist until the database management system assembles it. However, the programmer can ignore the physical data structure.

What if the physical data structure changes? Since application programs are not concerned with the physical data, they are not affected. Rather than modifying hundreds of application routines, the new physical data structure can be implemented by modifying only the database management system, so the application routines are data independent.

Advantages and Disadvantages

A database improves data integrity by reducing data redundancy and improving verification and security. Because the database permits centralized control, it clarifies data ownership. The database management system insulates the application routine from the physical data, thus promoting data independence. These are compelling arguments for implementing a database.

No improvement is without cost, however. One problem is efficiency. With a database management system between the application routine and the access method, I/O operations involve one more level of overhead. There is little question that a well-written program accessing traditional custom files will run faster than an equivalent program accessing a database.

Unfortunately, this kind of efficiency is defined primarily in hardware terms. In addition to execution time and memory, the total cost of any program includes development, coding, testing, and maintenance. A database helps to reduce each of these costs by promoting data independence. Another concern is the relationships between the data processed by several application routines. With a database, all applications can share a single copy of a given data element; with traditional custom files, that data element might be stored, redundantly, many times. From an organizational viewpoint, the efficiency argument loses much of its appeal.

There is, however, one legitimate objection to using a database—cost. Commercial database management systems are relatively expensive, and the cost of developing the database can be prohibitive. A typical organization might have hundreds of custom data files, all of which must, in some way, be merged. Additionally, every program that previously accessed a custom file must be rewritten.

These costs are concrete, representing dollars that must be spent now. The benefits—data integrity, clear data ownership, and data independence—are less concrete, accruing only in the future. Management is asked to spend a great deal in the short run for a somewhat questionable long-run payoff. Not surprisingly, many organizations have decided not to change.

Unfortunately, postponing the decision only makes the problem worse. While the cost of upgrading to a database may seem prohibitive, the cost of *not* upgrading may be even more so. The future computer professional will almost certainly deal with databases.

Implementing a Database

The key to implementing a database is the database management system. It allows a programmer to request specific data elements or logical data structures without regard for the physical data structure. In effect, the database management system creates a custom data structure at the time the data are requested.

Obviously, the data must still be stored on a physical device, and physical records, blocks, or sectors must still move between primary and secondary storage. Most database management

Fig. 24.6   A database management system relies on traditional access methods to read and write physical data.

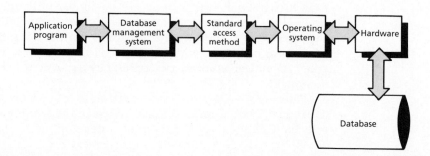

systems rely on the traditional access methods for physical I/O (Fig. 24.6). Given a request for selected data elements, the database management system identifies the physical record or records containing the data, issues the necessary physical I/O commands, extracts the requested data, and then returns them to the application routine.

Database Organization

The database consists of one or more (usually, more) related files. Pointers are sometimes used to link a master record to related secondary data (Fig. 24.7). Other database systems maintain a set of detailed indexes that show where key data elements are stored.

Some database systems impose a **hierarchical** structure on the data. For example, a university might use a hierarchical

Fig. 24.7   On many database management systems, pointers link a master record to related secondary records.

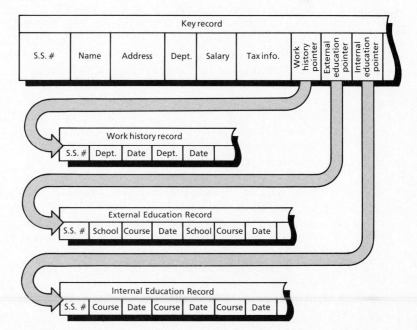

Fig. 24.8   In a hierarchical database, a parent record can have
one or more children. The database is typically
searched from top to bottom.

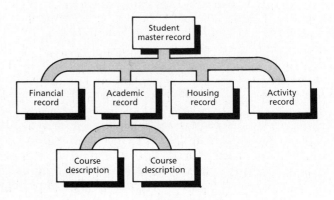

database to store student data (Fig. 24.8), with a student master
record pointing to that student's financial, academic, housing,
and activity records. These secondary records could, in turn,
point to lower level records. Records nearer the top of the hierarchy are called parents. Each parent can have one or more children. The academic record in Fig. 24.8 is a child of the student
record. It is also a parent in its own right, with two children.

Generally, while a parent can have many children, a child
can have only one parent. This limits the flexibility of a hierarchical database. On a **network database,** a child can have many
parents (Fig. 24.9). On a hierarchical database, the data search
always starts at the top and works down, through the hierarchy.
With a network database, it is possible to start almost anywhere
and move in any direction.

Many newer database systems are relational in nature. The
best way to visualize a **relational database** is as a table (Fig.
24.10). Each row holds one record (a set of related data elements), and each column holds a set of values (one per record)
for a single data element. Links between database files are defined by the elements' logical relationships.

A relational database user can access data by defining a logical data **view** (Fig. 24.11). The view represents the user's image
of the data. The database management system responds by

Fig. 24.9 In a network database, a child can have many parents, so a data search can start almost anywhere and move in almost any direction.

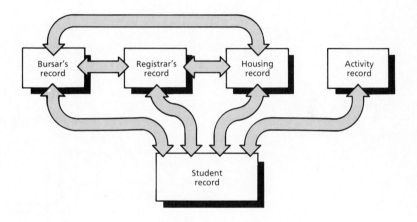

Fig. 24.10 A relational database represents data as a table consisting of rows (records) and columns (fields).

Columns

Name	Street address	City	State	Zip code
Melinda Atkins	142 Maple St.	Oxford	Ohio	450781718
Charles Baker	713 Main Street	Cincinnati	Ohio	457033304
Thomas Bates	42 South Blvd.	Atlanta	Georgia	352170315
Lisa Campanella	8 Tower Square	San Jose	California	953214450
Shen Chan	State Route 77	Binghamton	New York	127561495
Tomas Garcia	473 Dixie Highway	Lexington	Kentucky	434101236
.	.	.	.	.
.	.	.	.	.
.	.	.	.	.
Arthur White	Northside Mall	Orlando	Florida	214504372

File

Rows

Field

Record

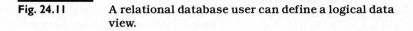

Fig. 24.11   A relational database user can define a logical data
                      view.

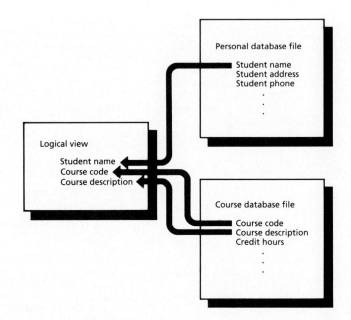

accessing one or more database files, assembling the data elements that comprise the view, and passing the newly created
logical data structure back to the user.

The Database Management System

Access to a database is controlled by a database management
system. The first database management systems were little
more than sophisticated access methods (Fig. 24.12). They were
physically part of a load module and supported a single application routine in a single partition. Today, most database management systems occupy their own partitions and are shared by
several application routines (Fig. 24.13), so all database access,
from *all* partitions, pass through a common routine. The result
is centralized control.

Fig. 24.12   Early database management systems were little more
than sophisticated access methods.

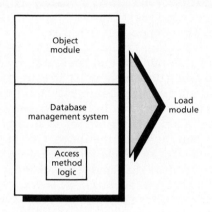

Fig. 24.13   Most database management systems occupy an
independent partition and deal concurrently with
several application routines.

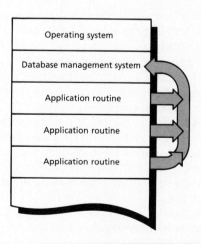

Summary

Early computer applications were cost justified and developed independently. Often, files were custom designed to fit each application. This led to a variety of problems, including data redundancy, questionable data integrity, unclear data ownership, and data-dependent software.

A database helps to solve all these problems. By minimizing data redundancy and assigning responsibility for the accuracy of a given data element to the functional group most affected by that element, data integrity can be improved. The fact that the database is centralized allows centralized ownership and control, often under a database administrator. The database management system insulates the application routine from the physical data, so the programmer can focus on true logical, data element I/O. This leads to data-independent software.

There are, of course, disadvantages. Technical people sometimes attack the efficiency of database I/O, but their concern is with hardware efficiency. Database management software is expensive, and the cost of creating the database and modifying existing programs to access it can be prohibitive.

A database management system allows a programmer to specify I/O at a logical, data element level. The database management system accepts the programmer's logical requests, performs necessary physical I/O operations, extracts the relevant data elements, and passes them back to the application routine, so the physical structure of the data is transparent to the programmer.

Some database management systems use pointers to link physical records, perhaps on different physical files. Others rely on indexes. Hierarchical databases define the relationships between data elements as a hierarchy, with parent structures pointing to child structures. Generally, a parent can have many children, but a child can have only one parent. This limits a hierarchical database to a one-way (top to bottom) data search. Network databases maintain multiple links, and a child can have more than one parent. Consequently, a data search can start at any point and move in any direction. Many modern databases are relational, with the relationships between data elements defined logically, rather than by pointers or indexes. A relational database user can often access the database by defining a logical data view.

Initially, database management systems started as sophisticated access methods functioning in a single partition. Today, most occupy their own partition, where they are shared by numerous application routines.

Key Words

data accessibility	data	hierarchical
database	dependency	database
database	data	network database
administrator	integrity	relational
database	data	database
management	redundancy	view
system		

Exercises

1. Why does treating each application independently lead to custom data files?

2. What is data redundancy? How does data redundancy affect data integrity?

3. With files customized to the application, who owns the data? Why? How does this affect data accessibility?

4. Programs that access custom files tend to be data dependent. Why? Why is data dependency a problem?

5. How does a database help to minimize data dependency?

6. How does a database help to define data ownership? What is a database administrator?

7. How does a database help to improve data accessibility?

8. How does a database promote data-independent programs? Why is data independence so important?

9. Technical people sometimes argue that database access is inefficient. Why? Why does management tend to dismiss this argument?

10. What anti-database arguments are taken seriously by management? Why?

11. Explain how a database management system converts logical, data-element I/O requests to physical I/O commands.

12. Explain how pointers and indexes are used to link the elements in a database.

13. Distinguish between a hierarchical database and a network database. Intuitively, which organization seems more flexible? Which one seems easiest to implement?

14. Briefly, what distinguishes a relational database from a network or hierarchical database?

15. Where is the database management system located; in other words, where in memory is it physically stored?

Appendixes

A

Number Systems, Data Types, and Codes

Number Systems

A decimal number consists of a series of digits—0, 1, 2, 3, 4, 5, 6, 7, 8, 9—written in precise relative positions. The positions are important; 23 and 32 are different numbers in spite of the fact that they contain the same two digits. The value of a given number is found by multiplying each digit by its place or positional value and adding the products. For example, 3582 represents:

```
  3 times 1000  =  3000
+ 5 times  100  =   500
+ 8 times   10  =    80
+ 2 times    1  =     2
                   ____
                   3582
```

Generally, any number's value is the sum of the products of its digit and place values.

Take a close look at the decimal place values 1, 10, 100, 1000, 10000, and so on. The pattern is obvious. Rather than writing all those zeros, you can use scientific notation, for example, writing 10000 as 10^4. Because any number raised to the zero power is (by definition) 1, you can write the decimal place values as the base (10) raised to a series of integer powers:

$$\ldots 10^8 \; 10^7 \; 10^6 \; 10^5 \; 10^4 \; 10^3 \; 10^2 \; 10^1 \; 10^0$$

A few general rules can be derived from this discussion of decimal numbers. First is the idea of place or positional value represented by the base (10) raised to a series of integer powers. The second is the use of the digit zero (0) to represent "nothing" in a given position. (How else could you distinguish 3 from 30?) Third, a total of ten digits (0 through 9) is needed to write decimal values. Finally, only values less than the base (in this case, 10) can be written with a single digit.

Binary Numbers

There is nothing to restrict the application of these rules to a base-10 number system. If the positional values are powers of 2, you have the framework of a binary or base-2 number system:

$$\ldots 2^8\ 2^7\ 2^6\ 2^5\ 2^4\ 2^3\ 2^2\ 2^1\ 2^0$$

As in any number system, the digit zero (0) is needed to represent nothing in a given position. Additionally, the binary number system needs only one other digit, 1. Given these digit and place values, you can find the value of any number by multiplying each digit by its place value and adding these products. For example, the binary number 1100011 is:

$$
\begin{array}{rcll}
1 \text{ times } 2^6 &=& 1 \text{ times } 64 &= 64 \\
+\,1 \text{ times } 2^5 &=& 1 \text{ times } 32 &= 32 \\
+\,0 \text{ times } 2^4 &=& 0 \text{ times } 16 &= 0 \\
+\,0 \text{ times } 2^3 &=& 0 \text{ times } 8 &= 0 \\
+\,0 \text{ times } 2^2 &=& 0 \text{ times } 4 &= 0 \\
+\,1 \text{ times } 2^1 &=& 1 \text{ times } 2 &= 2 \\
+\,1 \text{ times } 2^0 &=& 1 \text{ times } 1 &= \underline{1} \\
& & & 99
\end{array}
$$

The decimal number 2 is 10 in binary; the decimal number 4 is 100. Decimal 5 is 101 (1 four, 0 twos, and 1 one).

Octal and Hexadecimal

Other number systems, notably octal (base 8) and hexadecimal (base 16) are commonly used with computers. The octal number system uses powers of 8 to represent positional values and the digit values 0, 1, 2, 3, 4, 5, 6 and 7. The hexadecimal number system uses powers of 16 and the digits 0, 1, 2, 3, 4, 5, 6, 7, 8, 9, A, B, C, D, E, and F. The hexadecimal number FF is:

$$15 \text{ times } 16^1 = 240$$
$$+ 15 \text{ times } 16^0 = \underline{15}$$
$$255$$

There are no computers that work directly with octal or hex values; a computer is a binary machine. These two number systems are used simply because it is easy to convert between them and binary. Each octal digit is exactly equivalent to three binary digits (Fig. A.1) and each hexadecimal digit is exactly equivalent to four binary digits (Fig. A.2), so octal and hex can be used as shorthands for displaying binary values (Fig. A.3).

Data Types

Numeric Data

Because binary numbers are so well suited to electronic devices, computers are at their most efficient when working with pure binary. A typical computer is designed around a basic unit of binary data called a word (usually, 8, 16, or 32 bits). Normally, the high-order bit is set aside to hold a sign (0 for +, 1 for −) and the remaining bits are data bits. There is no provision for a decimal point; decimal point alignment is the programmer's responsibility. For example, the biggest binary value that can be stored on a 32-bit word computer is

01111111111111111111111111111111

which is 2,147,483,647 in decimal, while the limit on a 16-bit machine is

0111111111111111

or 32,767 in decimal.

Binary integers are fine for many applications, but at times, very large, very small, and fractional numbers are needed. With scientific notation, numbers are written as a decimal fraction

Fig. A.1

Each octal digit is exactly equivalent to three binary digits.

Octal	Binary	Octal	Binary
0	000	4	100
1	001	5	101
2	010	6	110
3	011	7	111

Fig. A.2

Each hexadecimal digit is exactly equivalent to four binary digits.

Hex	Binary	Hex	Binary
0	0000	8	1000
1	0001	9	1001
2	0010	A	1010
3	0011	B	1011
4	0100	C	1100
5	0101	D	1101
6	0110	E	1110
7	0111	F	1111

Fig. A.3

Because it is so easy to convert between octal or hexadecimal and binary, octal and hexadecimal are convenient shorthands for representing binary data.

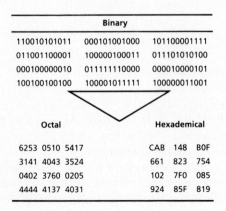

Binary		
110010101011	000101001000	101100001111
011001100001	100000100011	011101010100
000100000010	011111110000	000010000101
100100100100	100001011111	100000011001

Octal			Hexademical		
6253	0510	5417	CAB	148	B0F
3141	4043	3524	661	823	754
0402	3760	0205	102	7F0	085
4444	4137	4031	924	85F	819

followed by a power of 10; for example, the speed of light, 186,000 miles per second, is written as 0.186×10^6. Many computers can store and manipulate binary approximations of scientific numbers called real or floating-point numbers.

Certain applications, particularly business applications, demand precisely rounded decimal numbers. While any data type will do for whole numbers or integers, floating-point and binary numbers provide at best a close approximation to decimal fractions, so many computers support a form of decimal data. Generally, computers are at their least efficient when processing decimal data.

String Data

Computers are not limited to storing and manipulating numbers, however. Many applications call for such data as names, addresses, and product descriptions. These string values are typically stored as sets of characters, with each character represented by a code. Most modern computers use either ASCII or EBCDIC (Fig. A.4). On many computers, a single coded character occupies 1 byte, so the name "Lopez" would be stored in 5 consecutive bytes.

It is important to note that strings and numbers are different. For example, if you type the digit 1 followed by the digit 2, each character will be stored as a 1-byte string in memory. On a computer that uses the ASCII code, these two characters would appear as:

00110001 00110010

This is *not* the number 12. On a 16-bit computer, a pure bina 12 is stored as

0000000000001100

(Try using the "digit-times-place-value" rule.)

Since numbers and strings are different, in most ɟ ming languages you must distinguish strings from The positional value of each digit in a number is sigŋ you move from byte to byte, the positional values of ual bits have no meaning in a string. (The order of t' nificant, but arbitrary.)

Fig. A.4

Most modern computers use an 8-bit code such as EBCDIC or ASCII to represent characters.

Character	EBCDIC Binary	Hex	ASCII-8 Binary	Hex
A	1100 0001	C1	0100 0001	41
B	1100 0010	C2	0100 0010	42
C	1100 0011	C3	0100 0011	43
D	1100 0100	C4	0100 0100	44
E	1100 0101	C5	0100 0101	45
F	1100 0110	C6	0100 0110	46
G	1100 0111	C7	0100 0111	47
H	1100 1000	C8	0100 1000	48
I	1100 1001	C9	0100 1001	49
J	1101 0001	D1	0100 1010	4A
K	1101 0010	D2	0100 1011	4B
L	1101 0011	D3	0100 1100	4C
M	1101 0100	D4	0100 1101	4D
N	1101 0101	D5	0100 1110	4E
O	1101 0110	D6	0100 1111	4F
P	1101 0111	D7	0101 0000	50
Q	1101 1000	D8	0101 0001	51
R	1101 1001	D9	0101 0010	52
S	1110 0010	E2	0101 0011	53
T	1110 0011	E3	0101 0100	54
U	1110 0100	E4	0101 0101	55
V	1110 0101	E5	0101 0110	56
W	1110 0110	E6	0101 0111	57
X	1110 0111	E7	0101 1000	58
Y	1110 1000	E8	0101 1001	59
Z	1110 1001	E9	0101 1010	5A
0	1111 0000	F0	0011 0000	30
1	1111 0001	F1	0011 0001	31
2	1111 0010	F2	0011 0010	32
3	1111 0011	F3	0011 0011	33
4	1111 0100	F4	0011 0100	34
5	1111 0101	F5	0011 0101	35
6	1111 0110	F6	0011 0110	36
7	1111 0111	F7	0011 0111	37
8	1111 1000	F8	0011 1000	38
9	1111 1001	F9	0011 1001	39

Data normally enter a computer through an input device in string form. Most computers have special instructions to convert strings to numbers. Arithmetic operations are performed on the numbers, and the results are converted back to string form before they are sent to an output device. Most programming languages perform these data type conversions for you; assembler languages are an exception.

B
Summary of MS-DOS (PC-DOS) Commands

References

The following material is based on two primary sources:

1. IBM (1988). *Using Disk Operating System Version 4.00.* Armonk, New York: International Business Machine Corporation.
2. Zenith Data Systems (1988). *MS-DOS Version 3.3 Plus.* St. Joseph, Michigan: Zenith Data Systems Corporation.

It represents a brief summary of selected commands and filters. For additional detail, see the primary sources.

General

*Format of a command:

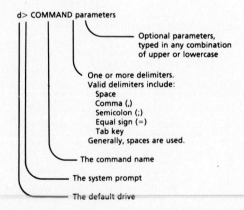

d> COMMAND parameters

Optional parameters, typed in any combination of upper or lowercase

One or more delimiters. Valid delimiters include:
Space
Comma (,)
Semicolon (;)
Equal sign (=)
Tab key
Generally, spaces are used.

The command name

The system prompt

The default drive

*Rules for defining a file name:

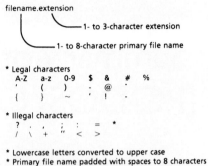

filename.extension

— 1- to 3-character extension

— 1- to 8-character primary file name

* Legal characters
A-Z	a-z	0-9	$	&	#	%
'	(	)	-	@	^	
{	}	~	'	!	-	

* Illegal characters
  | ? | . | ; | : | = | * |
  | / | \ | + | " | < | > |

* Lowercase letters converted to upper case
* Primary file name padded with spaces to 8 characters
* Extension padded with spaces to 3 characters
* Wild card characters

  ? Any single character
  * Any group of 1-8 characters

*Rules for defining path names:

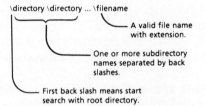

\directory \directory ... \filename

— A valid file name
with extension.

— One or more subdirectory
names separated by back
slashes.

— First back slash means start
search with root directory.

* To define a subdirectory name, use the rules for
  defining a file name without an extension.

* Maximum path name length is 64 characters.

* If path name does not start with a back slash,
  search begins with current working directory.

*Reserved device names:

CON PRN LPT1 AUX COM1
LPT2 LPT3 COM2 NUL CLOCK$

*Conventional file name extensions:

ASM	assembler source	EXE	executable file
BAK	backup file	FOR	FORTRAN source
BAS	BASIC source	LIB	library source
BAT	batch file	LST	ASCII list file
BIN	binary file	MAP	ASCII load module
COB	COBOL source	OBJ	object module
COM	command file	OVR	overlay file
DAT	ASCII data file	REF	cross-reference
DIF	difference file	TMP	temporary link
DOC	ASCII document	$$$	temporary work
DVD	device driver		

*Redirection parameters:

Parameter	Meaning	Example
<	Change source to a speci-fied file or device	<MYFILE.DAT
>	Change destination to a specified file or device	>PRN
>>	Change destination, usu-ally to an existing file, and append new output to it	>>HOLD.DAT
|	Pipe standard output to another command or to a filter	DIR | MORE

Commands

*CHDIR changes the current working directory.

CHDIR d:pathname
                  —— Path name of new working directory
        —— Drive identifier

* . designates the current working directory.

* .. is the parent of the current working directory.

* CHDIR with no parameters displays name of current working directory.

*CHKDSK checks a disk's directory and reports on its contents.

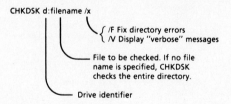

CHKDSK d:filename /x
           { /F Fix directory errors
           { /V Display "verbose" messages
      —— File to be checked. If no file name is specified, CHKDSK checks the entire directory.
    —— Drive identifier

*CLS clears the screen.

CLS (No parameters)

*COMP compares two files.

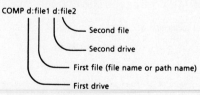

COMP d:file1 d:file2
           —— Second file
        —— Second drive
      —— First file (file name or path name)
    —— First drive

COMP is often used after COPY to verify results.

*COPY copies one or more files from a source to a destination.

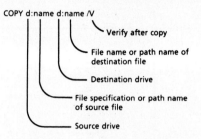

COPY d:name d:name /V

- Verify after copy
- File name or path name of destination file
- Destination drive
- File specification or path name of source file
- Source drive

* If no destination file name is given, the source file name is used. In this case, the drives must be different.

* The source and destination must differ in some way (file name, drive, and/or directory).

*DATE checks and/or sets the system date.

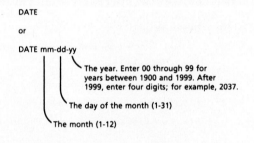

DATE

or

DATE mm-dd-yy

- The year. Enter 00 through 99 for years between 1900 and 1999. After 1999, enter four digits; for example, 2037.
- The day of the month (1-31)
- The month (1-12)

*DIR displays a directory's contents.

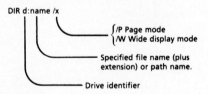

DIR d:name /x

- {/P Page mode
  {/W Wide display mode
- Specified file name (plus extension) or path name.
- Drive identifier

*Default drive selection.

B: Selects drive B

A: Selects drive A

*DISKCOMP compares the contents of two complete disks.

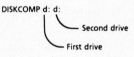

DISKCOMP d: d:

- Second drive
- First drive

Note: A /V option on a DISKCOPY command implies DISKCOMP.

*DISKCOPY copies the contents of one disk to another.

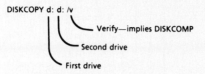

DISKCOPY d: d: /v

- Verify—implies DISKCOMP
- Second drive
- First drive

*ECHO controls the display of batch file commands and displays comments on the screen.

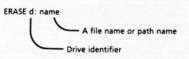

ECHO { ON — Commands displayed / OFF — Commands not displayed / message — Message displayed }

*ERASE (or DEL) erases a file or files.

ERASE d: name

- A file name or path name
- Drive identifier

*FORMAT formats a disk.

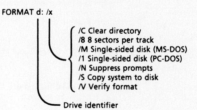

FORMAT d: /x

- /C Clear directory
- /8 8 sectors per track
- /M Single-sided disk (MS-DOS)
- /1 Single-sided disk (PC-DOS)
- /N Suppress prompts
- /S Copy system to disk
- /V Verify format
- Drive identifier

*GRAPHICS supports the output of graphic displays to a graphics printer.

GRAPHICS   (No parameters)

Note: Load GRAPHICS before loading application routine.

*MKDIR creates a new directory.

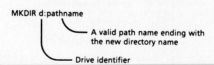

MKDIR d:pathname

- A valid path name ending with the new directory name
- Drive identifier

*PRINT sends selected files to the printer in the background.

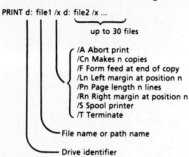

PRINT d: file1 /x d: file2 /x ...

up to 30 files

/A Abort print
/Cn Makes n copies
/F Form feed at end of copy
/Ln Left margin at position n
/Pn Page length n lines
/Rn Right margin at position n
/S Spool printer
/T Terminate

File name or path name

Drive identifier

*RECOVER salvages useful portions of a file or files on a disk containing bad sectors.

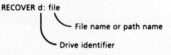

RECOVER d: file

File name or path name

Drive identifier

Note: If no file is specified, all files stored on the specified or default disk are recovered.

*RENAME (or REN) renames an existing file.

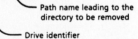

RENAME d: name filename

New file name

Old file name or pathname

Drive identifier

*RMDIR (or RD) removes the specified directory.

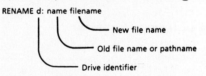

RMDIR d: pathname

Path name leading to the
directory to be removed

Drive identifier

Note: The directory to be removed must be empty.

*TIME checks and/or sets the system time.

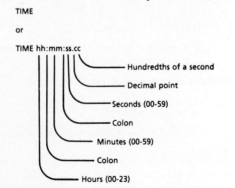

TIME

or

TIME hh:mm:ss.cc

Hundredths of a second

Decimal point

Seconds (00-59)

Colon

Minutes (00-59)

Colon

Hours (00-23)

*TREE displays the directory paths on the specified disk.

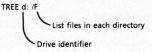

TREE d: /F

- List files in each directory

- Drive identifier

*TYPE displays the selected file's contents on the screen.

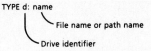

TYPE d: name

- File name or path name

- Drive identifier

*VER displays the MS-DOS version number.

VER (No parameters)

Filters

*FIND searches the specified file or files for a string, and displays all lines containing that string.

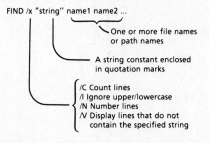

FIND /x "string" name1 name2 ...

- One or more file names
  or path names

- A string constant enclosed
  in quotation marks

/C Count lines
/I Ignore upper/lowercase
/N Number lines
/V Display lines that do not
  contain the specified string

*MORE reads text from the standard input device and displays it one screen at a time.

MORE

usually,

command ¦ MORE

- The pipe operator

- Command whose output is piped to MORE

*SORT sorts data into ascending order.

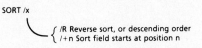

SORT /x

/R Reverse sort, or descending order
/+n Sort field starts at position n

These inserts go with msp. 687

This is insert #1

/4	Low-capacity 5.25-inch diskette
/F:360	Low-capacity 5.25-inch diskette
/8	8 sectors per track
/1	Single-sided diskette
/F:720	3.5-inch, 720 KB diskette
/S	Copy operating system to disk
/B	Allocate space for system files

This is insert #2

/D:name	Designate printer
/C	Cancel file from queue
/T	Cancel all files from queue
/Q	Limit number of files in queue
/B:n	Set size of internal buffer
/M:t	Set time
/U:t	Set wait time
/S:t	Set time slice

C
Summary of UNIX Commands

References

The material in this appendix is based primarily on the following three references:

1. Bourne, S.R. (1983). *The UNIX System*. Reading, Massachusetts: Addison-Wesley Publishing Company.
2. Parker, Tim (1990). *UNIX Survival Guide*. Reading, Massachusetts: Addison-Wesley Publishing Company.
3. Sobell, Mark G. (1984). *A Practical Guide to the UNIX System*. Menlo Park, California: The Benjamin Cummings Publishing Company.

It represents a brief summary of selected UNIX commands and utilities. For additional details, see the references or your UNIX system manual.

General

* Format of a command

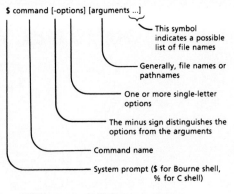

$ command [-options] [arguments ...]

— This symbol indicates a possible list of file names

— Generally, file names or pathnames

— One or more single-letter options

— The minus sign distinguishes the options from the arguments

— Command name

— System prompt ($ for Bourne shell, % for C shell)

* Fields are separated by one or more spaces.
* Fields enclosed in brackets [..] are optional.

* Rules for defining a file name:

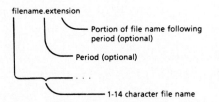

filename.extension

— Portion of file name following period (optional)

— Period (optional)

. . .

— 1-14 character file name

* Any character you can type is legal.

* Suggested characters include A-Z, a-z, 0-9, comma (,), and underscore (_).

* UNIX distinguishes between upper and lowercase.

* If you include a period in the file name, the characters following the period form the extension.

* The period and the extension count against the 14-character limit.

* You can code more than one period.

*Rules for defining path names:

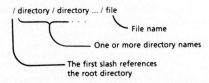

/ directory / directory ... / file

. . .

— File name

— One or more directory names

— The first slash references the root directory

* A directory is a type of file; thus the rules for defining a directory name are the same as the rules for defining a file name.

* If the path name starts with a directory name instead of a slash, UNIX starts searching with the working directory.

* Redirection parameters:

Operator	Meaning	Example
<	Change source to a specified file or device	<myfile
>	Change destination to a specified file or device	>tempfile
>>	Change destination, usually to an existing file, and append new output to it	>>master.pay
|	Pipe	cat file1 sort

Commands and Utilities

* *cat* displays the contents of a file or files.

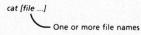

cat [file ...]
                └── One or more file names

* *cd* changes the working directory.

cd [directory]
              └── New working directory. If no directory
                  is coded, the home directory is assumed.

* *chmod* changes a file's access permissions.

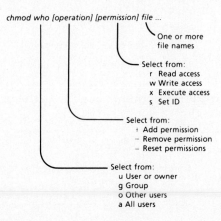

chmod who [operation] [permission] file ...
                                              └── One or more
                                                  file names
                                   └── Select from:
                                       r Read access
                                       w Write access
                                       x Execute access
                                       s Set ID
                          └── Select from:
                              + Add permission
                              − Remove permission
                              − Reset permissions
                 └── Select from:
                     u User or owner
                     g Group
                     o Other users
                     a All users

* *cp* copies a file or files.

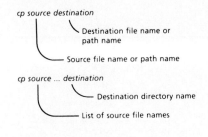

cp source destination
    Destination file name or
    path name
    Source file name or path name

cp source ... destination
    Destination directory name
    List of source file names

* *csh* activates the C shell.

csh
    No options or parameters

* *date* displays the system date and time.

date
    No options

* *ln* creates a link.

ln file1 [file2]
    * Normally, the new directory
    * If not specified, the working
      directory
    * If a file name is specified, it
      becomes another name (an
      alias) for file1
    Path name of existing file

* *logout* logs a user off the system.

logout
    No options or parameters

Note: On most systems, press control-D to log off.

* *lpr* sends the contents of a file to the printer.

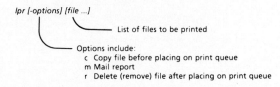

lpr [-options] [file ...]
    List of files to be printed
    Options include:
    c Copy file before placing on print queue
    m Mail report
    r Delete (remove) file after placing on print queue

* *ls* lists the contents of a directory or directories.

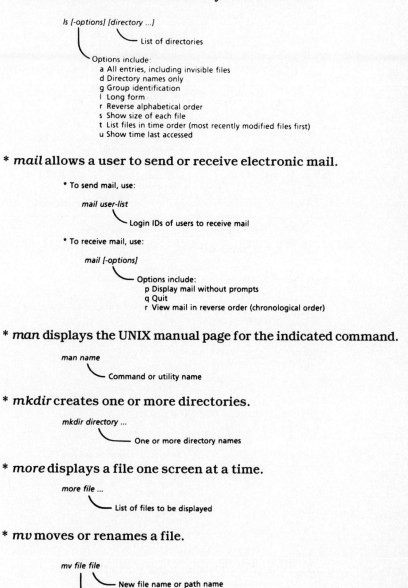

ls [-options] [directory ...]

List of directories

Options include:
a All entries, including invisible files
d Directory names only
g Group identification
l Long form
r Reverse alphabetical order
s Show size of each file
t List files in time order (most recently modified files first)
u Show time last accessed

* *mail* allows a user to send or receive electronic mail.

* To send mail, use:

mail user-list

Login IDs of users to receive mail

* To receive mail, use:

mail [-options]

Options include:
p Display mail without prompts
q Quit
r View mail in reverse order (chronological order)

* *man* displays the UNIX manual page for the indicated command.

man name

Command or utility name

* *mkdir* creates one or more directories.

mkdir directory ...

One or more directory names

* *more* displays a file one screen at a time.

more file ...

List of files to be displayed

* *mv* moves or renames a file.

mv file file

New file name or path name

Old file name or path name

mv file ... directory

New directory

List of files to be moved

* *passwd* changes a user's password.

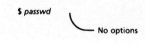

$ passwd
— No options

* *pr* prepares standard input or a file for printing.

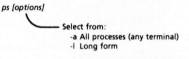

pr [-options] file ...
— List of files to be printed
— Options include:
    h   Header (argument following this option)
    l*n* Page length *n* lines
    m   Multiple columns
    +*n* Start numbering with page *n*
    -*n* Display *n* columns
    t   No header or trailer
    w*n* Line width *n* columns

* *ps* displays the status of a process.

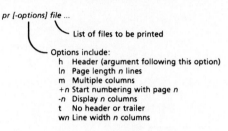

ps [options]
— Select from:
    -a All processes (any terminal)
    -l Long form

If no options are coded, displays status of all processes controlled by user's terminal.

* *pwd* displays the user's current working directory.

pwd
— No options

* *rm* deletes a file by removing a link.

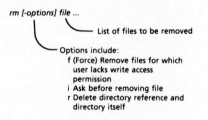

rm [-options] file ...
— List of files to be removed
— Options include:
    f (Force) Remove files for which
      user lacks write access
      permission
    i Ask before removing file
    r Delete directory reference and
      directory itself

* *rmdir* deletes one or more directories.

rmdir directory ...
— Pathnames of one or more empty directories

* *sh* activates the Bourne shell.

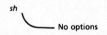

sh
— No options

* *sort* sorts the contents of a file.

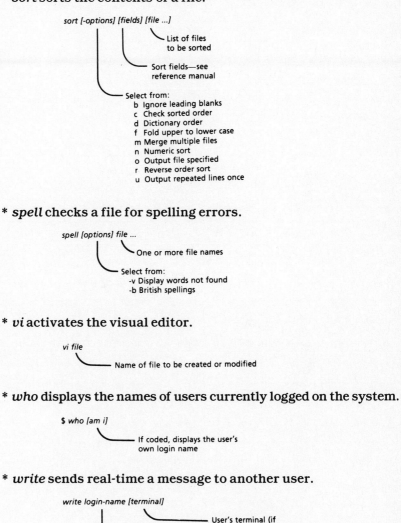

sort [-options] [fields] [file ...]

List of files
to be sorted

Sort fields—see
reference manual

Select from:
- b Ignore leading blanks
- c Check sorted order
- d Dictionary order
- f Fold upper to lower case
- m Merge multiple files
- n Numeric sort
- o Output file specified
- r Reverse order sort
- u Output repeated lines once

* *spell* checks a file for spelling errors.

spell [options] file ...

One or more file names

Select from:
- -v Display words not found
- -b British spellings

* *vi* activates the visual editor.

vi file

Name of file to be created or modified

* *who* displays the names of users currently logged on the system.

$ who [am i]

If coded, displays the user's
own login name

* *write* sends real-time a message to another user.

write login-name [terminal]

User's terminal (if
logged on more than one)

Login name of receiver

D
Selected OS/400 Commands

References

1. IBM Corporation (1990). *Application System/400. Programming: Command Reference Summary.* Rochester, Minnesota: International Business Machines Corporation. Publication Number SC21-8076.
2. IBM Corporation (1989). *Application System/400. Programming: Control Language Programmer's Guide.* Rochester, Minnesota: International Business Machines Corporation. Publication Number SC21-8077.
3. IBM Corporation (1988). *Application System/400. Programming: Control Language Reference.* Rochester, Minnesota: International Business Machines Corporation. Publication Number SBOF-0481, five volumes.

Commands

Command	Description
ANZPRB	Analyze problem. Allows the user to analyze or report problems that are not detected by the system.
	Required parameters: ANZTYPE
	Optional parameters: NETID, USERID, PASSWORD
BCHJOB	Batch job. Marks the beginning of a batch job in the batch input stream.
	Required parameters: none

Optional parameters: JOB, JOBQ, JOBPTY, OUTPTY, PRTTXT, RTGDTA, RQSDTA, SYNTAX, CURLIB, INLIBL, ENDSEV, LOG, LOGCLPGM, INQMSGRPY, PRTDEV, OUTQ, HOLD, DATE, SWS, MSGQ

CALL   Call program. Calls and starts the named program.

Required parameters: PGM

Optional parameters: PARM

CHGCURLIB   Change current library. Changes the current library to the named library.

Required parameters: CURLIB

Optional parameters: none

CHGJOB   Change job. Changes selected attributes of a job such as job queue, scheduling priority, message logging controls, date format, printer device, output queue, run priority, time slice, and others.

Required parameters: none

Optional parameters: JOB, JOBQ, JOBPTY, OUTPTY, PRTTXT, LOG, LOGCLPGM, INQMSGRPY, BRKMSG, STSMSG, PRTDEV, OUTQ, DDMCNV, DATE, DATFMT, DATSEP, SWS, RUNPTY, TIMESLICE, PURGE, DFTWAIT, DEVRCYACN, TSEPOOL

CHGPWD   Change password. Allows a user to specify a new password.

Required parameters: none

Optional parameters: none

CPYF   Copy file. Copies all or part of a database or external device file to a database or external device file.

Required parameters: FROMFILE, TOFILE

Optional parameters: FROMMBR, TOMBR, MBROPT, CRTFILE, PRINT, RCDFMT, FROMRCD, FROMKEY, TORCD, TOKEY, NBRRCDS, INCCHAR, INCREL, FMTOPT, SRCOPT, SRCSEQ, OUTFMT, ERRLVL, COMPRESS

CRTDUPOBJ   Create duplicate object. Copies a single object or a group of objects.

Required parameters: OBJ, FROMLIB, OBJTYPE

Optional parameters: TOLIB, NEWOBJ, DATA

CRTLIB	Create library. Adds a new library to the system.
	Required parameters: LIB
	Optional parameters: TYPE, AUT, ASP, TEXT
CRTPF	Create physical file. Creates a physical file in the database.
	Required parameters: FILE
	Optional parameters: SRCFILE, RCDLEN, SRCMBR, OPTION, SYSTEM, GENLVL, FLAG, FILETYPE, MBR, EXPDATE, MAXMBRS, MAINT, RECOVER, FRCACCPTH, SIZE, ALLOCATE, CONTIG, UNIT, FRCRATIO, IGCDTA, WAITFILE, WAITRCD, SHARE, DLTPCT, ALWUPD, ALWDLT, LVLCHK, AUT, TEXT
CRTUSRPRF	Create user profile. Identifies a user to the system and creates a user profile for that user.
	Required parameters: USRPRF
	Optional parameters: PASSWORD, SPCAUT, PWDEXP, USRCLS, SPCENV, DSPSGNINF, PWDEXPITV, LMTDEVSSN, MAXSTG, PTYLMT, CURLIB, INLPGM, INLMNU, LMTCPB, JOBD, GRFPRF, OWNER, GRPAUT, ACGCDE, DOCPWD, MSGQ, DLVRY, SEV, PRTDEV, OUTQ, ATNPGM, USROPT, AUT, TEXT
DLTF	Delete file. Deletes specified database or device files from the system.
	Required parameters: FILE
	Optional parameters: SYSTEM
DLTLIB	Delete library. Deletes the specified library from the system. All library members must be deleted before this command is issued.
	Required parameters: LIB
	Optional parameters: none
DSPJOBLOG	Display job log. Displays commands and related messages for a job.
	Required parameters: none
	Optional parameters: JOB, OUTPUT
DSPLIB	Display library. Displays the contents of one or more specified libraries.

Required parameters: none

Optional parameters: LIB, OUTPUT

DSPLIBL Display library list. Displays the system portion, the current library, and the user portion of the library list.

Required parameters: none

Optional parameters: OUTPUT

DSPMSG Display message. Displays messages in the specified message queue.

Required parameters: none

Optional parameters: MSGQ, MSGTYPE, START, SEV, OUTPUT

DSPOBJD Display object description. Displays the names and attributes of specified objects.

Required parameters: OBJ, OBJTYPE

Optional parameters: DETAIL, OUTPUT, OUTFILE, OUTMBR

DSPPFM Display physical file member. Displays the contents of a physical database file member.

Required parameters: FILE

Optional parameters: MBR, FROMRCD

DSPPGM Display program. Displays information about a program.

Required parameters: PGM

Optional parameters: OUTPUT

DSPPGMVAR Display program variable. Shows the current value of one or more program variables in a program being debugged.

Required parameters: PGMVAR

Optional parameters: START, LEN, OUTFMT, OUTPUT, PGM, RCRLVL

DSPUSRPRF Display user profile. Display the contents of a user profile.

Required parameters: USRPRF

Optional parameters: TYPE, OUTPUT, OUTFILE, OUTMBR

GO Go to menu. Displays the requested menu.

Required parameters: MENU

Optional parameters: none

PRTDEVADR   Print device addresses. Prints a configuration matrix of addresses for devices attached to a local workstation controller.

Required parameters: CTLD

Optional parameters: none

PWRDWNSYS   Power down system. Starts power down sequence.

Required parameters: none

Optional parameters: OPTION, DELAY, RESTART, IPLSRC

RSTLIB   Restore library. Restores user libraries that were previously saved to diskette, tape, or a save file.

Required parameters: SAVLIB, DEV

Optional parameters: VOL, SEQNBR, LABEL, ENDOPT, STRLIB, SAVF, OPTION, MBROPT, ALWOBJDIF, RSTLIB, RSTASP, OUTPUT

RSTOBJ   Restore object. Restores objects that were previously saved to diskette, tape, or a save file.

Required parameters: OBJ, DEV

Optional parameters: OBJTYPE, VOL, SEQNBR, LABEL, ENDOPT, SAVF, OPTION, FILEMBR, MBROPT, SAVDATE, SAVTIME, ALWOBJDIF, RSTLIB, RSTASP, OUTPUT

SAVLIB   Save library. Saves a copy of up to 50 specified libraries.

Required parameters: LIB, DEV

Optional parameters: VOL, SEQNBR, LABEL, EXPDATE, ENDOPT, STRLIB, SAVF, UPDHST, TGTRLS, CLEAR, PRECHK, ACCPTH, SAVFDTA, STG, DTACPR

SAVOBJ   Save object. Saves a copy of one or more objects.

Required parameters: OBJ, LIB, DEV

Optional parameters: OBJTYPE, VOL, SEQNBR, LABEL, EXPDATE, TGTRLS, ENDOPT, STRLIB, SAVF, UPDHST, CLEAR, PRECHK, FILEMBR, ACCPTH, SAVFDTA, STG, DTACPR

SBMJOB   Submit job. Submit a batch job.

Required parameters: none

Optional parameters: JOB, JOBD, USER, JOBQ, JOBPTY, OUTPTY, PRTTXT, RTGDTA, SYSLIBL, CURLIB, INLLIBL, LOG, LOGCLPGM, INQMSGRPY, PRTDEV, OUTQ, HOLD, DATA, SWS, DSPSBMJOB, MSGQ

SIGNOFF   Sign off. Ends an interactive job.

Required parameters: none

Optional parameters: LOG, DROP

SNDBRKMSG   Send break message. Used by the system operator to send an impromptu message to one or more message queues.

Required parameters: MSG, TOMSGQ

Optional parameters: MSGTYPE, RPYMSGQ

SNDMSG   Send message. Used by display station users to send a message to one or more message queues.

Required parameters: SNDMSG, TOUSR or TOMSGQ

Optional parameters: MSGTYPE, RPYMSGQ

SNDPTFORD   Send program temporary fix order. Allows user to send an order for a specific fix.

Required parameters: PTFID

Optional parameters: PTFPART, DELIVERY, RMTCPNAME, RMTNETID, ORDER, REORDER

STRDFU   Start data file utility. Starts the data file utility program.

Required parameters: none

Optional parameters: OPTION, DFUPGM, FILE, MBR

STROFC   Start office. Allows a user to access OfficeVision/400 functions.

Required parameters: none

Optional parameters: OPTION

STRPDM   Start programming development manager. Calls the programming development manager utility.

Required parameters: none

Optional parameters: none

STRQRY   Start query. Displays the query menu.

Required parameters: none

Optional parameters: none

WRKACTJOB Work with active jobs. Allows the user to work with performance and status information for active jobs.

Required parameters: none

Optional parameters: OUTPUT, RESET, SBS, CPUPCTLMT, RSPLMT, SEQ

WRKCFGSTS Work with configuration status. Display and work with configuration status functions.

Required parameters: CFGTYPE

Optional parameters: CFGD, OUTPUT, RMTLOCNAME

WRKLIB Work with libraries. Display and update libraries over which you have authority.

Required parameters: none

Optional parameters: LIB

WRKMBRPDM Work with members using PDM. Allows the user to work with lists of members.

Required parameters: none

Optional parameters: FILE, MBR, MBRTYPE

WRKOUTQ Work with output queue. Display and work with output queue status.

Required parameters: none

Optional parameters: OUTQ, OUTPUT

WRKPRB Work with problem. Starts the work with problem display.

Required parameters: none

Optional parameters: STATUS, PERIOD, HARDWARE, RESOURCE, FUNCTION, PGM, ORIGIN, SRVID

WRKQRY Work with query. Create, change, copy, delete, print, or run a query.

Required parameters: none

Optional parameters: none

WRKSYSSTS   Work with system status. Work with information about the
               system's current status.

               Required parameters: none

               Optional parameters: OUTPUT, RESET

WRKUSRPRF   Work with user profiles. Work with a list of user profiles.

               Required parameters: USRPRF

               Optional parameters: none

WRKWTR   Work with writers. Work with the status of printers and
               writers.

               Required parameters: none

               Optional parameters: WTR, DSPFMT, OUTPUT

E

Summary of VSE Job Control Statements

References

The primary reference for this appendix is IBM Publication *VSE Advanced Functions System Control Statements*. Portions of several of the generalized job control statements are taken directly from this publication. The excerpts are reprinted by permission from International Business Machines Corporation.

Statements

ASSGN, assigns a logical I/O unit to a physical device.

```
// ASSGN SYSxxx, address    [ {  ,X'cuu'       } ]
                            [ {  ,UA           } ]
                            [ {  ,IGN          } ]
                            [ {  ,SYSyyy       } ]
                            [ {  ,device-class } ]
                            [ {  ,device-type  } ]
```

where

> **SYSxxx** is the symbolic unit name:
> **address** is the physical device address expressed as
> X'cuu' where c = channel and uu = device, or
> UA which indicates that unit is unassigned, or
> IGN which indicates that the device is to be ignored (i.e., disabled), or

SYSyyy, which assigns SYSxxx to the same device as
SYSyyy, or
device-class, for example DISK or READER, or
device-type, for example 3330 or 2501.

A number of optional operands can be coded as well.

CLOSE closes a logical unit.

```
// CLOSE SYSxx    [  ( ,X'cuu'[,X'ss']  )  ]
                  [  { ,UA              }  ]
                  [  < ,IGN             >  ]
                  [  { ,ALT             }  ]
                  [  ( ,SYSyyy          )  ]
```

where parameters have the same meaning as in ASSGN.

DATE places a date in the communication region.

```
//    DATE    mm/dd/yy
```

or

```
//    DATE    dd/mm/yy
```

EXEC indicates end of control information for a job step and
identifies the phase which is to be loaded and executed.

```
//    EXEC    [programname].Go
```

or

```
//    EXEC    PROC = procname
```

where

   programname is the name of the program to be loaded and
   executed. If blank, the load module just produced by the linkage editor is assumed,
   GO indicates that the output of a compiler is to be link edited
   and executed, and
   procname is the name of a cataloged procedure.

EXTENT defines an area or extent of a direct access file.

```
//    EXTENT          [symbolic-unit],
                      [serial-number], [type],
                      [sequence-number],
                      [relative-track],
                      [number-of-tracks],
                      [split-cylinder-track],
```

where

>**symbolic unit** is the SYSxxx form symbolic = unit name of the desired volume. (If omitted, the unit from the last EXTENT is used. If this is the first or only EXTENT, the unit from the DTF is used.)
>
>**serial number** is the volume's serial number. (If omitted, the serial number from the last EXTENT is used. If this is the first or only EXTENT and no serial number is coded, the serial number is not checked.)
>
>**type** is 1 for a data area, 2 for an overflow area, 4 for an index area, and 8 for a split-cylinder data area;
>
>**sequence number** is the relative location of this extent within a multiextent file;
>
>**relative track** is relative track address of the track where the data extent (indexed sequential file) is to begin;
>
>**number of tracks** indicates the number of tracks to be assigned to this file;
>
>**split-cylinder track** indicates the upper track number for split-cylinder sequential files.

JOB indicates start of a job.

```
//    JOB      jobname [accounting information]
```

where

>**jobname** is the 1–8 alphanumeric character name of the job;
>
>**accounting information** is optional with the installation. (If specified, separate from the jobname by a blank.)

LBLTYP defines the amount of main storage to be reserved at link edit time or at execution time for label processing.

```
//    LBLTYP        ⎧ TAPE[ (nn) ] ⎫
                    ⎩ NSD (nn)     ⎭
```

where

TAPE(nn) is used to indicate that only tape labels and no nonsequential DASD file labels are to be processed; **NSD(nn)** indicates that nonsequential disk file labels are to be processed. (This also allows for other types as well. The nn indicates the largest number of extents to be processed for a single file.)

LIBDEF defines a library search list.

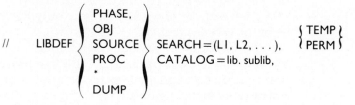

where

The first parameter, *member-type,* limits the search to a specific type of library member. Following SEARCH, code up to 15 sublibrary names. CATALOG defines the linkage editor or dump output sublibrary.

OPTION specifies job control options.

```
//    OPTION          option1[,option2 . . . ]
```

where

typical **options** include: LOG or NOLOG, DUMP or NODUMP, LINK or NOLINK, DECK or NODECK, LIST or NOLIST, LISTX or NOLISTX, SYM or NOSYM, XREF or NOXREF, ERRS or NOERRS, CATAL, STDLABEL, USRLABEL, PARSTD, 48C, 60C (60-character set), and SYSPARM.

RESET resets certain I/O assignments to the standard assignment, within the partition.

```
//    RESET          ⎧ SYS   ⎫
                     ⎨ PROG  ⎬
                     ⎪ ALL   ⎪
                     ⎩ SYSxxx⎭
```

where

>**SYS** resets all system logical units;
>**PROG** resets programmer logical units;
>**ALL** resets all logical units;
>**SYSxxx** resets the specified unit.

RSTRT allows programmer to restart a checkpointed program.

```
//    RSTRT       SYSxxx.nnnn[.filename]
```

where

>**SYSxxx** is the symbolic name of the device on which check-point records are stored;
>**nnnn** identifies the checkpoint record to be used for restarting;
>**filename** is the symbolic name of a disk file used for checkpoint (disk volumes hold multiple files).

UPSI allows the programmer to set program switches in the communications region:

```
//    UPSI nnnnnnnn
```

where

>**nnnnnnnn** represents the desired settings of the eight program switch bits—a 0 sets the associated switch to 0, a 1 sets the switch to a 1, and an X leaves the switch setting unchanged.

The symbol /* is an end-of-data file marker.
The symbol /& is an end-of-job marker.

Linkage Editor Control Statements

PHASE assigns a phase name and gives main storage load address for the phase.
INCLUDE indicates that an object module is to be included. If the

operands field is blank, the module is on SYSIPT; i.e., it's in object deck form.

ENTRY provides for an optional phase entry point.

ACTION specifies linkage-editor options.

Job Entry Control Language (JECL) Commands

JOB marks the start of a user job stream.

* $$ JOB   JNM = job-name, DISP = disposition, PRI = priority, CLASS = class

where

> Valid dispositions include H (hold then delete), L (hold then retain), D(execute automatically then delete), and K (execute automatically then retain).

EOJ marks the end of a user job stream.

* $$ EOJ

LST controls spooled printer output.

* $$ LST   DISP = disposition, PRI = priority, CLASS = class,
                FNO = form-number, JSEP = job separators,
                COPY = copies

PUN controls spooled card image output.

* $$ PUN   DISP = disposition, PRI = priority, CLASS = class,
                FNO = form-number, JSEP = job separators,
                COPY = copies, TADDR = tape-unit,
                PUN = punch-unit

ICCF Commands and the Editor

Commands

Command	Function
/DQ	Display POWER queues.
/LIB	List primary library directory.
/LIB COMM	List common library directory.

/LIST	List input area contents.
/LIST name	List contents of named library member.
/LP job	Display output for specified job.
/LOGON userid	Begin ICCF session.
/LOGOFF	End ICCF session.
/PURGE name	Delete named library member.
/RENAME name new	Change specified member name.
/SP job	Display status of specified job.

Common Macros

Macro	Function
ED	Start a full-screen editor session.
GETL job	Copy list output from specified job to print area. Mem = name parameter copies list output to named library member.
GETP job	Copy punch output from specified job to punch area. MEM = name option copies punch output to named library member.
SUBMIT job parms	Submit a job to VSE/POWER, where job is the job name and two common parameters are RETURN and PRINT.

Editor Commands

Command	Function
BACKWARD n	Scroll back n screens.
BOTTOM	Go to end of text.
CANCEL	End editor session.
DOWN n	Scroll forward n lines.
END	End editor session.
FILE name	Save named library member and end editor session.
FORWARD n	Scroll forward n screens.
GETFILE name	Retrieve named library member.
LOCATE text	Search from current position for pattern.
NEXT n	Scroll forward n lines.
QUIT	End editor session.
REPLACE name	Replace named library member.
SAVE name	Save named library member.
SEARCH text	Search from start of file for pattern.

TOP	Go to first line.
UP n	Scroll n lines toward start of text.

Editor Line Commands

Command	Function
An	Insert n lines.
Cn	Copy n lines to copy work area.
Dn	Delete n lines.
I	Insert text in copy work area.
Kn	Append n lines to copy work area.
Mn	Move n lines to copy work area.
"n	Duplicate line n times.
/	Make indicated line the current line.

F

Summary of MVS Job Control Language

References

The primary references for this appendix are:

1. IBM Publication GC28-1350. *MVS JCL Reference.*
2. Trombetta, M., and Finkelstein, S. C. (1989). *OS JCL and Utilities, A Comprehensive Treatment,* second edition.

The format for describing JCL statements in Figs. F.1, F.2, and F.3 is based on the IBM reference material.

General JCL Rules

JCL Statement Format

```
//name operation operands comments
```

Fields are separated by one or more blanks.
Operands are separated by commas.
Each operand consists of one or more parameters separated by commas.
Positional parameters derive their meaning from their relative positions.

Keyword parameters derive their meaning from a key word, and thus can be coded in any order.
A single JOB statement can be followed by one or more EXEC statements.
Each EXEC statement can be followed by one or more DD statements.

A jobname, stepname, or DDname may consist of from one to eight alphanumeric characters, the first of which must be alphabetic or one of the national characters (#, @, or $).

Continuing a JCL Statement

1. Break after any comma, and include the comma on the original line.
2. Code "/" in the first two columns of the continuation line.
3. Resume the coding of parameters anywhere between positions four and sixteen of the continuation line.

Rules for using parentheses: When the first subparameter is the only one coded, parentheses are not needed. When more than one subparameter or a positional subparameter other than the first one is coded, parentheses are needed.

The Job Statement

Function: Job separation. Secondary functions allow the programmer to pass accounting information and other parameters to the system. (See Fig. F.1.)

Parameters:
  accounting information: An installation-dependent positional parameter, normally containing an account number followed by other accounting information. It's operational but can, at the installation's request, be made a required parameter.
  programmer's name: Positional parameter consisting of a 1- to 20-character name composed of letters, numbers, and a period. If the field contains any other characters (a blank, for example) it must be enclosed in a set of apostrophes.
  MSGLEVEL = (jcl, allocations): Specifies the printing of job

Fig. F.1   The JOB statement.

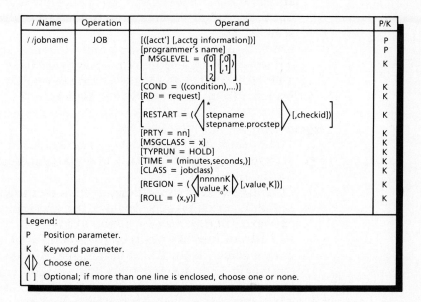

//Name	Operation	Operand	P/K
//jobname	JOB	[([acct'] [,acctg information])]	P
		[programmer's name]	P
		MSGLEVEL = ([0] [,0])	K
		[1] [,1]	
		[2]	
		[COND = ((condition),...)]	K
		[RD = request]	K
		RESTART = (* stepname [,checkid])	K
		stepname.procstep	
		[PRTY = nn]	K
		[MSGCLASS = x]	K
		[TYPRUN = HOLD]	K
		[TIME = (minutes,seconds,)]	K
		[CLASS = jobclass)	K
		[REGION = (nnnnnK [,value₁K])]	K
		value₀K	
		[ROLL = (x,y)]	K

Legend:

P   Position parameter.

K   Keyword parameter.

◁▷   Choose one.

[ ]   Optional; if more than one line is enclosed, choose one or none.

control statements and device allocation messages. The two positional subparameters are interpreted as follows.

JCL	Meaning
0	Print JOB statement only.
1	Print all JCL including that generated by cataloged procedures.
2	Print only JCL in job stream.

Allocations	Meaning
0	Print messages only if job abnormally terminates.
1	Print all messages.

COND = (condition . . . .): Normally coded on an EXEC statement. It allows a programmer to specify conditions for bypassing a job step. If coded on a JOB statement, the JOB COND is logically added to the EXEC COND(s).

RD=request: Allows for automatic restart and suppression of checkpoints.

RESTART=stepname: Requests step restart.

PRTY=nn: Priority within job class—low is zero; high is 13 or 15, depending on the version of JES (the job entry subsystem) used.

MSGCLASS=x: Allows the programmer to specify the device to which job scheduler messages are to be spooled.

TYPRUN=HOLD: Holds the job in the input queue until the operator issues a RELEASE command.

TYPRUN = SCAN: Checks JCL for syntax errors, but does not execute job.

TIME=(minutes, seconds): Normally coded on an EXEC statement. If coded on the JOB statement, sets a time limit for the entire job.

CLASS=jobclass: Specifies the job's class. The job class is normally specified as a single letter, and indicates the job's external priority.

REGION=nnnnnK: Another parameter that is more commonly coded on an EXEC statement. If coded on the JOB statement, the parameter sets an upper limit on the amount of main storage space allocated to any job step: thus, you must allow enough space for the biggest step.

The EXEC Statement

Function: Identifies the specific program (directly or through a cataloged procedure) to be executed. (See Fig. F.2.)

Parameters:

PGM=program name, or **PROC=procedure name,** or just plain **procedure name.** The first positional parameter. It fulfills the primary function of the EXEC statement. If no keyword is coded, PROC is assumed.

COND=(condition 1, condition 2, . . .): Allows the programmer to specify conditions for bypassing the job step.

PARM=value: Allows the programmer to pass parameters to a program.

ACCT=(accounting information): A rarely used parameter that allows the programmer to provide jobstep accounting information. Accounting information is usually passed through the JOB statement.

Fig. F.2   The EXEC statement.

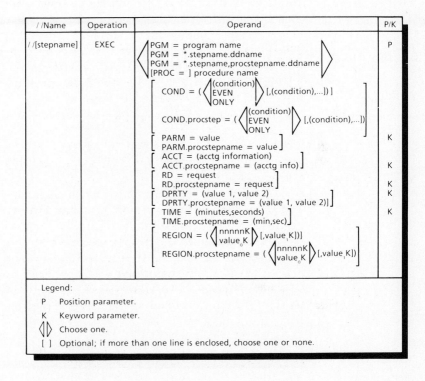

//Name	Operation	Operand	P/K
//[stepname]	EXEC	PGM = program name PGM = *.stepname.ddname PGM = *.stepname,procstepname.ddname [PROC =] procedure name	P
		COND = ((condition)/EVEN/ONLY [,(condition),...])]	
		COND.procstep = ((condition)/EVEN/ONLY [,(condition),...])	
		PARM = value PARM.procstepname = value]	K
		ACCT = (acctg information) ACCT.procstepname = (acctg info)]	K
		RD = request RD.procstepname = request]	K
		DPRTY = (value 1, value 2) DPRTY.procstepname = (value 1, value 2)]]	K
		TIME = (minutes,seconds) TIME.procstepname = (min,sec)]	K
		REGION = (nnnnnK/value$_0$K [,value$_1$K])] REGION.procstepname = (nnnnnK/value$_0$K [,value$_1$K])	

Legend:
P   Position parameter.
K   Keyword parameter.
◁▷   Choose one.
[ ] Optional; if more than one line is enclosed, choose one or none.

RD=request: As on the JOB statement, allows for automatic restart and suppression of checkpoints.
DPRTY = (value 1, value 2): The dispatching priority determines which of the several programs concurrently resident in memory gets first access to the processor in the event of the conflicts.
TIME = (minutes, seconds): Sets a time limit for the job step.
REGION = nnnnnK: Sets a limit on the amount of storage available to the jobstep.

The DD statement

Function: Specifies details—physical location, logical configuration—of data sets. (See Fig. F.3.)

Fig. F.3   The DD statement. Except for *, DATA, and DUMMY, all parameters are keyword.

//Name	Operation	Operand	P/K

//⎡ ddname
procstepname.
ddname ⎤
	DD	⎡ DSNAME = identification ⎤
		⎣ DSN = identification ⎦
		[UNIT = (unit information)]
		⎡ VOLUME = (volume information) ⎤
		⎣ VOL = (volume information) ⎦
		⎡ DCB = (attributes)
		        ⎧dsname
		DCB = (⎨ *.stepname.ddname ⎬ [,attributes])
		        ⎩ *.stepname.procstep.ddname
		[LABEL = (label information)]
		DISP = ([status] [,disposition])
		SYSOUT = x
		SYSOUT = (x ⎡,progname⎤ [,form#])
		      ⎣ ⎦
		[SPACE = (direct access space)]
			K
			
			K
			K
			
			K
			
			K
			K
			K
			
			K

		⎧ * ⎫ [,DCB = ([BLKSIZE = block] [,BUFNO = number])] ⎨ DATA ⎬	P
		DUMMY,...	P
		DDNAME = ddname	K

Legend:

P   Positional parameter

K   Keyword parameter

⟨⟩   Choose one.

[ ] Optional; if more than one line is enclosed, choose one or none.

Parameters: *DSNAME* or *DSN* identifies a data set by name.

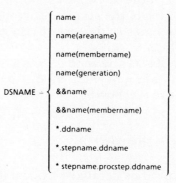

DSNAME = ⎧ name
name(areaname)
name(membername)
name(generation)
&&name
&&name(membername)
*.ddname
*.stepname.ddname
* stepname.procstep.ddname ⎫

UNIT: Requests a particular type of physical I/O device:

$$\text{UNIT} = (\begin{bmatrix} \text{address} \\ \text{type} \\ \text{group} \end{bmatrix} \begin{bmatrix} ,\text{P} \\ ,\text{n} \end{bmatrix} \quad [,\text{DEFER}] \ [,\text{SEP}=(\text{list of ddnames})] \ )$$

Units can be requested by actual channel/device address (address), by IBM model number (2400 is a particular model of tape drive—this is the "type" option), or by a general group name as defined by the installation. The second positional subparameter allows the programmer to specify parallel mounting of all the volumes in a multivolume file by indicating the actual number of volumes; if the number of volumes is specified in the VOL parameter, the programmer simply codes "P." The DEFER subparameter, the third positional subparameter, postpones a volume mount message until the actual OPEN macro is executed. The SEP subparameter is a keyword subparameter that indicates data sets listed as part of the subparameter are to be placed on physically separate devices—if, for example, a program were to access both input and output disk data sets, the SEP subparameter could cause these data sets to be maintained on separate disk volumes, thus minimizing head movement.

The second form of the UNIT parameter:

UNIT = AFF = ddname

allows the data set to be mounted on the same physical device used by a previous data set (referenced by DDNAME) in the job.

VOLUME or VOL: Allows for the specification of volumes; i.e., specific tape volumes or disk volumes.

$$\text{VOLUME}=([\text{PRIVATE}] \begin{bmatrix} ,\text{RETAIN} \\ , \end{bmatrix} \begin{bmatrix} ,\text{VOLSEQ\#} \\ , \end{bmatrix} \begin{bmatrix} ,\text{volcount} \\ , \end{bmatrix} [,] \begin{bmatrix} \text{SER}=(\text{list of serial numbers}) \\ \text{REF}=\text{dsname} \\ \text{REF}=*.\text{ddname} \\ \text{REF}=*.\text{stepname.ddname} \\ \text{REF}=*.\text{stepname.procstep.ddname} \end{bmatrix})$$

The primary option is the SER or REF subparameter that allows the programmer to specify either a specific volume or a group of volumes directly, by serial number, or indirectly by referring back to a prior job step. The PRIVATE subparameter means that no other output data set may be allocated to this volume without a specific volume request.

RETAIN keeps the volume mounted between job steps. The third positional subparameter allows the programmer to indicate that processing is to begin with a volume other than the first one on a multivolume file. The fourth positional subparameter allows the programmer to specify the number of volumes in a multivolume file.

DCB: Specifies details about actual data format.

LABEL: Specifies the label type and the relative file number on a multifile tape volume.

$$\text{LABEL}=(\text{ [data set seq\#]}\begin{bmatrix}\text{,SL}\\\text{,SUL}\\\text{,NSL}\\\text{,NL}\\\text{,BLP}\end{bmatrix}\begin{bmatrix}\text{,PASSWORD}\\\text{,NOPWREAD}\end{bmatrix}\begin{bmatrix}\text{,IN}\\\text{,OUT}\end{bmatrix}\text{[,]}\begin{bmatrix}\text{EXPDT=yyddd}\\\text{RETPD=nnnn}\end{bmatrix})$$

The first subparameter, which is positional, indicates the relative file number on a multifile volume; if omitted, relative file #1 is assumed. The second positional subparameter identifies the label type. PASSWORD indicates that a password must be entered before any access to the data set is permitted. NOPWREAD requires a password for write operations only. Specifying "IN" or "OUT" as the third positional subparameter allows the programmer to override a program specification of INOUT access in the OPEN macro for BSAM files; it's of primary importance to FORTRAN programmers. The final subparameter allows for the specification of an expiration date or retention period.

DISP: Specifies the status and disposition of a data set. The first positional subparameter indicates the status of the data set at the beginning of the job step. The second subparameter indicates what is to be done with the data set at the conclusion of the job step, while the third subparameter indicates the disposition in the event of abnormal jobstep termination.

$$DISP = (\begin{bmatrix} SHR \\ NEW \\ OLD \\ MOD \end{bmatrix} \begin{bmatrix} ,DELETE \\ ,KEEP \\ ,PASS \\ ,CATLG \\ ,UNCATLG \end{bmatrix} \begin{bmatrix} ,UNCATLG \\ ,CATLG \\ ,DELETE \\ ,KEEP \end{bmatrix})$$

SYSOUT: Specifies the use of a standard system output device.

SYSOUT = (class, program-name, form-name)

The class is usually A for the printer and B for the punch, although an installation can define its own output classes. Use the program name subparameter to identify a program (other than the job entry subsystem) that is to write the data; use the form-name subparameter to identify the output form you want used.

SPACE: Specifies the amount of direct access space to be allocated to a data set.

$$SPACE = (\begin{Bmatrix} TRK \\ CYL \\ blocksize \end{Bmatrix} ,(quantity \begin{bmatrix} ,increment \\ , \end{bmatrix} \begin{bmatrix} ,directory \\ ,index \end{bmatrix}) \begin{bmatrix} ,RLSE \end{bmatrix} \begin{bmatrix} ,CONTIG \\ ,MXIG \\ ,ALX \\ , \end{bmatrix} [,ROUND])$$

The programmer can request tracks (TRK), cylinders (CYL), or blocks of a given size. Following specification of the type of space required, the programmer requests an amount of space, asking first, through a series of positional subparameters, for a primary allocation, next, for a secondary allocation in the event that the primary allocation proves to be insufficient, and finally for directory or index space. View the entire "quantity" request as a single positional subparameter, with the quantity, increment, and index sub-subparameters being enclosed in a set of parentheses.

The RLSE subparameter allows the programmer to return all unused space to the system at the conclusion of the job step. CONTIG allows the programmer to request contiguous space, MXIG allows for the allocation of the largest contiguous free area on the volume (as long as it's larger than the request), and

ALX provides the five largest contiguous free areas on the volume (again, with a "larger than the request" restriction). ROUND causes space allocated by blocks to be aligned on cylinder boundaries.

DUMMY: Causes the I/O operations specified on the DD statement to be bypassed.

* or DATA: The asterisk or (*) character in the operands portion of the DD statement indicates that data follow in the job stream; this parameter is often used to indicate that punched card or card image data are to be read through the system input device.

DATA implies the same thing, but allows for the inclusion of cards or card images with // in the first two columns.

DDNAME: Postpones definition of data set parameters until a subsequent DD statement with the specified DDNAME is encountered.

Special DD Statements

The JOBLIB statement

//JOBLIB DD DSN = library-name,DISP = SHR

Allows programs in a private library to be loaded and executed. The JOBLIB statement follows the JOB statement and makes the library available to all subsequent job steps; the JOBLIB, SYSCHK, and JOBCAT statements are the only DD statements that can legally precede the first EXEC statement.

The STEPLIB statement

//STEPLIB DD DSN = library-name,DISP = SHR

like the JOBLIB statement, allows programs in private library to be loaded and executed. The STEPLIB statement follows the EXEC statement and is effective for a single job step only.

The SYSUDUMP statement

//SYSUDUMP DD SYSOUT = class

Provides an abnormal termination dump of the load module.

The SYSCHK statement

//SYSCHK DD DISP = OLD,DSN = dataset-name

Describes a checkpoint data set. Follows the JOB statement and the JOBLIB statement if present.

GLOSSARY

This glossary contains brief definitions intended to convey a sense of the meanings of selected key words. For more precise definitions see:

The American National Dictionary for Information Processing, American National Standards Institute, 1430 Broadway, New York, New York 10018.

The ISO Vocabulary of Data Processing, published by The International Standards Organization.

Absolute address. An address assigned to each memory location in a computer. Generally, an address relative to the very first location in memory.

Access method. A software routine that translate a programmer's logical request for input or output into the physical commands required by the external device.

Active queue. The OS/400 dispatching queue.

Address. A location in memory.

Address translation. The translation from relative form to an absolute address.

Agent process. A process on a host computer that represents the link to a computer network.

Analog. Continuous. Contrast with digital.

Architecture. *See* Computer architecture.

Arithmetic and logic unit. The part of a computer's processor that executes instructions.

Assembler language. A programming language in which one mnemonic source statement is coded for each machine-level instruction.

AS/400. An IBM midrange computer system.

Background. A low-priority fixed-length partition.

Backup. Extra hardware, software, or data intended to keep a computer system running in the event that one or more components fail.

Backward reference. A reference that tells the operating system to look at a previous JCL statement.

Base address. Generally, the absolute address of a program's or module's entry point.

Basic control (BC) mode PSW. On an IBM System/370 computer, a form of PSW used when the dynamic address translation feature is disabled.

Batch file. A set of MS-DOS commands, stored as a file, that can be referenced by name. When referenced, the commands are executed in sequence.

Baud. The basic measure of data communication speed. Signal events per second.

Bit. A binary digit.

Block device. A UNIX device (normally disk) that holds files.

Block. To store several logical records in one physical record.

Boot. A routine, read into main memory when the computer is activated, that reads the rest of the operating system into memory. *See also* Initial program load.

Bourne shell. The standard UNIX shell.

Buffer. Temporary storage used to compensate for the different speeds of adjacent devices.

Buffer pool. A set of buffers in memory. Under UNIX, all block I/O takes place through the buffer pool.

Bus. A set of parallel wires used to transmit data, commands, or power.

Byte. Eight bits. On many computer systems, the smallest addressable unit of memory.

C shell. A UNIX shell related to the C programming language.

Carrier signal. In data communication, a signal with a constant frequency and amplitude that is used to transmit data.

Cataloged procedure. A set of pre-coded JCL statements inserted into the job stream by the operating system.

CAW. *See* Channel address word.

CCB. *See* Command control block.

CCW. *See* Channel command word.

Central processing unit. *See* Processor.

Channel. A device used to attach input, output, and secondary storage devices to a large computer system.

Channel address word (CAW). On an IBM System/370 computer, a word located at main memory address 72 that specifies the address where a channel program begins.

Channel command word (CCW). A single instruction in an IBM System/ 370 channel program.

Channel program. One or more CCWs that control a sequence of channel operations. More generally, a set of primitive commands that control an I/O operation.

Channel queue. The queue for I/O operations during a channel-busy condition.

Channel status word (CSW). On an IBM System/370 computer, a doubleword at main memory address 64 through which a channel communicates its status to the main processor.

Character device. Under UNIX, such

nonblock devices as printers and terminals.

Child. In UNIX, the second copy of a process. In a database, a record that is linked, in some way, to a higher level record. *Contrast with* Parent.

Clock. The processor component that generates the regular electronic pulses that drive a computer.

Close. The instruction that signals the operating system when a program is finished accessing a file or peripheral device.

Closed architecture. Hardware or an operating system that is designed to discourage customizing or modification.

Cluster. Under MS-DOS, the unit used in allocating disk space.

CMS. *See* Conversation monitor system.

Collision detection. A data transmission technique in which a terminal or host computer transmits a message and listens for a collision with another message. If such a collision is detected, the message is retransmitted after a random interval.

Command. (1) A control signal that tells a hardware component to perform a specific function; for example, a fetch command. (2) A request from a programmer, an operator, or a user to an operating system asking that a specific function be performed; for example, a request to load a program.

Command control block (CCB). Under VSE, a PIOCS block that points to a channel program.

Command driven. An operating system whose main control module is the command processor.

Command language. A language for communicating with an operating system.

Command name. In OS/400 command language, a series of concatenated abbreviations that uniquely defines a command.

Command processor. An operating system module that reads, interprets, and carries out commands.

COMMAND.COM. The MS-DOS command processor, or shell.

Common data management. Under OS/400, a set of data management routines that are common to all file types.

Communication vector table (CVT). Under IBM's OS, a table that holds system constants and pointers to most of the key control blocks.

Compiler. A support program that reads a source module, translates the source statements to machine language, and outputs a complete binary object module.

Composite object. An object composed of two or more other objects.

Computation migration. The transfer of tasks between hosts in a computer network.

Computer architecture. The physical structure of a computer; in particular, the way in which a computer's components are linked together.

Computer program. A series of instructions that guides a computer through some process.

Condition code. A two-bit code in an IBM System/370 computer that supports decision logic.

Configuration table. A table used in UNIX to list all peripheral devices attached to the system.

Contextual help. A help feature that selects the information to be displayed based on what the user was doing when he or she requested help.

Contiguous. Adjacent to.

Control block. The block that holds

control information for an active program.

Control language. OS/400's command language.

Control language program. Under OS/400, a program comprised of control language commands.

Control program (CP) Under IBM's VM/SP, the operating system that manages the real computer.

Control unit, instruction. *See* Instruction control unit.

Control unit, I/O. An electronic device that links an I/O device to a channel.

Conversational monitor system (CMS). Under IBM's VM/SP, a virtual operating system that simulates a personal computer, thus combining the interactive nature of a PC and the resources of a large mainframe.

Core image library. *See* Load module library.

CP. *See* Control program.

CPU. Acronym for central processing unit. *See* Processor.

CSW. *See* Channel status word.

Current library. Under OS/400, the user's default library.

Current PSW. On an IBM System/370, a special register that holds the address of the next instruction to be executed.

CVT. *See* Communication vector table.

Data access. The act of reading and/or writing data.

Data accessibility. The availability of data to the user.

Database. A collection of related data. Generally, an integrated, centralized collection of an organization's data.

Database administrator. The person in an MIS group with unambiguous responsibility for data. Generally, the person responsible for installing and maintaining the database management system.

Database file. Under OS/400, a file that is part of a database.

Database management system. Software that controls access to a database.

Data communication. The act of transmitting data between two or more independent devices.

Data communication monitor. A module used to mange the partition and serve as an interface to the communication media in a time-sharing system.

Data communication software. Application and system software that controls data communication.

Data control block (DCB). Under IBM's OS, a series of constants and addresses that describe the characteristics of the physical and logical records.

Data dependency. A condition that occurs when a program's logic is excessively dependent on its physical data structure. Data-dependent programs are difficult to maintain.

Data element. A single, meaningful unit of data.

Data extent block (DEB). Under IBM's OS, an extension of the DCB that is not accessible to the programmer.

Data integrity. The reliability of data. Loosely, data accuracy.

Data management. Storing data in such a way that they can be retrieved when needed.

Data migration. The transfer of files and selected data elements between hosts in a computer network.

Data redundancy. The same data recorded in several different files.

Data segment. In UNIX, a private segment that follows the text segment and holds the program's data.

Data structure. An organized set of data. Examples include a list, an array, and a file.

DCB. *See* Data control block.

DD statement. An IBM OS/JCL statement that defines a peripheral device.

Deadlock. A consequence of poor resource management that occurs when two programs each control a resource needed by the other and neither is willing to give in.

DEB. *See* Data extent block.

Default. The value assumed by a system when the programmer fails to code a particular parameter.

Default drive. The drive that the operating system assumes will hold programs, routines, and data files.

Define the file (DTF). A VSE macro that sets key data parameters and specifies an access method.

Delimiter. A flag used to separate data items or fields.

Demand paging. The process of bringing pages into memory as they are referenced.

Demodulation. Filtering a carrier signal to extract the data.

Device driver. A file that describes the access rules for a particular physical device.

Device number. Under UNIX, a number that uniquely defines an external device.

Digital. Discrete data. Contrast with analog.

Directory. The list of files stored on a disk. *See also* Root directory; Subdirectory; Working directory.

Disk. A flat, platelike surface on which data can be stored magnetically.

Diskette. A thin, flexible magnetic disk often used on small computer systems.

Dispatcher. An operating system routine used to manage processor time.

Displacement. A number of memory locations away from a base address. A location relative to a base address.

DOS/VSE. An IBM batch-oriented, multiprogramming operating system popular on small mainframes. The current version is called VSE.

DTF. *See* Define the file.

Dynamic address translation. The process of changing relative segment and/or page addresses to absolute addresses during execution of an instruction.

Dynamic memory management. Allocation of memory space to application programs as the space is needed.

Editor. A program that allows a user to enter, maintain, and store source data or source code.

Entry point. The address of the first instruction to be executed in a program or routine.

ESD. *See* External symbol dictionary.

E-time or Execution time. The time during which an instruction is executed by the arithmetic and logic unit.

Event. In UNIX, the event signal generated by the death of a process.

Event-wait. A routine that causes UNIX to search the process table and wake every process waiting for that event.

EXCP. *See* Execute channel program.

exec. A UNIX system call that overlays a process with new text and data segments.

EXEC statement. Under VSE and OS/JCL, a statement used to identify a program (or cataloged procedure) to be executed.

Execute channel program (EXCP). Under VSE, a PIOCS macro that generates the instructions needed to execute a channel program.

exit. A UNIX system call that signals a process's completion.

Extended architecture mode. An IBM System/370 operating mode that uses a 31-bit address. The PSW that supports this mode.

Extended control (EC) mode PSW. On an IBM System/370 computer, a form of PSW that implies virtual memory.

Extension. Part of a file name. Often used to assign the file name to a particular category. Generally, follows a period.

External interrupt. On an IBM System/370 computer, an interrupt that comes from the operator's console, another processor, or the timer.

External paging device. A storage device used to hold application programs on a virtual memory system.

External reference. A reference by an object module to logic that is not part of that object module.

External symbol dictionary (ESD). A table of unresolved external references placed by the compiler at the beginning of the object module.

File. A collection of related records.

File allocation table. Under MS-DOS, a table, stored on disk, containing an entry for each cluster on the disk.

File description. A set of attributes associated with an OS/400 file.

File descriptor. Under UNIX, a small, nonnegative integer used to identify an open file to a user's process.

File name. The name used to identify a file.

File system. An operating system routine that manages directories and allocates disk space. The routine that allows programmers and users to access data and programs by name.

Filter. A routine that accepts input from the standard input device, modifies the data in some way, and sends the results to the standard output device.

Fixed-partition memory management. A memory management technique in which the available memory space is divided into several fixed-length partitions, and one program is loaded into each partition.

Floppy disk. *See* Diskette.

Foreground. A high-priority fixed-length partition.

fork. A UNIX system call that creates a new process.

Format. To prepare a disk for use.

Fragmentation. Chunks of unused space spread throughout memory as a result of dynamic memory management.

Front-end device. A peripheral device that manages data communication.

Hard disk. A rigid disk. *Contrast with* floppy disk, or diskette.

Help, or help feature. On-line reference information that is available on request.

Hierarchical database. A hierarchically structured database.

Home directory. The file selected by UNIX as the working directory when a user logs on.

Host. An individual end-user computer in a computer network.

i-list. A region on a UNIX disk that holds the i-nodes.

Image. In UNIX, an execution environment that consists of program and data storage, the contents of general-purpose registers, the status of open files, the current directory, and other key elements.

INCLUDE statement. Under VSE and OS/JCL, a statement used to specify external references to the linkage editor.

init. When UNIX is booted, the "original ancestor" that creates one system process for each terminal channel.

Initial program load (IPL). The process of copying the resident operating system into real memory.

Initiator/terminator. Under IBM's OS, a transient module that starts and ends tasks.

i-node. An entry on the i-list in UNIX.

i-node table. A UNIX table listing the i-nodes of all open files.

Input. Providing data to a computer.

Input/output block (IOB). Under OS, a block that links the DCB to the channel program.

Input/output control system (IOCS). The operating system module that assumes responsibility for communicating directly with input, output, and secondary storage devices.

Instruction. One step in a program. Each instruction tells the com- puter to perform one of its basic functions.

Instruction address. On an IBM System/370 computer, the PSW field that holds the address of the next instruction to be executed.

Instruction control unit. The part of a computer's processor that decides which instruction will be executed next.

Instruction length code. On an IBM System/370 computer, a BC mode field that indicates the length of the current instruction.

Interface. On a small computer, an electronic component, often a board, that links an external device to a computer. More generally, an electronic component that links two different devices.

Interpreter. A support program that reads a single source statement, translates that statement to machine language, executes those machine-level instructions, and then moves on to the next source statement.

Interrupt. An electronic signal that causes a computer to stop what it is doing and transfer control to the operating system in such a way that the task being performed at the time of the interrupt can later be resumed.

Interrupt handler. An operating system routine that responds to an interrupt.

Interrupt vector table. A table that holds the addresses (interrupt vectors) of several interrupt handler routines.

Interruption code. On an IBM System/370 computer, a code showing the cause of an interrupt.

i-number. Under UNIX, an i-node's offset from the beginning of the i-list.

Invisible file. On UNIX, a file whose name is not displayed when a directory is listed.

I/O control unit. *See* Control unit, I/O.

I/O interrupt. On an IBM System/370 computer, an interrupt that occurs when the channel signals the processor that an I/O operation is completed.

I/O processor. On a multiprocessing system, an independent processor that controls input and output operations.

IOB. *See* Input/output block.

IOCS. *See* Input/output control system.

IO.SYS. Under MS-DOS, a hardware-dependent module that issues physical data transfer commands. The MS-DOS input/output control system.

IPL. *See* Initial program load.

I-time, or Instruction time. The time during which the next instruction is fetched from main memory and interpreted by the processor's instruction control unit.

JCL. *See* Job control language.
JECL. *See* Job entry control language.
JES. *See* Job entry subsystem.
Job. A set of related tasks or related activities.
Job control language (JCL). A batch-oriented language used to identify jobs, identify the program or programs to be executed, define peripheral device requirements, and pass other information to the operating system.
Job control program. Under VSE, a routine that loads job steps or tasks.
Job entry control language. A set of commands for communicating with VSE/POWER.
Job entry subsystem (JES). Under OS, a job management routine that reads the job stream and assigns jobs to class queues.
Job management. The OS routines that dispatch, enqueue, schedule, initiate, and terminate jobs or tasks.
Job name. The name chosen by the programmer to identify a job.
JOB statement. Under VSE or OS/ JCL, a statement used to separate and identify jobs.
Job step. A single program in a job.
Job stream. A series of jobs submitted, in batch mode, to the operating system. Generally, the job stream holds control statements, source code, and data.

Kernel. Under UNIX, the portion of the operating system that is hardware dependent.
Keyword parameter. A parameter that derives its meaning from its name, not its position.

LAN. *See* Local area network.
Library. A collection of related files or programs.
Library list. Under OS/400, a list of the libraries available to a user.
Licensed internal code. The IBM AS/ 400's microcode.
Line. A data communication medium.
Linkage editor. A system program that combines object modules to form a load module and outputs the load module to a library.
LIOCS. *See* Logical I/O control system.
Load module. A complete machine-level program in a form ready to be loaded into main memory and executed.
Load module library. A library that holds ready to execute load modules.
Loader. A system program that combines object modules to form a load module, and then loads the program into main memory. Similar to a linkage editor, except that a loader does not output the load module to a library.
Local. Data transmission between two devices without boosting or filtering the signals. Generally limited to a mile or two.
Local area network (LAN). A computer network that relies on local data transmission.
Logical I/O. Input or output operations performed without regard for the physical structure of the data. Under traditional data management, a request for a logical record.
Logical I/O control system (LIOCS). Input or output operations performed without regard for the physical structure of the data. Under traditional data management, a request for a logical record.
Logical unit block (LUB). Under VSE, a

table that lists the symbolic names of physical I/O devices. Each table entry points to a PUB table entry.

Login name. Name used to begin a session in UNIX.

LUB. *See* Logical unit block.

Machine check interrupt. On an IBM System/370 computer, the interrupt that occurs when a computer's self-checking circuitry detects a hardware failure.

Machine cycle. The basic operating cycle of a processor during which a single instruction is fetched, interpreted, and executed.

Machine language. Binary instructions that can be stored in main memory, fetched, and executed by a computer.

Macro. A set of precoded source statements added to a source module by an assembler in response to a source reference.

Main memory. Memory that can be directly accessed by the processor.

MAIN menu. Under OS/400, the user's default initial menu.

Main processor. On a multiprocessing computer, the primary processor. Sometimes used as a synonym for processor.

Masking. A method used to determine whether to acknowledge an interrupt.

Master scheduler. The OS dispatcher.

Member. Under IBM's OS, a module or data file on a partitioned data set. Under VSE, a program, file, or procedure on a subdirectory.

Memory management. Allocating memory to programs and routines.

Memory protection. Ensuring that the various users on a multiple-user system do not interfere with each other's memory space.

Menu. A list of choices.

Message slot transmission. Controlling access to a network by continuously transmitting several message slots. A terminal or host computer can transmit data only through an open slot.

Microcode. Instructions stored on read-only memory.

Minidisk. A portion of a sharable device, such as disk, in a virtual machine environment. A virtual disk.

Modem. Acronym for modulator/demodulator.

Modulation. Adding data to a carrier signal.

MS-DOS. A popular microcomputer operating system.

MSDOS.SYS. Under MS-DOS, a hardware-independent module that implements logical I/O. The MS-DOS file system.

Multiple-access bus. A network configuration in which computers are linked to a common bus. Generally limited to local area networks.

Multiple-bus architecture. A computer architecture in which more than one bus line is used to link components.

Multiprocessing. One computer with two or more independent processors.

Multiprogramming. One processor concurrently executing several programs.

Network. Two or more computers linked by communication lines.

Network database. A database organized as a network. Generally, a parent can have many children, and a child can have many parents.

Network operating system. An operating system for a computer network.

Network server. The computer that manages a network.

New PSW. On an IBM System/370 computer, a field located in main memory that holds the address of an interrupt handling routine in the operating system.

Noise. Electronic interference.

Noncontiguous. Separated. For example, a program's pages can be stored in widely separated regions of memory.

Nucleus. Another name for the resident operating system.

Object. An entity in an object-oriented system.

Object management. A set of OS/400 functions that store, retrieve, and maintain objects without regard for their type.

Object module. A machine-level translation of a programmer's source code.

Object module library. A library of object modules.

Old PSW. On an IBM System/370 computer, a field located in memory that holds the PSW associated with the program that was executing at the time an interrupt occurred.

On-line education. On-line tutorials that can be accessed interactively.

Open. To prepare a file for processing.

Open data path. On an OS/400 system, a link to a file created at open time and recorded in a user file control block.

Operand. The portion of an instruction that specifies the registers and memory locations that are to participate in the operation.

Operating system. A collection of program modules that control the operation of the computer. A typical operating system allocates resources, schedules programs, controls access to input and output devices, and manages data.

Operation. A single logical function.

Operation code. The portion of an instruction that specifies the operation to be performed.

OS/VS1. An IBM virtual storage operating system that relies on fixed-partition memory management to manage virtual memory space.

OS/VS2. An IBM virtual storage operating system that relies on dynamic memory management to mange virtual memory space.

OS/400. The operating system for an IBM AS/400.

Output. Sending information out from a computer.

Overlay. Storing a program module in the memory space previously allocated to another, no longer needed module of the same program.

Page. A fixed-length independently addressed portion of a program that can be loaded into noncontiguous memory.

Page address registers. A set of registers that hold the base addresses of the most recently accessed pages. Typically, these registers are searched in parallel with dynamic address translation.

Page fault. An interrupt generated when a virtual address references a page that is not in real storage.

Page frame table. A table that holds flags indicating each real memory page's status (i.e., free or in use). Used by the operating system to allocate main memory space.

Page pool. The region of real memory used to hold active application program pages on a virtual memory system.

Page table. A program listing the base addresses of all pages in a program.

Page table location register. A register that holds the address of the current program's page table.

Paging. (1) The process of dividing a program into fixed-length pages. (2) The process of swapping pages between the real page pool and the external paging device.

Parameter. A single operand on a job control language statement.

Parent. In UNIX, the first copy of a process created in response to the *fork* routine. In a database, a record that is linked, in some way, to one or more lower level records. *Contrast with* child.

Partition. A portion of memory used to hold one program on a fixed-portion memory management system.

Partition management. Management of multiple users' access to processor time, memory space, and peripheral devices in a single partition of a multiprogramming system.

Partitioned data set. A library on an IBM mainframe running under OS.

Password. A unique string of characters that identifies a user.

Pathname. The name used to find a file referenced through more than one subdirectory.

PC-DOS. A version of MS-DOS used on IBM personal computers.

PDS. *See* Partitioned data set.

Phase. Under VSE, a load module.

Physical I/O. The act of transferring a physical block of data to or from a peripheral device.

Physical I/O control system (PIOCS). Under VSE, a series of macros that allow a programmer to request physical I/O operations.

Physical unit block (PUB). A table that lists the peripheral devices attached to a VSE system.

PIOCS. *See* Physical I/O control system.

Pipe. An operator that causes one utility's standard output to be used as the standard input to another utility.

Platform. A set of hardware and software that forms a unique computing environment.

Pointer. An address stored in memory that provides a link to a related field, file, record, control block, etc.

Polling. Asking a series of terminals, or checking a series of buffers, one by one, to see if they have data to transmit. A technique for determining who gets to transmit data next.

Positional parameter. A parameter whose meaning is determined by its position in the operands field.

PRB. *See* Program request block.

Prepaging. The process of predicting the demand for a new page and bringing it into memory before it is actually needed.

Primitive command. A machine-level hardware command, such as a fetch or a seek.

Privileged instruction. An instruction that can be executed only by an operating system routine.

Problem state. A state in which a computer is executing an application program.

Process. Under UNIX, the execution of an image.

Process file table. Under UNIX, a table listing a process's open files.

Process id. Under UNIX, a number that identifies a process.

Process table. Under UNIX, a table used by the dispatcher, containing one entry for each process.

Process id. Under UNIX, a number that identifies a process.

Processor, or Central processing unit. The component of a computer that selects and executes instructions. The processor contains a clock, an instruction control unit, an arithmetic and logic unit, and registers.

Program. *See* Computer program.

Program interrupt. On an IBM System/370 computer, an interrupt that results from an illegal or invalid instruction.

Program name. A name that identifies a load module stored in a library.

Program request block (PRB). Under OS, a request block that indicates the existence of an active task.

Program status word (PSW). The IBM System/370 instruction counter.

Programming development manager. A licensed IBM AS/400 software product that defines a program development environment.

Prompt. A brief message printed or displayed by a program or by the operating system asking the user to provide input.

Protection key. On an IBM System/370 computer, a 4-bit key, stored in the PSW, that is used by hardware to prevent one program from destroying memory belonging to another.

Protocol. A set of rules for establishing communication between two devices.

Pseudocomputer. In UNIX, an imaginary machine on which the user perceives an image to be executing.

PSW. *See* Program status word.

PUB. *See* Physical unit block.

Queuing. Placing application programs on a waiting line (or queue) for eventual loading into main memory.

Ready state. A state in which a program is ready to resume processing.

Real computer. The physical computer in a virtual machine environment.

Real address area. Virtual space equal to available real memory.

Real memory. Actual, physical main memory space.

Real partition. A partition in the real address area that can be used to hold all or part of an application program.

Redirection. An operator used to override or change the standard input or output device.

Reentrant. A program attribute that allows the same copy of a program to be used by two or more programmers. Generally, a reentrant program does not modify itself.

Region. A portion of memory (real or virtual) allocated dynamically to an application program.

Register. High-speed temporary storage used to hold data, instructions, or control information in the processor.

Relational database. A database whose organization is based on the logical relationship between data elements.

Relative address. An address relative to a reference point.

Relative record number. The location of a record relative to the beginning of a file. Given the actual track and sector of the first record in the file, it is possible to compute the address of any other record given its relative record number.

Remote. Distant data transmission in which the signal has been boosted and filtered.

Request block. Under OS, a control block that describes the detailed contents of a given partition or region.

Resident. An operating system module that directly supports an application program as it runs and thus must remain in main memory.

Resource management. An operating system responsibility on many large, multiprogramming computer systems. Often includes managing processor time, main memory space, and access to secondary storage devices.

Resource sharing. Sharing peripheral devices over a network.

Response time. Time elapsed between entering a transaction and seeing the first character of the system's response appear on the screen.

Restart interrupt. On an IBM System/370 computer, an interrupt that allows an operator or another processor to start a program.

Ring network. A computer network configuration in which the host computers are linked to form a ring.

Roll-in/roll-out. A memory management technique used on time-shared systems in which programs are rolled out to secondary storage between transactions and then rolled back into main memory when a transaction arrives.

Root directory. The directory created when a disk is formatted.

Routing queue. Under OS/400, a queue maintained by work management to determine when jobs are started.

SAA. See Systems Applications Architecture.

Scheduler. An operating system module used to determine which program will be loaded into main memory when space becomes available.

Search index. An OS/400 help feature that allows a user to request help information by key word.

Secondary storage. Nonvolatile memory such as disk or magnetic tape used for the long-term storage of program instructions and data.

Segment. A variable-length, independently addressed portion of a program that can be loaded into noncontiguous memory.

Segment table. A table stored in the operating system listing the entry points of each of a program's segments.

Segment table location register. A register that holds the address of the current program's segment table.

Segmentation. The process of dividing programs into independently addressed segments.

Segmentation and paging. The process of dividing programs into logical segments and subdividing those segments into fixed-length pages.

Service processor. On an AS/400 system, an independent processor that performs IPL functions and monitors the system processor.

Session. An interactive job. The work performed between sign-on and sign-off.

Shared virtual area. An area of virtual memory that holds pagable routines designed to be shared by all partitions.

Shell. (1) A way to visualize the command processor's relationship to the operating system. (2) In UNIX, a command interpreter treated like an application program, allowing replacement of the standard shell with a custom shell.

Shell script. A UNIX batch file.

Signal. An electronic pulse that can be sensed by the operating system. For example, the death of a UNIX process generates a signal.

Signal degradation. The tendency of an electronic signal to die down or lose intensity with distance.

Sign-on. The act of starting an interactive session.

Single-bus architecture. A computer architecture in which all internal components are linked by a single bus line.

Single-level storage. An AS/400 feature that treats both main and secondary storage as a single, contiguous virtual memory.

Source code. Program instructions written in a source language such as BASIC, COBOL, FORTRAN, or Pascal.

Source module. A set of program statements written in a source language.

Source statement library. A program library that holds assembler or compiler source modules.

Spooling. On input, transferring data to secondary storage and holding them for eventual processing. On output, transferring data to secondary storage for eventual output to an output device.

Stack segment. A private segment at the end of a UNIX image that holds control information.

Star network. A computer network configuration in which each host is linked to a central "star" machine.

Step name. The name of the job step being executed.

Subdirectory. Under UNIX and MS-DOS, a file that holds directory entries. A subdirectory is listed in the root directory or in a higher level subdirectory.

Sublibrary. Under VSE, a second-level library that lists members in a directory.

Subparameter. On a JCL statement, a field that provides detailed specifications for a parameter; for example, the label type in an OS/JCL DD statement LABEL parameter.

Subsystem. Under OS/400, a set of work management resources that supports a group of related jobs.

Super block. The region on a UNIX disk that identifies the disk, defines the sizes of its regions, and tracks free blocks.

Supervisor. Another name for the resident operating system.

Supervisor request block (SVRB). Under OS, a request block that indicates a supervisor call interrupt is being processed in support of the partition.

Supervisory state. The state in which a computer is executing a supervisor routine.

SVC interrupt. On an IBM System/370 computer, an interrupt that occurs in response to an SVC instruction.

SVRB. *See* Supervisor request block.

Swapping. Moving processes or pages between main memory and an external paging device.

Symbolic name. Under VSE, a logical name used to identify an I/O device.

Synchronous. Control of timing by equally spaced clock signals or pulses.

SYSGEN (system generation). The act of creating a custom version of an operating system.

SYSRES. A device, usually a disk pack, that is the source of the operating system on a customer's computer.

System data segment. A segment of a UNIX process that contains data accessed by the operating system when the process is active. The system data segment is part of the process, but not the user's image.

System directory. A directory maintained by the VM/SP control program with one entry for each virtual machine.

System file table. A table maintained by UNIX that lists the i-nodes of all open files.

System input. The default input device.

System mask. On an IBM System/370 computer, a mask that determines whether I/O and external interrupts will be acknowledged.

System output. The default output device.

Systems Applications Architecture. A set of procedures and guidelines that supports common applications on IBM's PS/2, AS/400, and System/370 platforms.

Switching. Establishing a data communication path.

Task. A single program or routine in memory.

Task control block (TCB). Under OS, a control block that defines the status of a single partition or region.

Task input/output table (TIOT). Under OS, a table listing all the DDNAMES from the job step's DD statements with pointers to other information defined in each DD statement.

Task management. Under OS, the routines that manage a program as it runs, generally handling interrupts.

TCB. *See* Task control block.

Terminal. The end point of a communication line. An I/O device that consists of a keyboard, a screen, and (sometimes) a printer.

Text segment. In a UNIX image or process, the segment that holds executable code. Generally, the text segment is reentrant.

Text table. A UNIX table that keeps track of active text segments by listing each current text segment, its primary and secondary addresses, and a count of the number of processes sharing it.

Thrashing. A situation that occurs when paging on a virtual memory system is so frequent that little time is left for useful work.

Time-sharing. A set of techniques that allows multiple users, each controlling an independent terminal, to share a single computer.

Time-slicing. A processor management technique in which an application program is given a discrete "slice" of time in which to complete its work. If the work is not completed during a single time slice, the program loses control of the processor and must return to the end of the queue to await another turn.

TIOT. *See* Task input/output table.

Token passing. A network access technique in which an electronic signal called a token is transmitted continuously from host to host or terminal to terminal. A given host or terminal can transmit a message only when it holds the token.

Transient. An operating system module that resides on disk and is read into main memory only when needed.

Transient area. The area in main memory where application programs are loaded.

Transparent. Hidden; for example, details associated with the real computer that are hidden by the operating system in a virtual machine environment are said to be transparent.

UCB. *See* Unit control block.

Unit control block (UCB). Under OS, a list of the peripheral devices attached to a computer.

UNIX. A popular multiprogramming operating system developed by AT&T.

User file control block. An OS/400 control block that identifies an open data path.

User ID. A code that identifies a user at sign-on time.

User interface manager. The OS/400 command processor.

User profile. A set of attributes that defines a user's operating environment.

Utilities. Routines such as assemblers, compilers, linkage editors, loaders, line editors, sort routines, debugging features, library management routines, and so on.

V = R area. *See* Virtual-equals-real area.

View. A logical data structure.

Virtual address area. Virtual space over and above the available real memory.

Virtual-equals-real area. The region of memory where virtual, real, and absolute addresses match.

Virtual machine. A functional simulation of a computer and its associated devices, including an operating system.

Virtual memory. A memory management technique in which only active portions of a program are actually loaded into main memory.

Virtual operating system. The operating system in a virtual machine environment that controls application programs.

Virtual peripheral device. Peripheral devices in a virtual machine environment that are simulated by the real operating system.

VM/SP. Acronym for virtual machine system product, an IBM operating system that supports virtual machines.

VSE. A popular operating system on small IBM mainframe computers. Formerly called DOS/VSE.

VSE/POWER. The VSE spooler.

WAIT. A macro used to drop a program into a wait state while an I/O operation is executing.

wait. A UNIX system call that puts a process to sleep.

Wait state. The state in which a program is waiting for the completion of some event such as an I/O operation.

Wide area network. A network in which some or all of the computers are remote.

Wild card. A character used to generalize parameters. Especially useful for making backup copies of selected files or an entire disk.

Word. The basic storage unit around which a computer system is designed. On all but the smallest microcomputers, a word consists of two or more bytes.

Work entry. A set of OS/400 parameters that defines a job's routing information.

Work management. A set of OS/400 procedures that enqueues and schedules jobs.

Work station. A microcomputer linked to a local area network.

Working directory. The directory currently being used.

Index